# RUMBLE



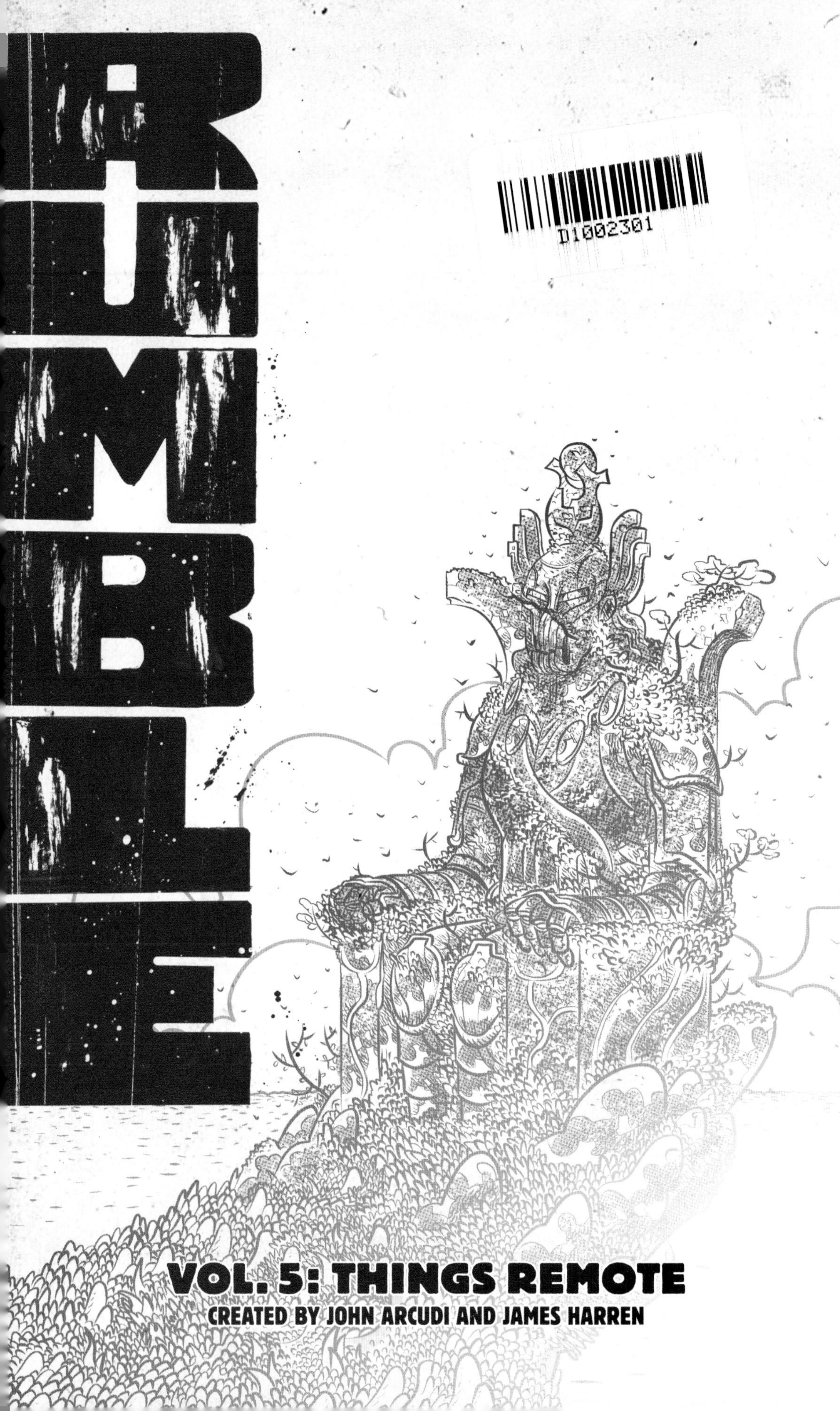

## VOL. 5: THINGS REMOTE

CREATED BY JOHN ARCUDI AND JAMES HARREN

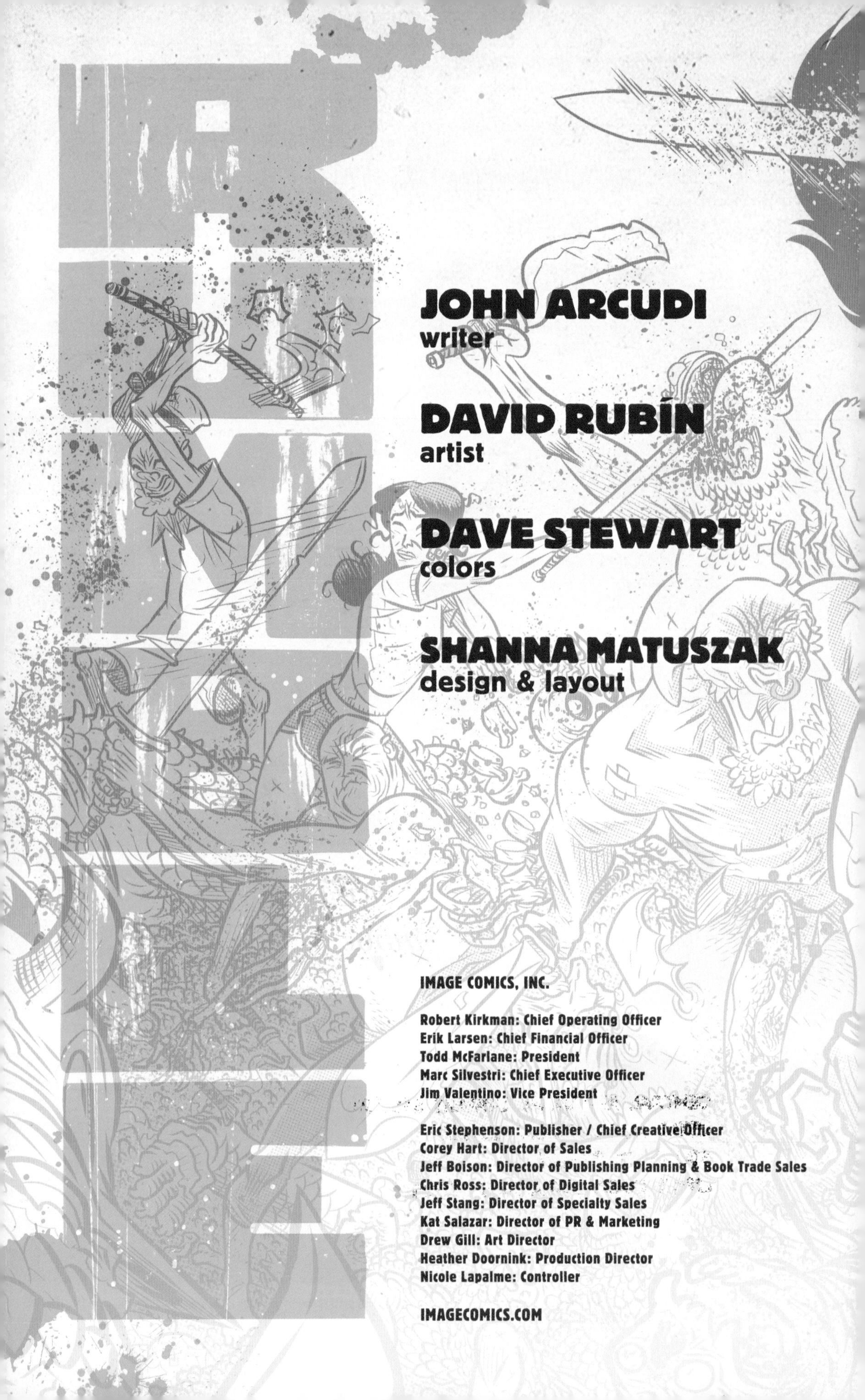

**JOHN ARCUDI**
writer

**DAVID RUBÍN**
artist

**DAVE STEWART**
colors

**SHANNA MATUSZAK**
design & layout


**IMAGE COMICS, INC.**

Robert Kirkman: Chief Operating Officer
Erik Larsen: Chief Financial Officer
Todd McFarlane: President
Marc Silvestri: Chief Executive Officer
Jim Valentino: Vice President

Eric Stephenson: Publisher / Chief Creative Officer
Corey Hart: Director of Sales
Jeff Boison: Director of Publishing Planning & Book Trade Sales
Chris Ross: Director of Digital Sales
Jeff Stang: Director of Specialty Sales
Kat Salazar: Director of PR & Marketing
Drew Gill: Art Director
Heather Doornink: Production Director
Nicole Lapalme: Controller

**IMAGECOMICS.COM**

**RUMBLE, VOL. 5: THINGS REMOTE.** First printing. February 2019. Published by Image Comics, Inc. Office of publication: 2701 NW Vaughn St., Suite 780, Portland, OR 97210. Copyright © 2019 John Arcudi & David Rubín. All rights reserved. Contains material originally published in single magazine form as RUMBLE 2017 #6-10. "Rumble," its logos, and the likenesses of all characters herein are trademarks of John Arcudi & David Rubín, unless otherwise noted. "Image" and the Image Comics logos are registered trademarks of Image Comics, Inc. No part of this publication may be reproduced or transmitted, in any form or by any means (except for short excerpts for journalistic or review purposes), without the express written permission of John Arcudi & David Rubín, or Image Comics, Inc. All names, characters, events, and locales in this publication are entirely fictional. Any resemblance to actual persons (living or dead), events, or places, without satirical intent, is coincidental. Printed in the USA. For information regarding the CPSIA on this printed material call: 203-595-3636. For international rights, contact: foreignlicensing@imagecomics.com. ISBN: 978-1-5343-1042-1.

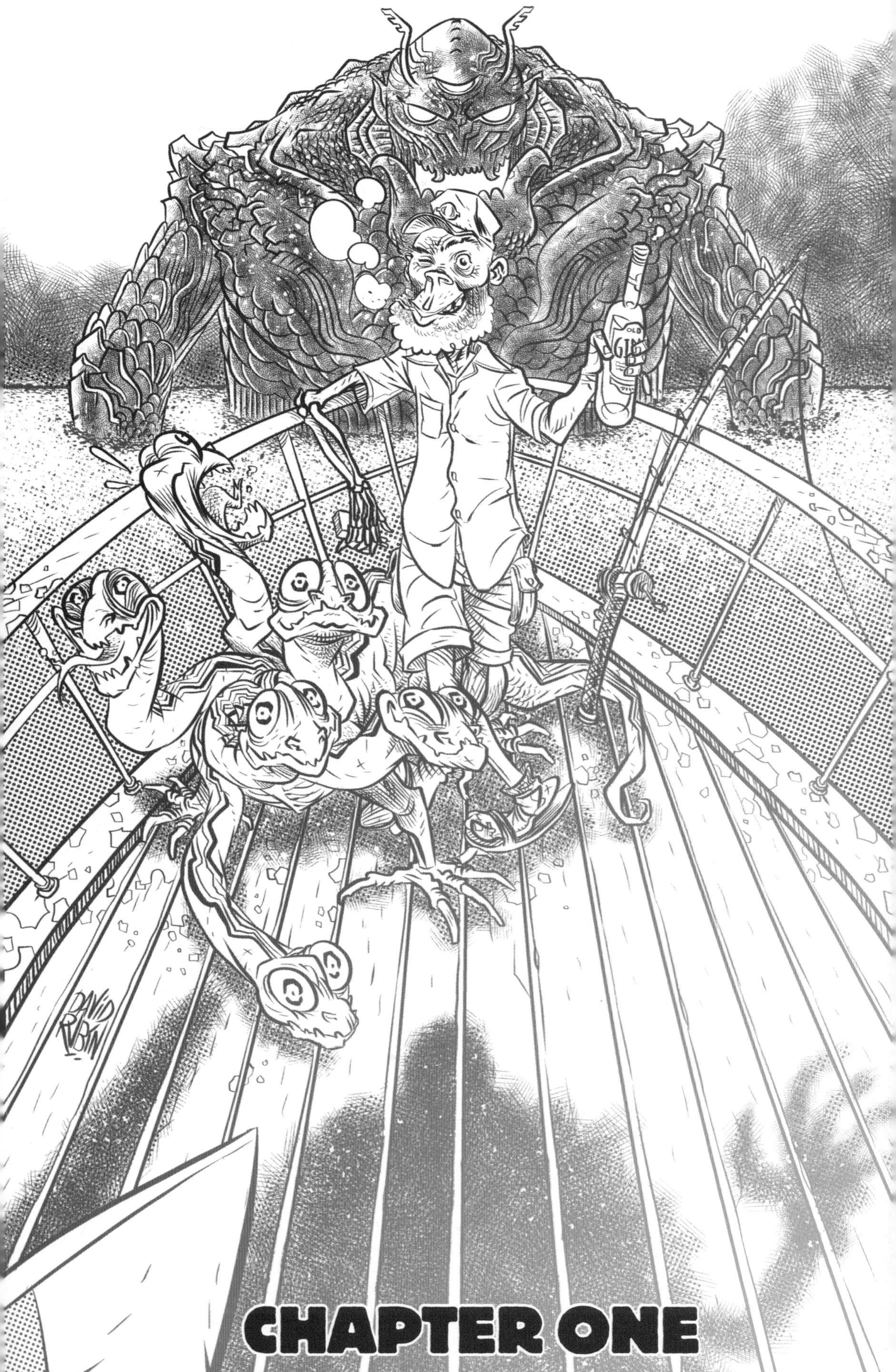

# CHAPTER ONE

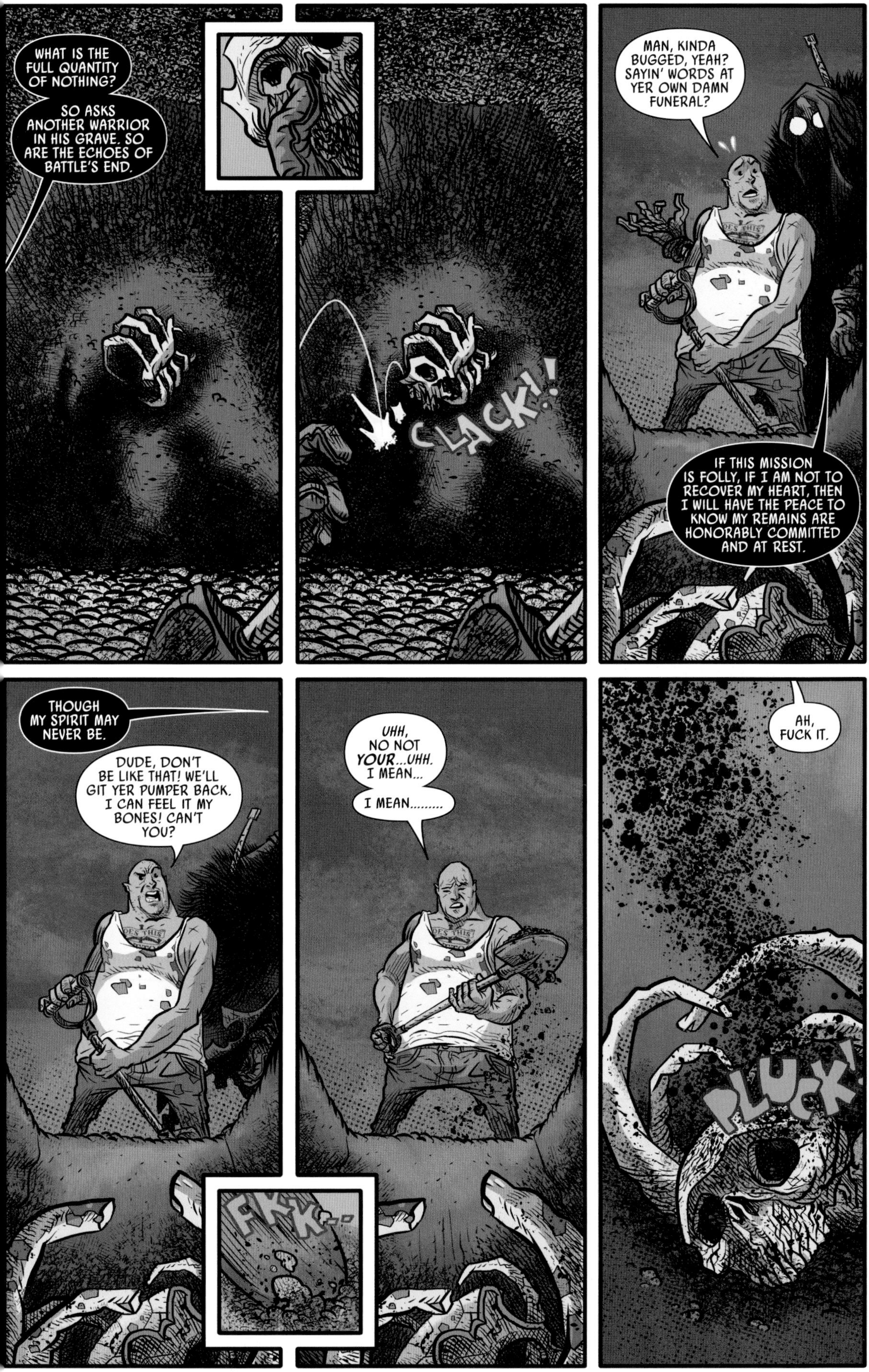
WHAT IS THE FULL QUANTITY OF NOTHING?
SO ASKS ANOTHER WARRIOR IN HIS GRAVE. SO ARE THE ECHOES OF BATTLE'S END.
CLACK!!
MAN, KINDA BUGGED, YEAH? SAYIN' WORDS AT YER OWN DAMN FUNERAL?
IF THIS MISSION IS FOLLY, IF I AM NOT TO RECOVER MY HEART, THEN I WILL HAVE THE PEACE TO KNOW MY REMAINS ARE HONORABLY COMMITTED AND AT REST.
THOUGH MY SPIRIT MAY NEVER BE.
DUDE, DON'T BE LIKE THAT! WE'LL GIT YER PUMPER BACK. I CAN FEEL IT MY BONES! CAN'T YOU?
FKK-
UHH, NO NOT YOUR...UHH. I MEAN...
I MEAN.........
AH, FUCK IT.
PLUCK!

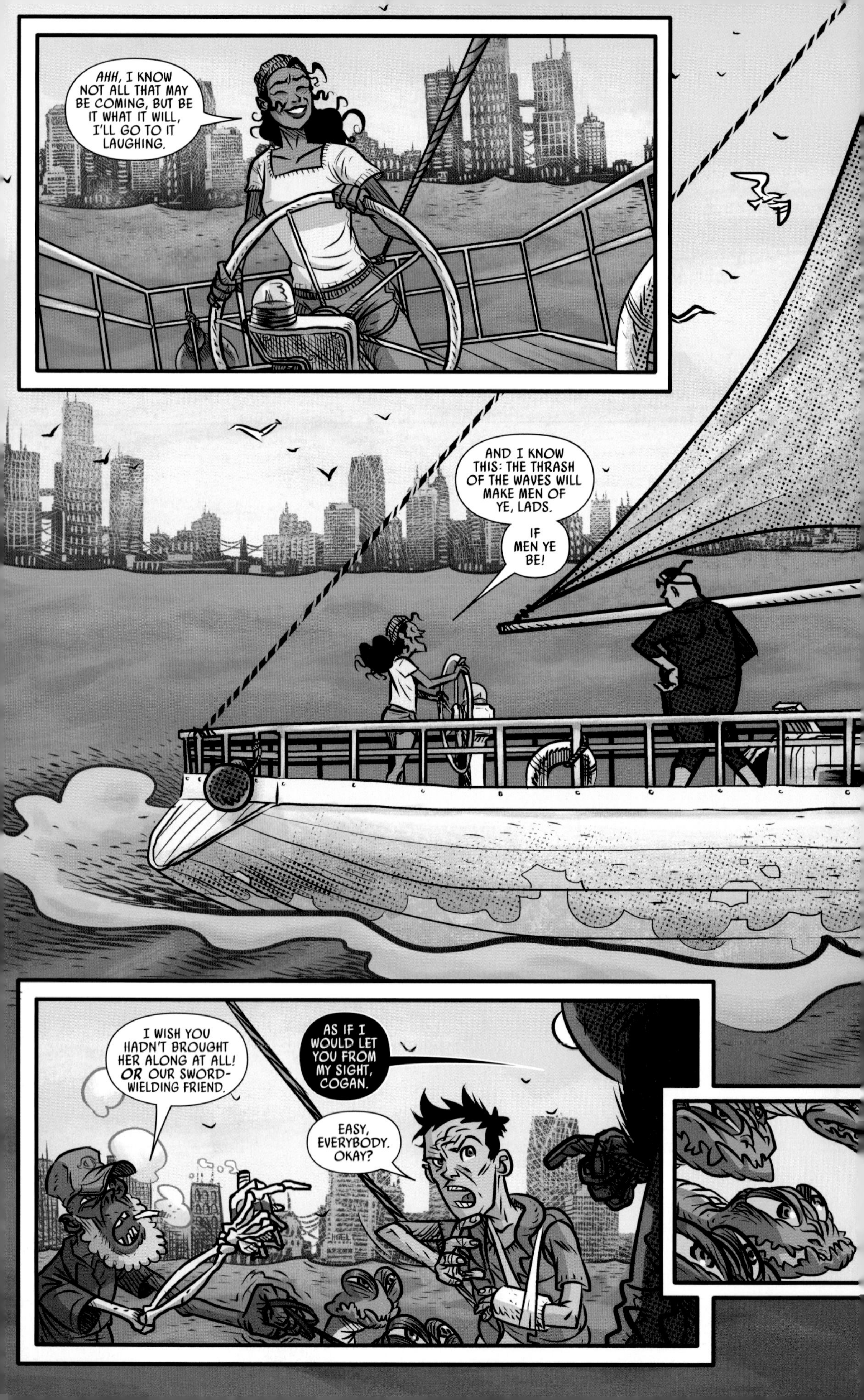
AHH, I KNOW NOT ALL THAT MAY BE COMING, BUT BE IT WHAT IT WILL, I'LL GO TO IT LAUGHING.
AND I KNOW THIS: THE THRASH OF THE WAVES WILL MAKE MEN OF YE, LADS.
IF MEN YE BE!
I WISH YOU HADN'T BROUGHT HER ALONG AT ALL! OR OUR SWORD-WIELDING FRIEND.
AS IF I WOULD LET YOU FROM MY SIGHT, COGAN.
EASY, EVERYBODY. OKAY?

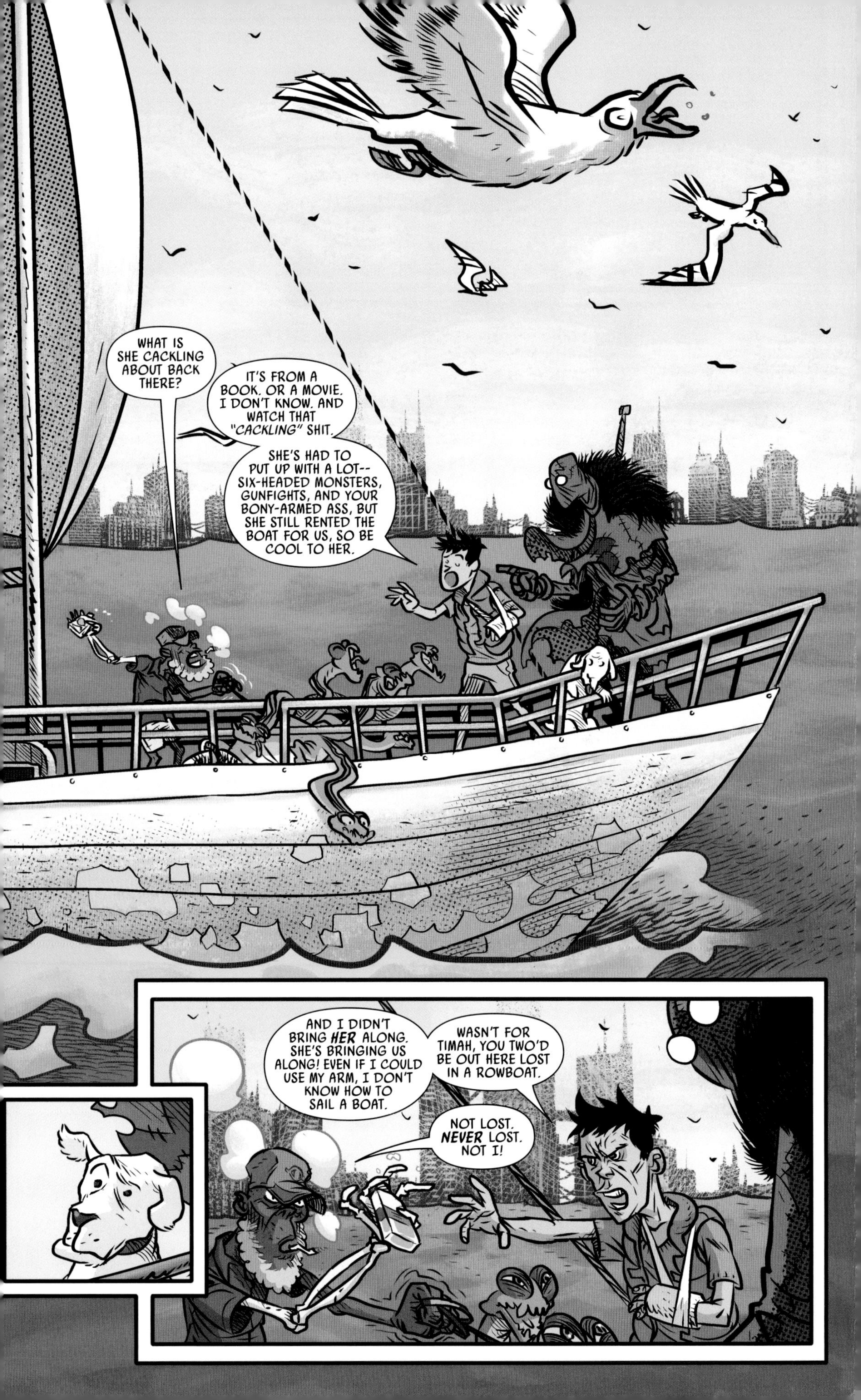
WHAT IS SHE CACKLING ABOUT BACK THERE?
IT'S FROM A BOOK. OR A MOVIE. I DON'T KNOW. AND WATCH THAT "CACKLING" SHIT.
SHE'S HAD TO PUT UP WITH A LOT-- SIX-HEADED MONSTERS, GUNFIGHTS, AND YOUR BONY-ARMED ASS, BUT SHE STILL RENTED THE BOAT FOR US, SO BE COOL TO HER.
AND I DIDN'T BRING HER ALONG. SHE'S BRINGING US ALONG! EVEN IF I COULD USE MY ARM, I DON'T KNOW HOW TO SAIL A BOAT.
WASN'T FOR TIMAH, YOU TWO'D BE OUT HERE LOST IN A ROWBOAT.
NOT LOST. NEVER LOST. NOT I!

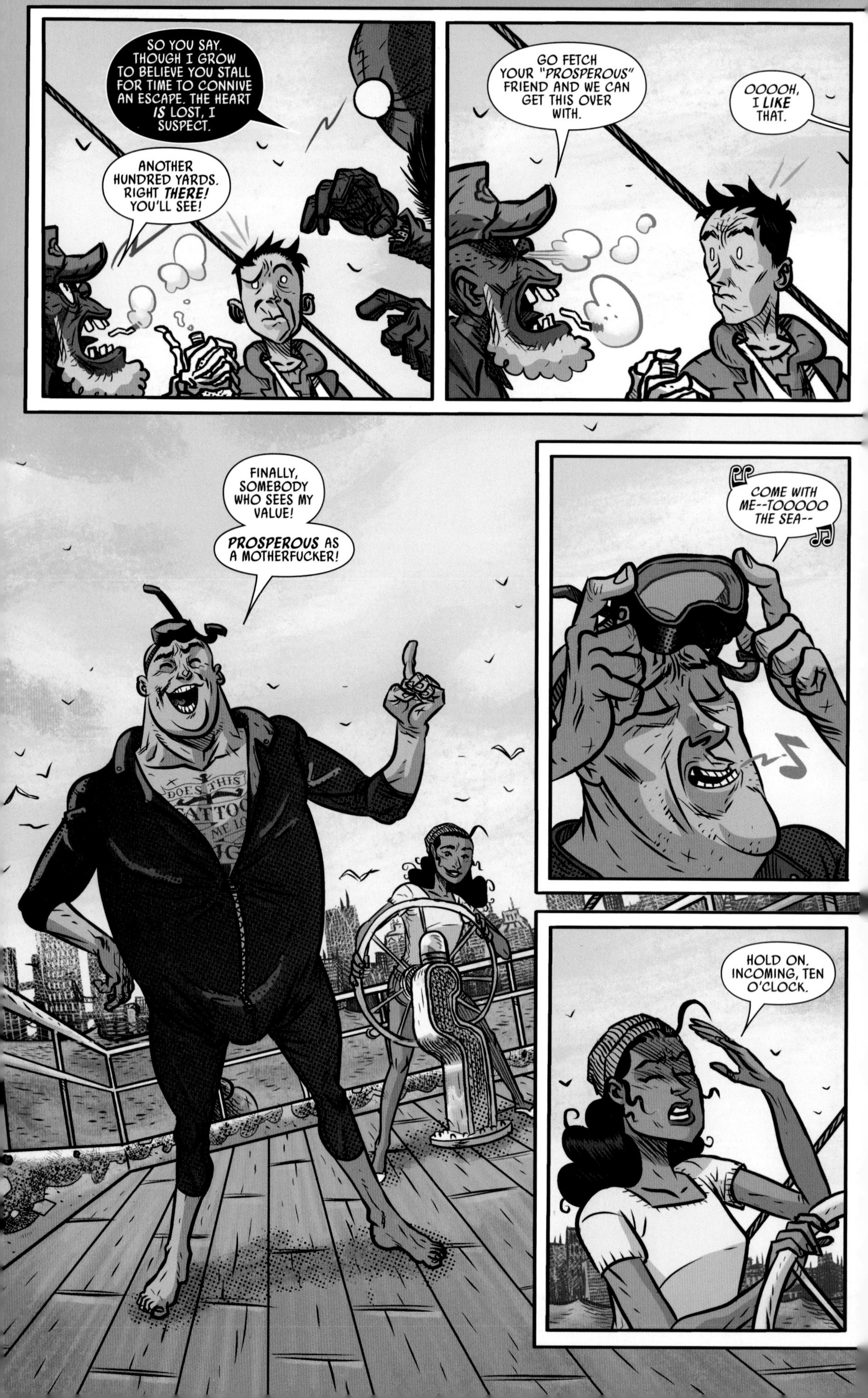
SO YOU SAY. THOUGH I GROW TO BELIEVE YOU STALL FOR TIME TO CONNIVE AN ESCAPE. THE HEART *IS* LOST, I SUSPECT.
ANOTHER HUNDRED YARDS. RIGHT *THERE!* YOU'LL SEE!
GO FETCH YOUR "*PROSPEROUS*" FRIEND AND WE CAN GET THIS OVER WITH.
OOOOH, I *LIKE* THAT.
FINALLY, SOMEBODY WHO SEES MY VALUE!
*PROSPEROUS* AS A MOTHERFUCKER!
DOES THIS TATTOO
COME WITH ME--TOOOOO THE SEA--
HOLD ON. INCOMING, TEN O'CLOCK.

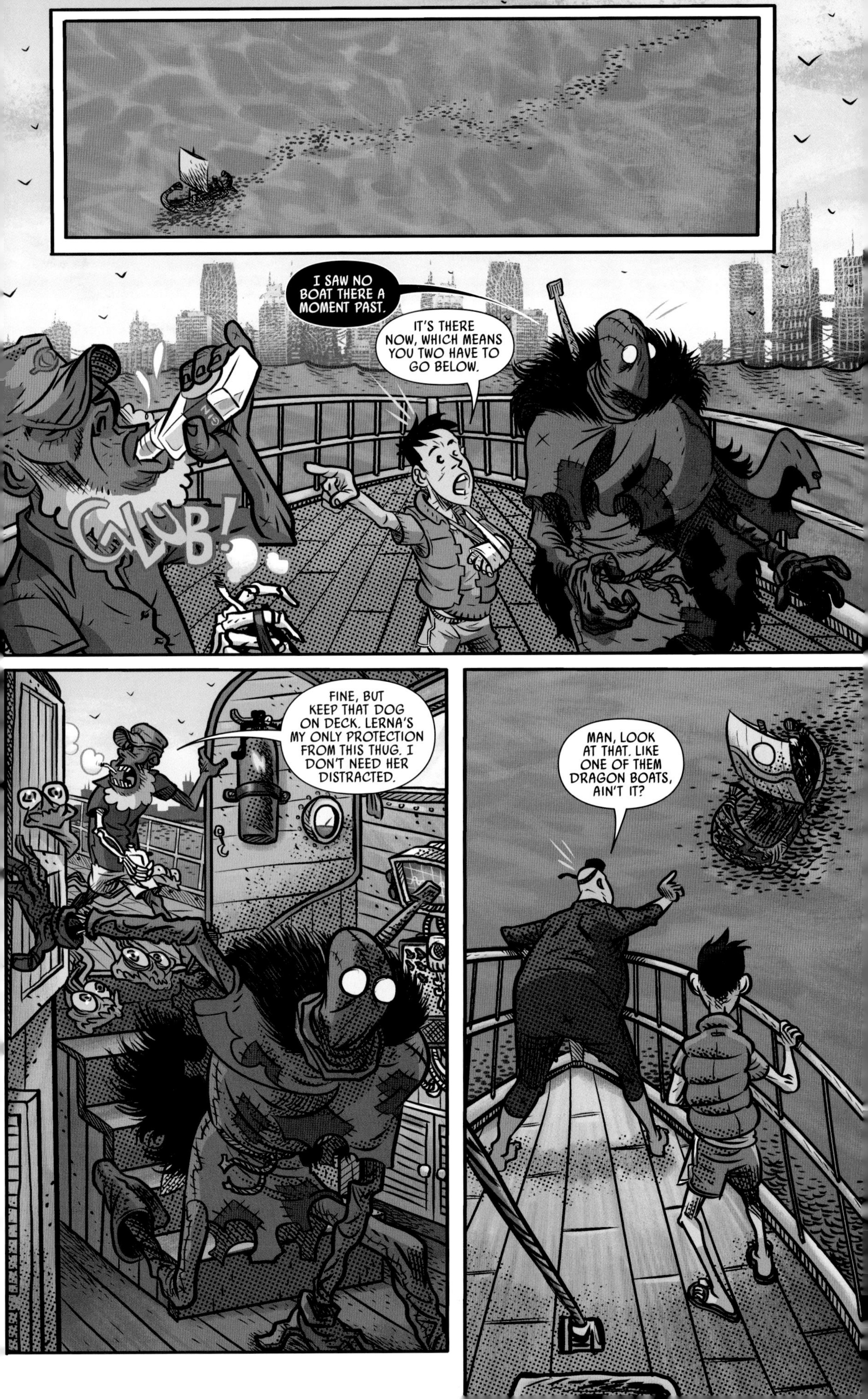
I SAW NO BOAT THERE A MOMENT PAST.
IT'S THERE NOW, WHICH MEANS YOU TWO HAVE TO GO BELOW.
GLUB!
GIN
FINE, BUT KEEP THAT DOG ON DECK. LERNA'S MY ONLY PROTECTION FROM THIS THUG. I DON'T NEED HER DISTRACTED.
MAN, LOOK AT THAT. LIKE ONE OF THEM DRAGON BOATS, AIN'T IT?

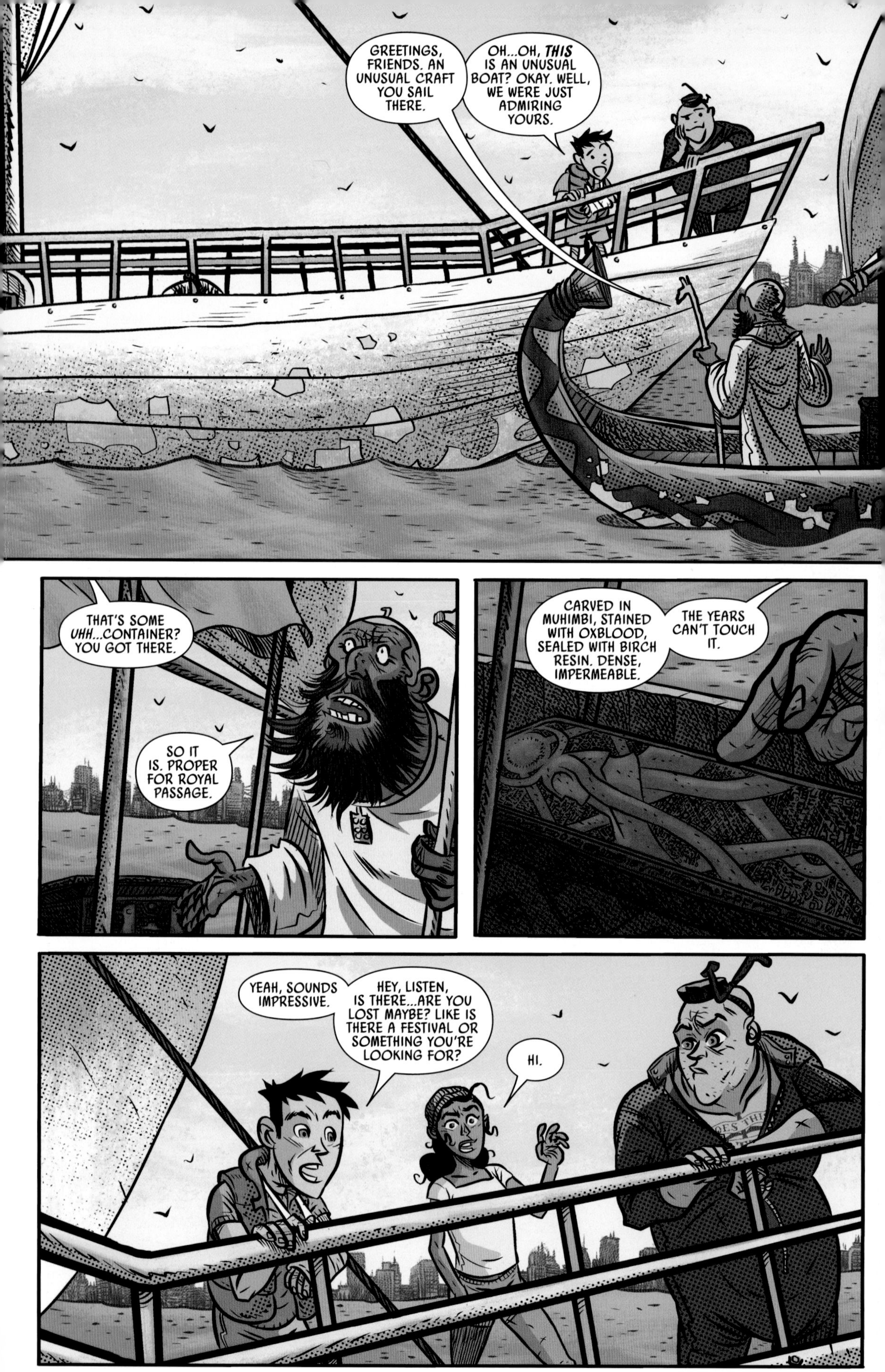
GREETINGS, FRIENDS. AN UNUSUAL CRAFT YOU SAIL THERE.
OH...OH, *THIS* IS AN UNUSUAL BOAT? OKAY. WELL, WE WERE JUST ADMIRING YOURS.
THAT'S SOME *UHH*...CONTAINER? YOU GOT THERE.
SO IT IS. PROPER FOR ROYAL PASSAGE.
CARVED IN MUHIMBI, STAINED WITH OXBLOOD, SEALED WITH BIRCH RESIN. DENSE, IMPERMEABLE.
THE YEARS CAN'T TOUCH IT.
YEAH, SOUNDS IMPRESSIVE.
HEY, LISTEN, IS THERE...ARE YOU LOST MAYBE? LIKE IS THERE A FESTIVAL OR SOMETHING YOU'RE LOOKING FOR?
HI.

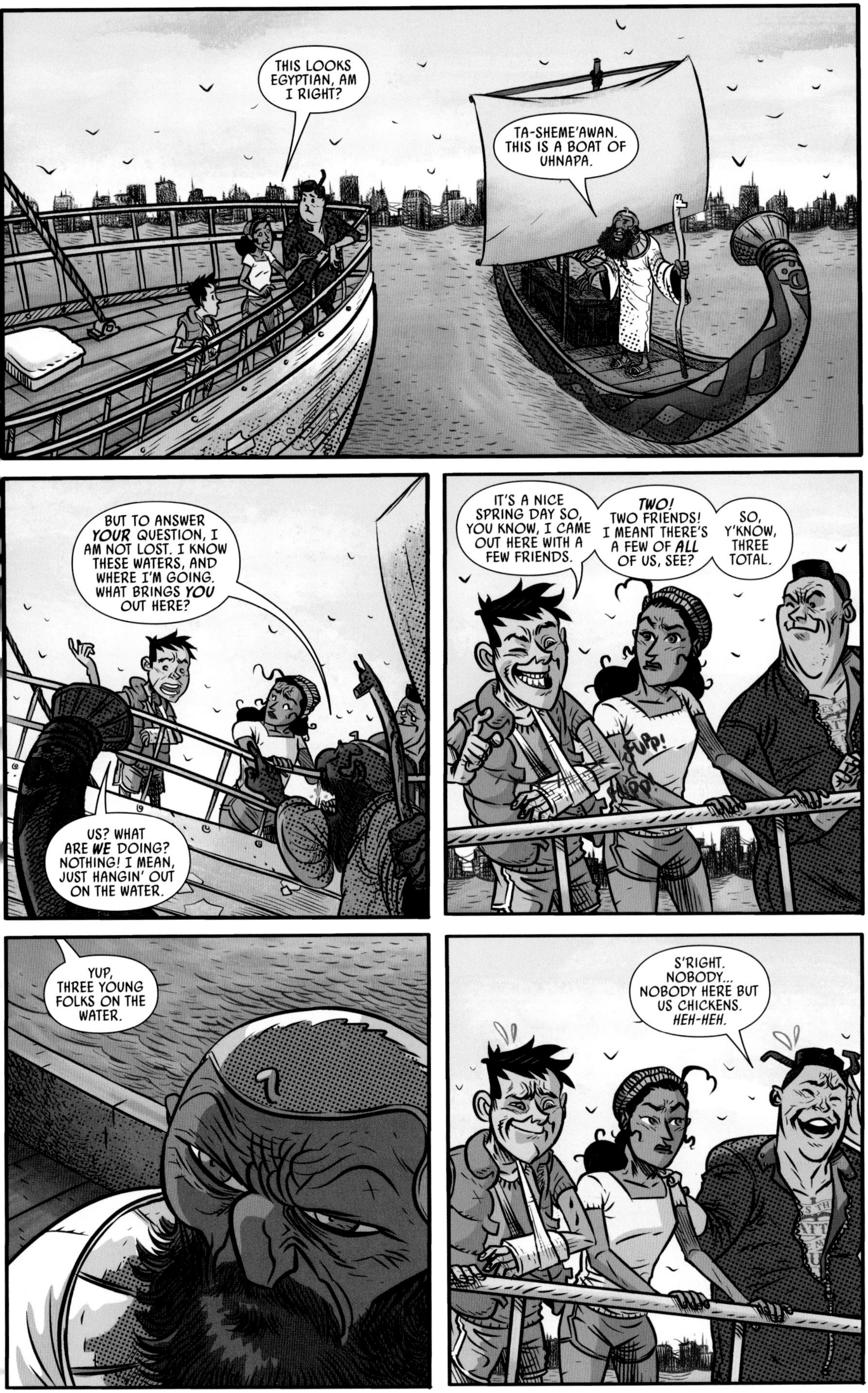
THIS LOOKS EGYPTIAN, AM I RIGHT?
TA-SHEME'AWAN. THIS IS A BOAT OF UHNAPA.
BUT TO ANSWER YOUR QUESTION, I AM NOT LOST. I KNOW THESE WATERS, AND WHERE I'M GOING. WHAT BRINGS YOU OUT HERE?
US? WHAT ARE WE DOING? NOTHING! I MEAN, JUST HANGIN' OUT ON THE WATER.
IT'S A NICE SPRING DAY SO, YOU KNOW, I CAME OUT HERE WITH A FEW FRIENDS.
TWO! TWO FRIENDS! I MEANT THERE'S A FEW OF ALL OF US, SEE?
SO, Y'KNOW, THREE TOTAL.
YUP, THREE YOUNG FOLKS ON THE WATER.
S'RIGHT. NOBODY... NOBODY HERE BUT US CHICKENS. HEH-HEH.

I'D HOPED I'D SUPPLIED MYSELF WITH ENOUGH GIN TO TOLERATE YOUR PRESENCE.

NOR DOES ALCOHOL PROVIDE ADEQUATE NUTRITION TO REMEDY THAT BARE, DEAD ARM OF YOURS.

PERHAPS NO SUCH A QUANTITY EXISTS.

A SOBERING MEMENTO OF THE *LAST* TIME I WAS ALONE WITH YOU. MY RELUCTANCE TO REPEAT THAT SCENARIO IS WELL FOUNDED.

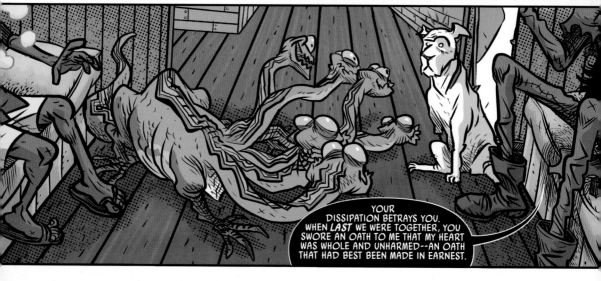

YOUR DISSIPATION BETRAYS YOU. WHEN *LAST* WE WERE TOGETHER, YOU SWORE AN OATH TO ME THAT MY HEART WAS WHOLE AND UNHARMED--AN OATH THAT HAD BEST BEEN MADE IN EARNEST.

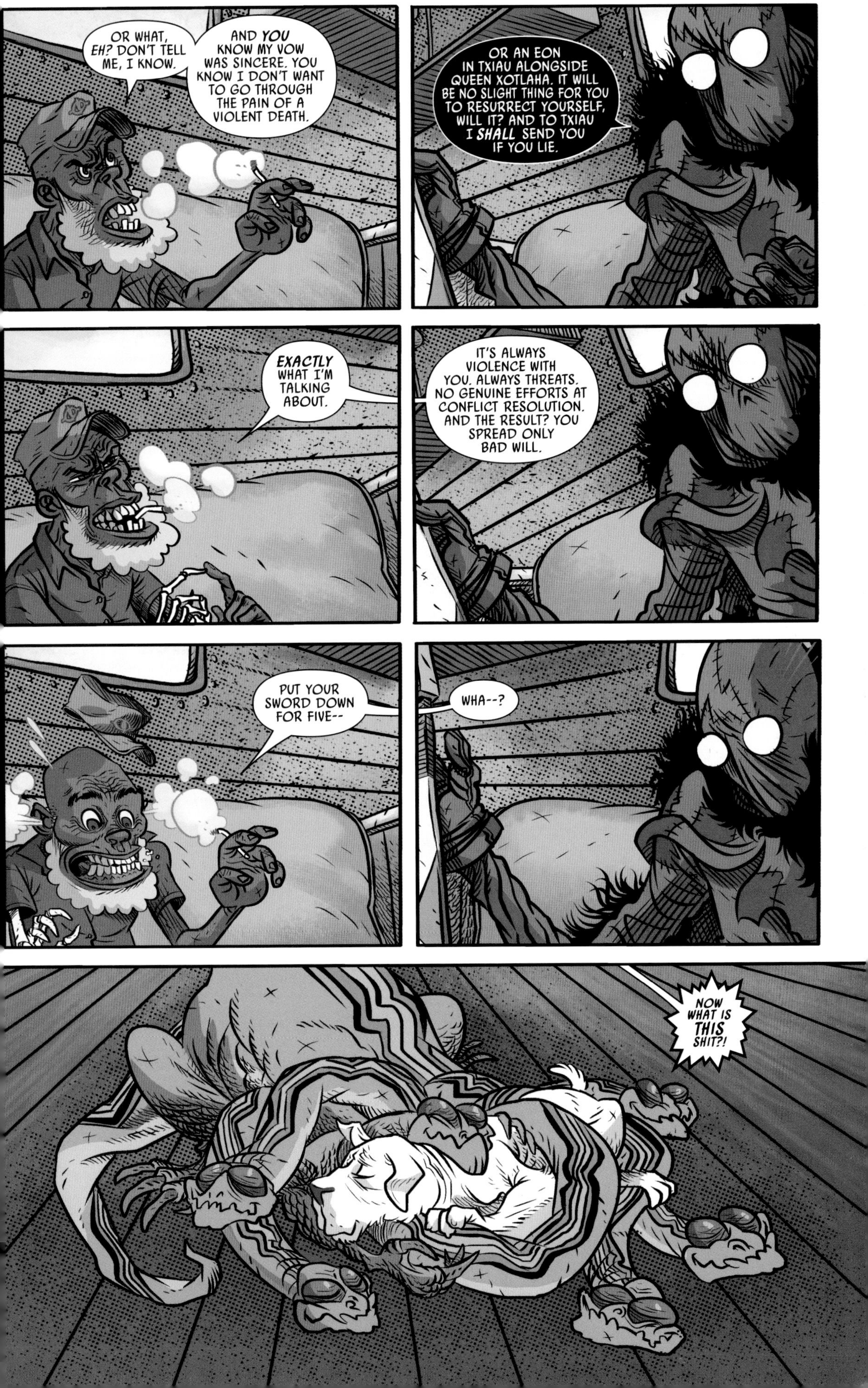
OR WHAT, EH? DON'T TELL ME, I KNOW.
AND YOU KNOW MY VOW WAS SINCERE. YOU KNOW I DON'T WANT TO GO THROUGH THE PAIN OF A VIOLENT DEATH.
OR AN EON IN TXIAU ALONGSIDE QUEEN XOTLAHA. IT WILL BE NO SLIGHT THING FOR YOU TO RESURRECT YOURSELF, WILL IT? AND TO TXIAU I SHALL SEND YOU IF YOU LIE.
EXACTLY WHAT I'M TALKING ABOUT.
IT'S ALWAYS VIOLENCE WITH YOU. ALWAYS THREATS. NO GENUINE EFFORTS AT CONFLICT RESOLUTION. AND THE RESULT? YOU SPREAD ONLY BAD WILL.
PUT YOUR SWORD DOWN FOR FIVE--
WHA--?
NOW WHAT IS THIS SHIT?!

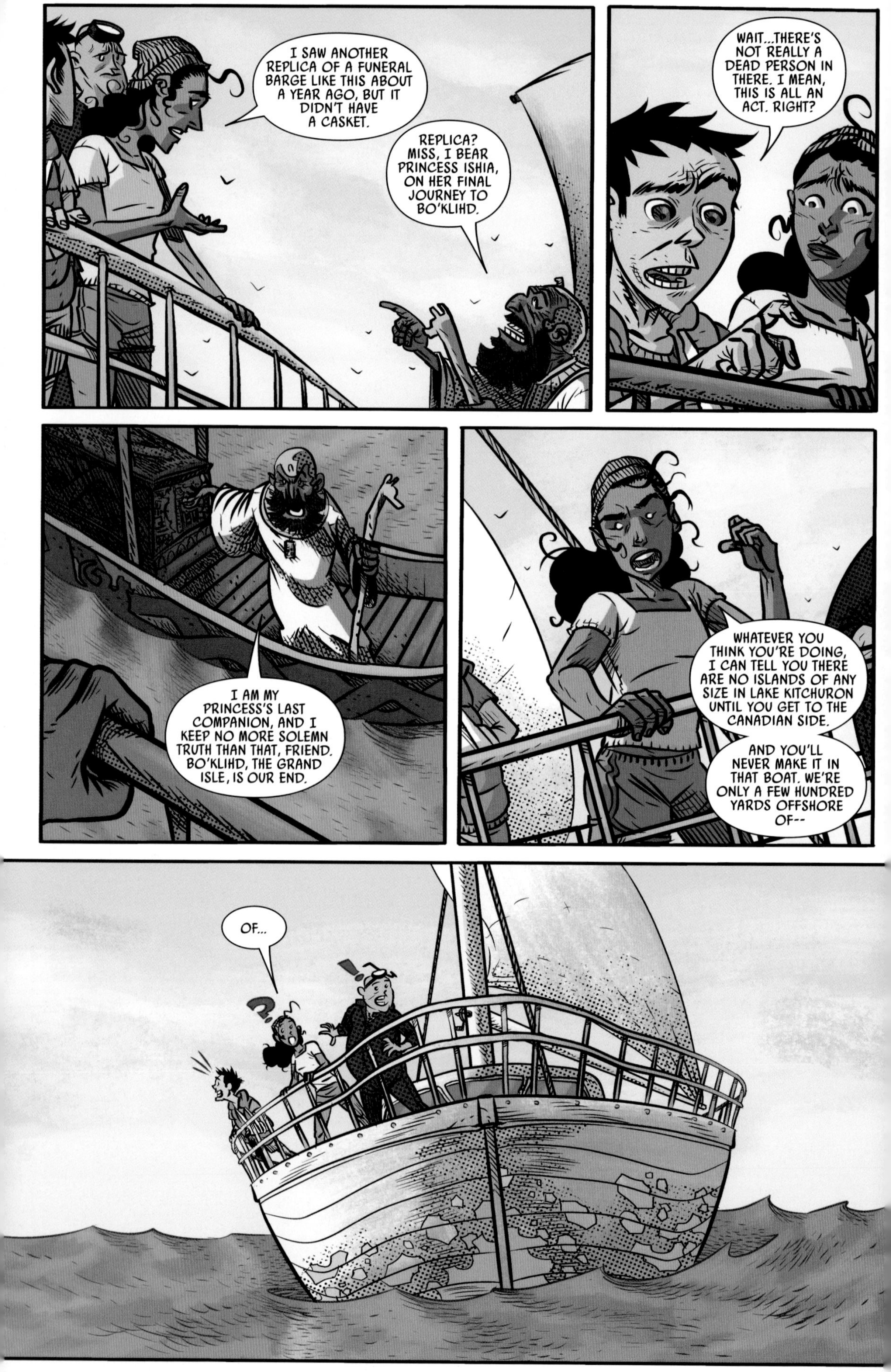
I SAW ANOTHER REPLICA OF A FUNERAL BARGE LIKE THIS ABOUT A YEAR AGO, BUT IT DIDN'T HAVE A CASKET.
REPLICA? MISS, I BEAR PRINCESS ISHIA, ON HER FINAL JOURNEY TO BO'KLIHD.
WAIT...THERE'S NOT REALLY A DEAD PERSON IN THERE. I MEAN, THIS IS ALL AN ACT. RIGHT?
I AM MY PRINCESS'S LAST COMPANION, AND I KEEP NO MORE SOLEMN TRUTH THAN THAT, FRIEND. BO'KLIHD, THE GRAND ISLE, IS OUR END.
WHATEVER YOU THINK YOU'RE DOING, I CAN TELL YOU THERE ARE NO ISLANDS OF ANY SIZE IN LAKE KITCHURON UNTIL YOU GET TO THE CANADIAN SIDE.
AND YOU'LL NEVER MAKE IT IN THAT BOAT. WE'RE ONLY A FEW HUNDRED YARDS OFFSHORE OF--
OF...

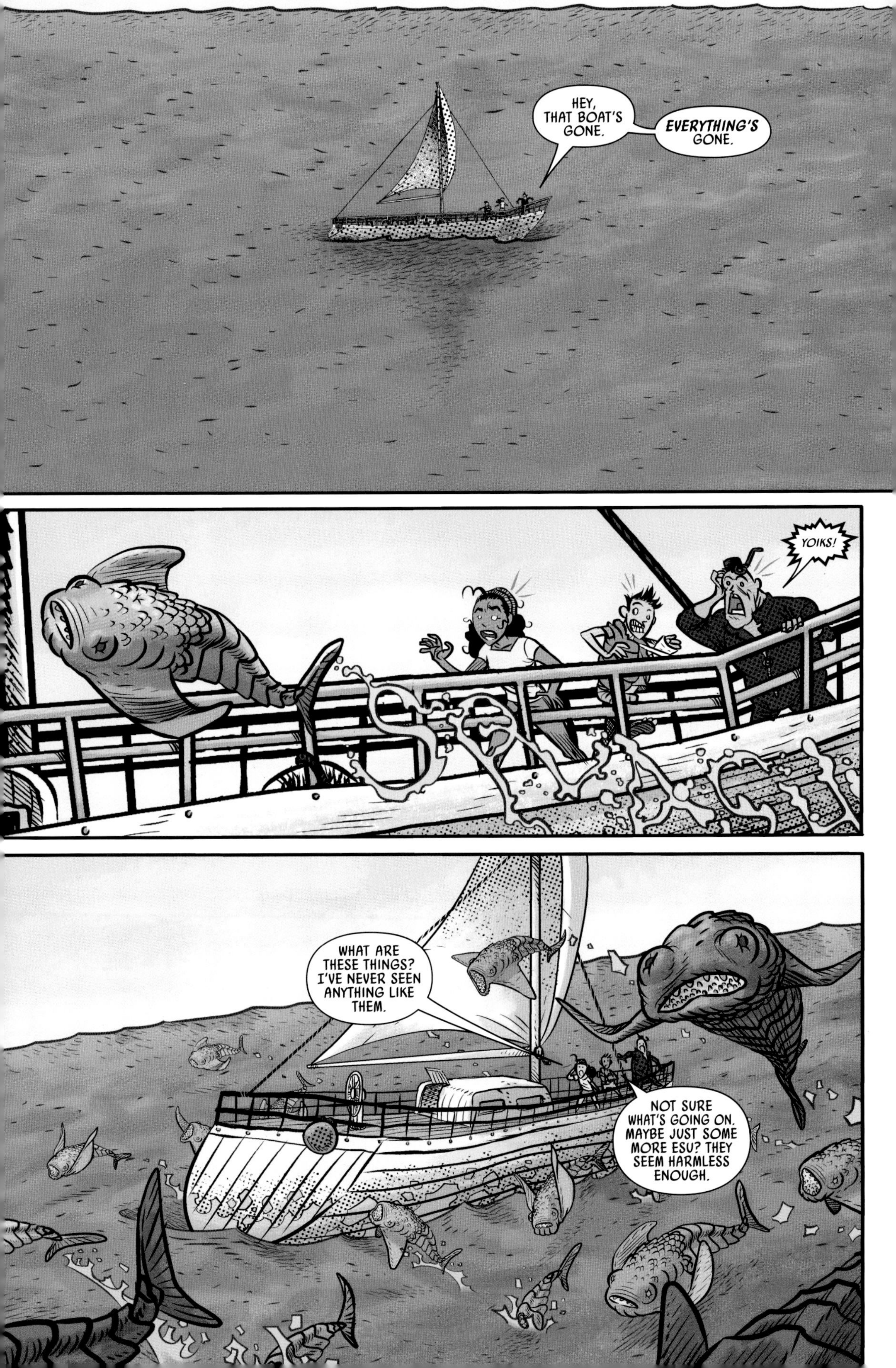

HEY, THAT BOAT'S GONE.
*EVERYTHING'S* GONE.
YOIKS!
WHAT ARE THESE THINGS? I'VE NEVER SEEN ANYTHING LIKE THEM.
NOT SURE WHAT'S GOING ON. MAYBE JUST SOME MORE ESU? THEY SEEM HARMLESS ENOUGH.

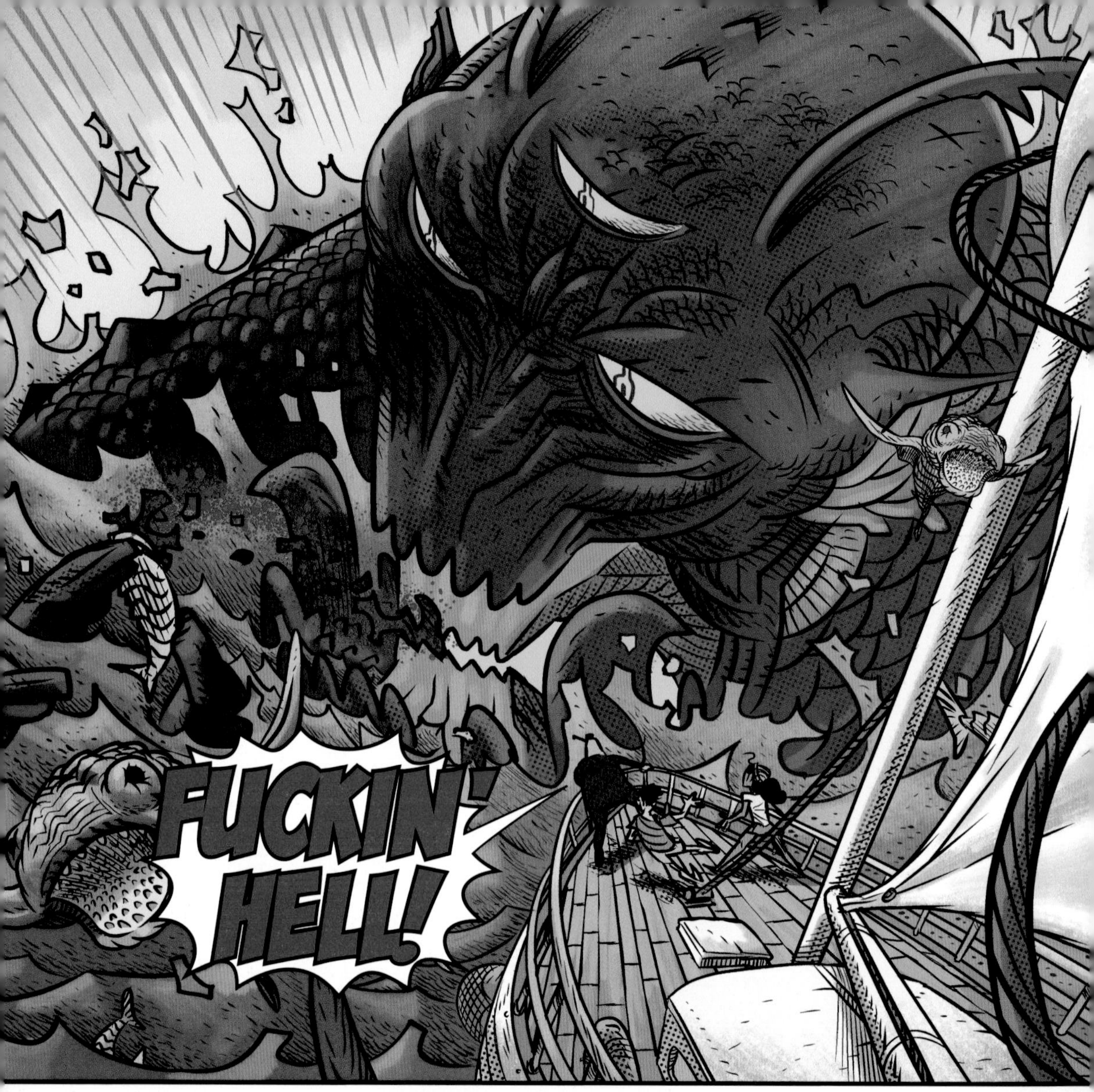
FUCKIN' HELL!

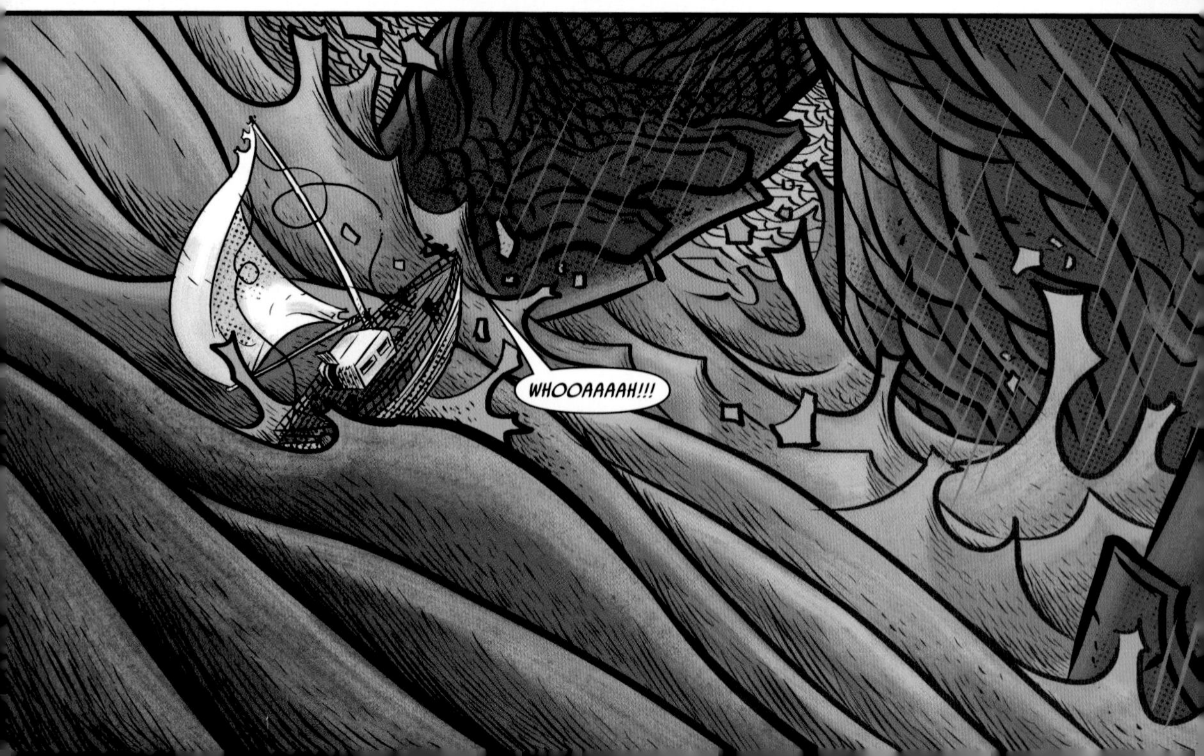
WHOOAAAAH!!!

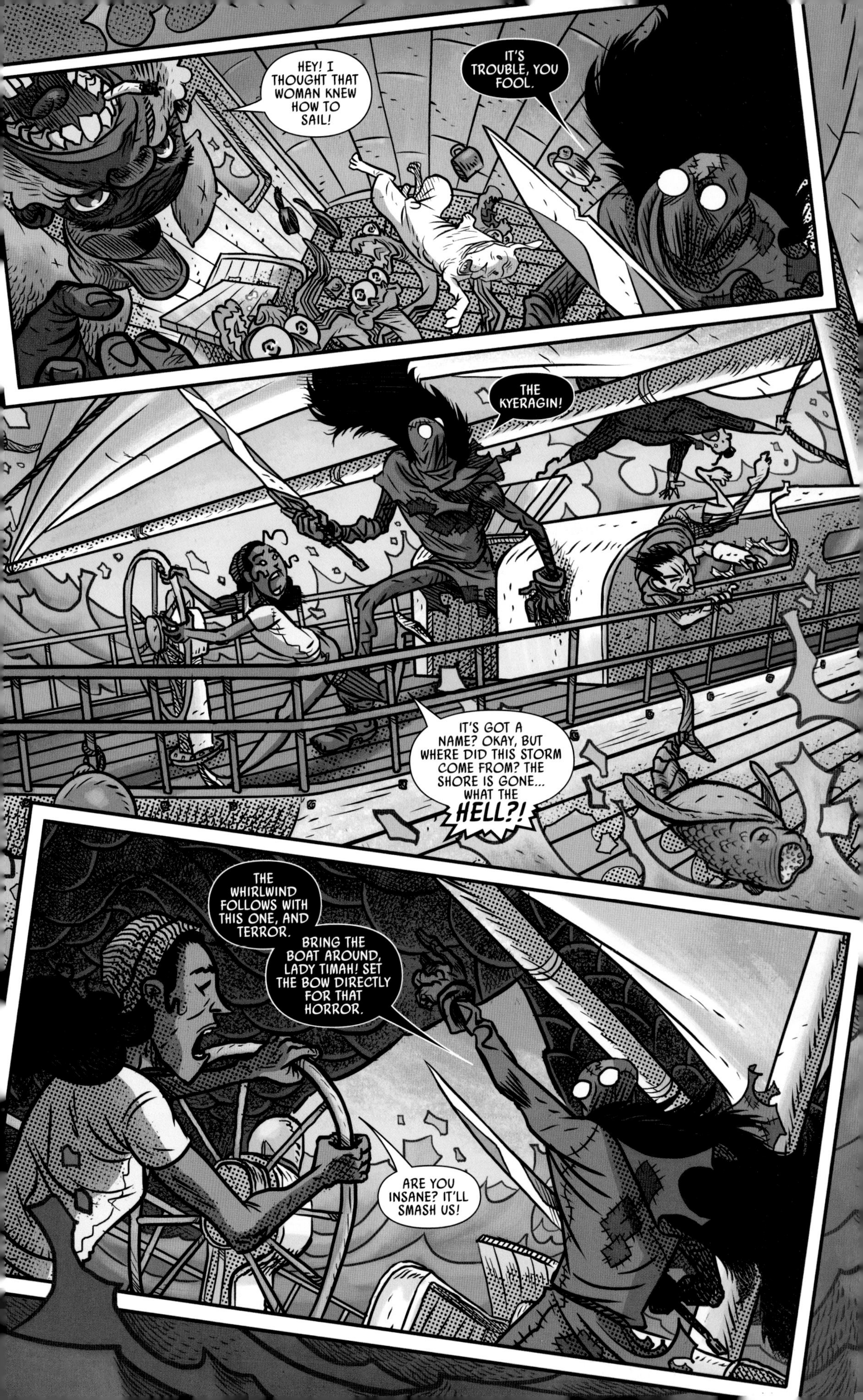
HEY! I THOUGHT THAT WOMAN KNEW HOW TO SAIL!
IT'S TROUBLE, YOU FOOL.
THE KYERAGIN!
IT'S GOT A NAME? OKAY, BUT WHERE DID THIS STORM COME FROM? THE SHORE IS GONE... WHAT THE HELL?!
THE WHIRLWIND FOLLOWS WITH THIS ONE, AND TERROR.
BRING THE BOAT AROUND, LADY TIMAH! SET THE BOW DIRECTLY FOR THAT HORROR.
ARE YOU INSANE? IT'LL SMASH US!

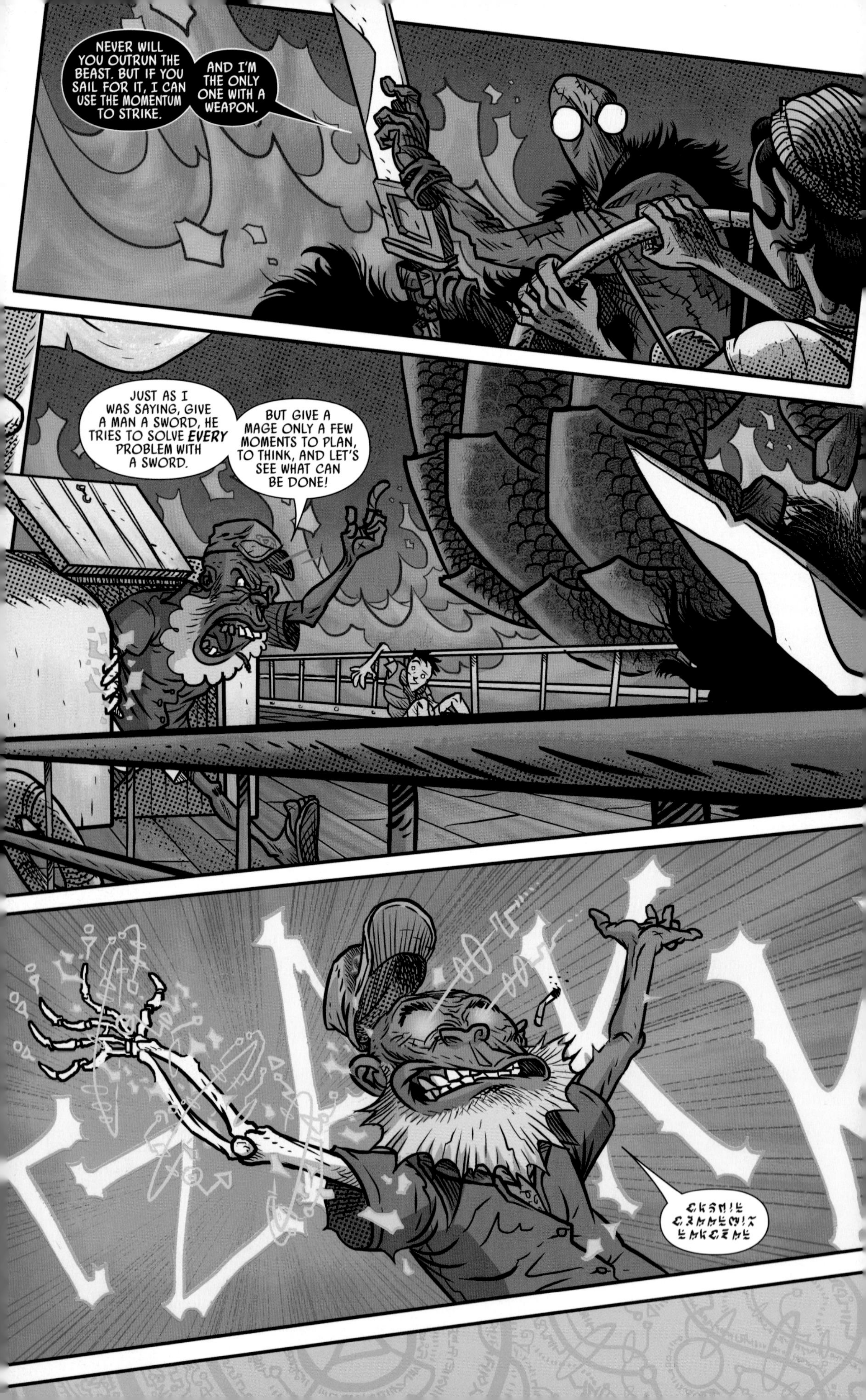
NEVER WILL YOU OUTRUN THE BEAST. BUT IF YOU SAIL FOR IT, I CAN USE THE MOMENTUM TO STRIKE.
AND I'M THE ONLY ONE WITH A WEAPON.
JUST AS I WAS SAYING, GIVE A MAN A SWORD, HE TRIES TO SOLVE EVERY PROBLEM WITH A SWORD.
BUT GIVE A MAGE ONLY A FEW MOMENTS TO PLAN, TO THINK, AND LET'S SEE WHAT CAN BE DONE!

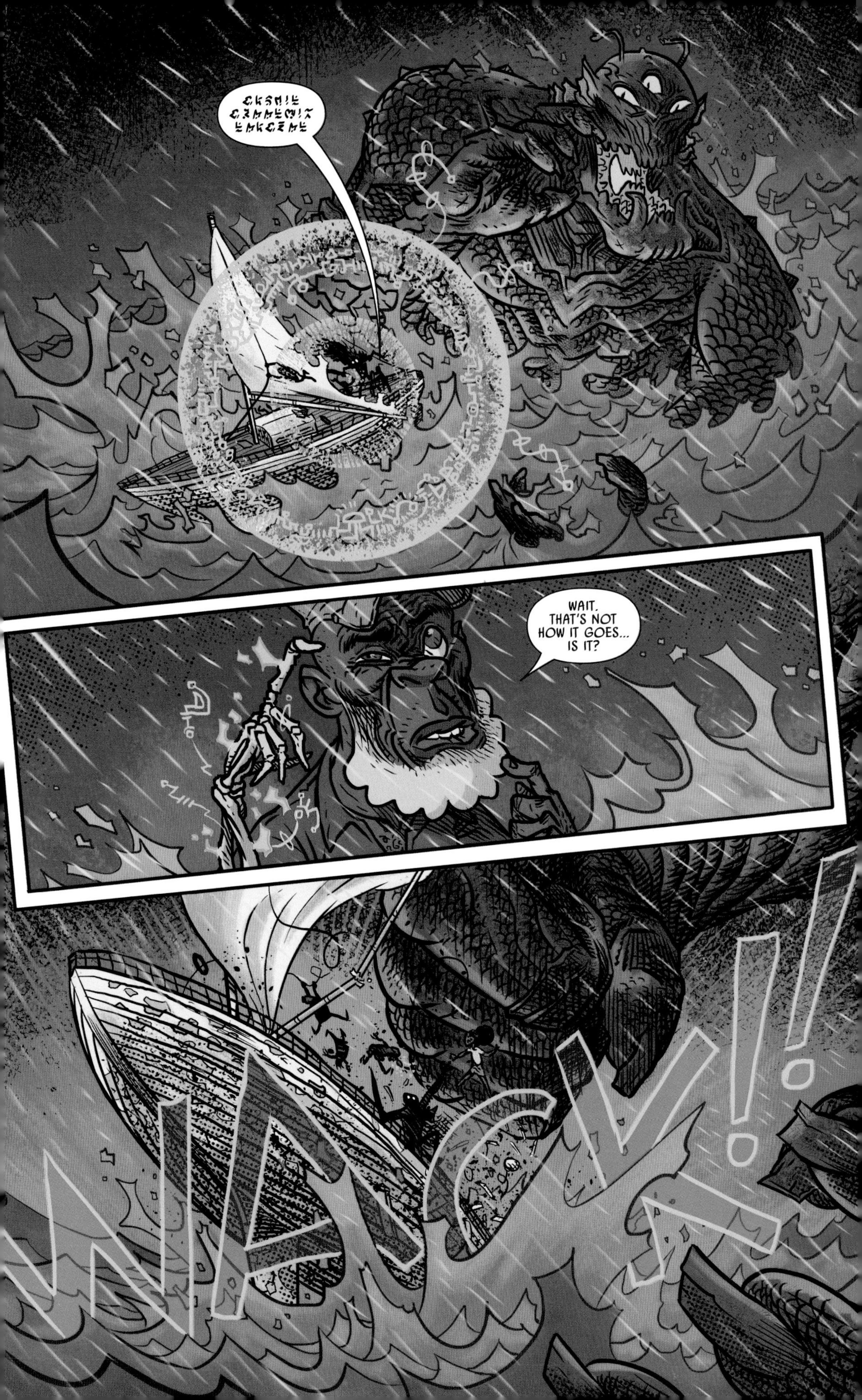
WAIT. THAT'S NOT HOW IT GOES... IS IT?

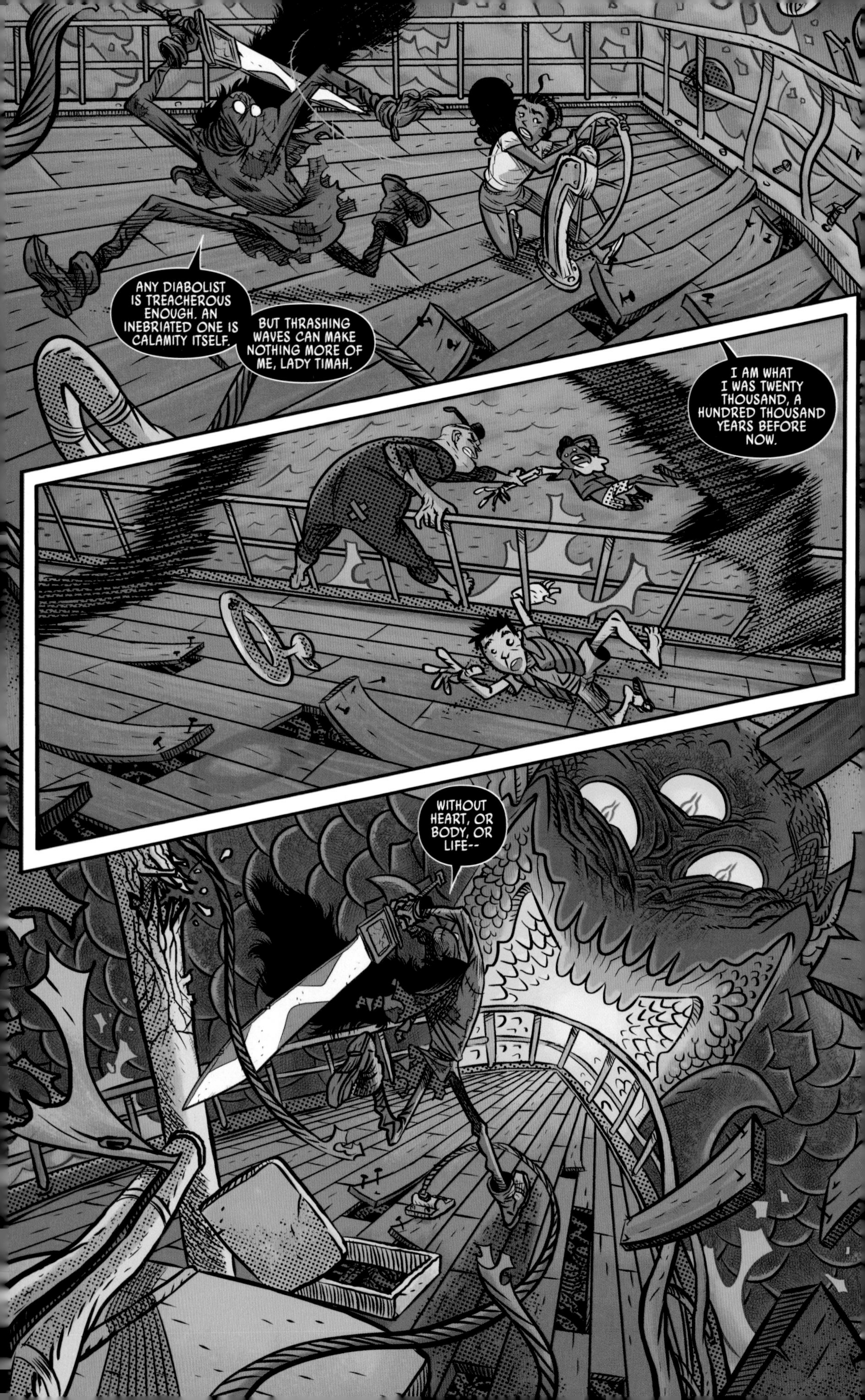
ANY DIABOLIST IS TREACHEROUS ENOUGH. AN INEBRIATED ONE IS CALAMITY ITSELF.
BUT THRASHING WAVES CAN MAKE NOTHING MORE OF ME, LADY TIMAH.
I AM WHAT I WAS TWENTY THOUSAND, A HUNDRED THOUSAND YEARS BEFORE NOW.
WITHOUT HEART, OR BODY, OR LIFE--

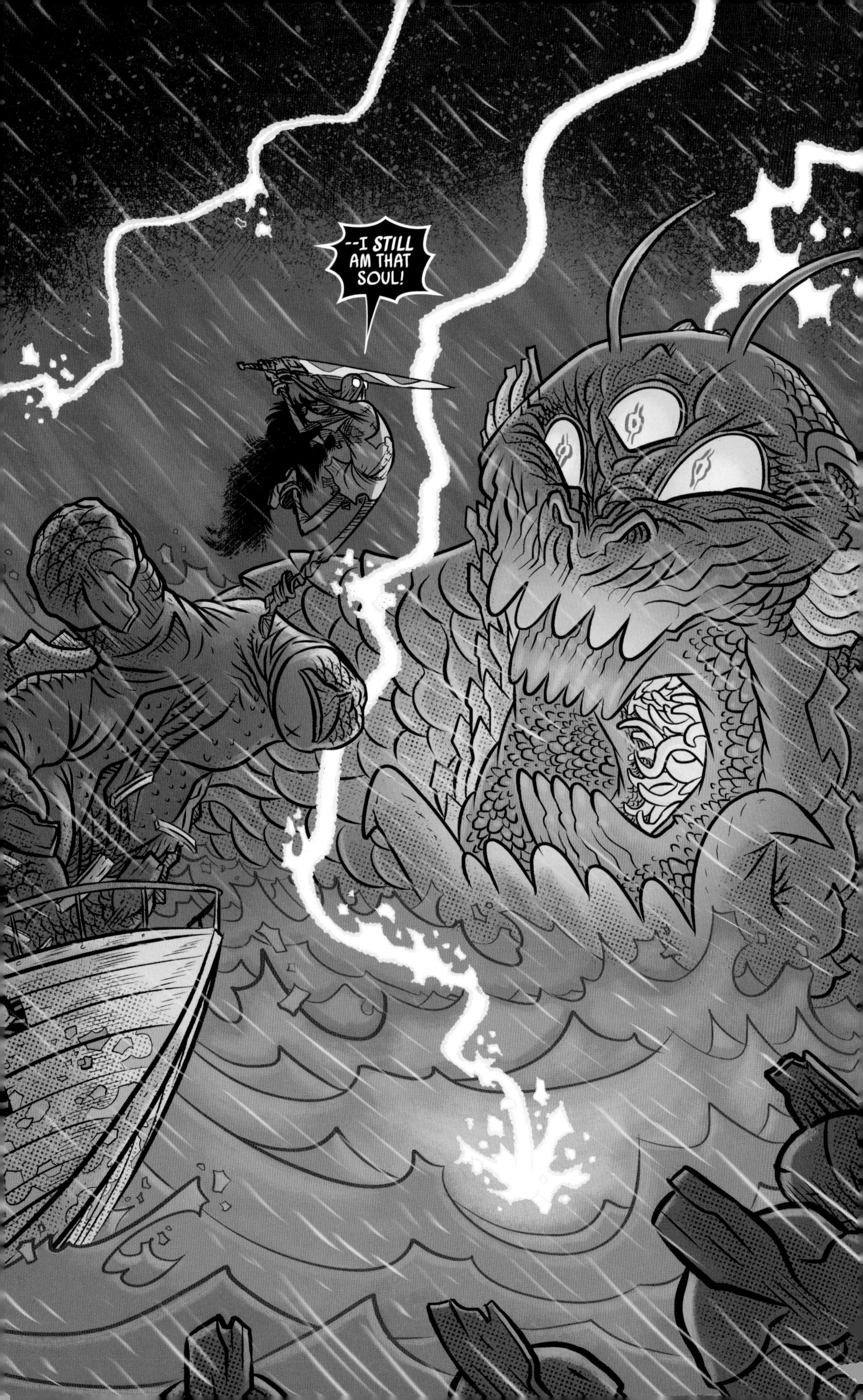
--I STILL AM THAT SOUL!

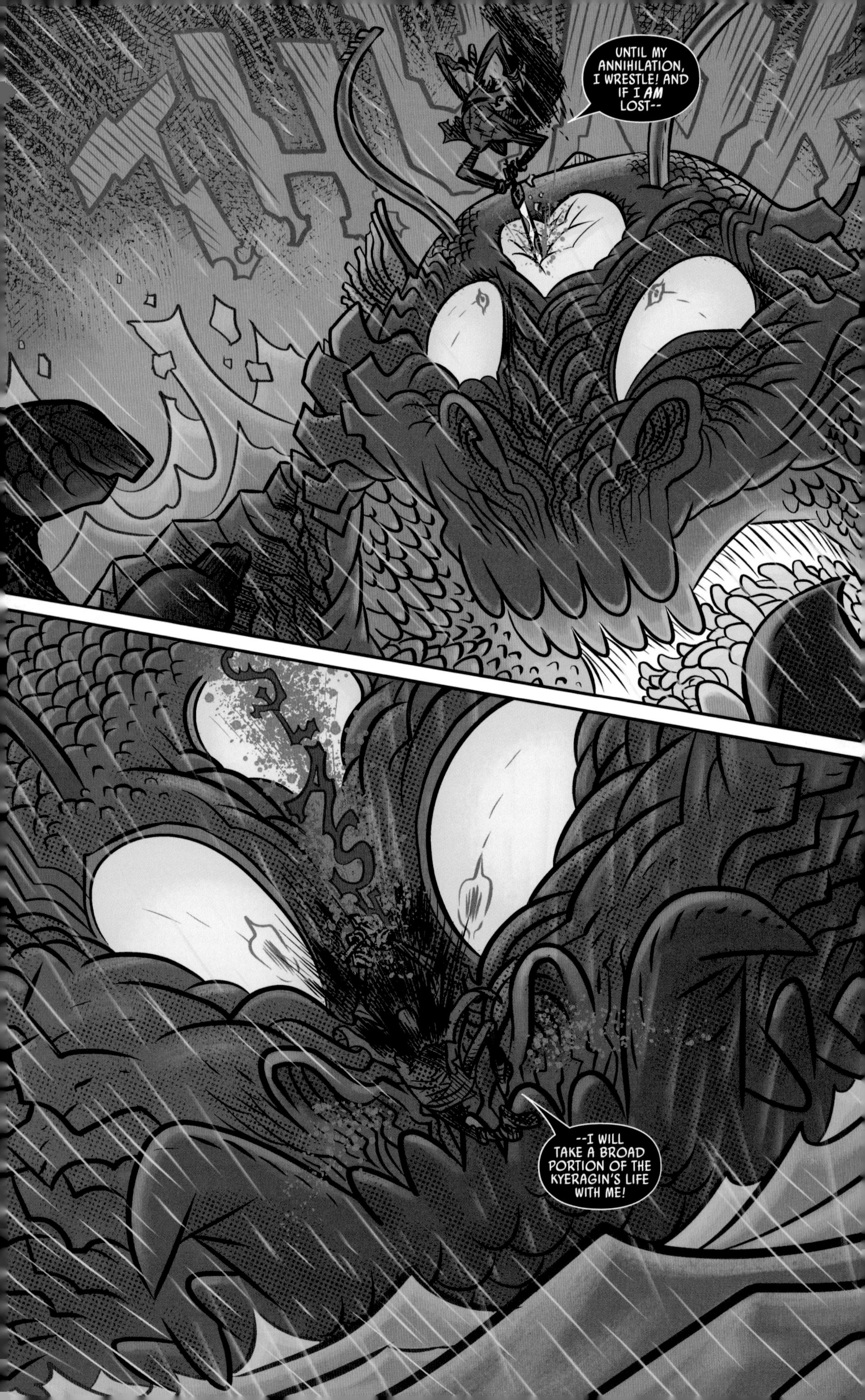
UNTIL MY ANNIHILATION, I WRESTLE! AND IF I AM LOST--
--I WILL TAKE A BROAD PORTION OF THE KYERAGIN'S LIFE WITH ME!

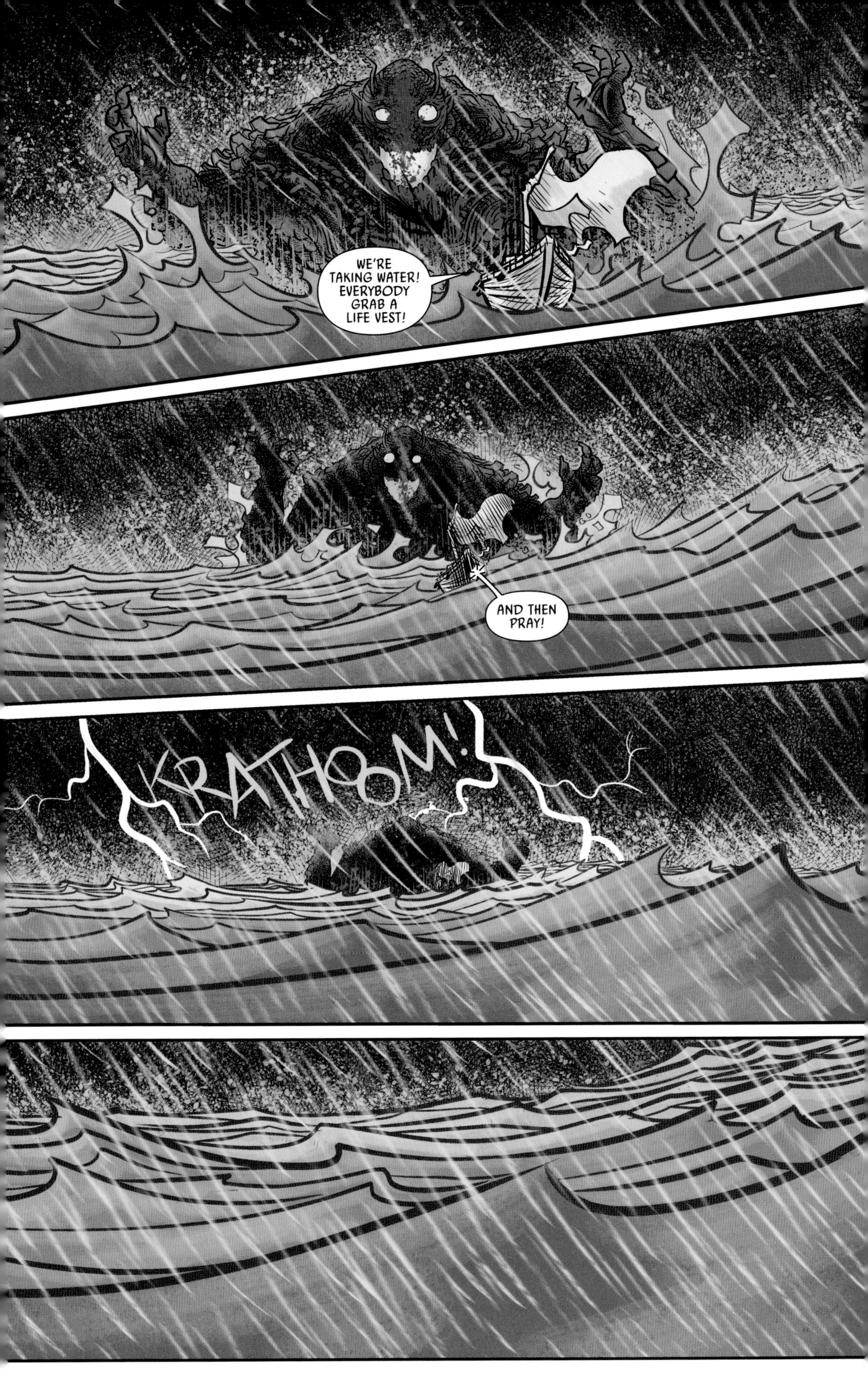
WE'RE TAKING WATER! EVERYBODY GRAB A LIFE VEST!
AND THEN PRAY!
KRATHOOM!

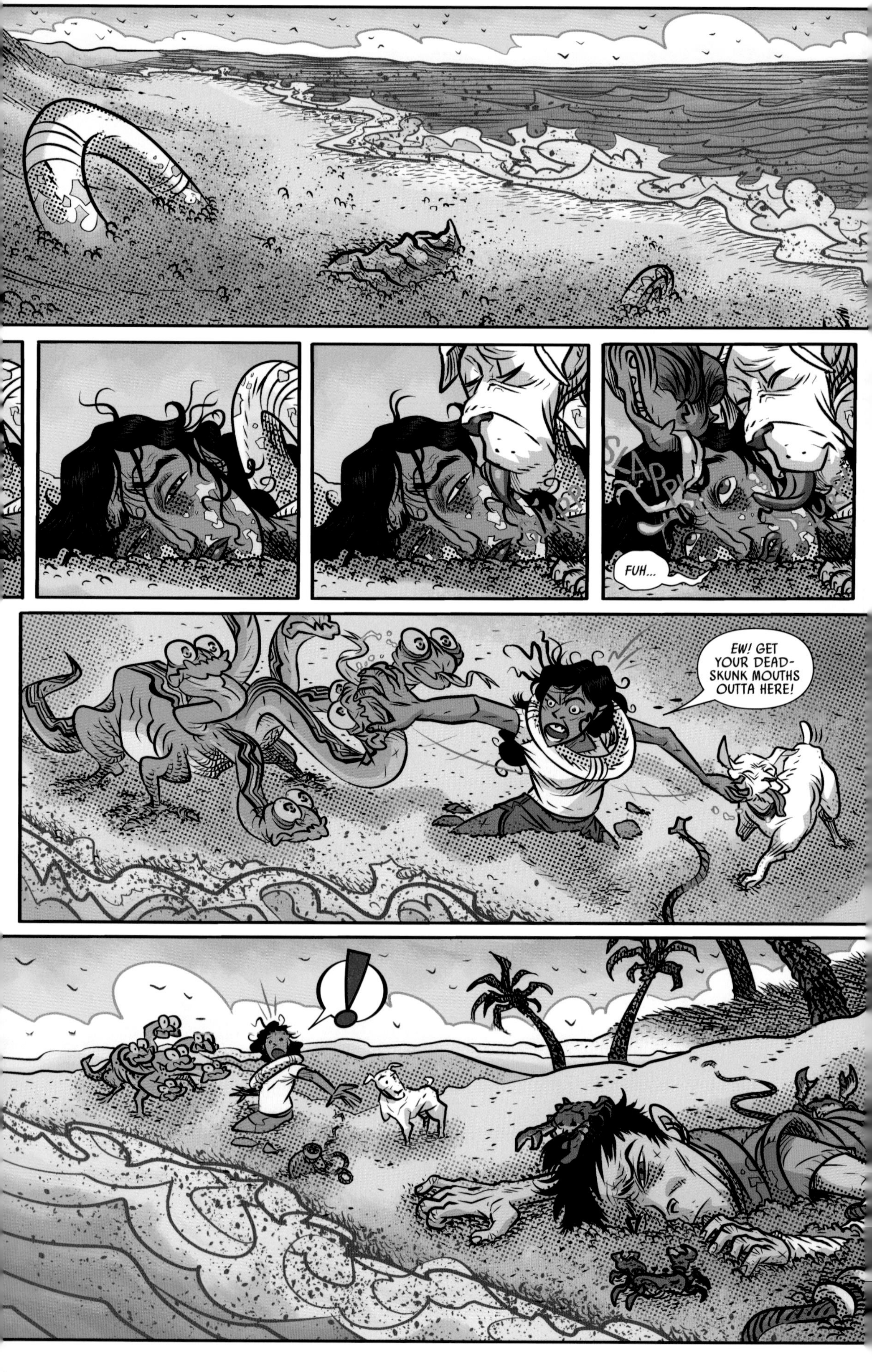
SLAPP!
FUH...
EW! GET YOUR DEAD-SKUNK MOUTHS OUTTA HERE!
!

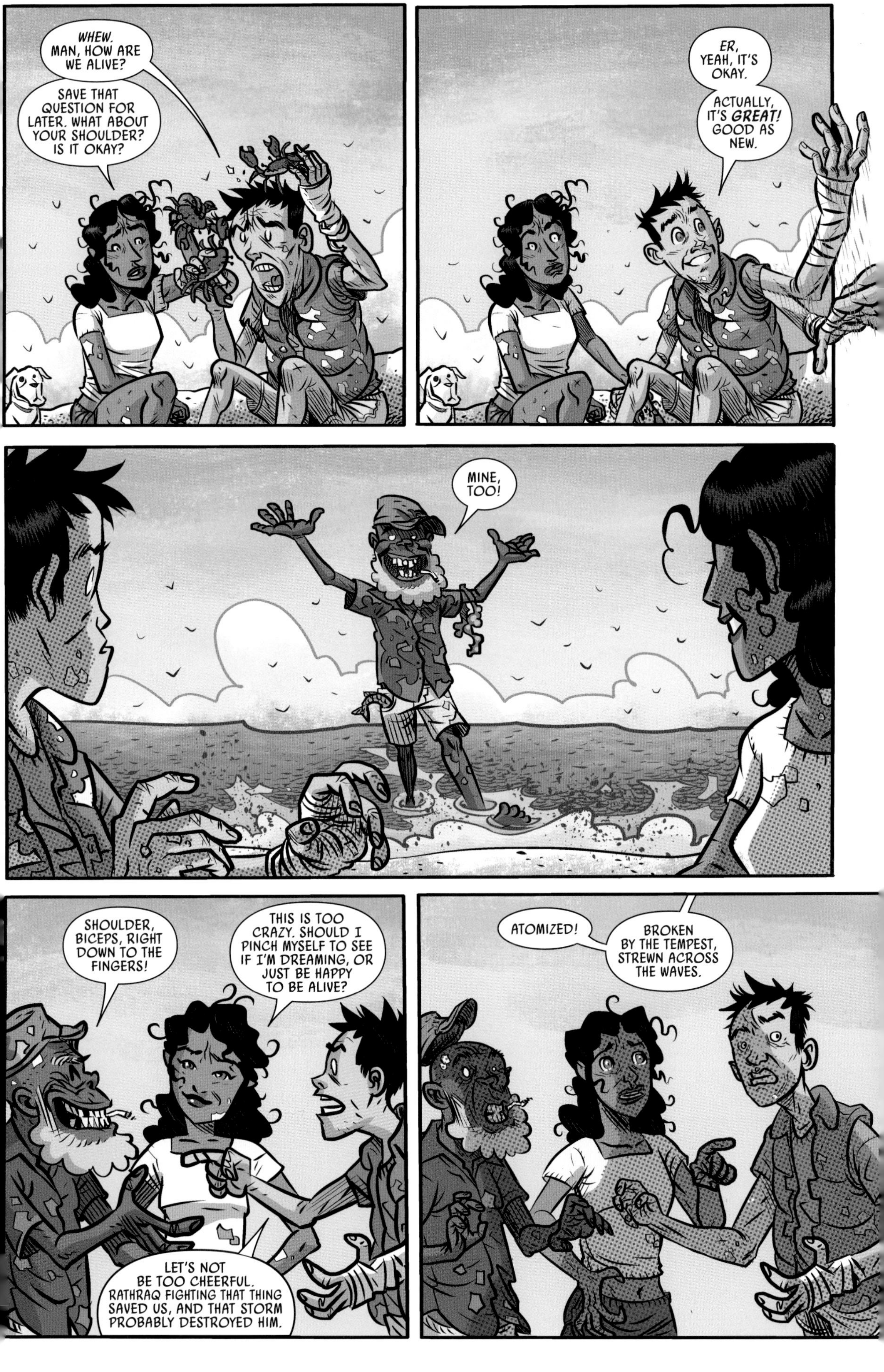
WHEW. MAN, HOW ARE WE ALIVE?
SAVE THAT QUESTION FOR LATER. WHAT ABOUT YOUR SHOULDER? IS IT OKAY?
ER, YEAH, IT'S OKAY.
ACTUALLY, IT'S **GREAT!** GOOD AS NEW.
MINE, TOO!
SHOULDER, BICEPS, RIGHT DOWN TO THE FINGERS!
THIS IS TOO CRAZY. SHOULD I PINCH MYSELF TO SEE IF I'M DREAMING, OR JUST BE HAPPY TO BE ALIVE?
LET'S NOT BE TOO CHEERFUL. RATHRAQ FIGHTING THAT THING SAVED US, AND THAT STORM PROBABLY DESTROYED HIM.
BROKEN BY THE TEMPEST, STREWN ACROSS THE WAVES.
ATOMIZED!

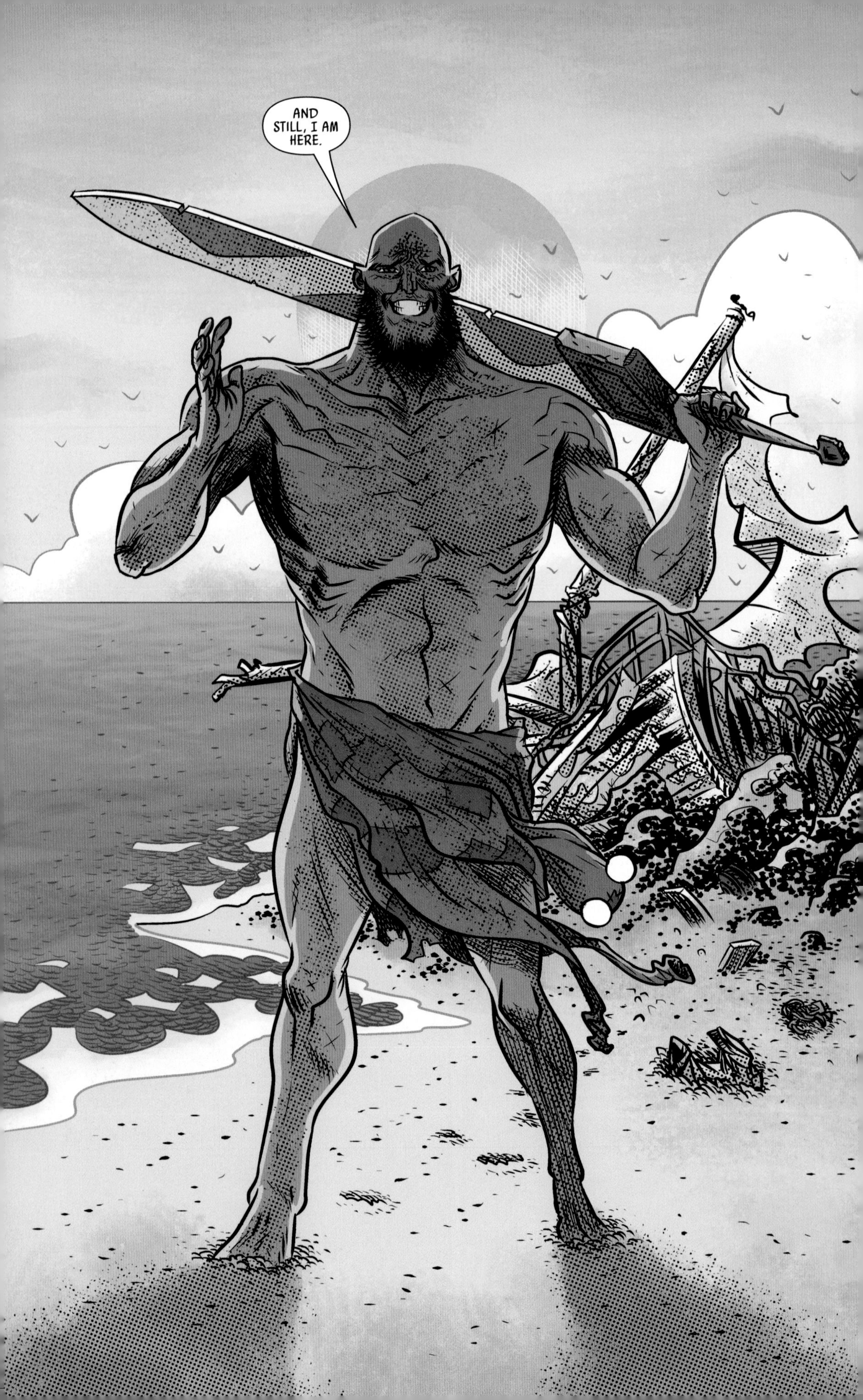
AND STILL, I AM HERE.

# RUMBLE

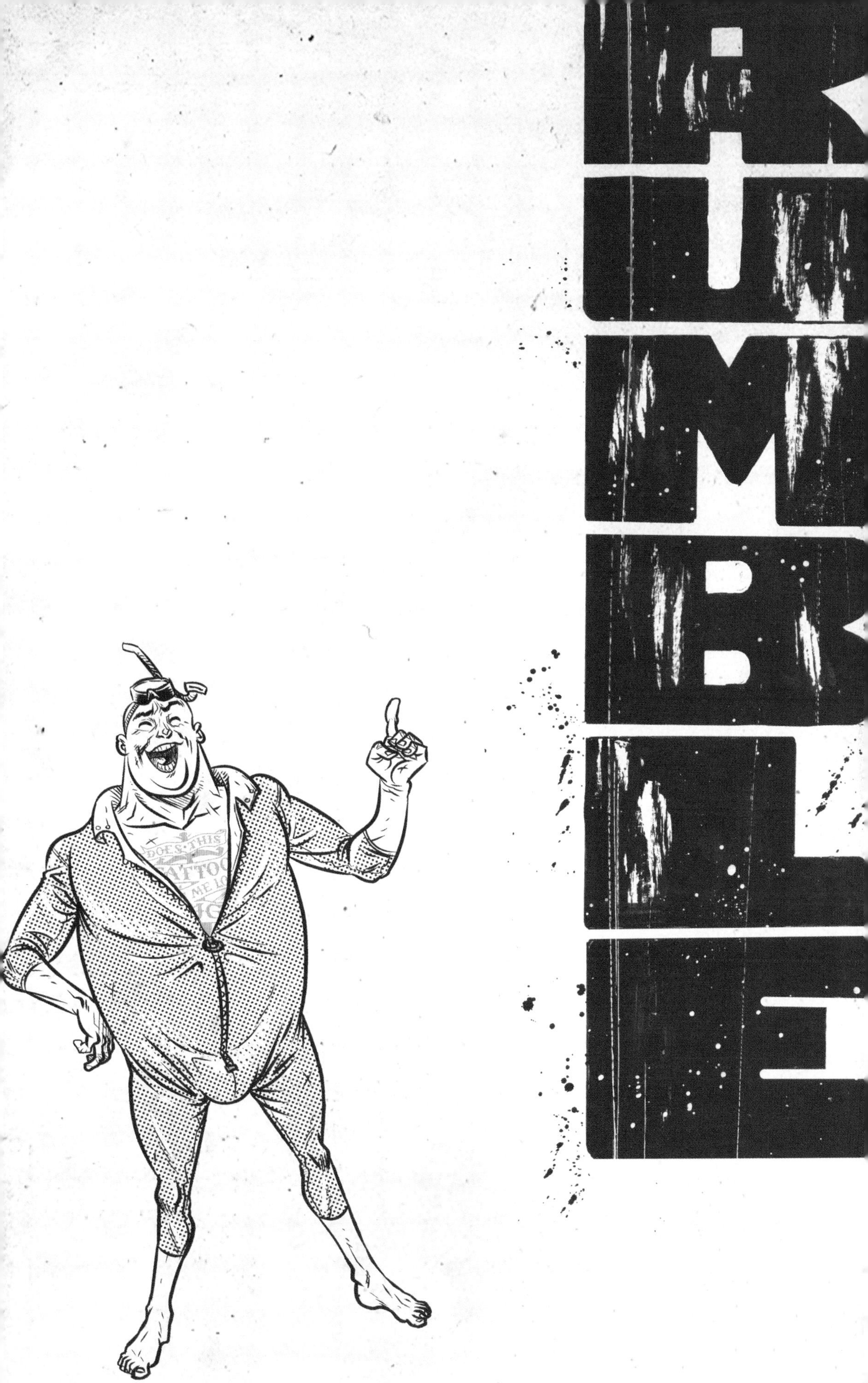
DOES THIS

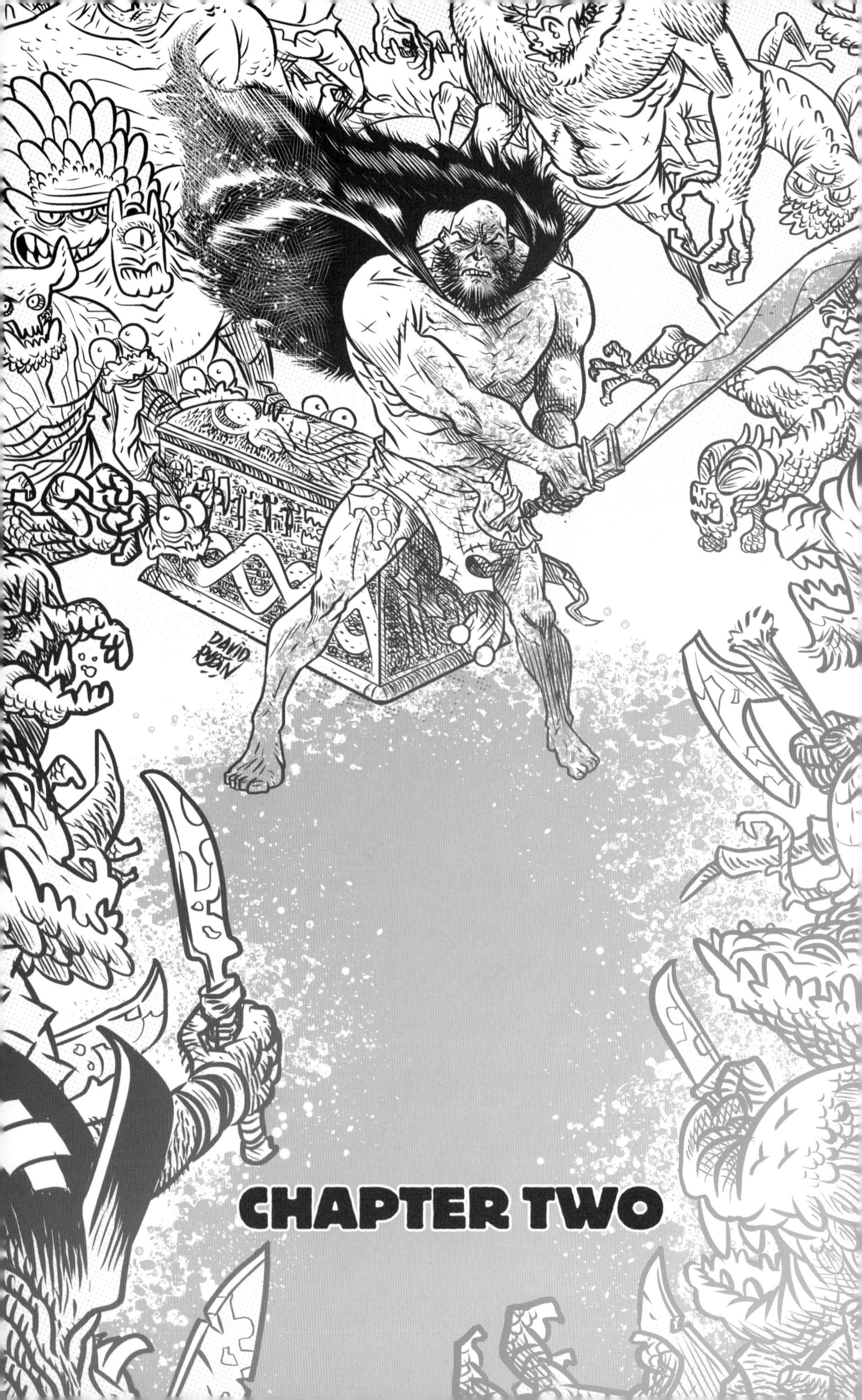
DAVID RUBIN

# CHAPTER TWO

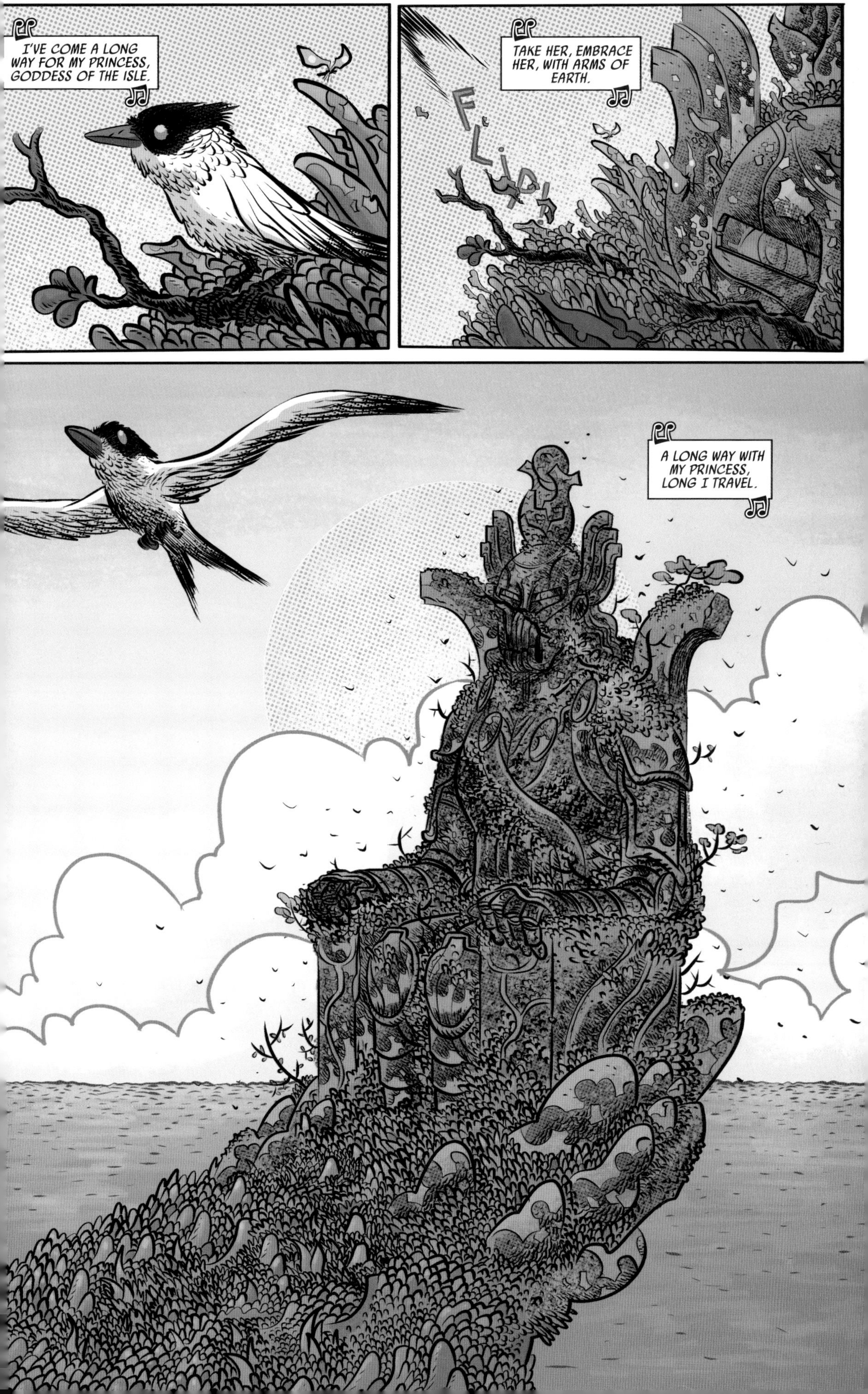

I'VE COME A LONG WAY FOR MY PRINCESS, GODDESS OF THE ISLE.
TAKE HER, EMBRACE HER, WITH ARMS OF EARTH.
FLIP!
A LONG WAY WITH MY PRINCESS, LONG I TRAVEL.

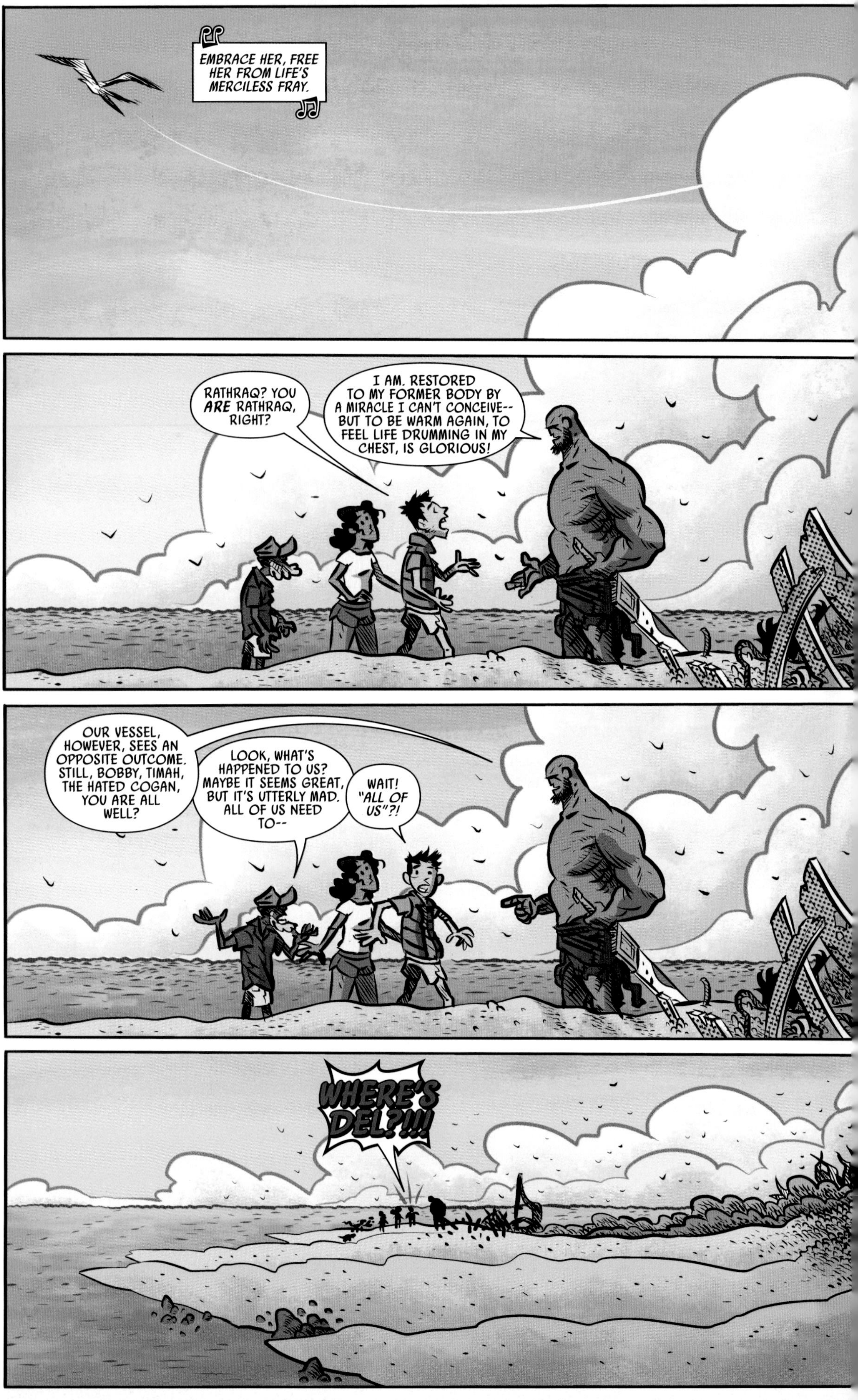
EMBRACE HER, FREE HER FROM LIFE'S MERCILESS FRAY.
RATHRAQ? YOU ARE RATHRAQ, RIGHT?
I AM. RESTORED TO MY FORMER BODY BY A MIRACLE I CAN'T CONCEIVE-- BUT TO BE WARM AGAIN, TO FEEL LIFE DRUMMING IN MY CHEST, IS GLORIOUS!
OUR VESSEL, HOWEVER, SEES AN OPPOSITE OUTCOME. STILL, BOBBY, TIMAH, THE HATED COGAN, YOU ARE ALL WELL?
LOOK, WHAT'S HAPPENED TO US? MAYBE IT SEEMS GREAT, BUT IT'S UTTERLY MAD. ALL OF US NEED TO--
WAIT! "ALL OF US"?!
WHERE'S DEL?!!!

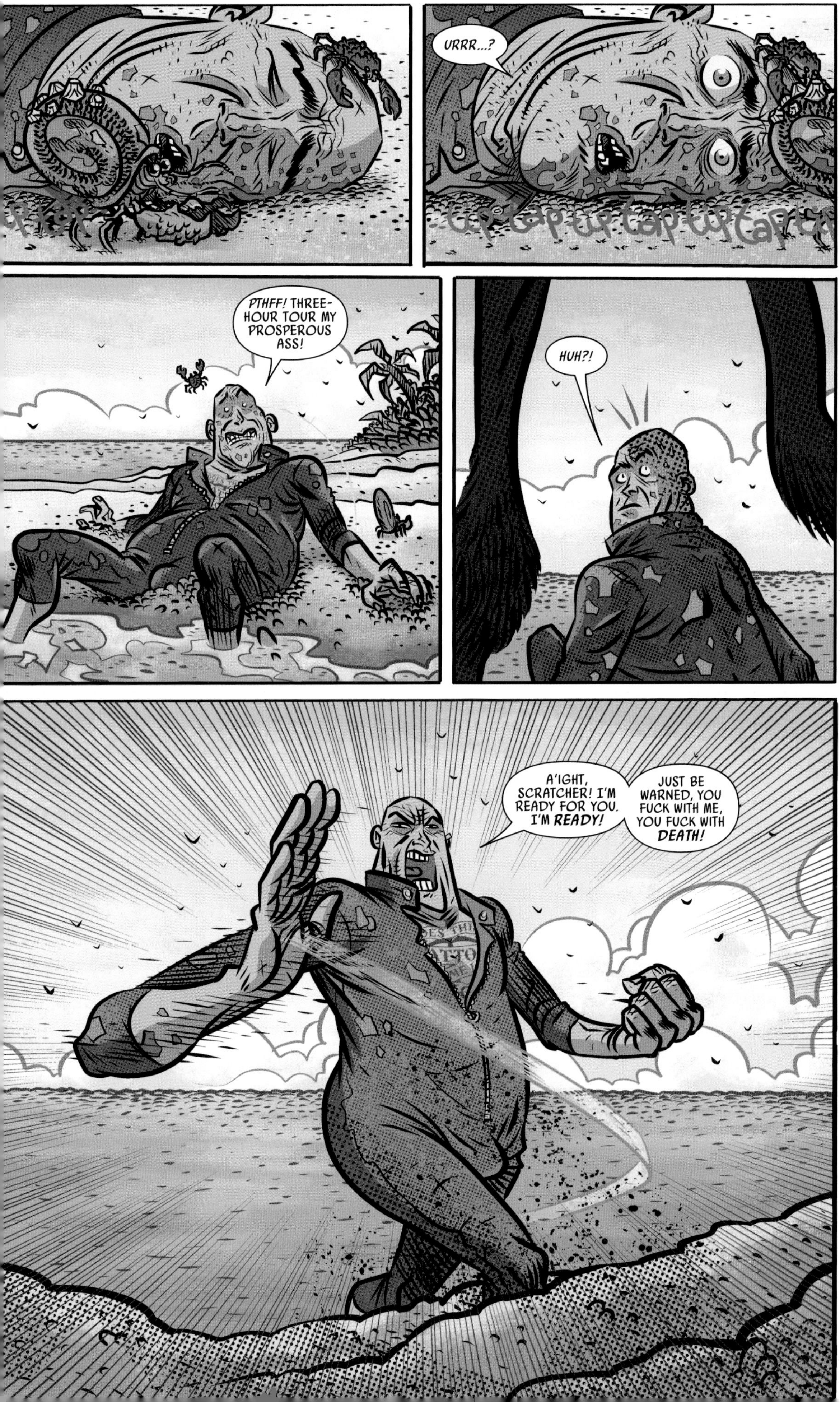
tap
URRR...?
tip tap tip tap tip tap
PTHFF! THREE-HOUR TOUR MY PROSPEROUS ASS!
HUH?!
A'IGHT, SCRATCHER! I'M READY FOR YOU. I'M **READY!**
JUST BE WARNED, YOU FUCK WITH ME, YOU FUCK WITH **DEATH!**

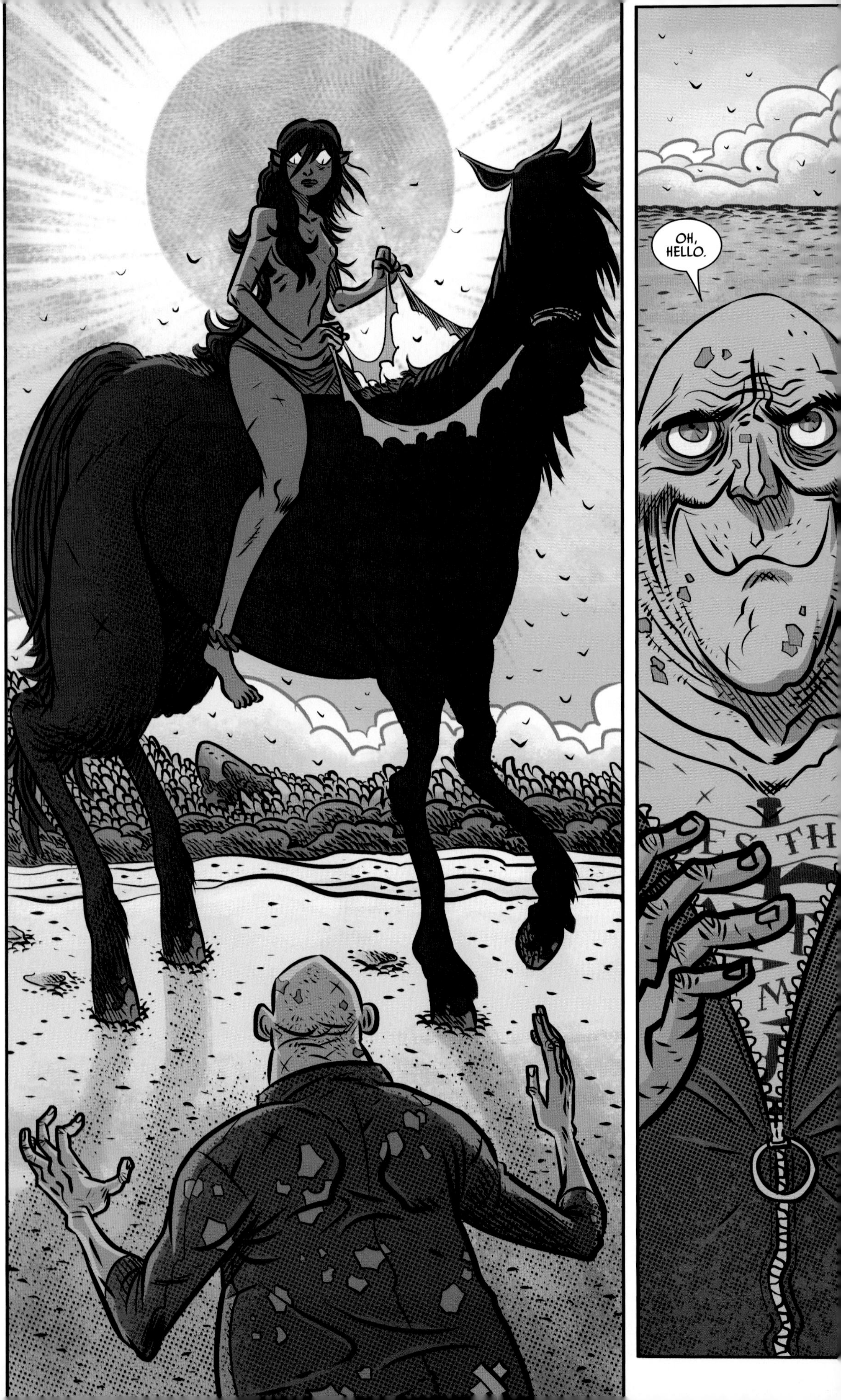
OH, HELLO.

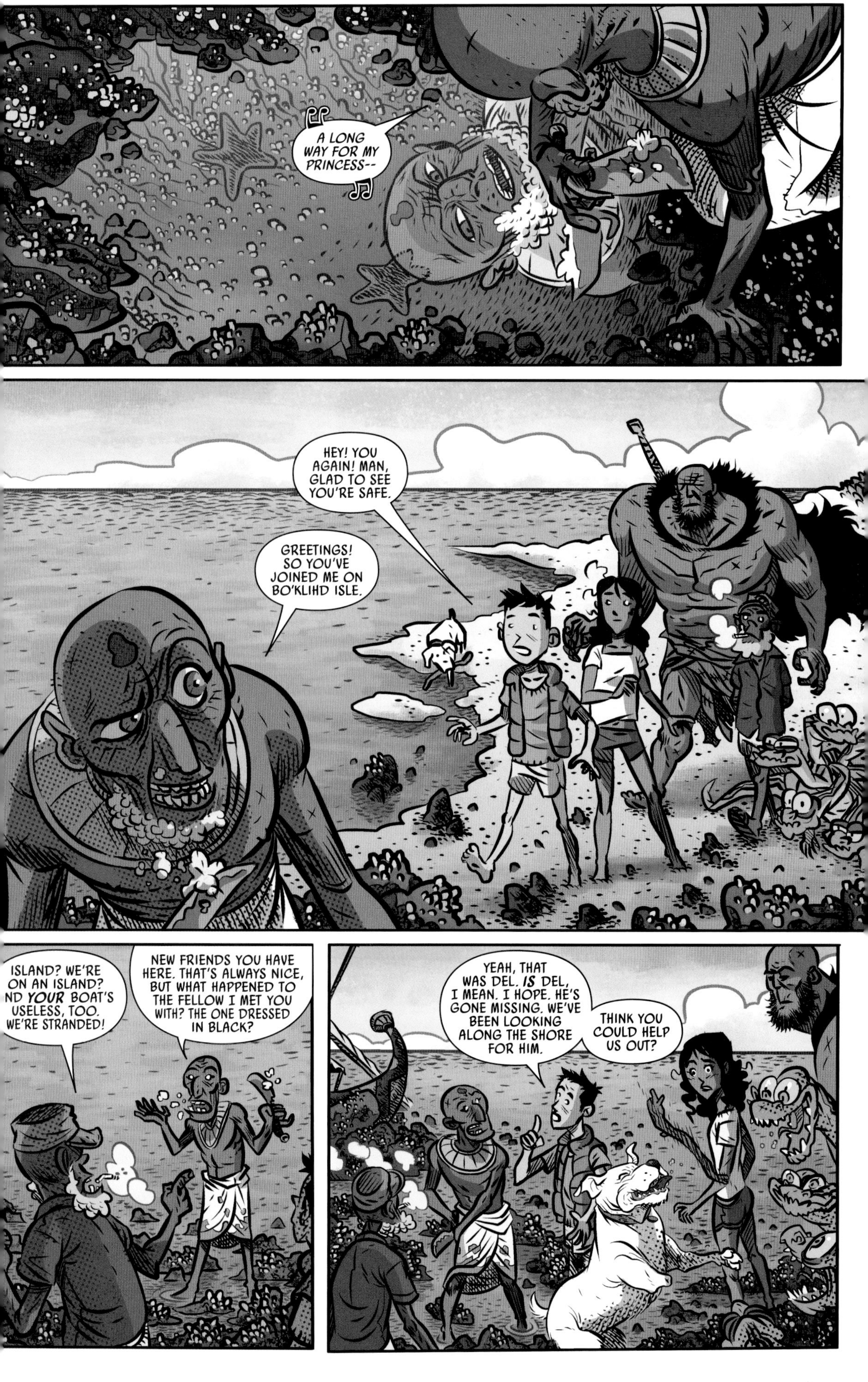
A LONG WAY FOR MY PRINCESS--
HEY! YOU AGAIN! MAN, GLAD TO SEE YOU'RE SAFE.
GREETINGS! SO YOU'VE JOINED ME ON BO'KLIHD ISLE.
ISLAND? WE'RE ON AN ISLAND? ND *YOUR* BOAT'S USELESS, TOO. WE'RE STRANDED!
NEW FRIENDS YOU HAVE HERE. THAT'S ALWAYS NICE, BUT WHAT HAPPENED TO THE FELLOW I MET YOU WITH? THE ONE DRESSED IN BLACK?
YEAH, THAT WAS DEL. *IS* DEL, I MEAN. I HOPE. HE'S GONE MISSING. WE'VE BEEN LOOKING ALONG THE SHORE FOR HIM.
THINK YOU COULD HELP US OUT?

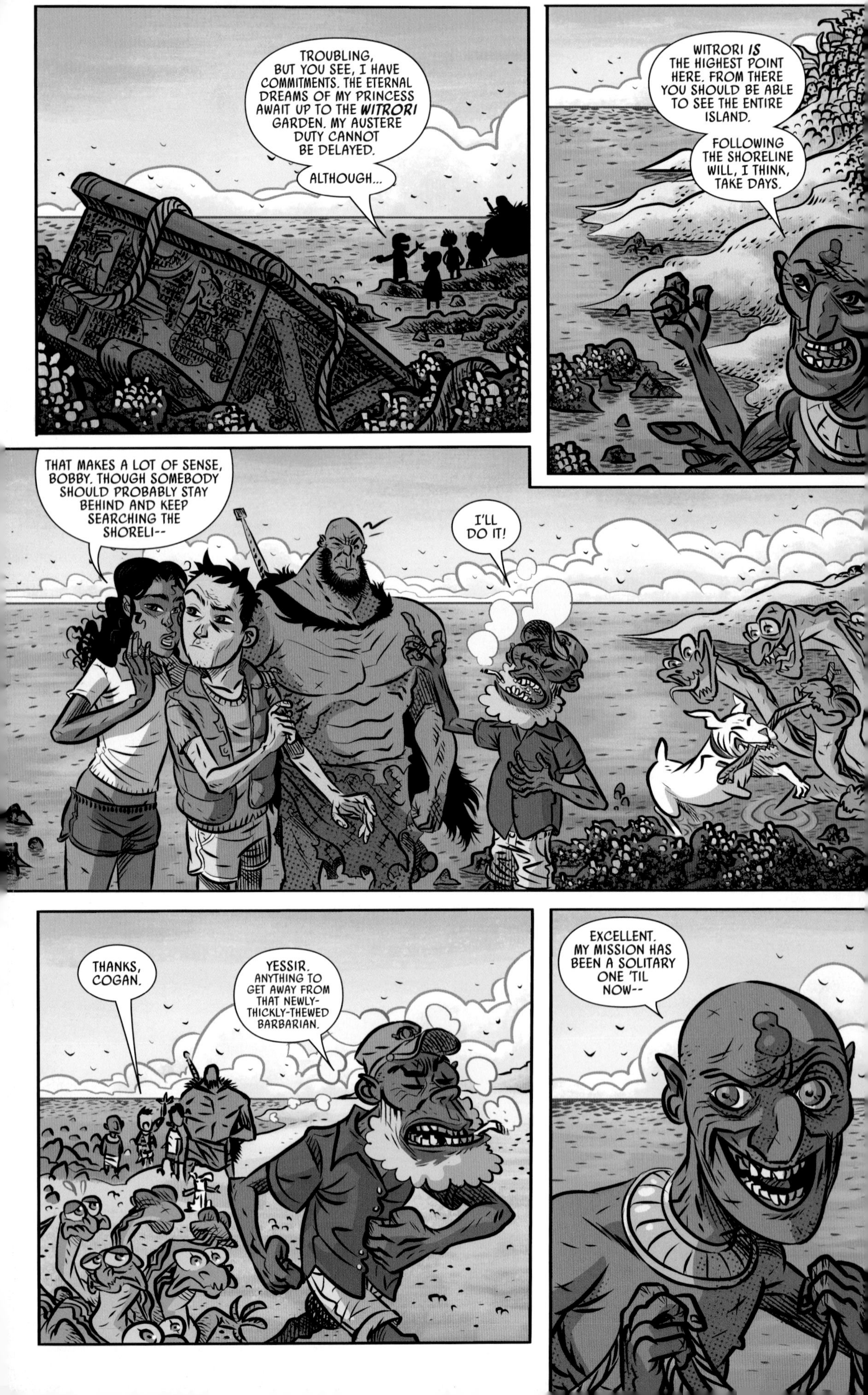

TROUBLING, BUT YOU SEE, I HAVE COMMITMENTS. THE ETERNAL DREAMS OF MY PRINCESS AWAIT UP TO THE WITRORI GARDEN. MY AUSTERE DUTY CANNOT BE DELAYED.
ALTHOUGH...
WITRORI IS THE HIGHEST POINT HERE. FROM THERE YOU SHOULD BE ABLE TO SEE THE ENTIRE ISLAND.
FOLLOWING THE SHORELINE WILL, I THINK, TAKE DAYS.
THAT MAKES A LOT OF SENSE, BOBBY. THOUGH SOMEBODY SHOULD PROBABLY STAY BEHIND AND KEEP SEARCHING THE SHORELI--
I'LL DO IT!
THANKS, COGAN.
YESSIR. ANYTHING TO GET AWAY FROM THAT NEWLY-THICKLY-THEWED BARBARIAN.
EXCELLENT. MY MISSION HAS BEEN A SOLITARY ONE 'TIL NOW--

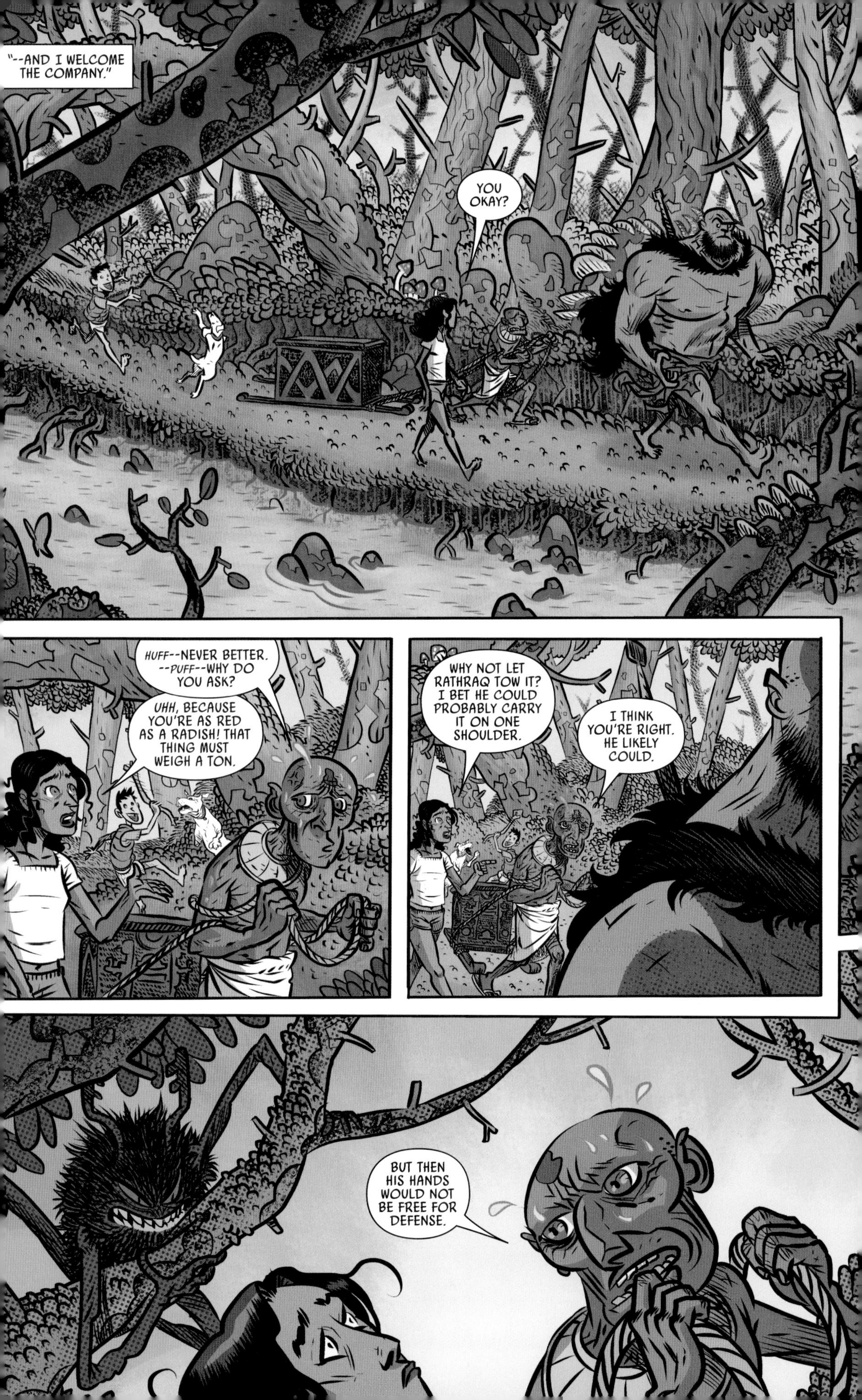
"--AND I WELCOME THE COMPANY."
YOU OKAY?
HUFF--NEVER BETTER. --PUFF--WHY DO YOU ASK?
UHH, BECAUSE YOU'RE AS RED AS A RADISH! THAT THING MUST WEIGH A TON.
WHY NOT LET RATHRAQ TOW IT? I BET HE COULD PROBABLY CARRY IT ON ONE SHOULDER.
I THINK YOU'RE RIGHT. HE LIKELY COULD.
BUT THEN HIS HANDS WOULD NOT BE FREE FOR DEFENSE.

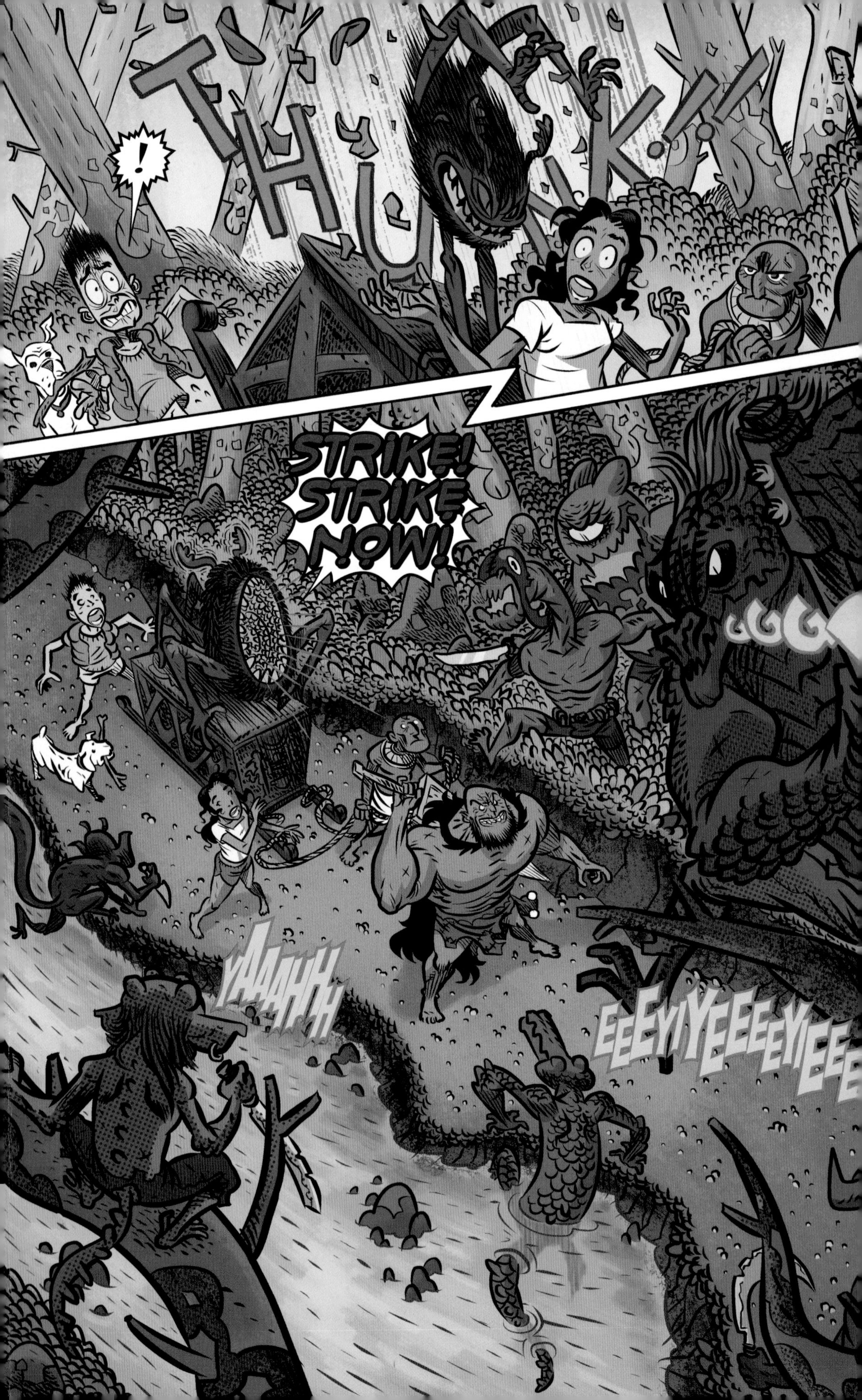
THUNK!!
!
STRIKE! STRIKE NOW!
GGG
YAAAHHH
EEEYIYEEEEEYIEEE

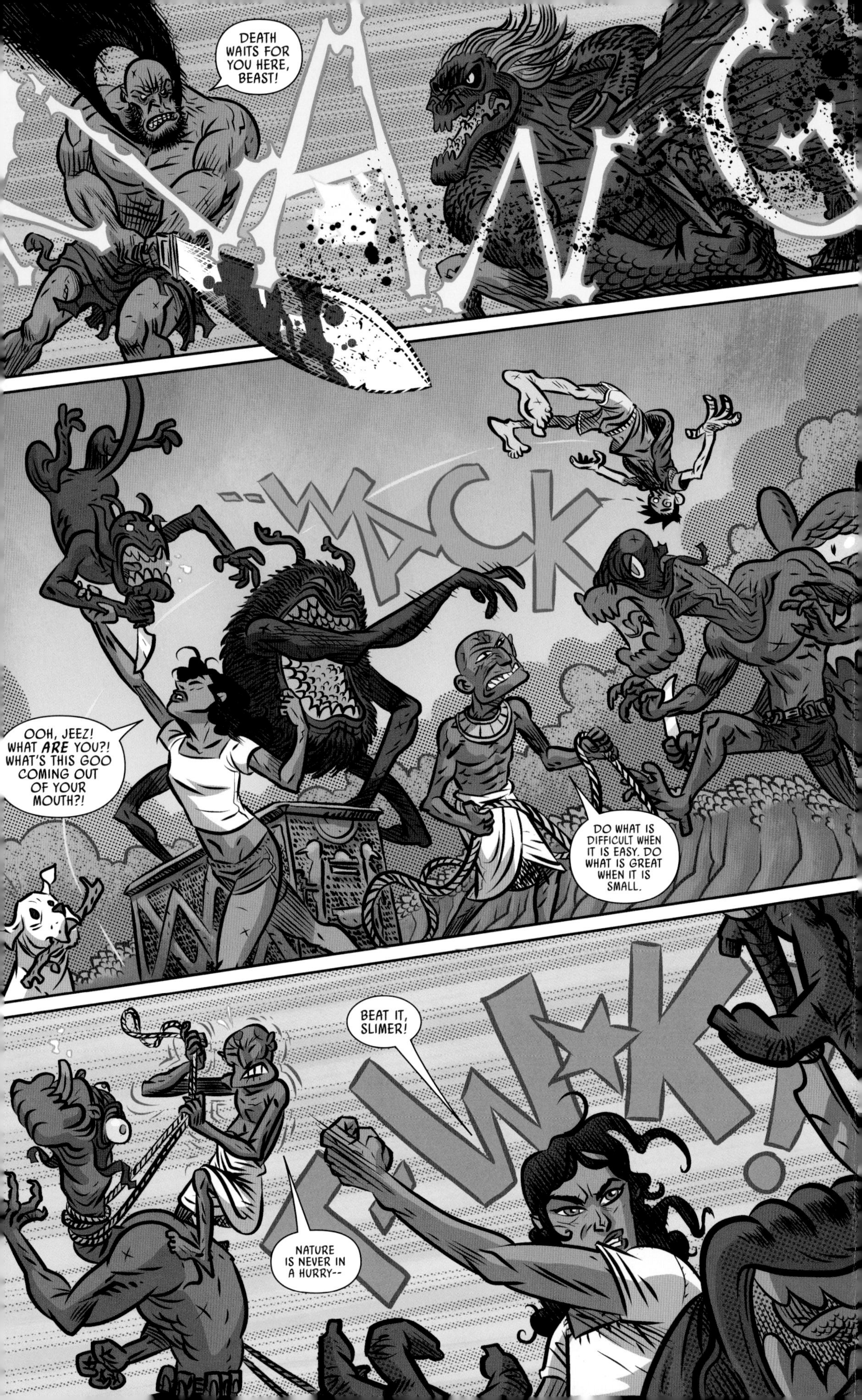
DEATH WAITS FOR YOU HERE, BEAST!
--WACK
OOH, JEEZ! WHAT *ARE* YOU?! WHAT'S THIS GOO COMING OUT OF YOUR MOUTH?!
DO WHAT IS DIFFICULT WHEN IT IS EASY. DO WHAT IS GREAT WHEN IT IS SMALL.
BEAT IT, SLIMER!
NATURE IS NEVER IN A HURRY--

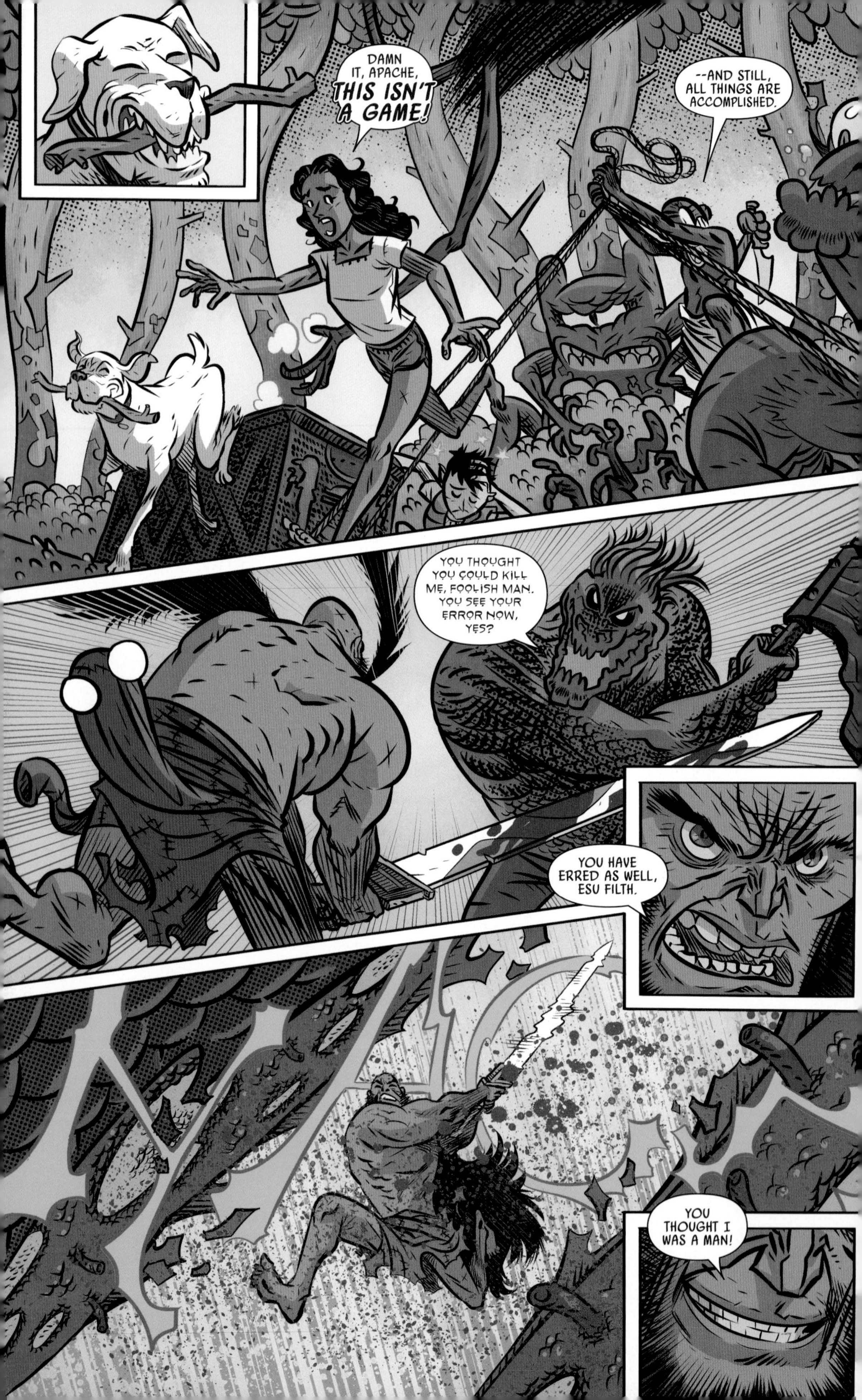
DAMN IT, APACHE, THIS ISN'T A GAME!
--AND STILL, ALL THINGS ARE ACCOMPLISHED.
YOU THOUGHT YOU COULD KILL ME, FOOLISH MAN. YOU SEE YOUR ERROR NOW, YES?
YOU HAVE ERRED AS WELL, ESU FILTH.
YOU THOUGHT I WAS A MAN!

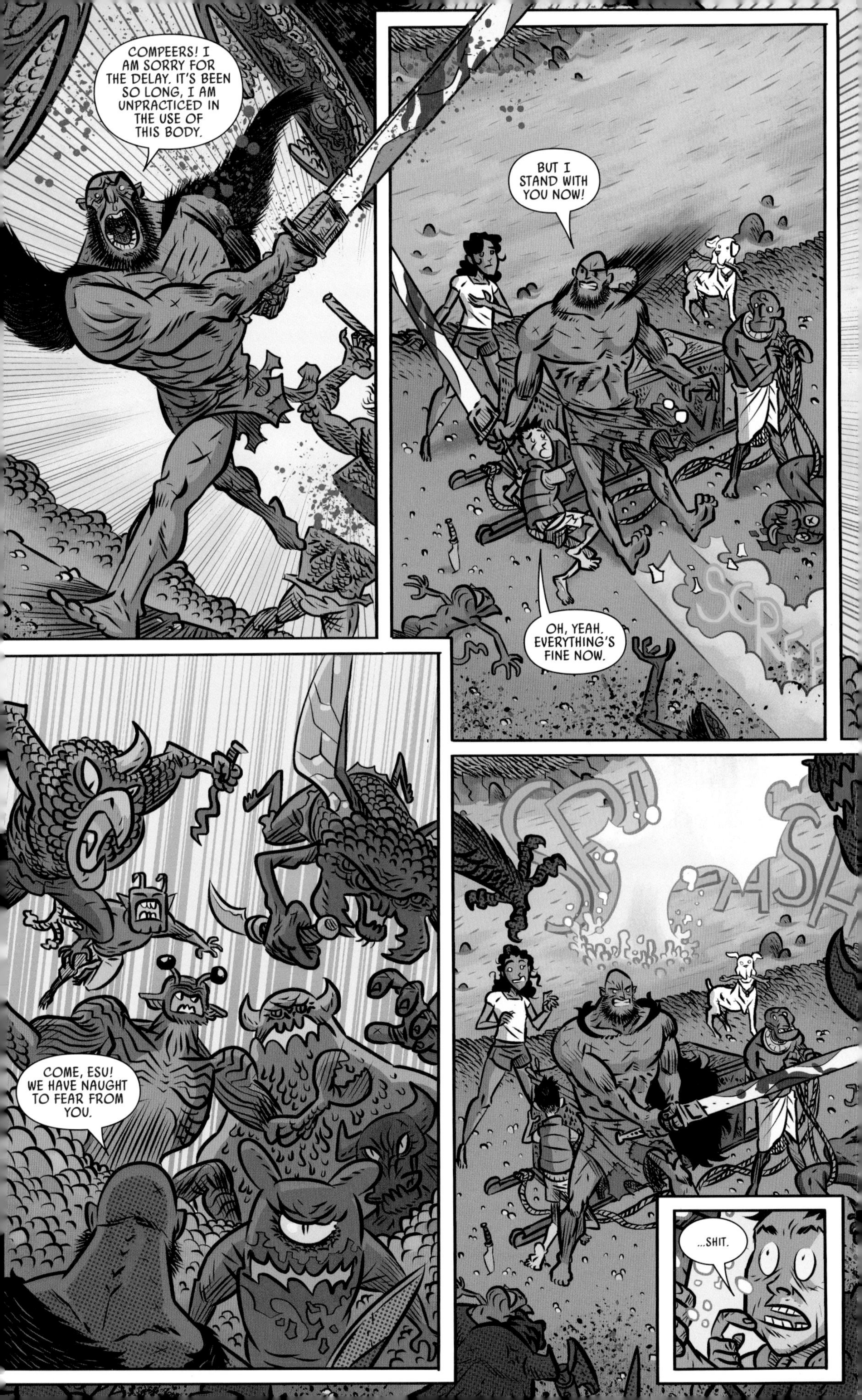
COMPEERS! I AM SORRY FOR THE DELAY. IT'S BEEN SO LONG, I AM UNPRACTICED IN THE USE OF THIS BODY.
BUT I STAND WITH YOU NOW!
OH, YEAH. EVERYTHING'S FINE NOW.
COME, ESU! WE HAVE NAUGHT TO FEAR FROM YOU.
...SHIT.

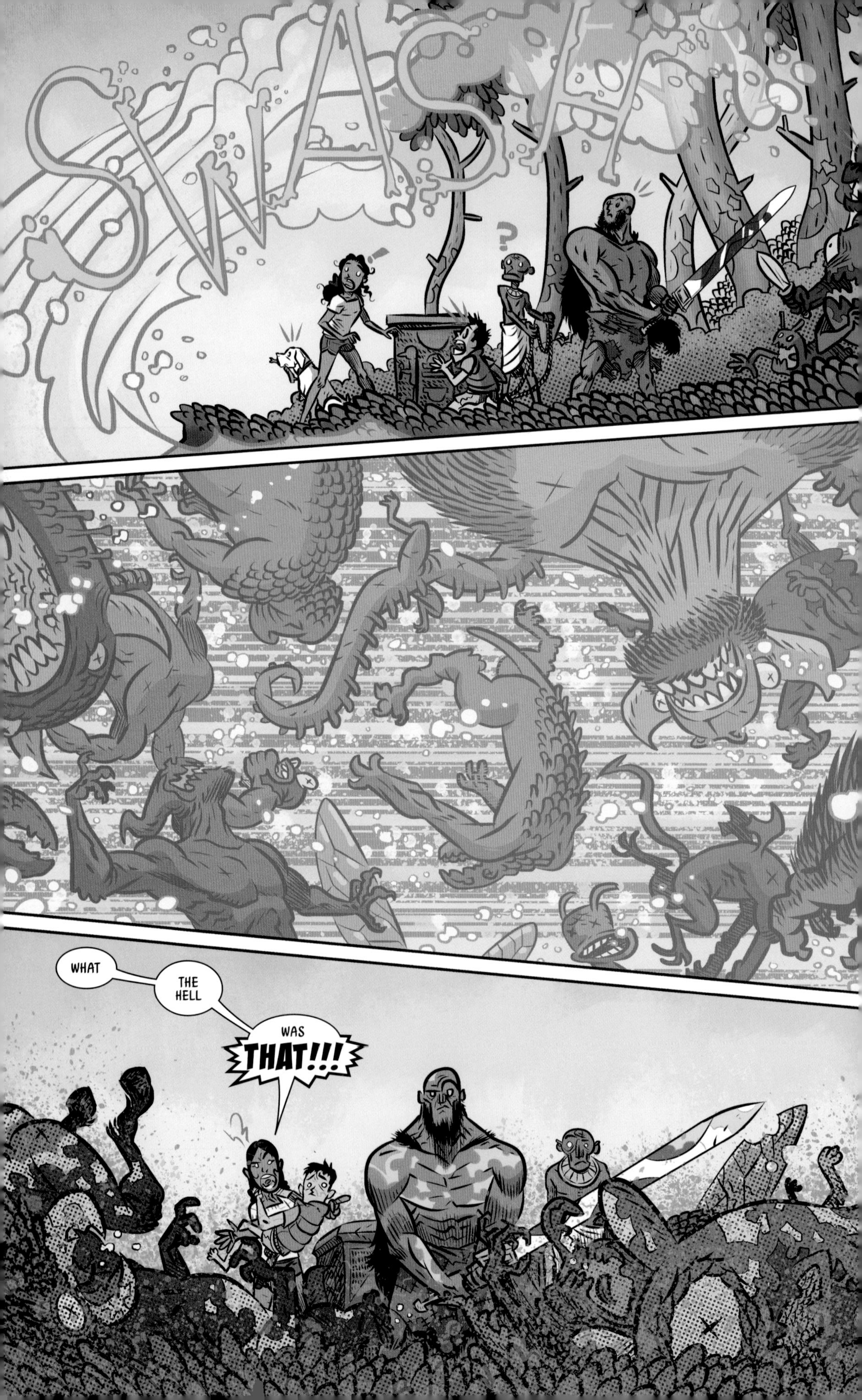
SWASH
?
WHAT
THE HELL
WAS
THAT!!!

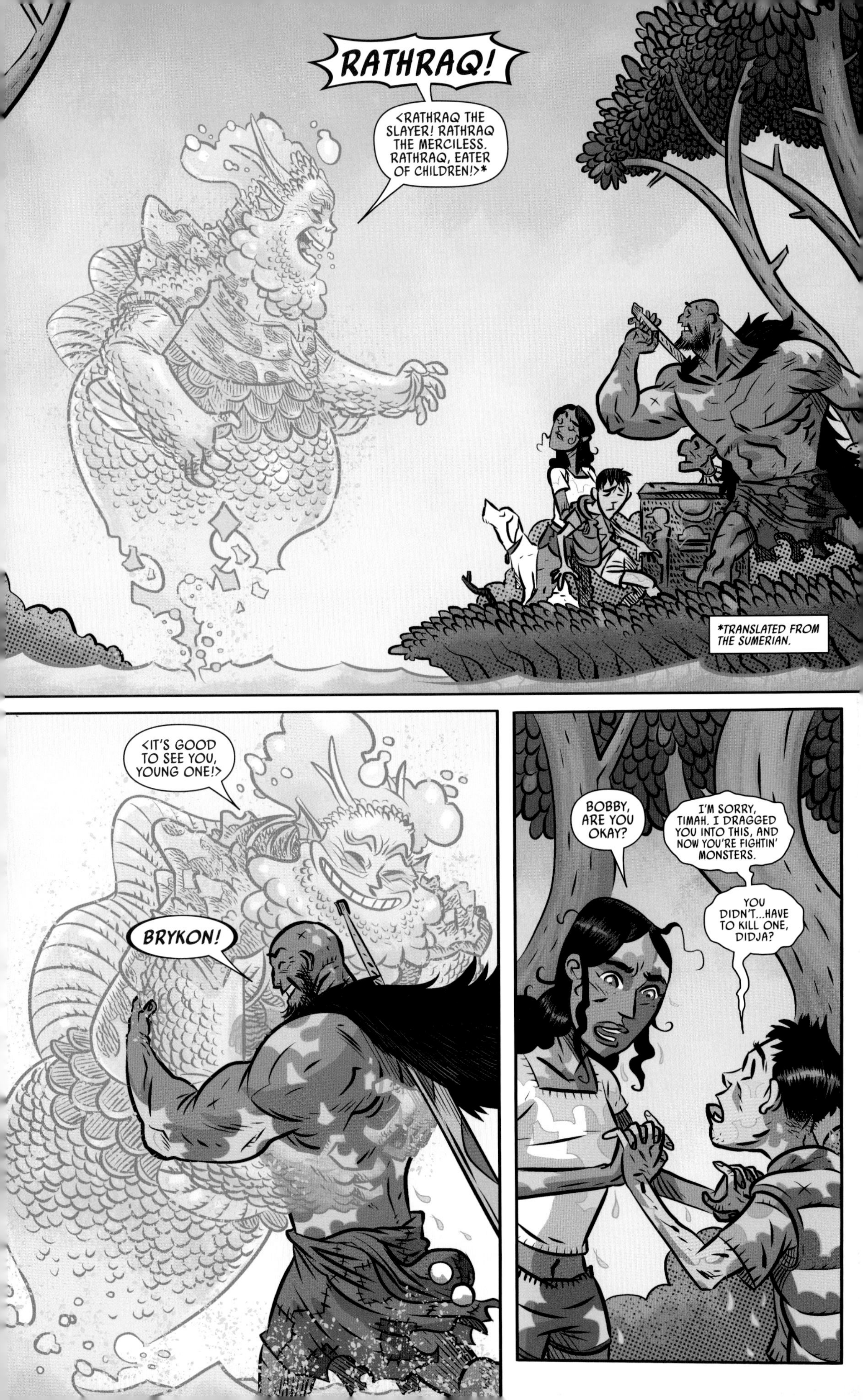
RATHRAQ!
<RATHRAQ THE SLAYER! RATHRAQ THE MERCILESS. RATHRAQ, EATER OF CHILDREN!>*
*TRANSLATED FROM THE SUMERIAN.
<IT'S GOOD TO SEE YOU, YOUNG ONE!>
BRYKON!
BOBBY, ARE YOU OKAY?
I'M SORRY, TIMAH. I DRAGGED YOU INTO THIS, AND NOW YOU'RE FIGHTIN' MONSTERS.
YOU DIDN'T...HAVE TO KILL ONE, DIDJA?

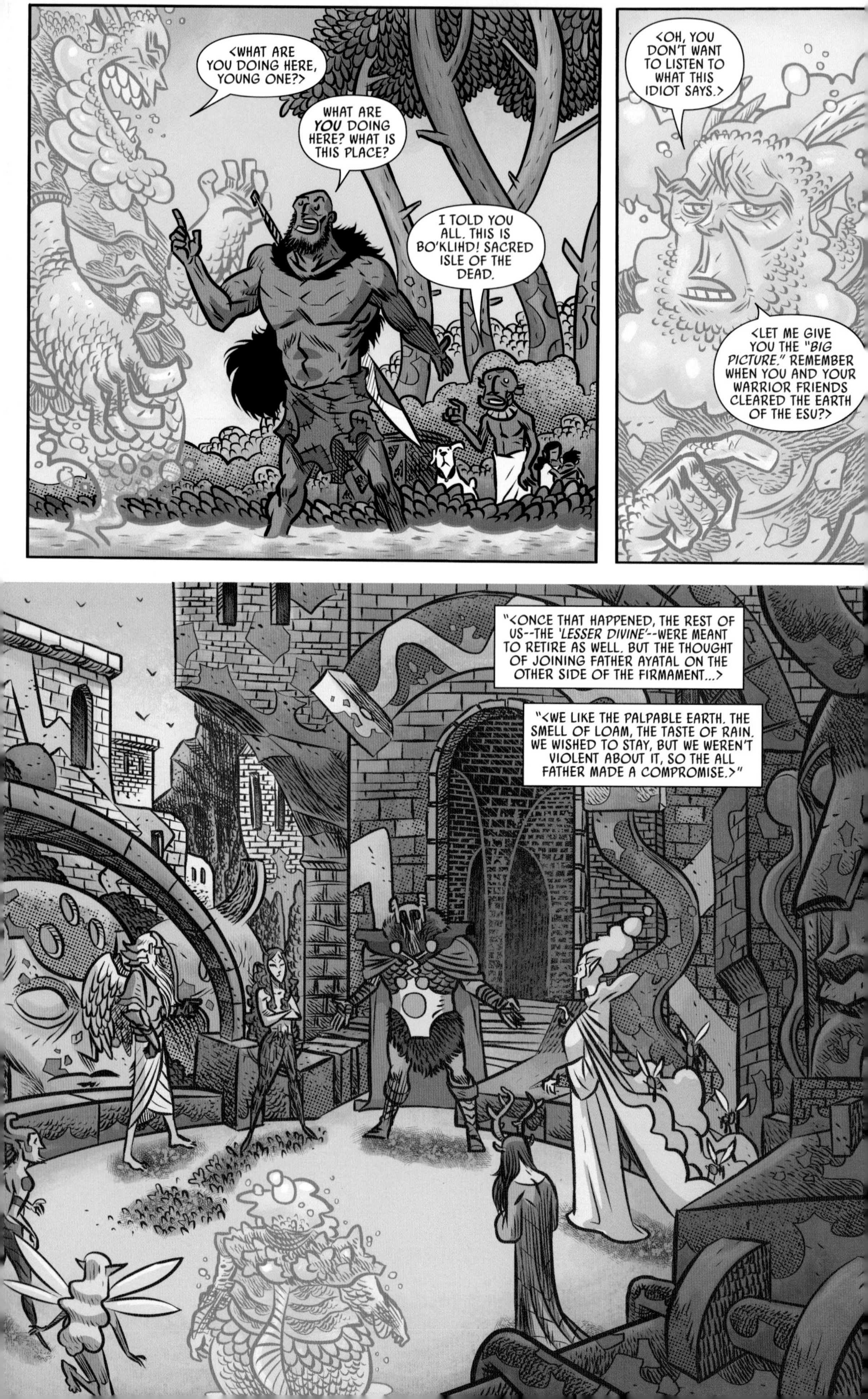

<WHAT ARE YOU DOING HERE, YOUNG ONE?>
WHAT ARE *YOU* DOING HERE? WHAT IS THIS PLACE?
I TOLD YOU ALL. THIS IS BO'KLIHD! SACRED ISLE OF THE DEAD.
<OH, YOU DON'T WANT TO LISTEN TO WHAT THIS IDIOT SAYS.>
<LET ME GIVE YOU THE "*BIG PICTURE.*" REMEMBER WHEN YOU AND YOUR WARRIOR FRIENDS CLEARED THE EARTH OF THE ESU?>
"<ONCE THAT HAPPENED, THE REST OF US--THE '*LESSER DIVINE*'--WERE MEANT TO RETIRE AS WELL. BUT THE THOUGHT OF JOINING FATHER AYATAL ON THE OTHER SIDE OF THE FIRMAMENT...>
"<WE LIKE THE PALPABLE EARTH. THE SMELL OF LOAM, THE TASTE OF RAIN. WE WISHED TO STAY, BUT WE WEREN'T VIOLENT ABOUT IT, SO THE ALL FATHER MADE A COMPROMISE.>"

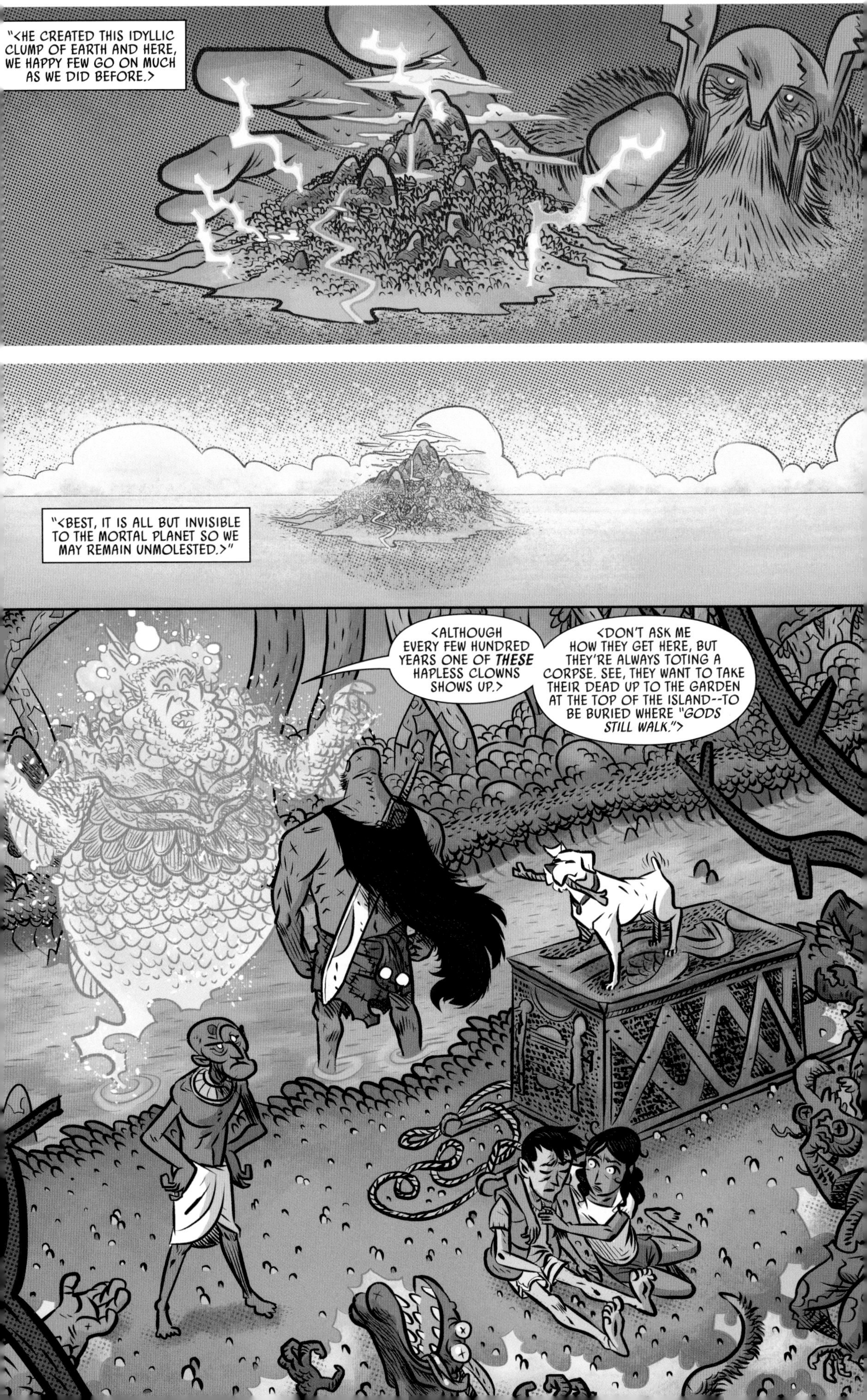
"<HE CREATED THIS IDYLLIC CLUMP OF EARTH AND HERE, WE HAPPY FEW GO ON MUCH AS WE DID BEFORE.>
"<BEST, IT IS ALL BUT INVISIBLE TO THE MORTAL PLANET SO WE MAY REMAIN UNMOLESTED.>"
<ALTHOUGH EVERY FEW HUNDRED YEARS ONE OF *THESE* HAPLESS CLOWNS SHOWS UP.>
<DON'T ASK ME HOW THEY GET HERE, BUT THEY'RE ALWAYS TOTING A CORPSE. SEE, THEY WANT TO TAKE THEIR DEAD UP TO THE GARDEN AT THE TOP OF THE ISLAND--TO BE BURIED WHERE *"GODS STILL WALK."*>

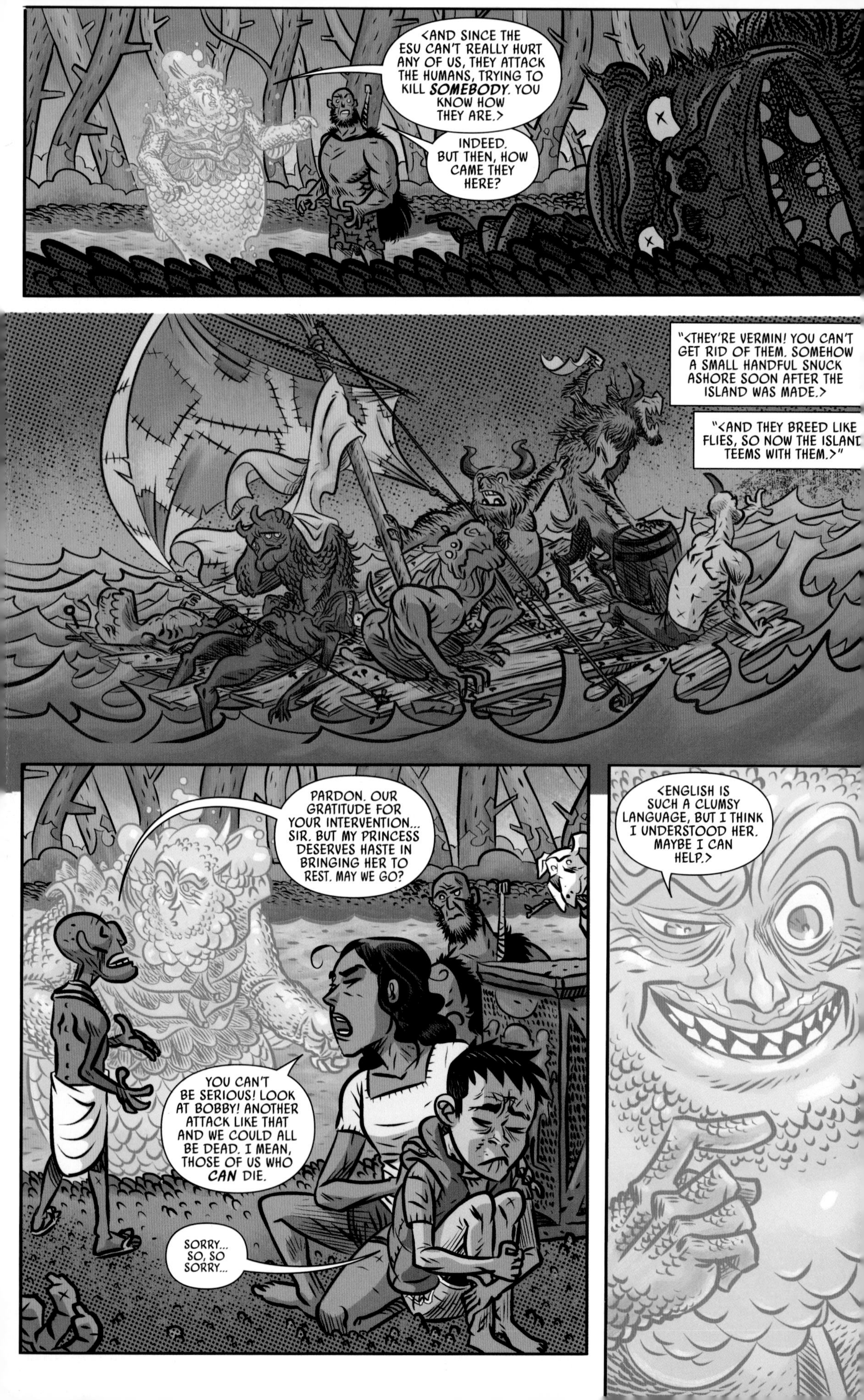
<AND SINCE THE ESU CAN'T REALLY HURT ANY OF US, THEY ATTACK THE HUMANS, TRYING TO KILL SOMEBODY. YOU KNOW HOW THEY ARE.>
INDEED. BUT THEN, HOW CAME THEY HERE?
"<THEY'RE VERMIN! YOU CAN'T GET RID OF THEM. SOMEHOW A SMALL HANDFUL SNUCK ASHORE SOON AFTER THE ISLAND WAS MADE.>
"<AND THEY BREED LIKE FLIES, SO NOW THE ISLAND TEEMS WITH THEM.>"
PARDON. OUR GRATITUDE FOR YOUR INTERVENTION... SIR. BUT MY PRINCESS DESERVES HASTE IN BRINGING HER TO REST. MAY WE GO?
YOU CAN'T BE SERIOUS! LOOK AT BOBBY! ANOTHER ATTACK LIKE THAT AND WE COULD ALL BE DEAD. I MEAN, THOSE OF US WHO CAN DIE.
SORRY... SO, SO SORRY...
<ENGLISH IS SUCH A CLUMSY LANGUAGE, BUT I THINK I UNDERSTOOD HER. MAYBE I CAN HELP.>

I DON'T LIKE IT. EVEN IF I DO HAVE MY ARM BACK, I DON'T LIKE IT.

SOME MAGIC ISLAND THAT GRANTS WISHES? THAT *NEVER* TURNS OUT WELL!

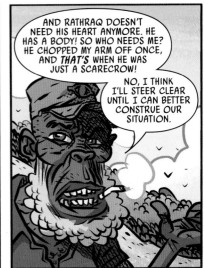

AND RATHRAQ DOESN'T NEED HIS HEART ANYMORE. HE HAS A BODY! SO WHO NEEDS ME? HE CHOPPED MY ARM OFF ONCE, AND *THAT'S* WHEN HE WAS JUST A SCARECROW!

NO, I THINK I'LL STEER CLEAR UNTIL I CAN BETTER CONSTRUE OUR SITUATION.

WOULD YOU LOOK AT THIS, LERNA. HOOF PRINTS.

AN EQUINE PRESENCE IS AFOOT. SURE. WHY NOT? BUT WE'RE NOT LOOKING FOR A HORSE.

JUST A SKINHEAD WHO EATS LIKE ONE.

GLUG!

SNIFF
SNIFF
SNIFF
SNIFF

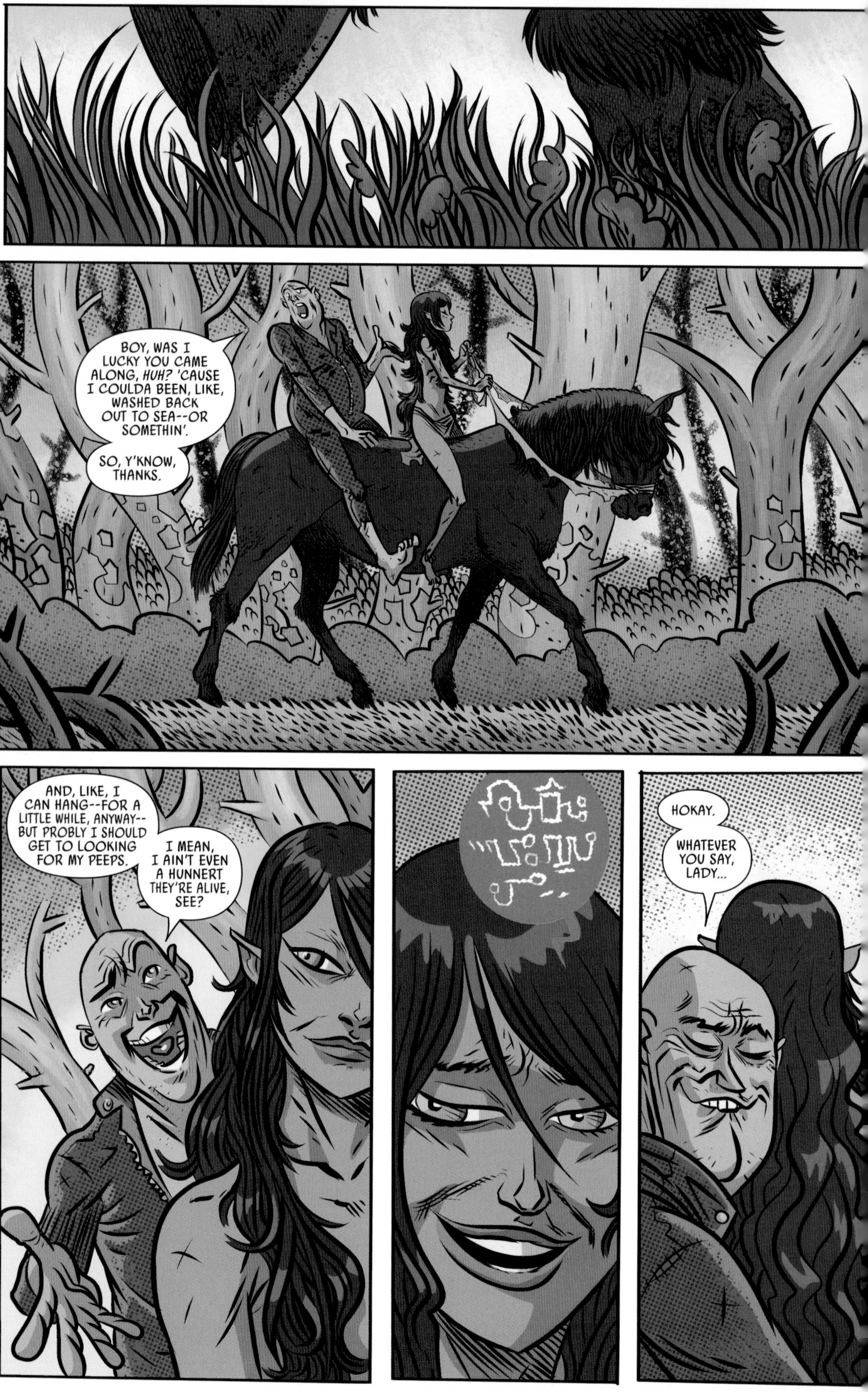
BOY, WAS I LUCKY YOU CAME ALONG, HUH? 'CAUSE I COULDA BEEN, LIKE, WASHED BACK OUT TO SEA--OR SOMETHIN'.
SO, Y'KNOW, THANKS.
AND, LIKE, I CAN HANG--FOR A LITTLE WHILE, ANYWAY--BUT PROBLY I SHOULD GET TO LOOKING FOR MY PEEPS.
I MEAN, I AIN'T EVEN A HUNNERT THEY'RE ALIVE, SEE?
HOKAY.
WHATEVER YOU SAY, LADY...

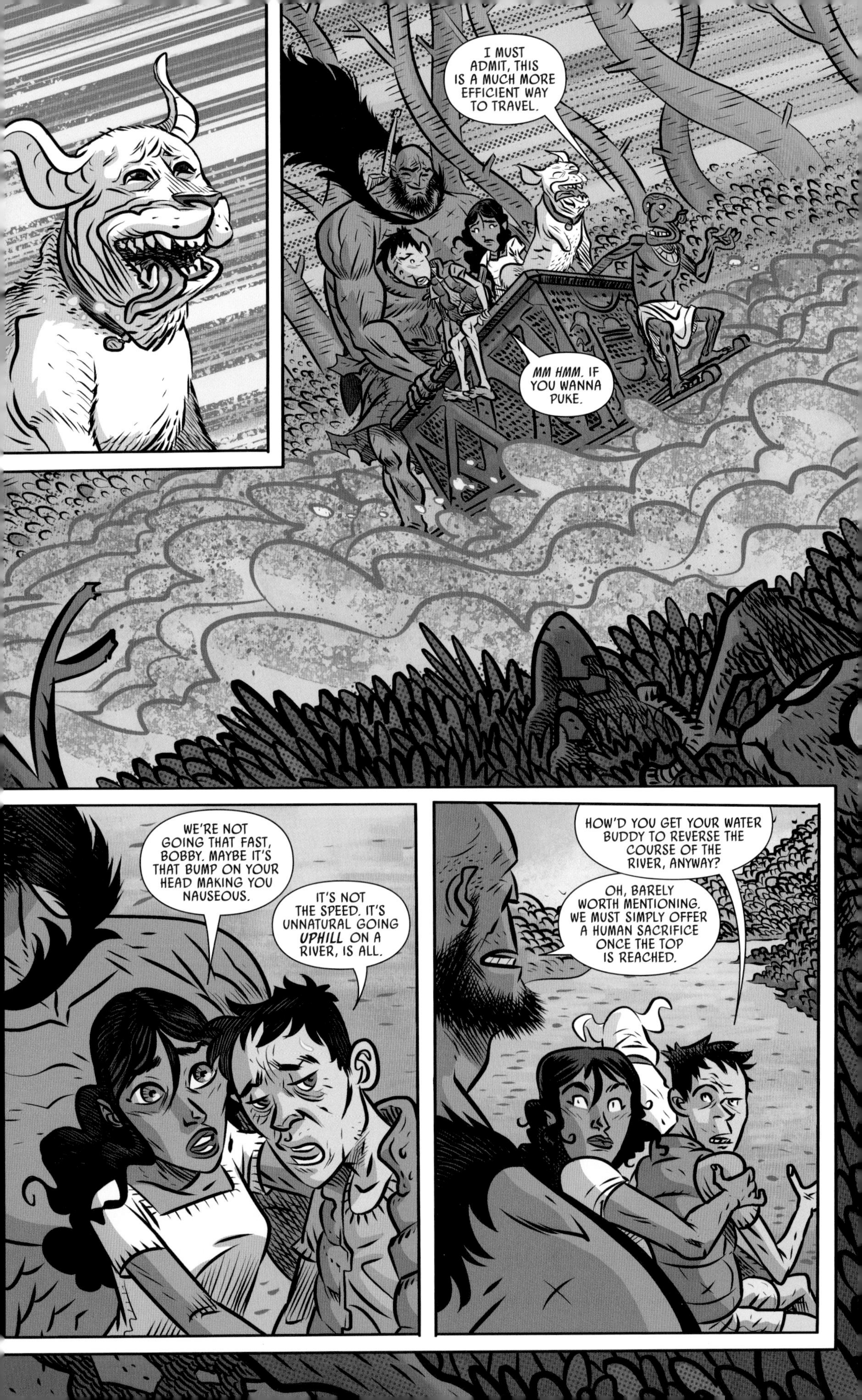
I MUST ADMIT, THIS IS A MUCH MORE EFFICIENT WAY TO TRAVEL.
MM HMM. IF YOU WANNA PUKE.
WE'RE NOT GOING THAT FAST, BOBBY. MAYBE IT'S THAT BUMP ON YOUR HEAD MAKING YOU NAUSEOUS.
IT'S NOT THE SPEED. IT'S UNNATURAL GOING *UPHILL* ON A RIVER, IS ALL.
HOW'D YOU GET YOUR WATER BUDDY TO REVERSE THE COURSE OF THE RIVER, ANYWAY?
OH, BARELY WORTH MENTIONING. WE MUST SIMPLY OFFER A HUMAN SACRIFICE ONCE THE TOP IS REACHED.

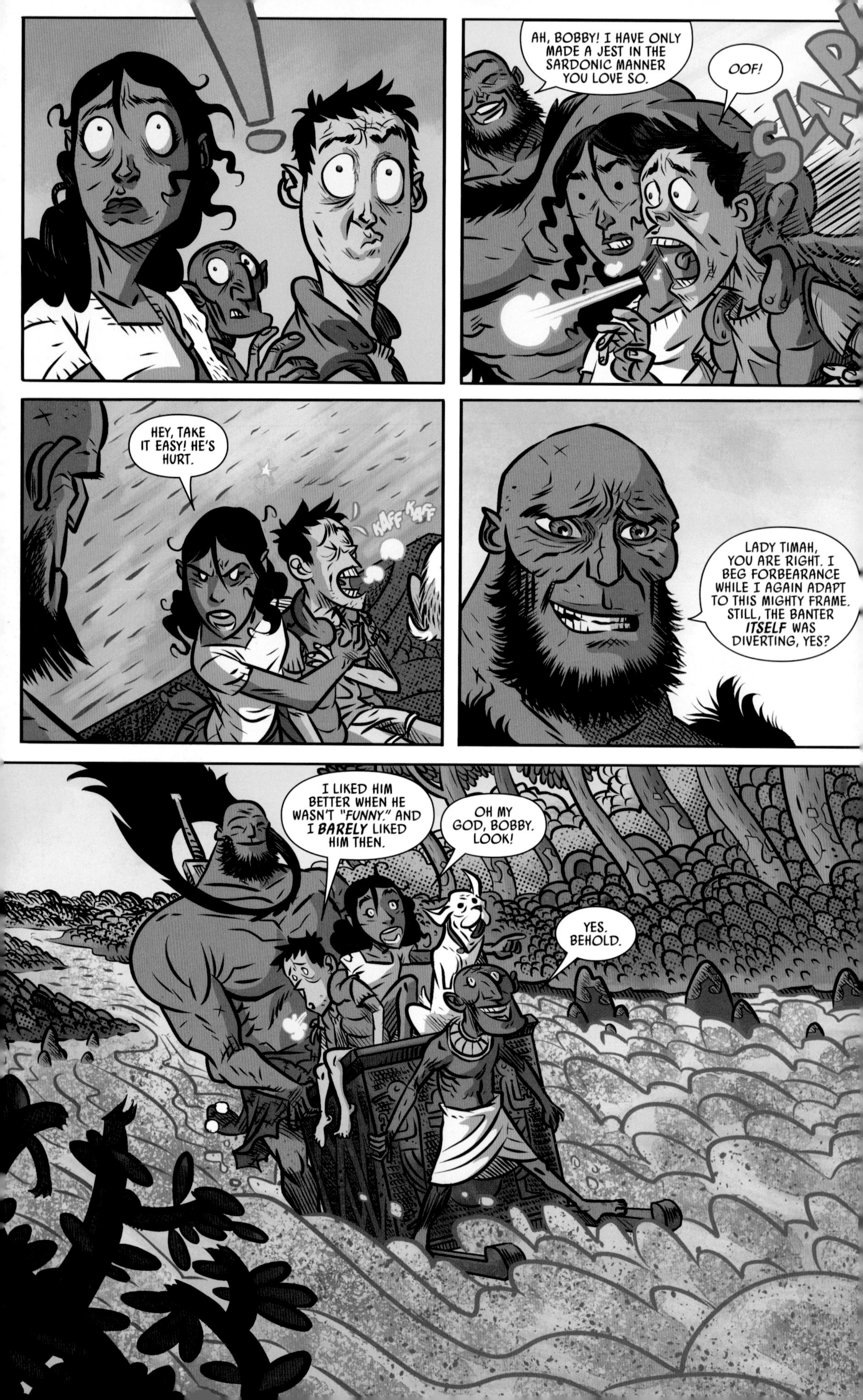

AH, BOBBY! I HAVE ONLY MADE A JEST IN THE SARDONIC MANNER YOU LOVE SO.
OOF!
SLAP!
HEY, TAKE IT EASY! HE'S HURT.
KAFF KAFF
LADY TIMAH, YOU ARE RIGHT. I BEG FORBEARANCE WHILE I AGAIN ADAPT TO THIS MIGHTY FRAME. STILL, THE BANTER *ITSELF* WAS DIVERTING, YES?
I LIKED HIM BETTER WHEN HE WASN'T "*FUNNY.*" AND I ***BARELY*** LIKED HIM THEN.
OH MY GOD, BOBBY. LOOK!
YES. BEHOLD.

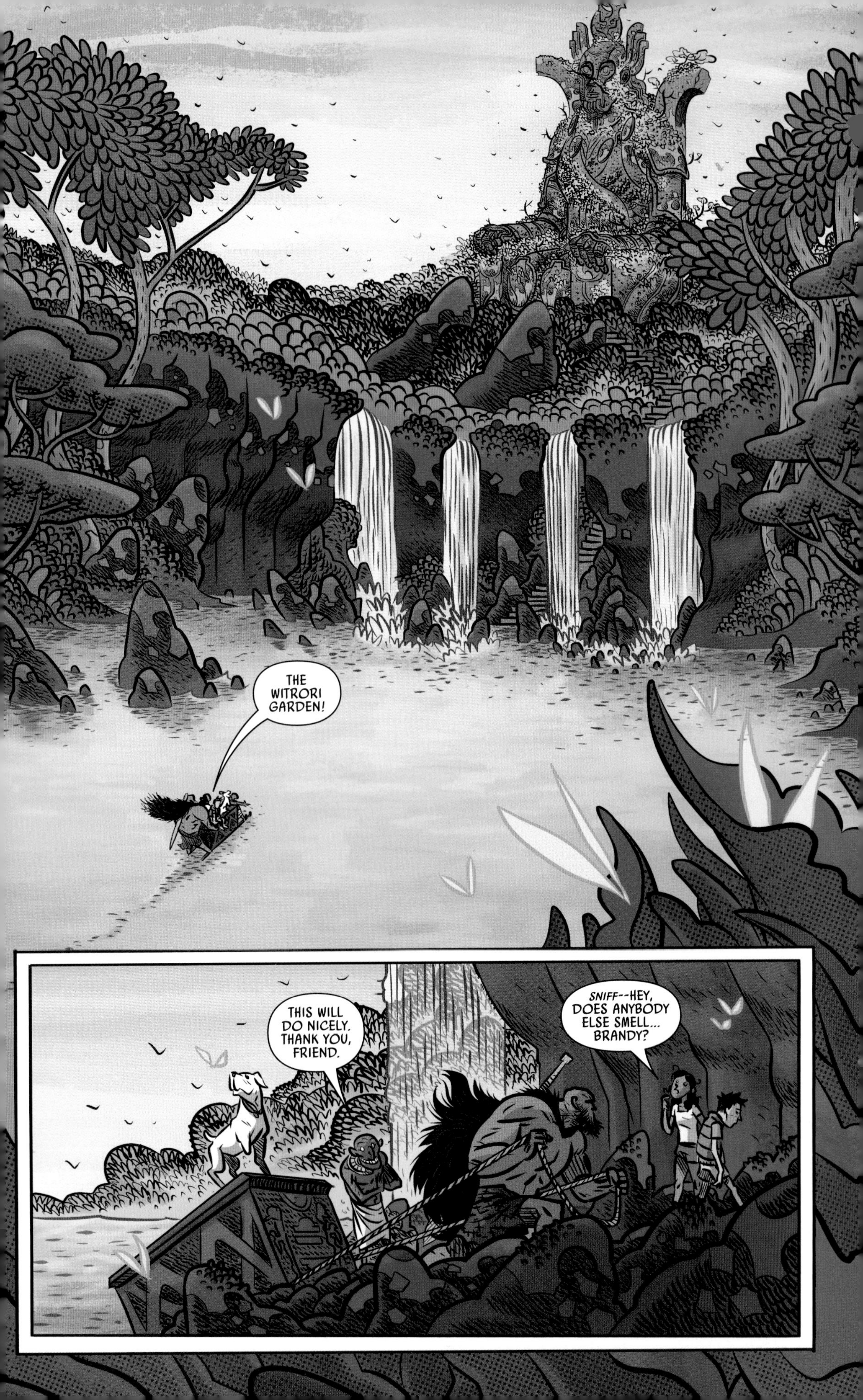
THE WITRORI GARDEN!
THIS WILL DO NICELY. THANK YOU, FRIEND.
SNIFF--HEY, DOES ANYBODY ELSE SMELL... BRANDY?

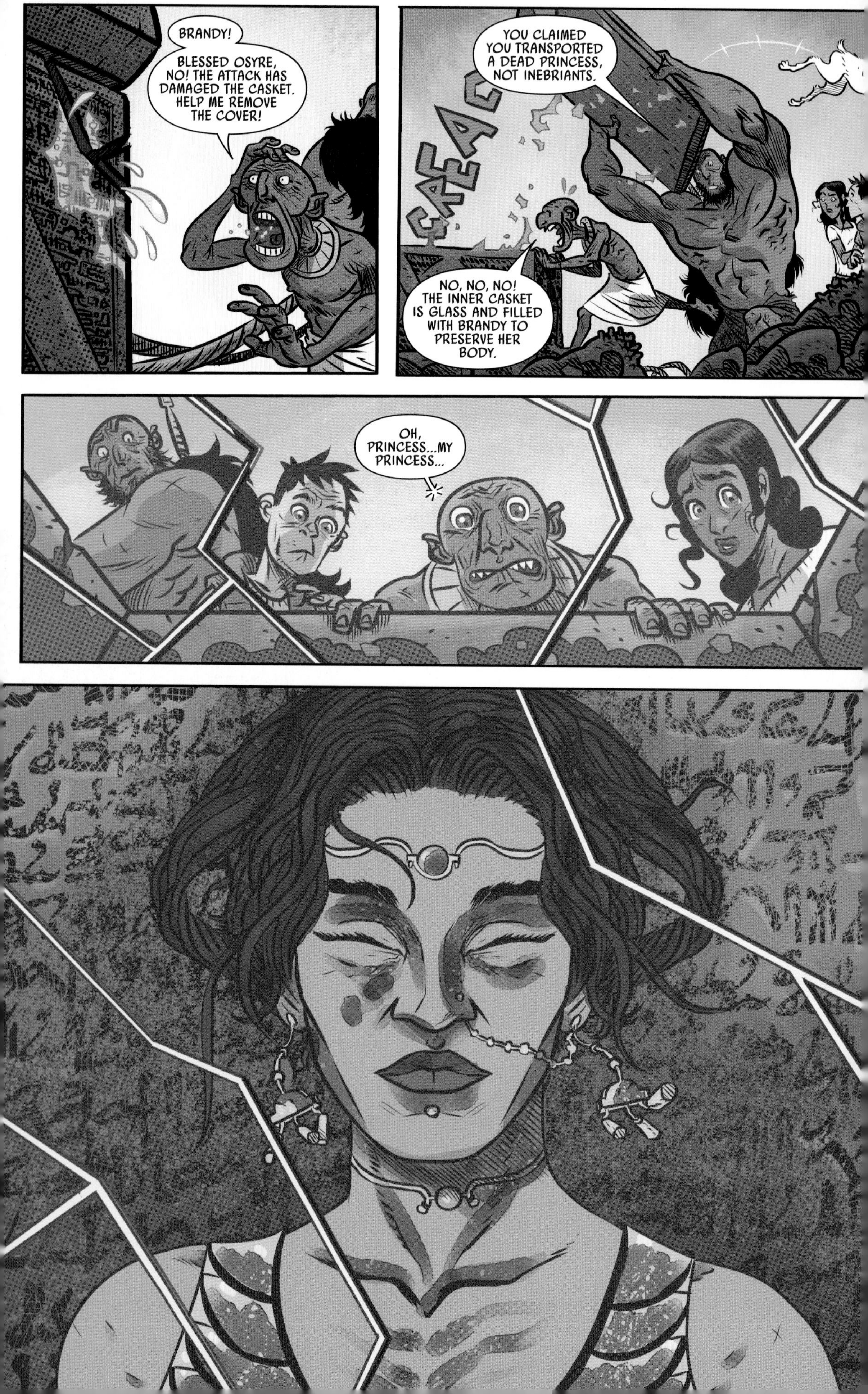
BRANDY!
BLESSED OSYRE, NO! THE ATTACK HAS DAMAGED THE CASKET. HELP ME REMOVE THE COVER!
YOU CLAIMED YOU TRANSPORTED A DEAD PRINCESS, NOT INEBRIANTS.
CREAC
NO, NO, NO! THE INNER CASKET IS GLASS AND FILLED WITH BRANDY TO PRESERVE HER BODY.
OH, PRINCESS...MY PRINCESS...

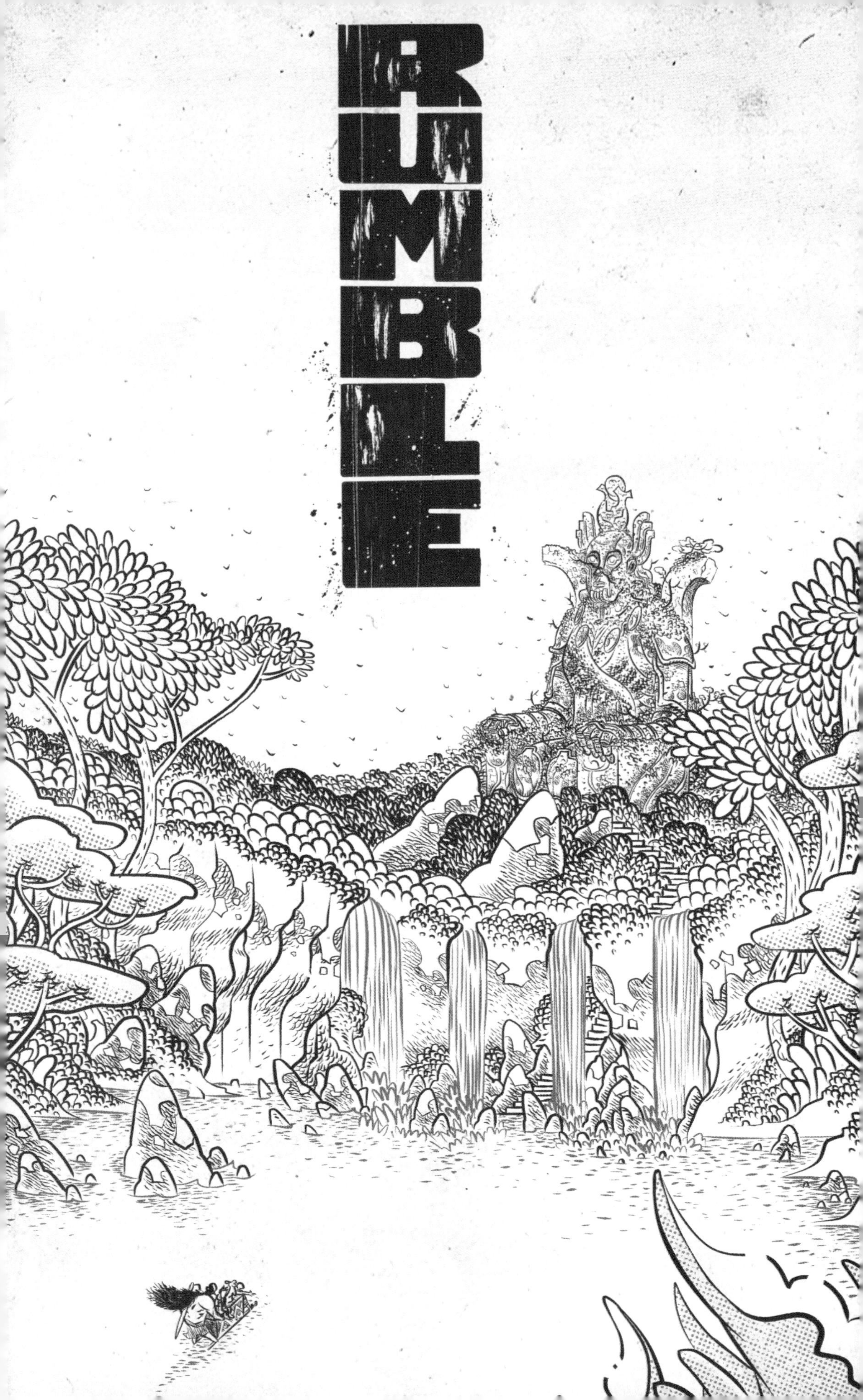
RUMBLE

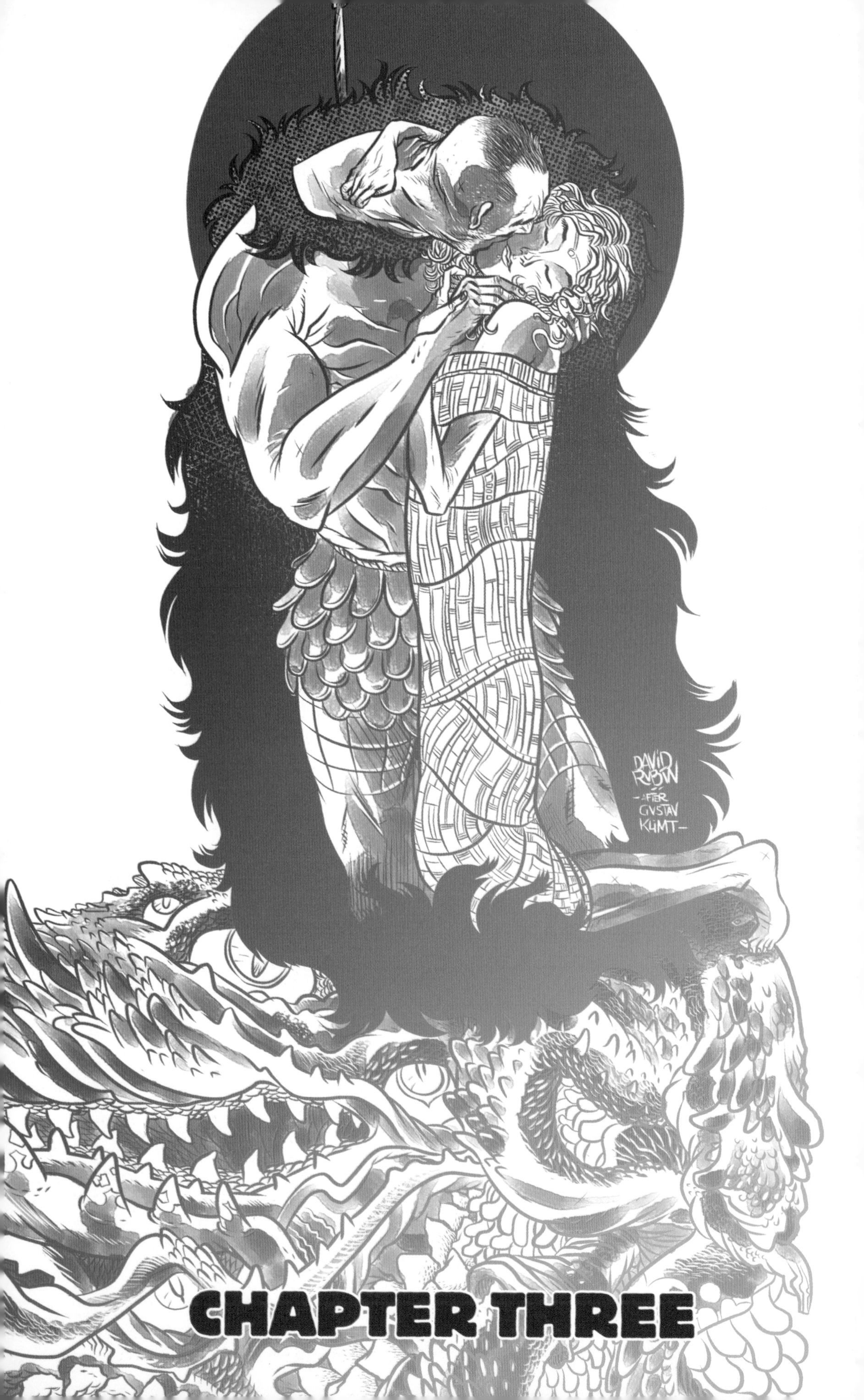
DAVID RUBIN
-AFTER
GUSTAV
KLIMT-

# CHAPTER THREE

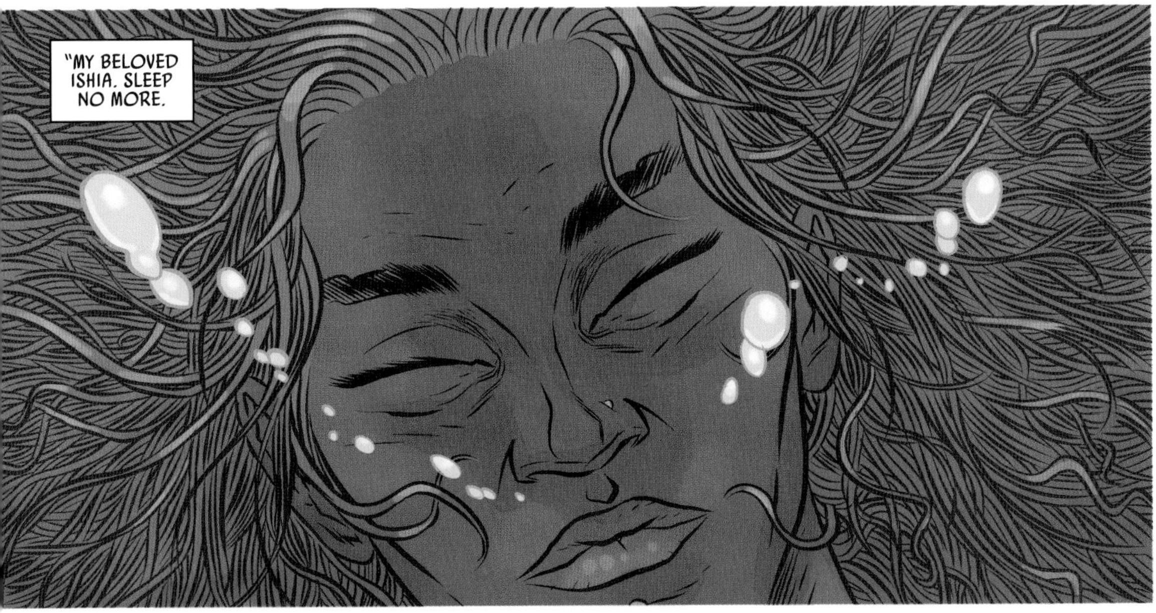
"MY BELOVED ISHIA. SLEEP NO MORE.

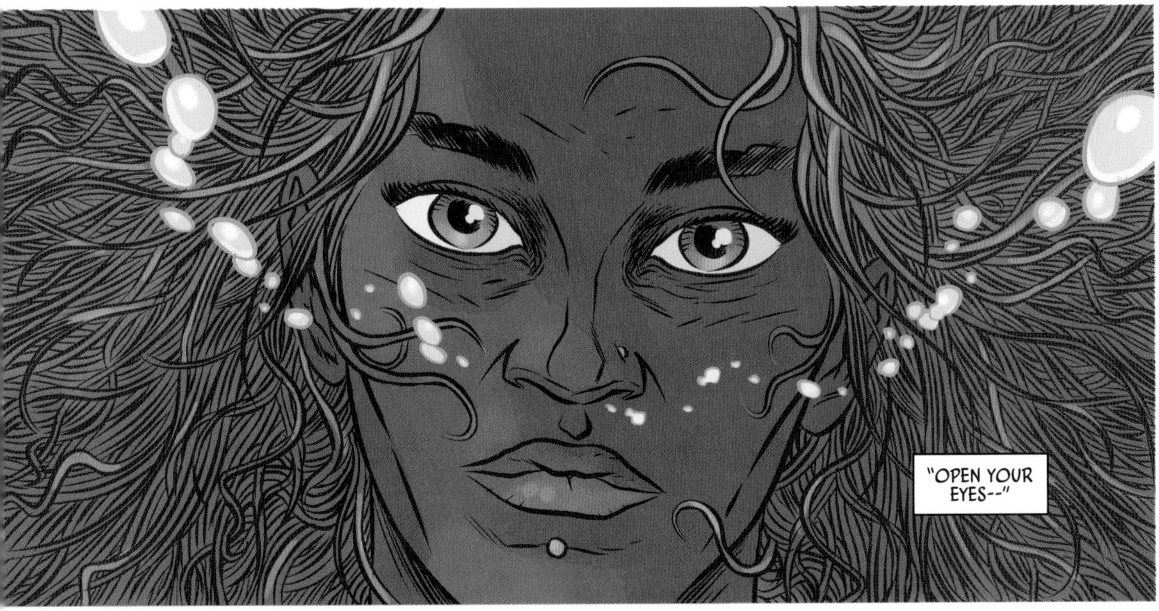
"OPEN YOUR EYES--"

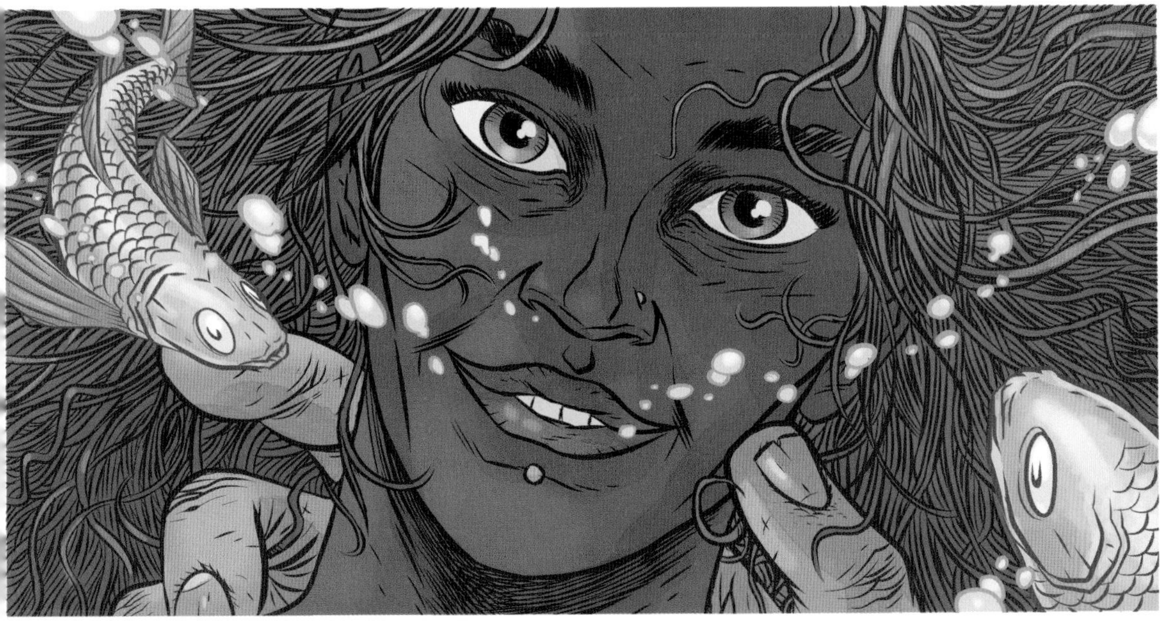

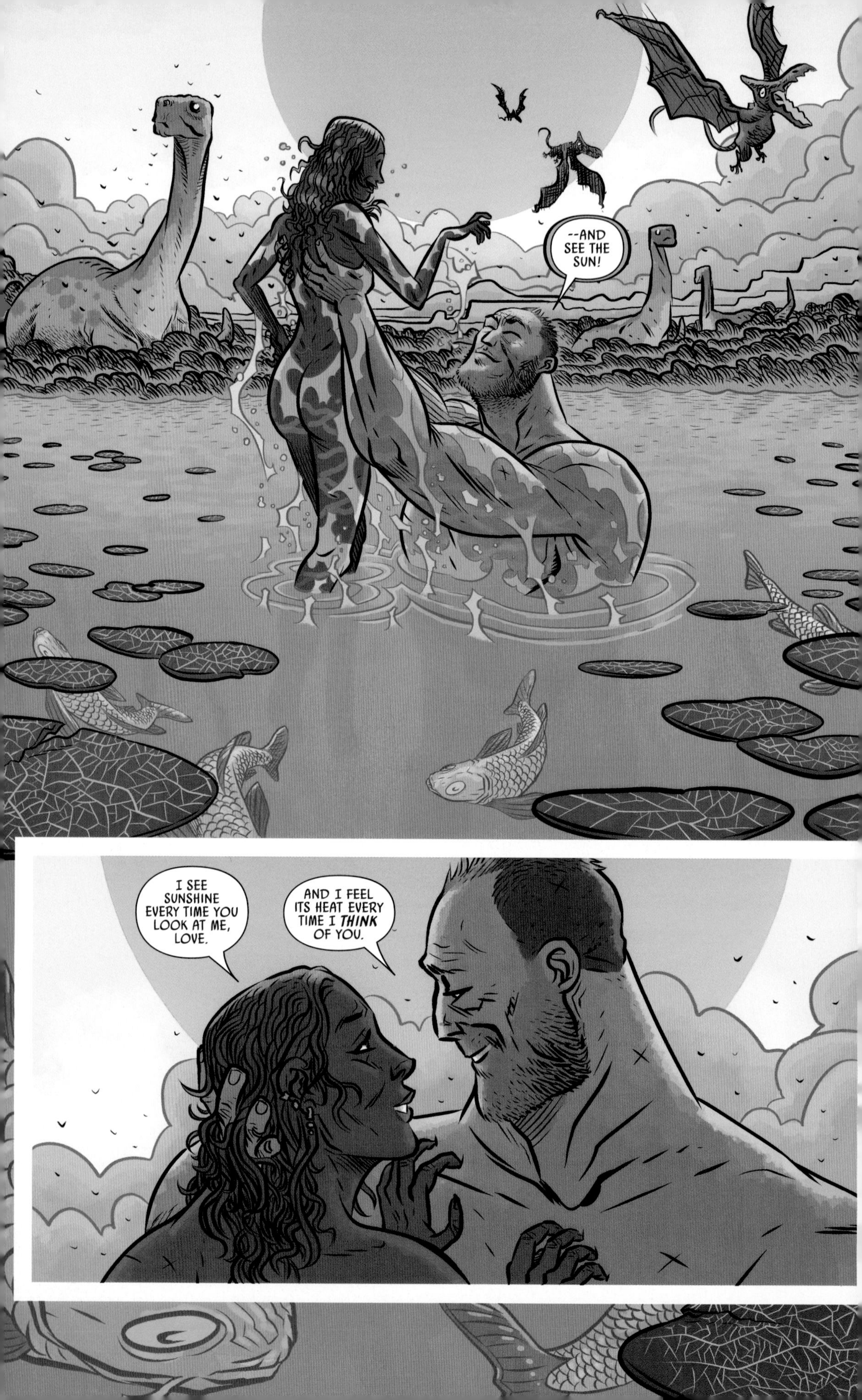
--AND SEE THE SUN!
I SEE SUNSHINE EVERY TIME YOU LOOK AT ME, LOVE.
AND I FEEL ITS HEAT EVERY TIME I *THINK* OF YOU.

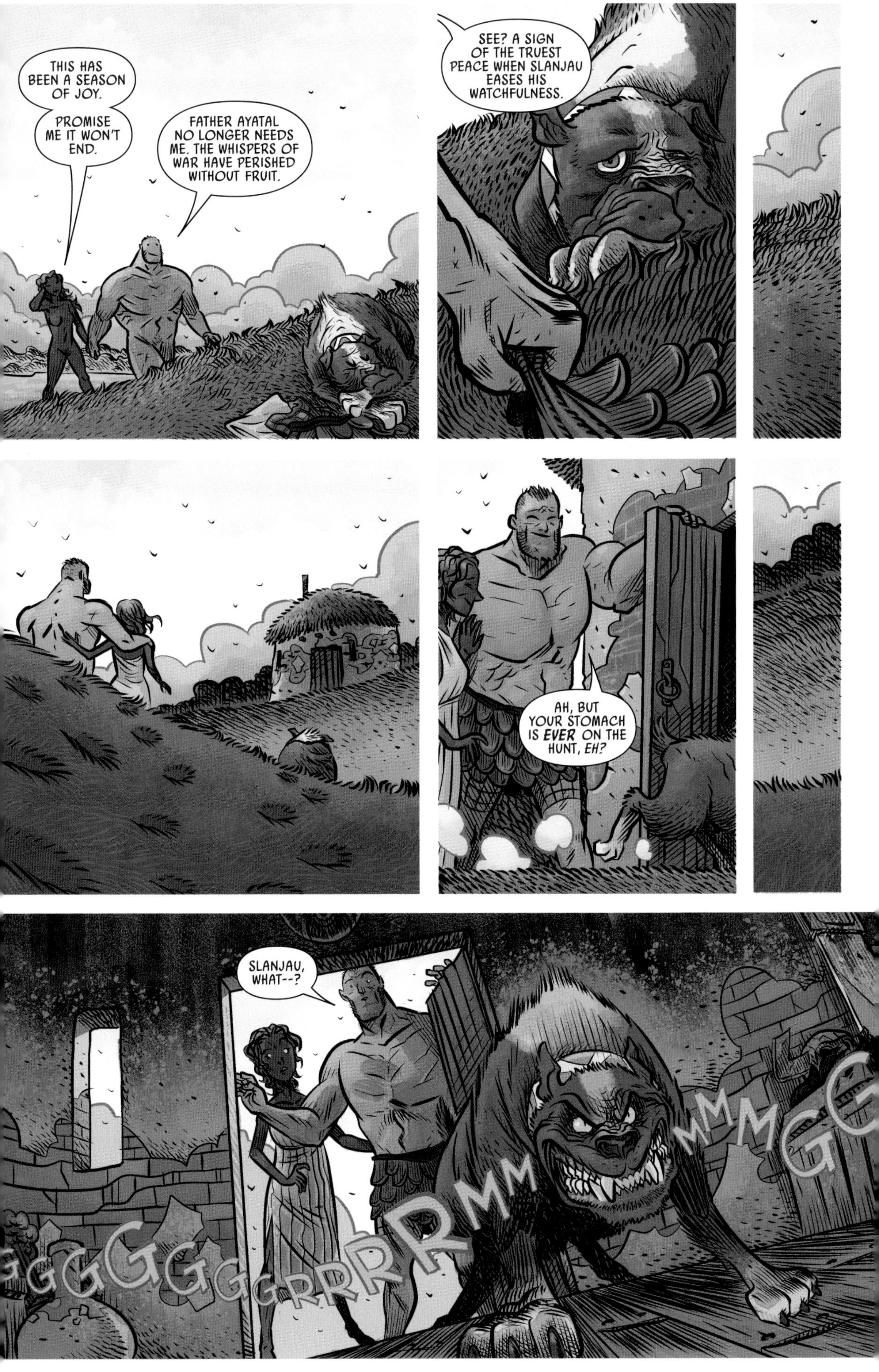
THIS HAS BEEN A SEASON OF JOY.
PROMISE ME IT WON'T END.
FATHER AYATAL NO LONGER NEEDS ME. THE WHISPERS OF WAR HAVE PERISHED WITHOUT FRUIT.
SEE? A SIGN OF THE TRUEST PEACE WHEN SLANJAU EASES HIS WATCHFULNESS.
AH, BUT YOUR STOMACH IS *EVER* ON THE HUNT, EH?
SLANJAU, WHAT--?
GGGGGGRRRRRMMMMMMGG

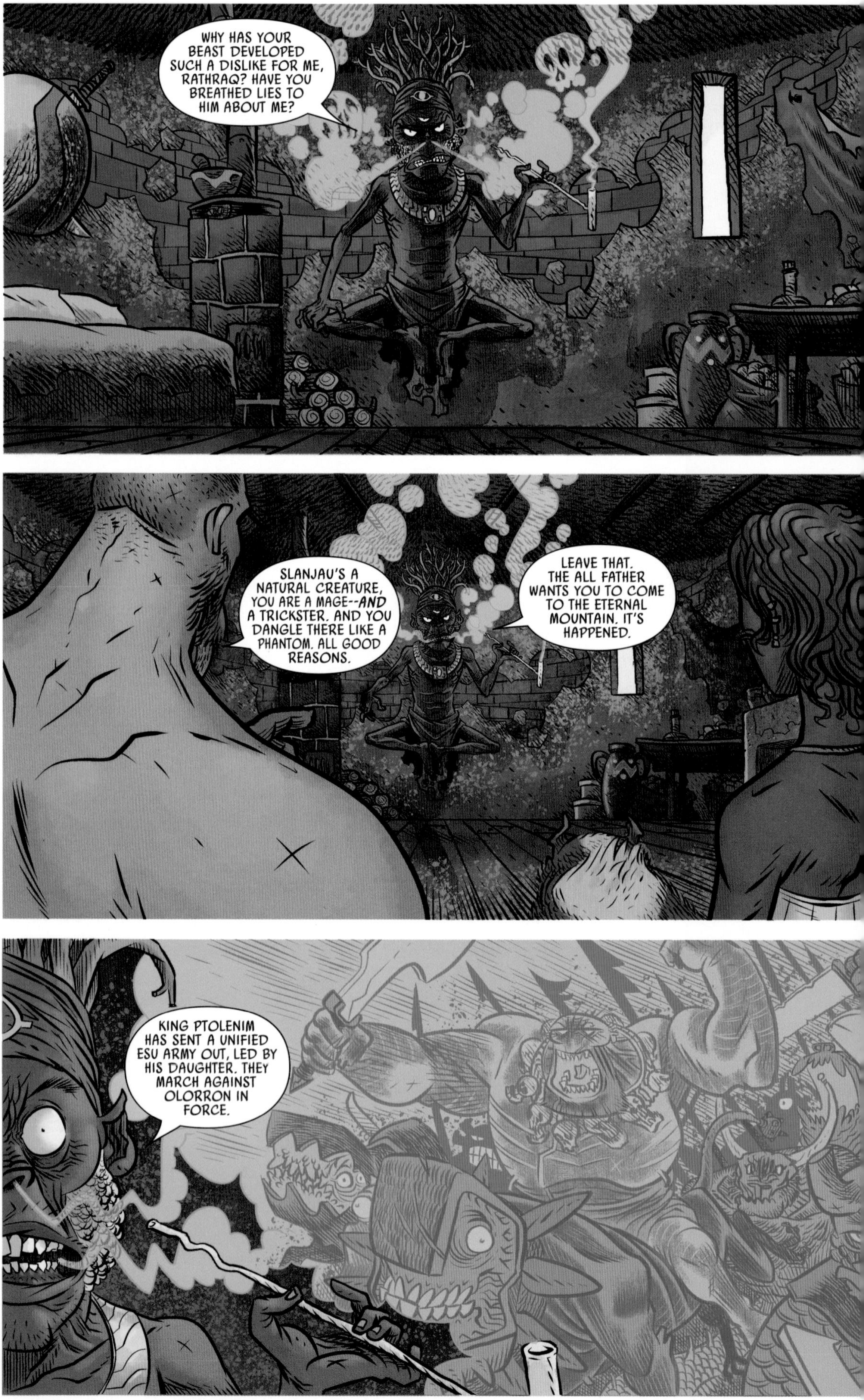
WHY HAS YOUR BEAST DEVELOPED SUCH A DISLIKE FOR ME, RATHRAQ? HAVE YOU BREATHED LIES TO HIM ABOUT ME?
SLANJAU'S A NATURAL CREATURE, YOU ARE A MAGE--AND A TRICKSTER. AND YOU DANGLE THERE LIKE A PHANTOM. ALL GOOD REASONS.
LEAVE THAT. THE ALL FATHER WANTS YOU TO COME TO THE ETERNAL MOUNTAIN. IT'S HAPPENED.
KING PTOLENIM HAS SENT A UNIFIED ESU ARMY OUT, LED BY HIS DAUGHTER. THEY MARCH AGAINST OLORRON IN FORCE.

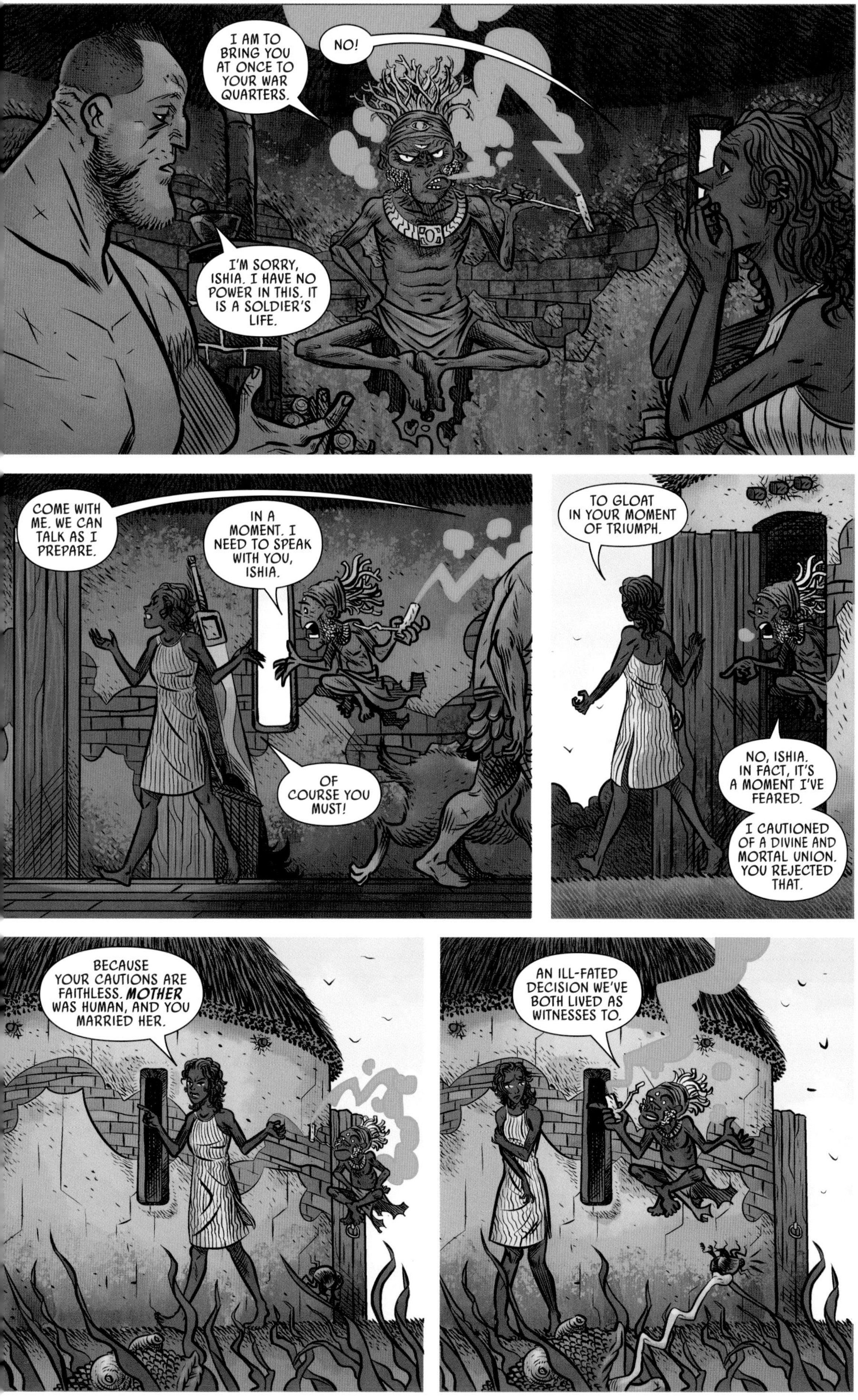
I AM TO BRING YOU AT ONCE TO YOUR WAR QUARTERS.
NO!
I'M SORRY, ISHIA. I HAVE NO POWER IN THIS. IT IS A SOLDIER'S LIFE.
COME WITH ME. WE CAN TALK AS I PREPARE.
IN A MOMENT. I NEED TO SPEAK WITH YOU, ISHIA.
OF COURSE YOU MUST!
TO GLOAT IN YOUR MOMENT OF TRIUMPH.
NO, ISHIA. IN FACT, IT'S A MOMENT I'VE FEARED.
I CAUTIONED OF A DIVINE AND MORTAL UNION. YOU REJECTED THAT.
BECAUSE YOUR CAUTIONS ARE FAITHLESS. MOTHER WAS HUMAN, AND YOU MARRIED HER.
AN ILL-FATED DECISION WE'VE BOTH LIVED AS WITNESSES TO.

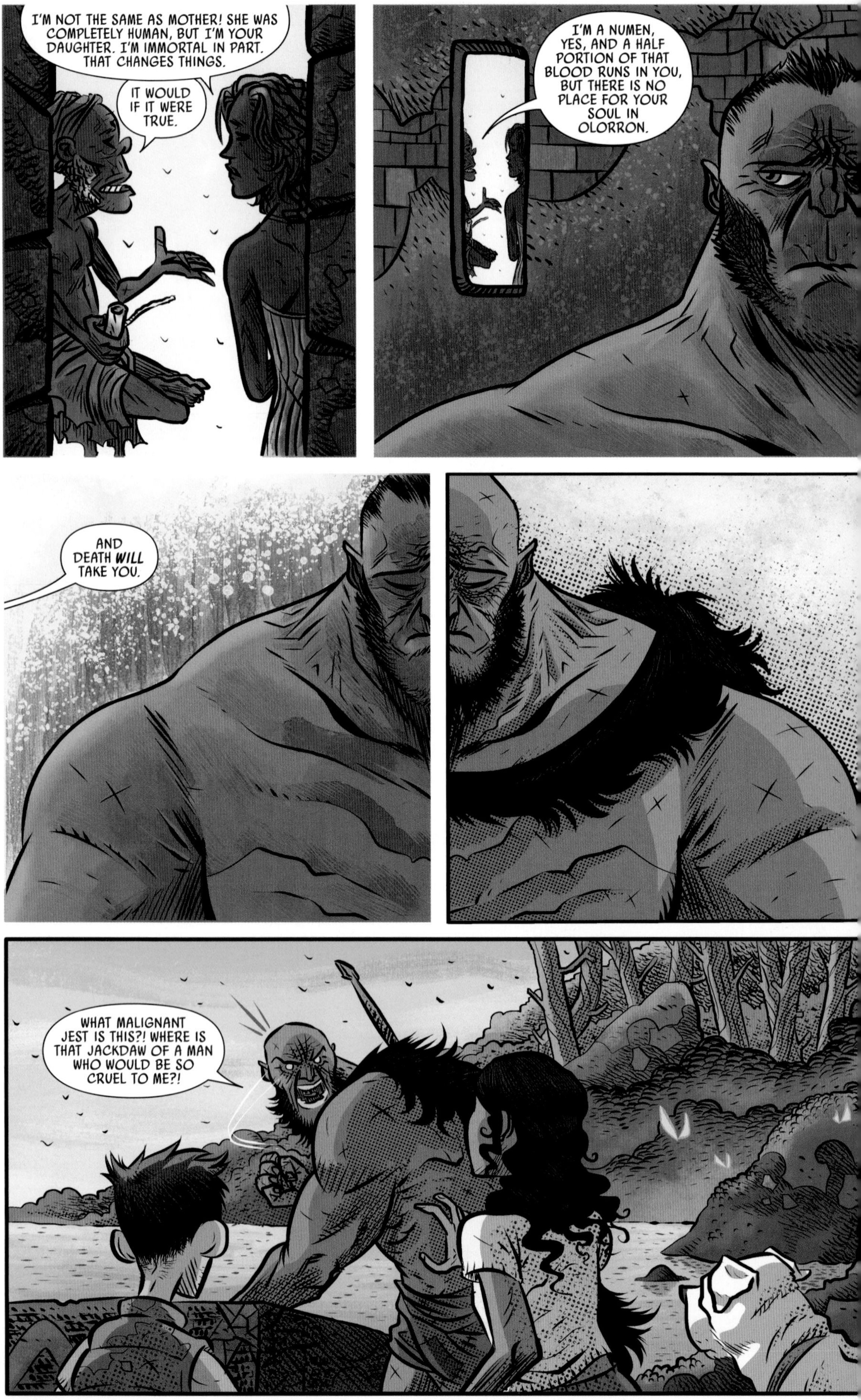
I'M NOT THE SAME AS MOTHER! SHE WAS COMPLETELY HUMAN, BUT I'M YOUR DAUGHTER. I'M IMMORTAL IN PART. THAT CHANGES THINGS.
IT WOULD IF IT WERE TRUE.
I'M A NUMEN, YES, AND A HALF PORTION OF THAT BLOOD RUNS IN YOU, BUT THERE IS NO PLACE FOR YOUR SOUL IN OLORRON.
AND DEATH WILL TAKE YOU.
WHAT MALIGNANT JEST IS THIS?! WHERE IS THAT JACKDAW OF A MAN WHO WOULD BE SO CRUEL TO ME?!

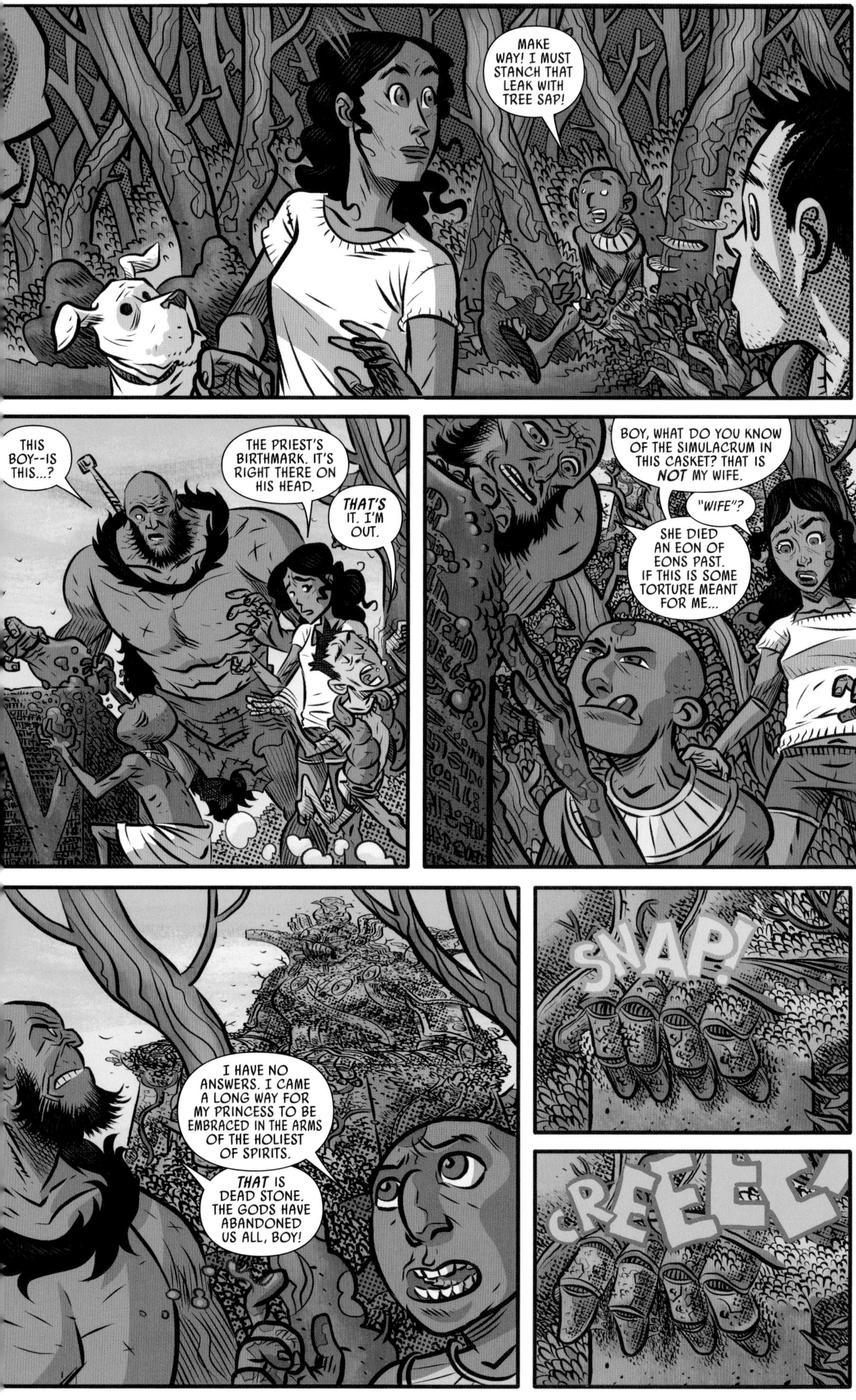
MAKE WAY! I MUST STANCH THAT LEAK WITH TREE SAP!
THIS BOY--IS THIS...?
THE PRIEST'S BIRTHMARK. IT'S RIGHT THERE ON HIS HEAD.
THAT'S IT. I'M OUT.
BOY, WHAT DO YOU KNOW OF THE SIMULACRUM IN THIS CASKET? THAT IS NOT MY WIFE.
"WIFE"?
SHE DIED AN EON OF EONS PAST. IF THIS IS SOME TORTURE MEANT FOR ME...
I HAVE NO ANSWERS. I CAME A LONG WAY FOR MY PRINCESS TO BE EMBRACED IN THE ARMS OF THE HOLIEST OF SPIRITS.
THAT IS DEAD STONE. THE GODS HAVE ABANDONED US ALL, BOY!
SNAP!
CREEEE

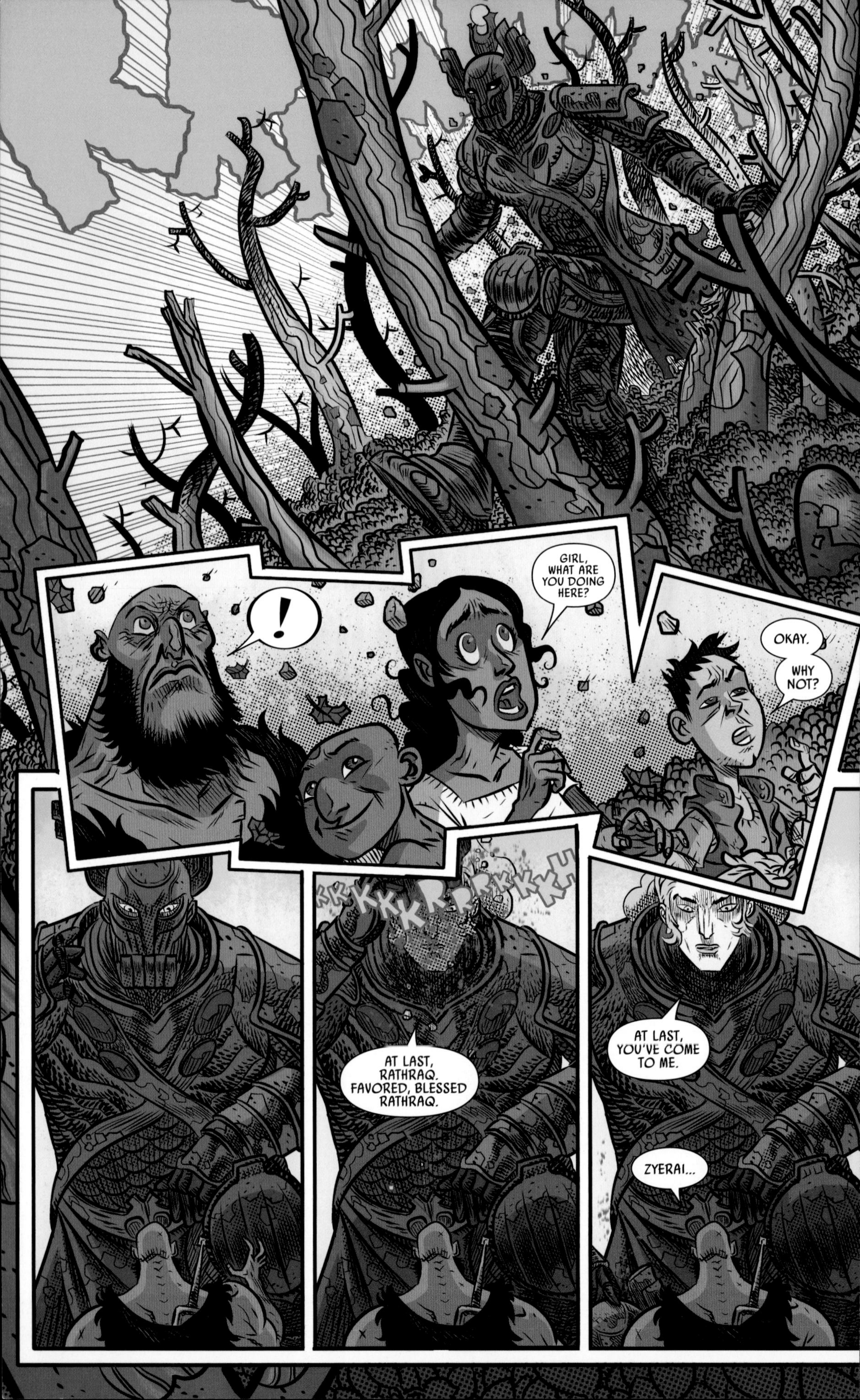
!
GIRL, WHAT ARE YOU DOING HERE?
OKAY.
WHY NOT?
KKKKRRRRKKKKH
AT LAST, RATHRAQ. FAVORED, BLESSED RATHRAQ.
AT LAST, YOU'VE COME TO ME.
ZYERAI...

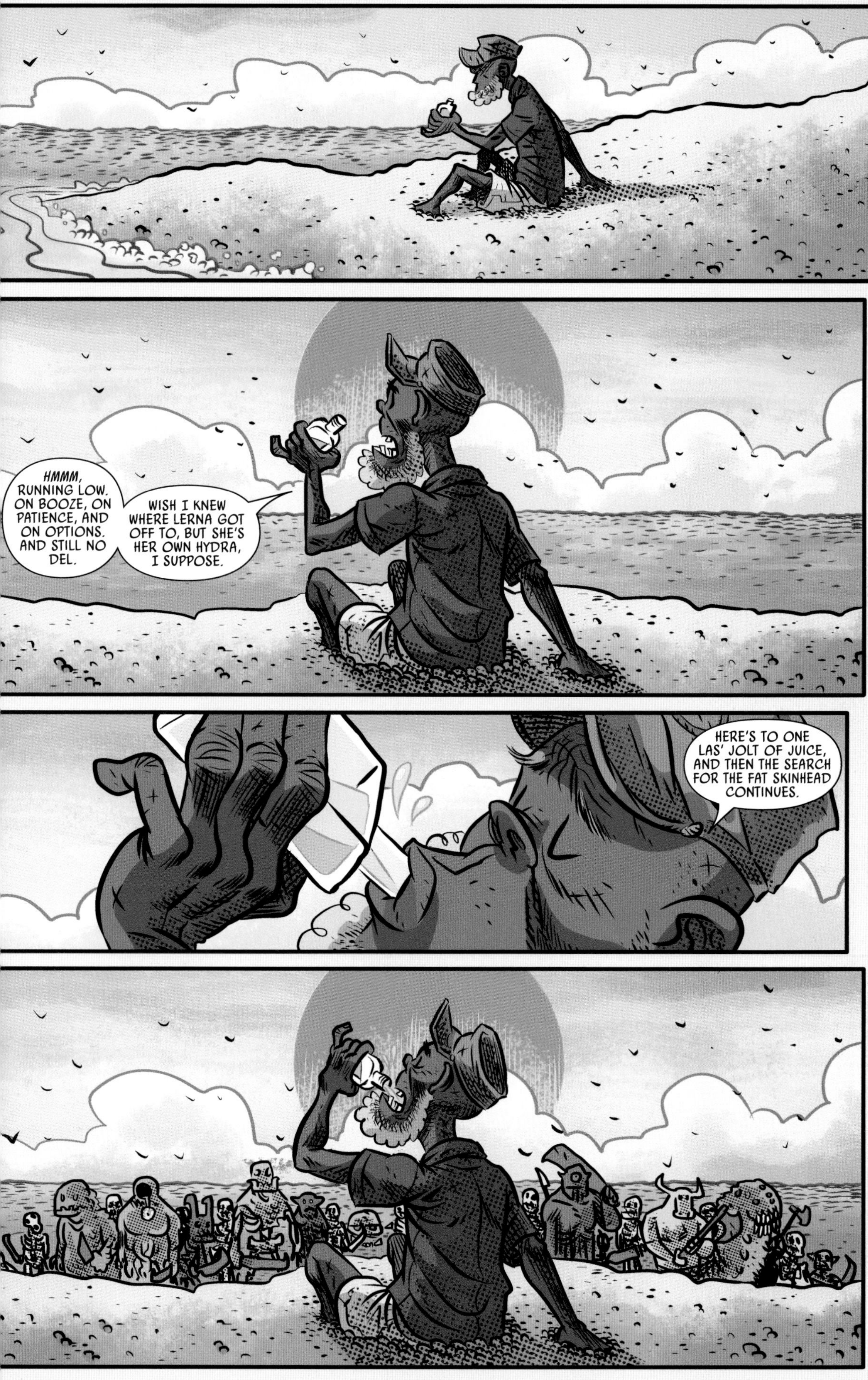
HMMM, RUNNING LOW. ON BOOZE, ON PATIENCE, AND ON OPTIONS. AND STILL NO DEL.
WISH I KNEW WHERE LERNA GOT OFF TO, BUT SHE'S HER OWN HYDRA, I SUPPOSE.
HERE'S TO ONE LAS' JOLT OF JUICE, AND THEN THE SEARCH FOR THE FAT SKINHEAD CONTINUES.

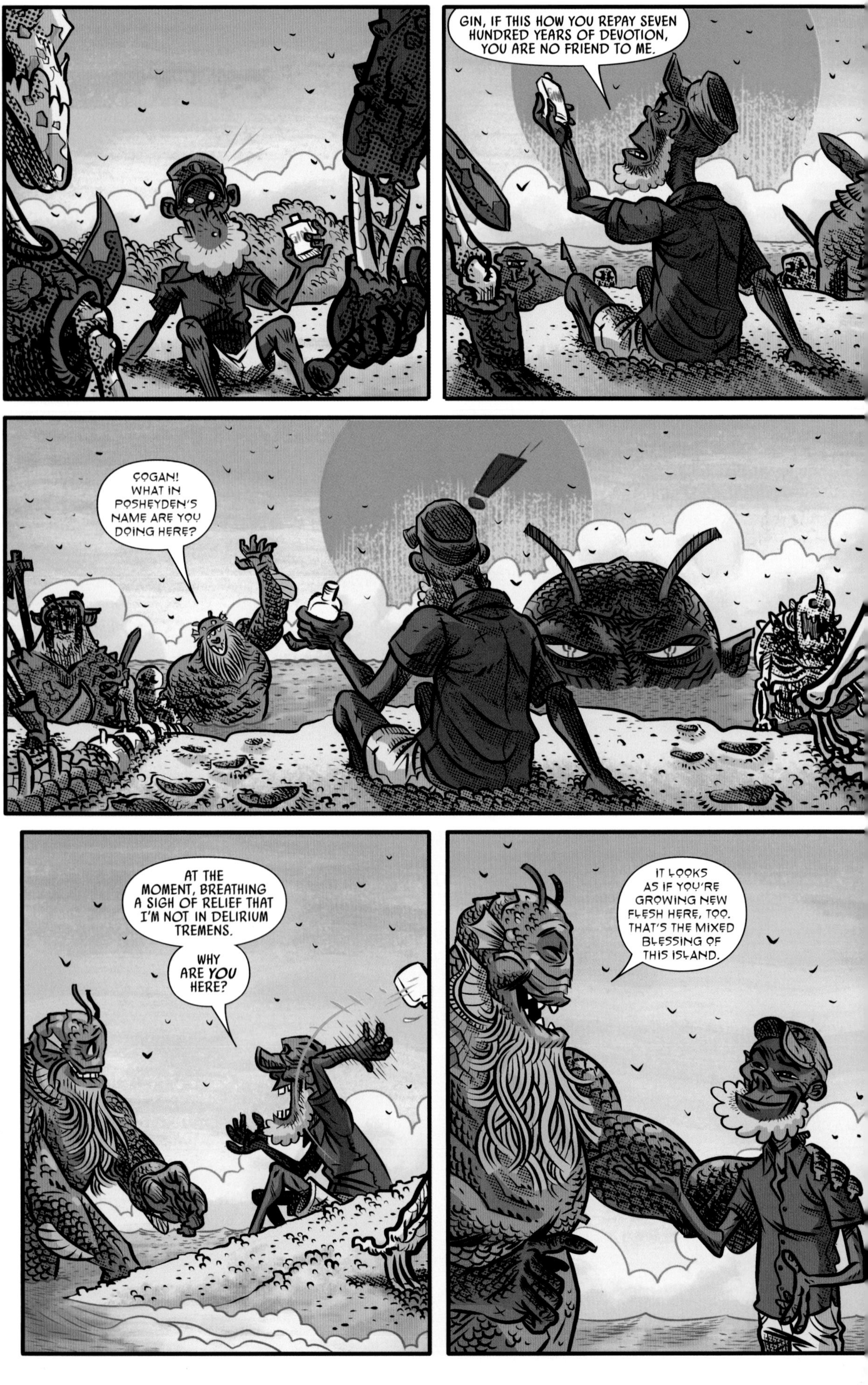
GIN, IF THIS HOW YOU REPAY SEVEN HUNDRED YEARS OF DEVOTION, YOU ARE NO FRIEND TO ME.
ÇOGAN! WHAT IN POSHEYDEN'S NAME ARE YOU DOING HERE?
AT THE MOMENT, BREATHING A SIGH OF RELIEF THAT I'M NOT IN DELIRIUM TREMENS.
WHY ARE *YOU* HERE?
IT LOOKS AS IF YOU'RE GROWING NEW FLESH HERE, TOO. THAT'S THE MIXED BLESSING OF THIS ISLAND.

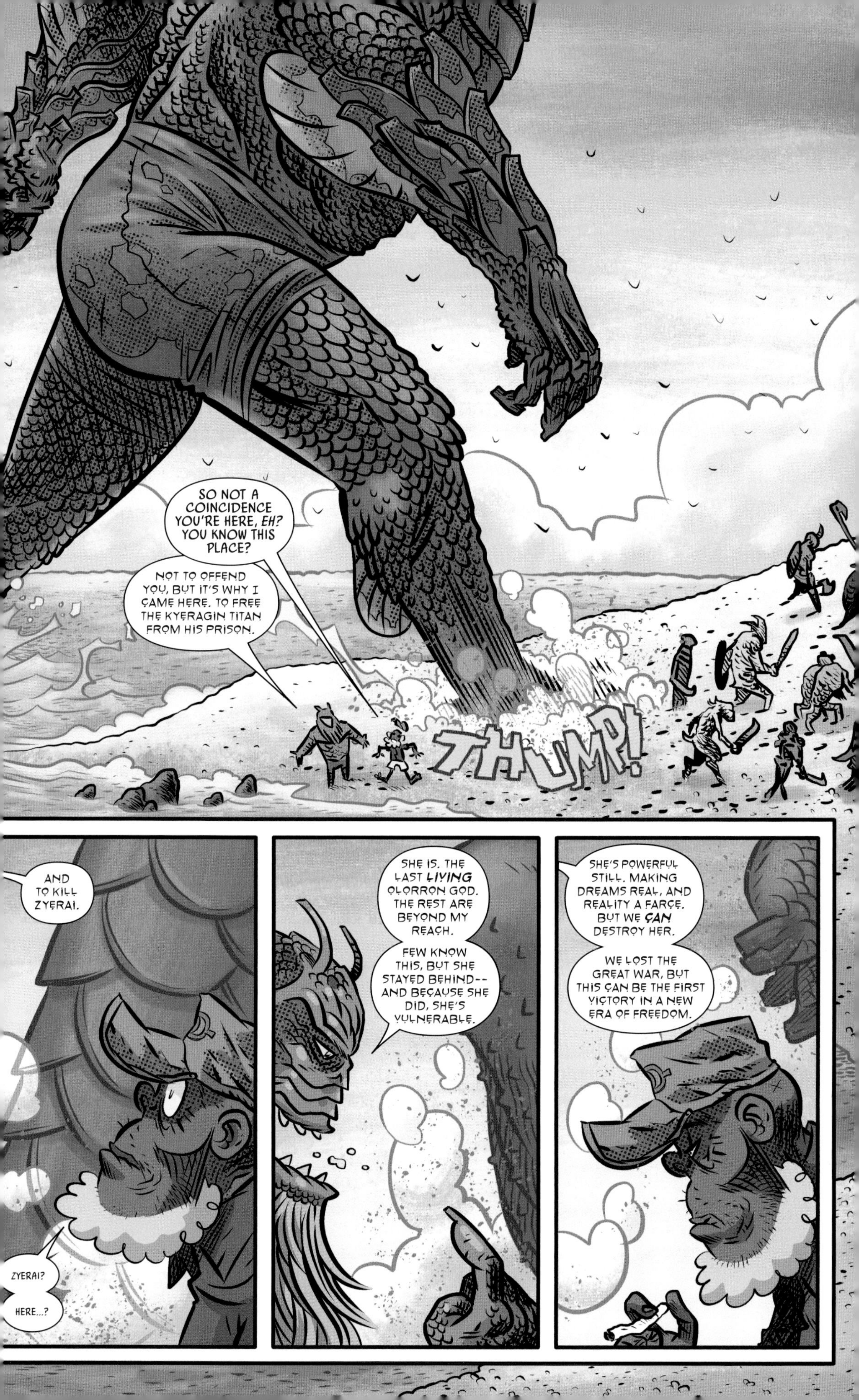
SO NOT A COINCIDENCE YOU'RE HERE, EH? YOU KNOW THIS PLACE?
NOT TO OFFEND YOU, BUT IT'S WHY I CAME HERE. TO FREE THE KYERAGIN TITAN FROM HIS PRISON.
THUMP!
AND TO KILL ZYERAI.
ZYERAI?
HERE...?
SHE IS. THE LAST LIVING OLORRON GOD. THE REST ARE BEYOND MY REACH.
FEW KNOW THIS, BUT SHE STAYED BEHIND-- AND BECAUSE SHE DID, SHE'S VULNERABLE.
SHE'S POWERFUL STILL. MAKING DREAMS REAL, AND REALITY A FARCE. BUT WE CAN DESTROY HER.
WE LOST THE GREAT WAR, BUT THIS CAN BE THE FIRST VICTORY IN A NEW ERA OF FREEDOM.

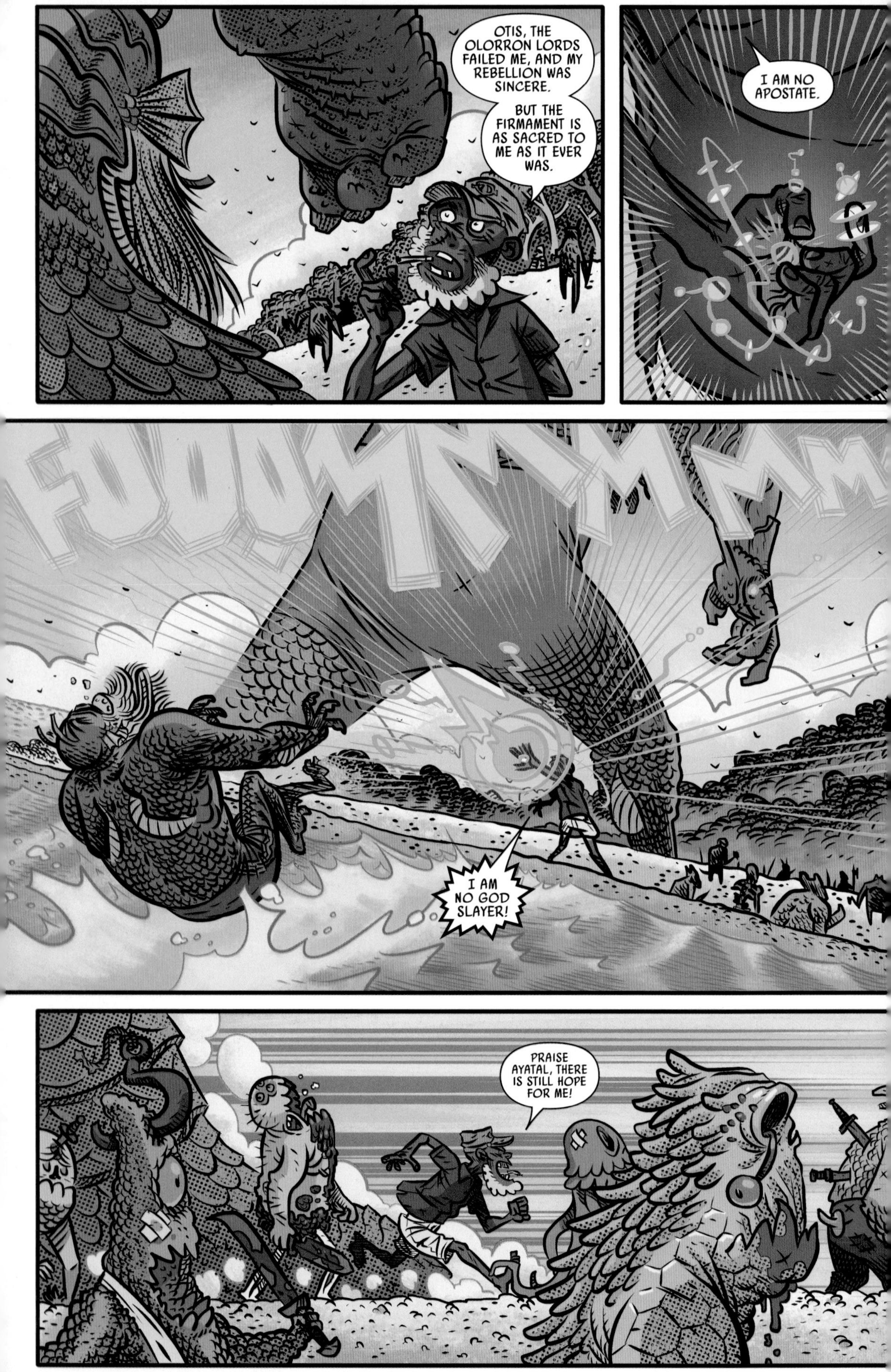
OTIS, THE OLORRON LORDS FAILED ME, AND MY REBELLION WAS SINCERE.
BUT THE FIRMAMENT IS AS SACRED TO ME AS IT EVER WAS.
I AM NO APOSTATE.
I AM NO GOD SLAYER!
PRAISE AYATAL, THERE IS STILL HOPE FOR ME!

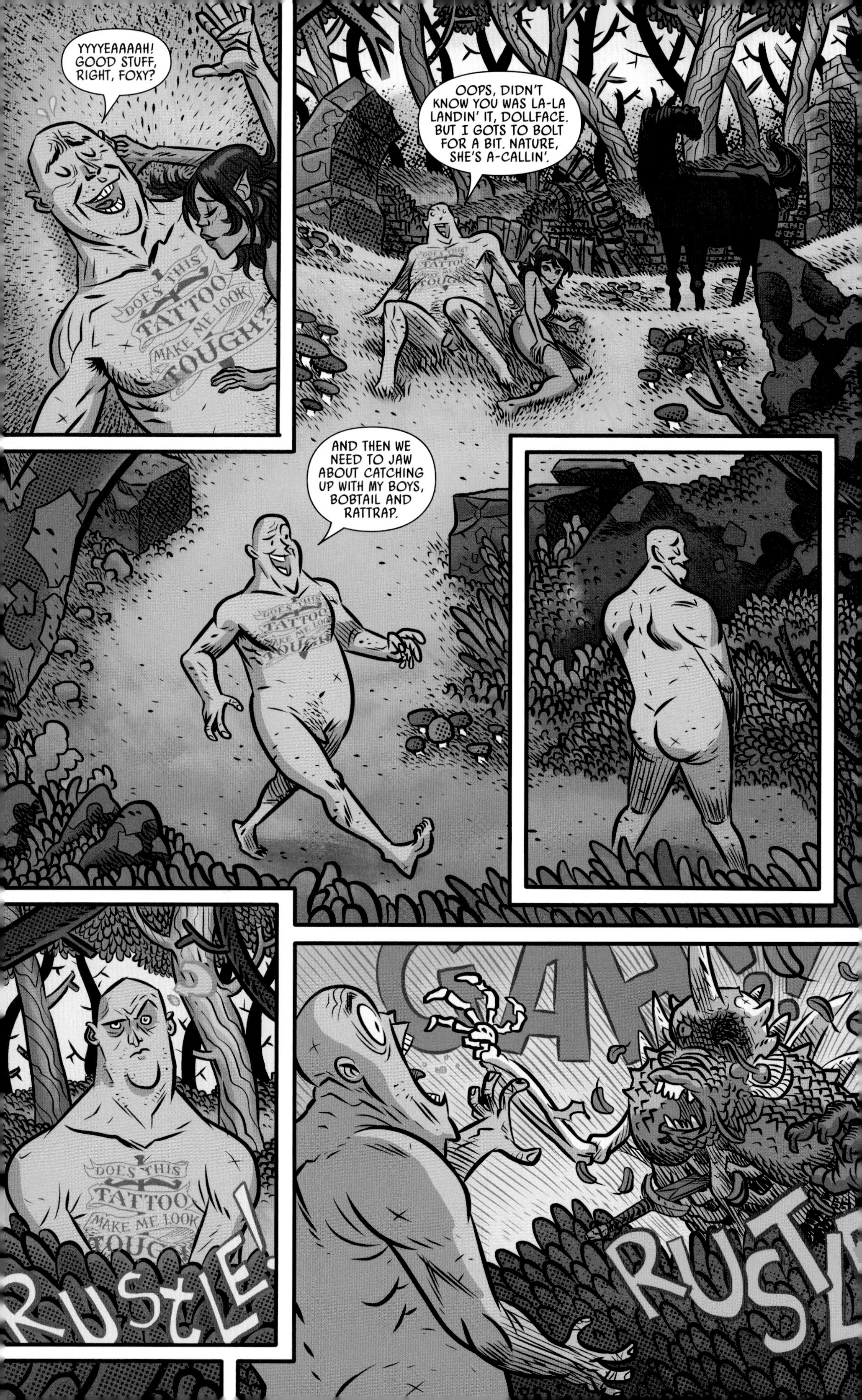
YYYYEAAAAH! GOOD STUFF, RIGHT, FOXY?
OOPS, DIDN'T KNOW YOU WAS LA-LA LANDIN' IT, DOLLFACE. BUT I GOTS TO BOLT FOR A BIT. NATURE, SHE'S A-CALLIN'.
AND THEN WE NEED TO JAW ABOUT CATCHING UP WITH MY BOYS, BOBTAIL AND RATTRAP.
RUSTLE!

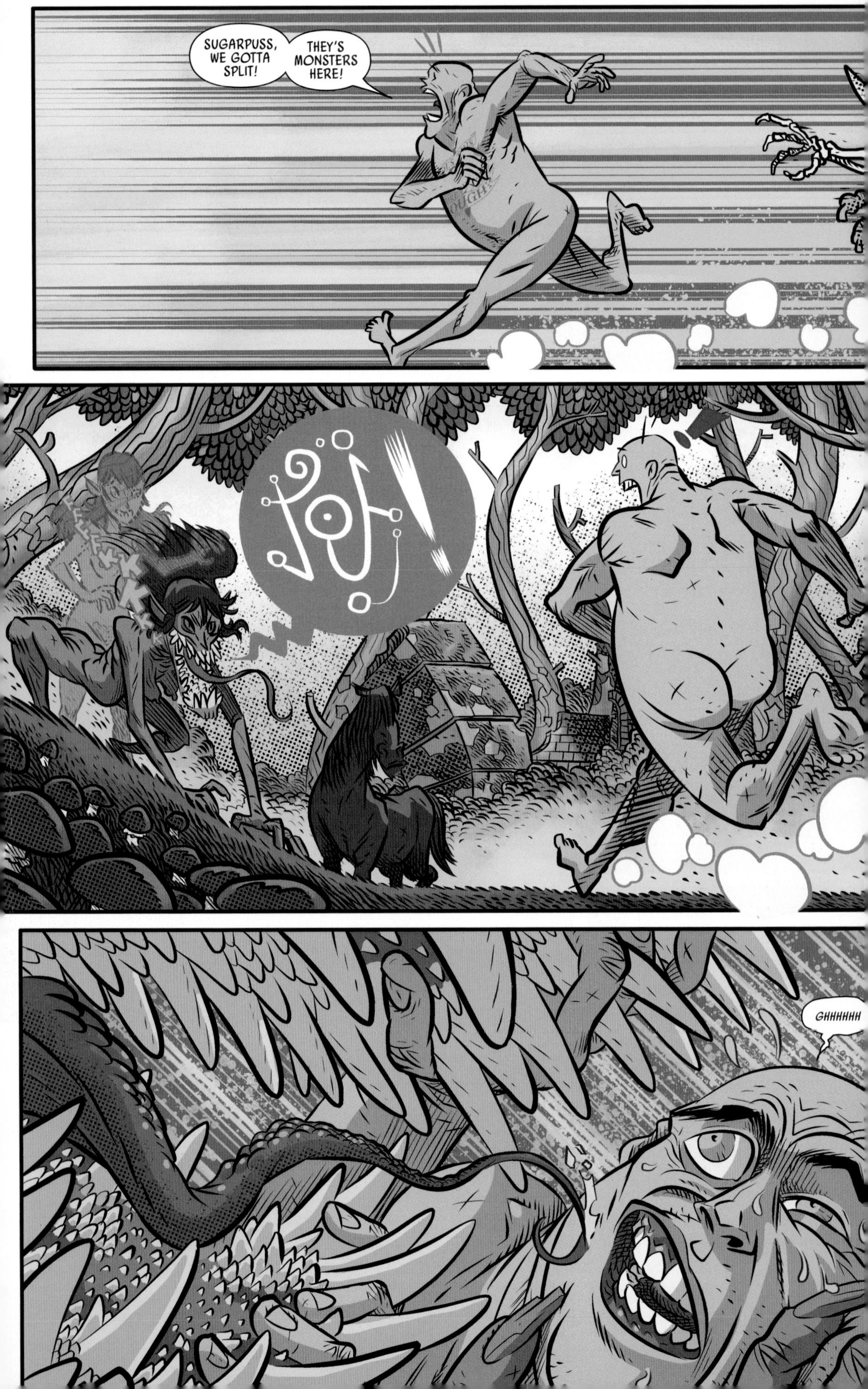
SUGARPUSS, WE GOTTA SPLIT!
THEY'S MONSTERS HERE!
GHHHHHH

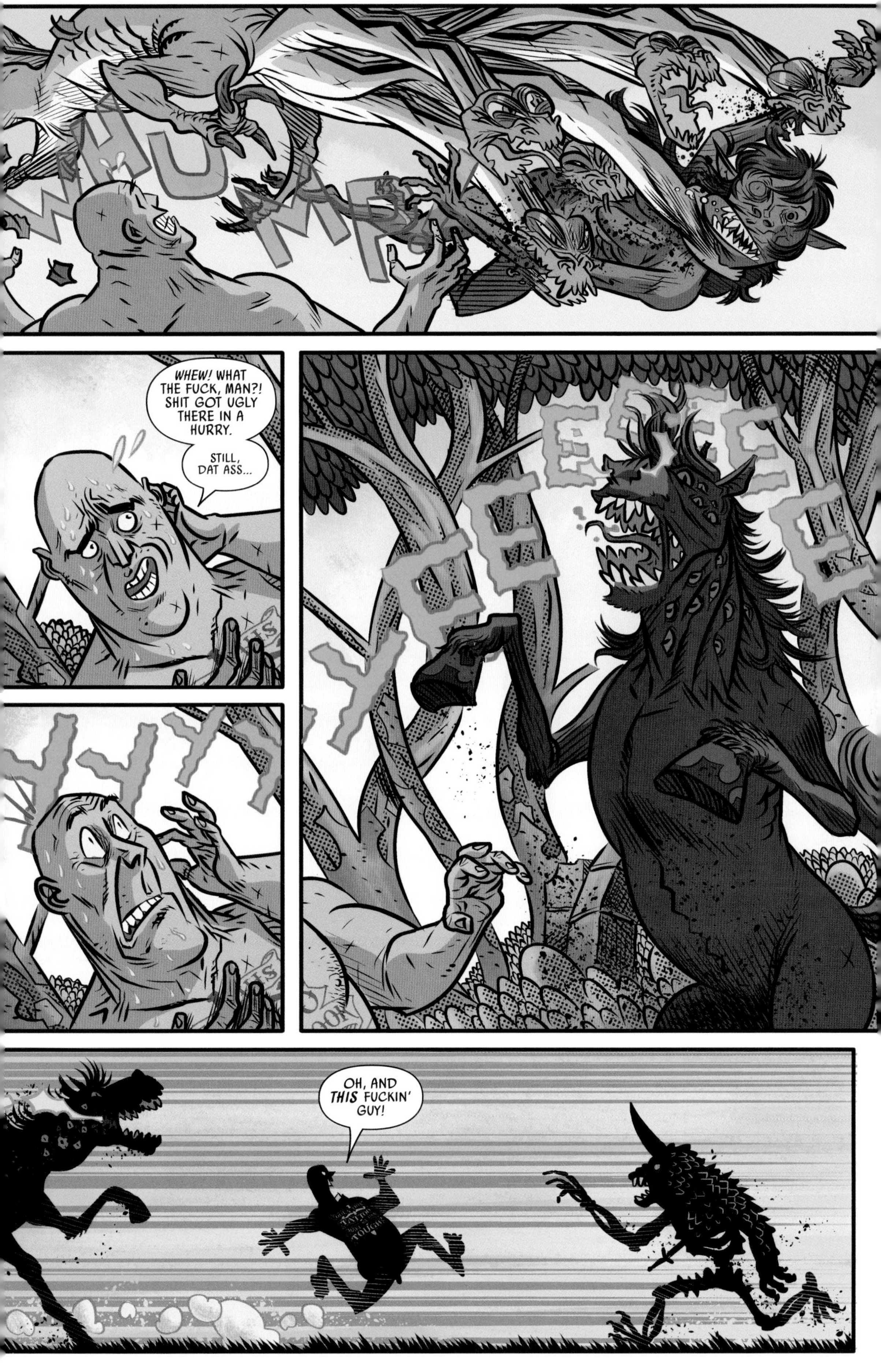
WHUMP
*WHEW!* WHAT THE FUCK, MAN?! SHIT GOT UGLY THERE IN A HURRY.
STILL, DAT ASS...
OH, AND *THIS* FUCKIN' GUY!

CAN'T RUN, CAN'T HIDE.

DOES TATTOO MAKE ME LOOK TOUGH?

GAPP!!

ONLY ONE OPTION!!!

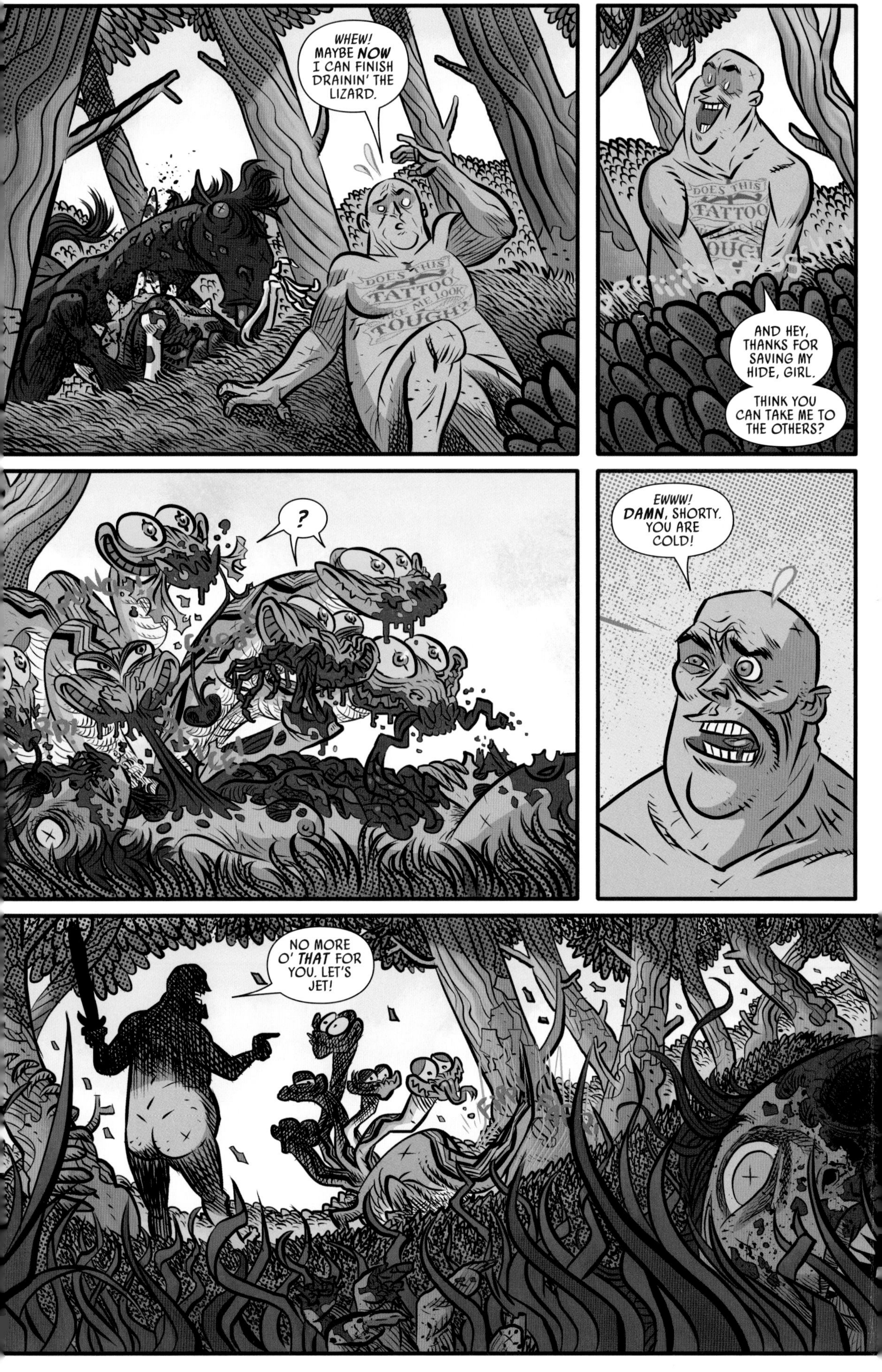
WHEW! MAYBE NOW I CAN FINISH DRAININ' THE LIZARD.
AND HEY, THANKS FOR SAVING MY HIDE, GIRL.
THINK YOU CAN TAKE ME TO THE OTHERS?
?
EWWW! DAMN, SHORTY. YOU ARE COLD!
NO MORE O' THAT FOR YOU. LET'S JET!

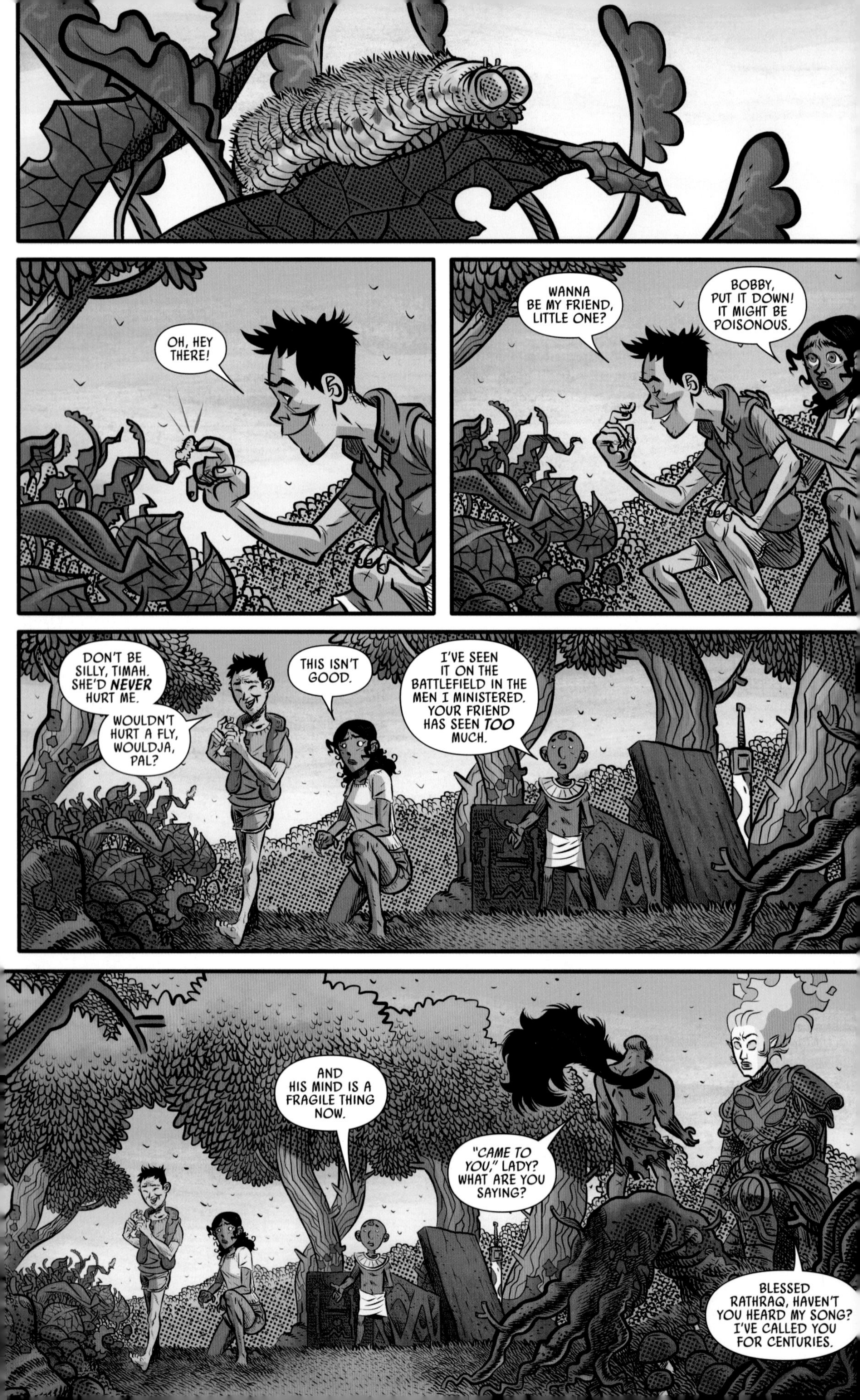
OH, HEY THERE!
WANNA BE MY FRIEND, LITTLE ONE?
BOBBY, PUT IT DOWN! IT MIGHT BE POISONOUS.
DON'T BE SILLY, TIMAH. SHE'D NEVER HURT ME.
WOULDN'T HURT A FLY, WOULDJA, PAL?
THIS ISN'T GOOD.
I'VE SEEN IT ON THE BATTLEFIELD IN THE MEN I MINISTERED. YOUR FRIEND HAS SEEN TOO MUCH.
AND HIS MIND IS A FRAGILE THING NOW.
"CAME TO YOU," LADY? WHAT ARE YOU SAYING?
BLESSED RATHRAQ, HAVEN'T YOU HEARD MY SONG? I'VE CALLED YOU FOR CENTURIES.

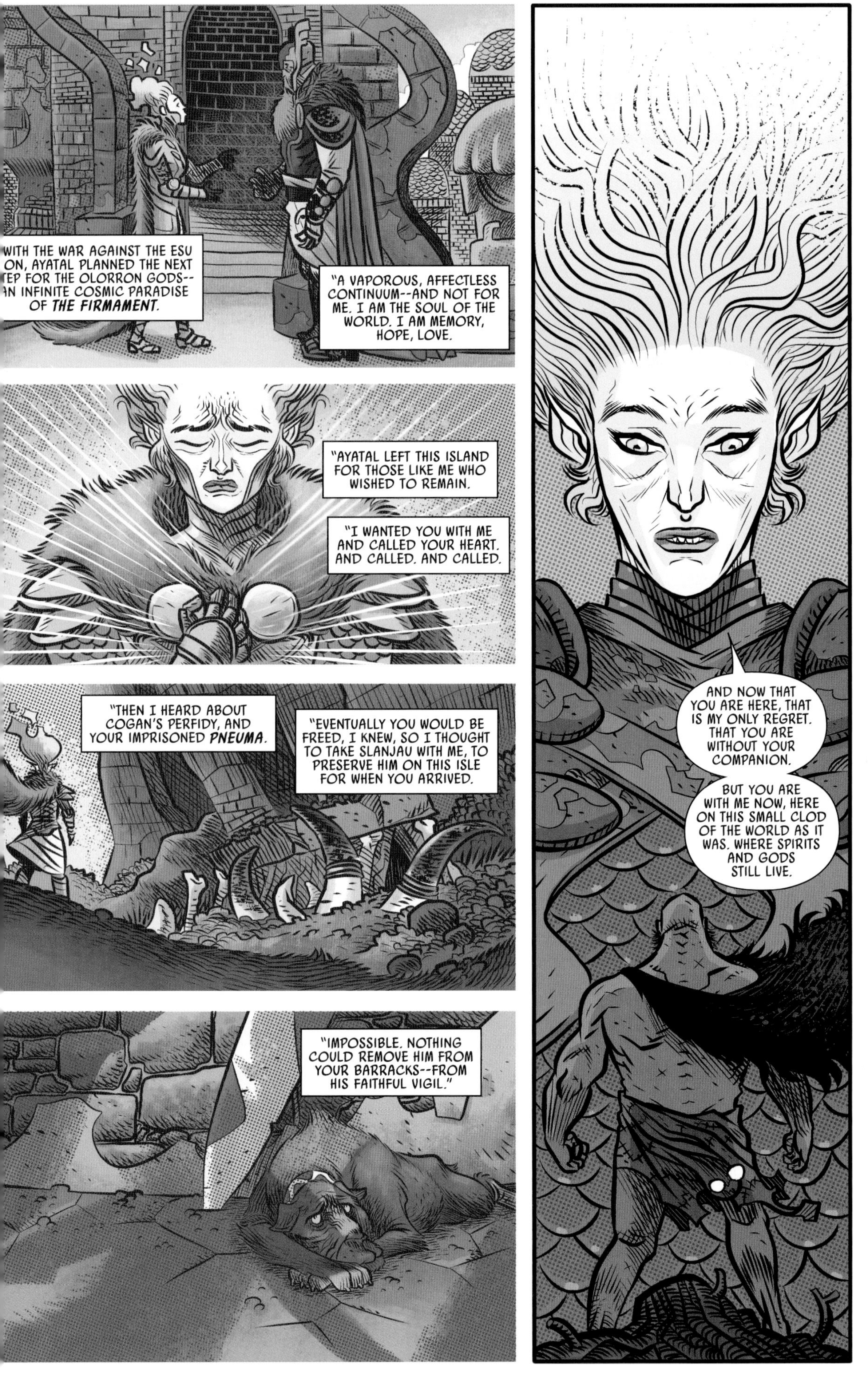
WITH THE WAR AGAINST THE ESU ON, AYATAL PLANNED THE NEXT TEP FOR THE OLORRON GODS--N INFINITE COSMIC PARADISE OF ***THE FIRMAMENT***.
"A VAPOROUS, AFFECTLESS CONTINUUM--AND NOT FOR ME. I AM THE SOUL OF THE WORLD. I AM MEMORY, HOPE, LOVE.
"AYATAL LEFT THIS ISLAND FOR THOSE LIKE ME WHO WISHED TO REMAIN.
"I WANTED YOU WITH ME AND CALLED YOUR HEART. AND CALLED. AND CALLED.
"THEN I HEARD ABOUT COGAN'S PERFIDY, AND YOUR IMPRISONED ***PNEUMA***.
"EVENTUALLY YOU WOULD BE FREED, I KNEW, SO I THOUGHT TO TAKE SLANJAU WITH ME, TO PRESERVE HIM ON THIS ISLE FOR WHEN YOU ARRIVED.
"IMPOSSIBLE. NOTHING COULD REMOVE HIM FROM YOUR BARRACKS--FROM HIS FAITHFUL VIGIL."
AND NOW THAT YOU ARE HERE, THAT IS MY ONLY REGRET. THAT YOU ARE WITHOUT YOUR COMPANION.
BUT YOU ARE WITH ME NOW, HERE ON THIS SMALL CLOD OF THE WORLD AS IT WAS. WHERE SPIRITS AND GODS STILL LIVE.

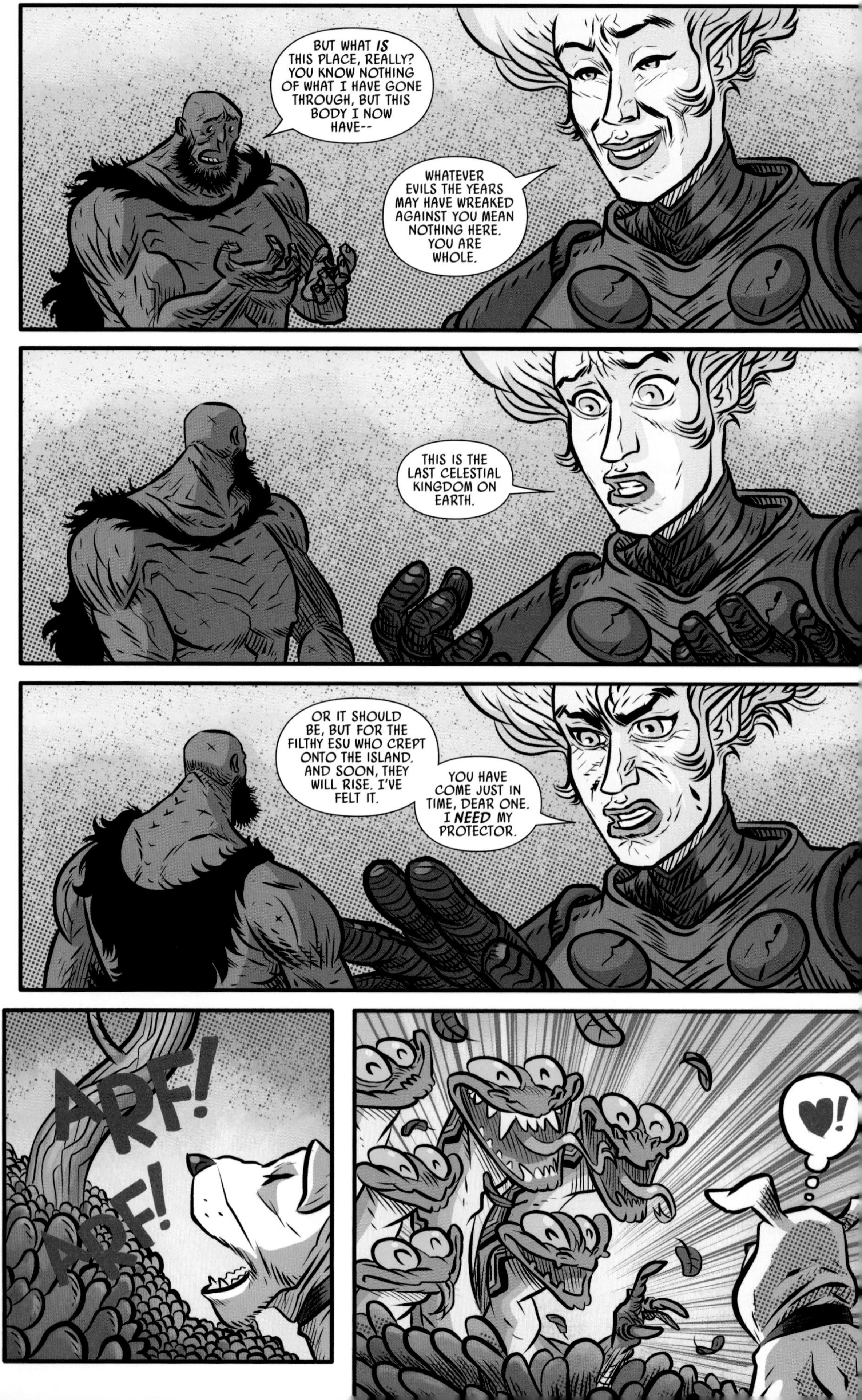
BUT WHAT **IS** THIS PLACE, REALLY? YOU KNOW NOTHING OF WHAT I HAVE GONE THROUGH, BUT THIS BODY I NOW HAVE--
WHATEVER EVILS THE YEARS MAY HAVE WREAKED AGAINST YOU MEAN NOTHING HERE. YOU ARE WHOLE.
THIS IS THE LAST CELESTIAL KINGDOM ON EARTH.
OR IT SHOULD BE, BUT FOR THE FILTHY ESU WHO CREPT ONTO THE ISLAND. AND SOON, THEY WILL RISE. I'VE FELT IT.
YOU HAVE COME JUST IN TIME, DEAR ONE. I **NEED** MY PROTECTOR.
ARF!
ARF!
♥!

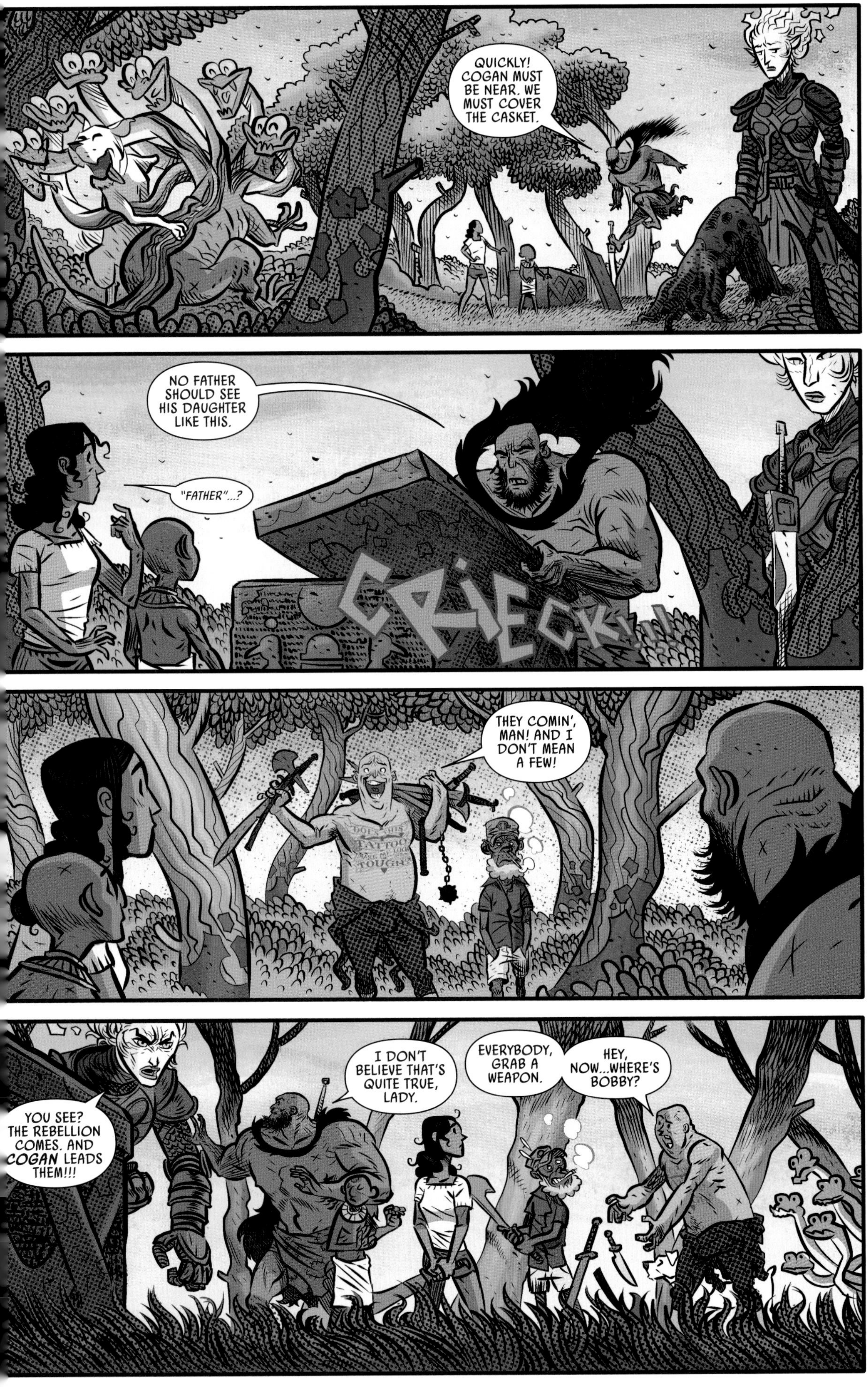
QUICKLY! COGAN MUST BE NEAR. WE MUST COVER THE CASKET.
NO FATHER SHOULD SEE HIS DAUGHTER LIKE THIS.
"FATHER"...?
CRIECK!!!
THEY COMIN', MAN! AND I DON'T MEAN A FEW!
YOU SEE? THE REBELLION COMES. AND COGAN LEADS THEM!!!
I DON'T BELIEVE THAT'S QUITE TRUE, LADY.
EVERYBODY, GRAB A WEAPON.
HEY, NOW...WHERE'S BOBBY?

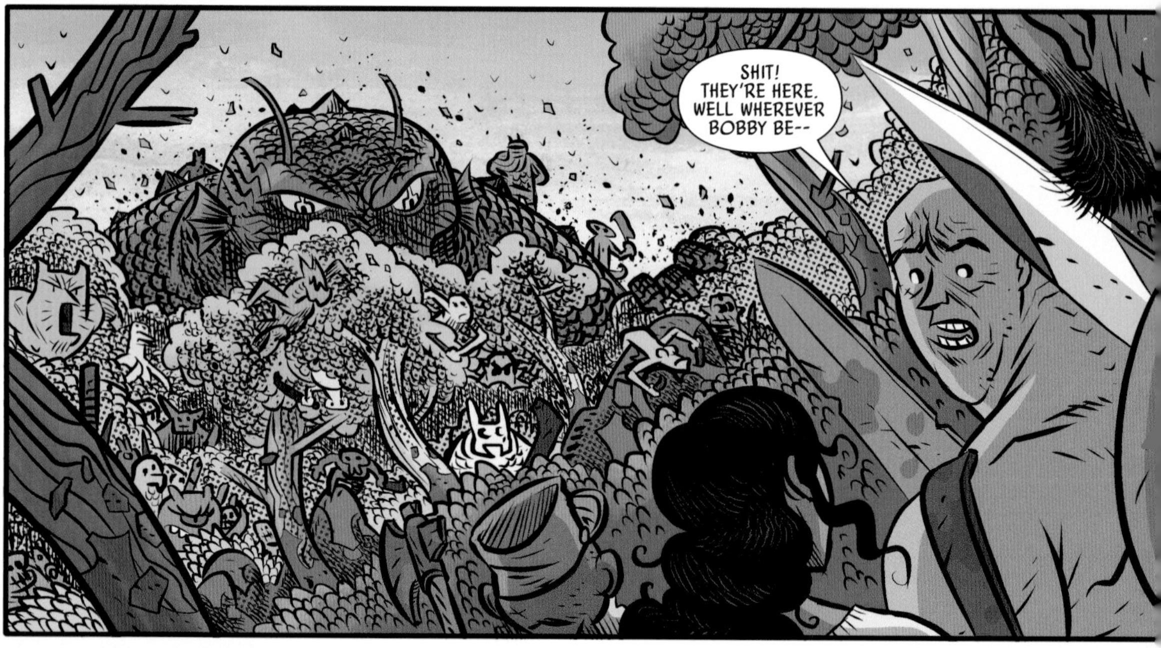
SHIT! THEY'RE HERE. WELL WHEREVER BOBBY BE--

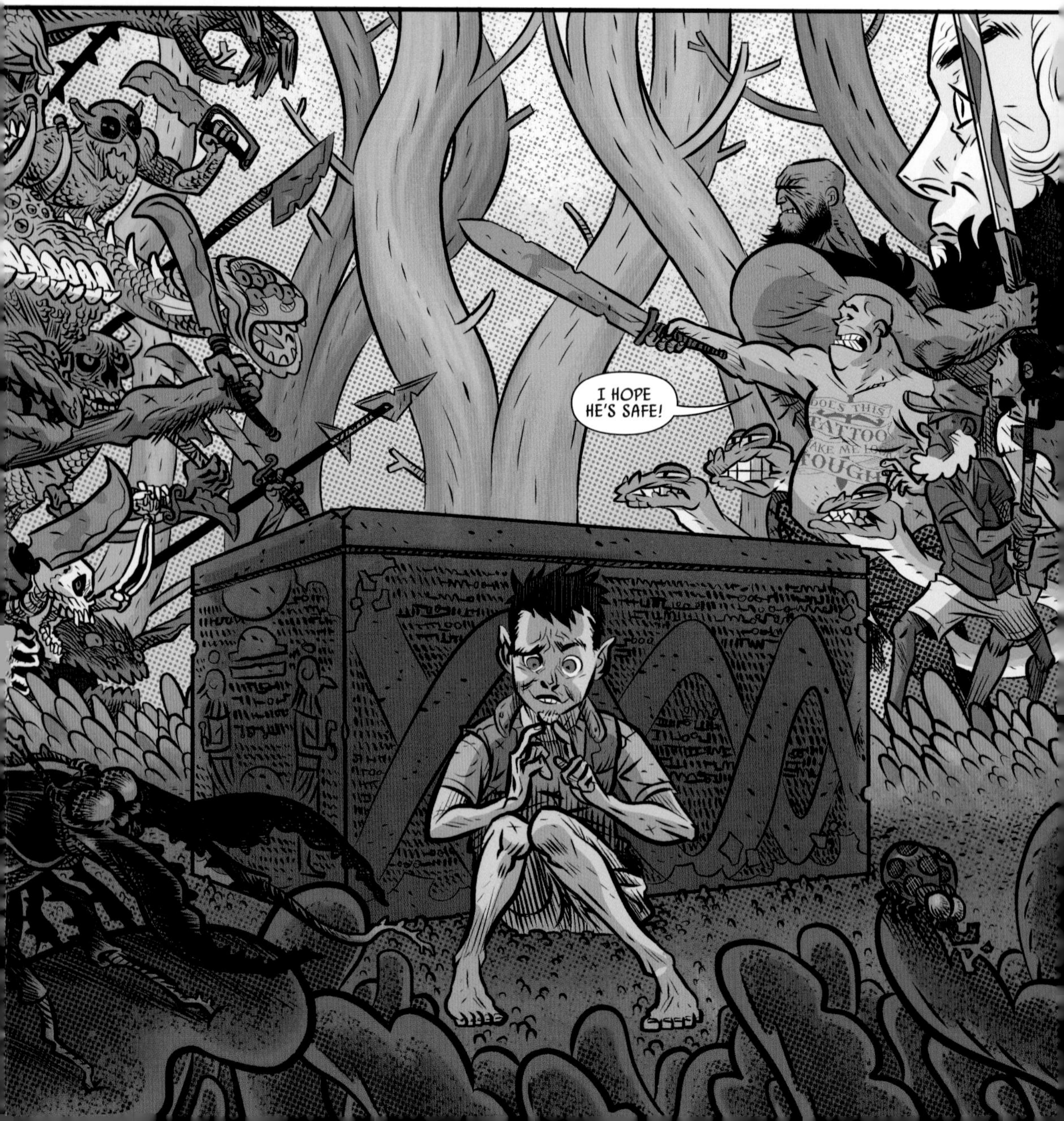
I HOPE HE'S SAFE!

# RUMBLE

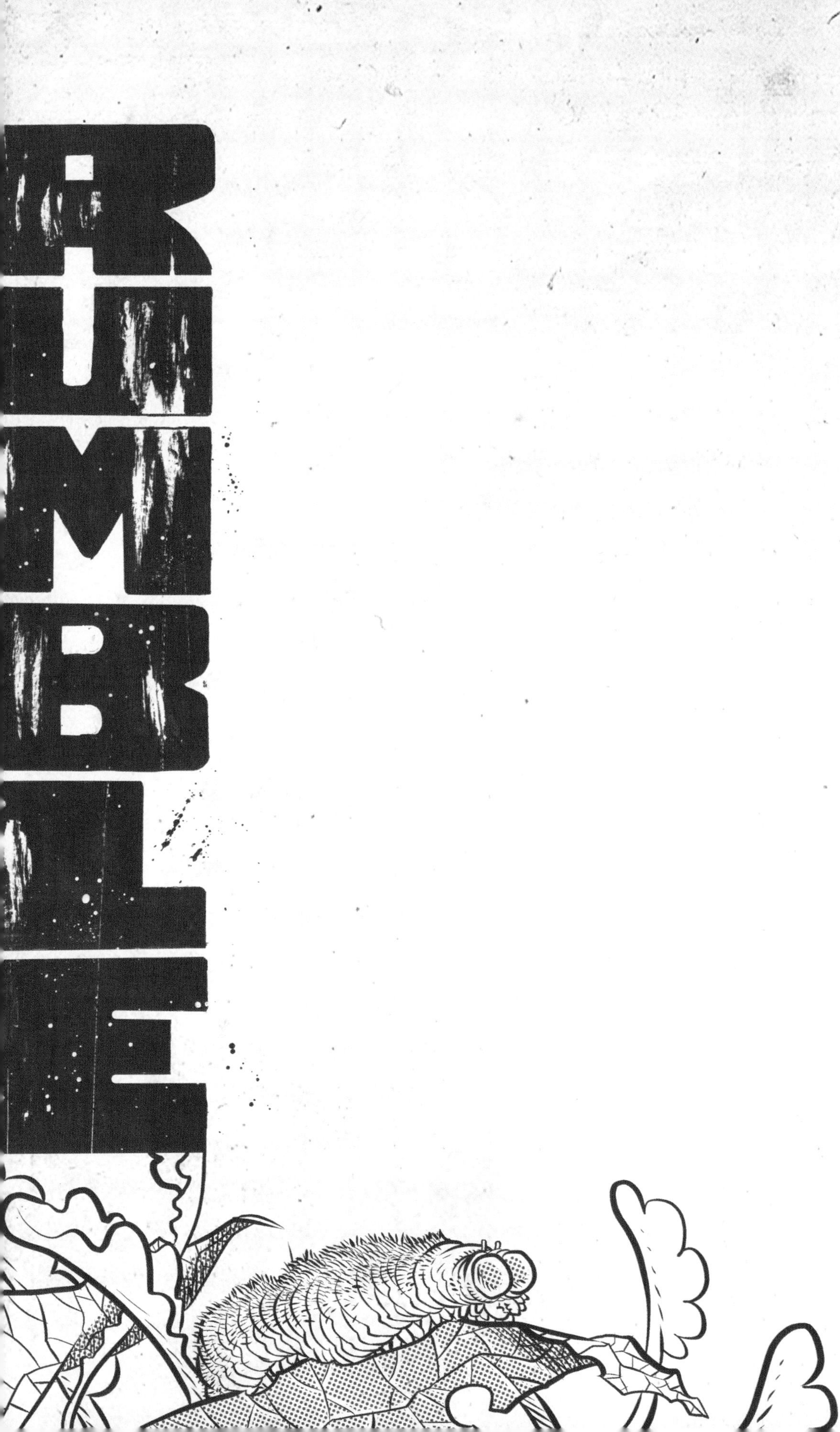

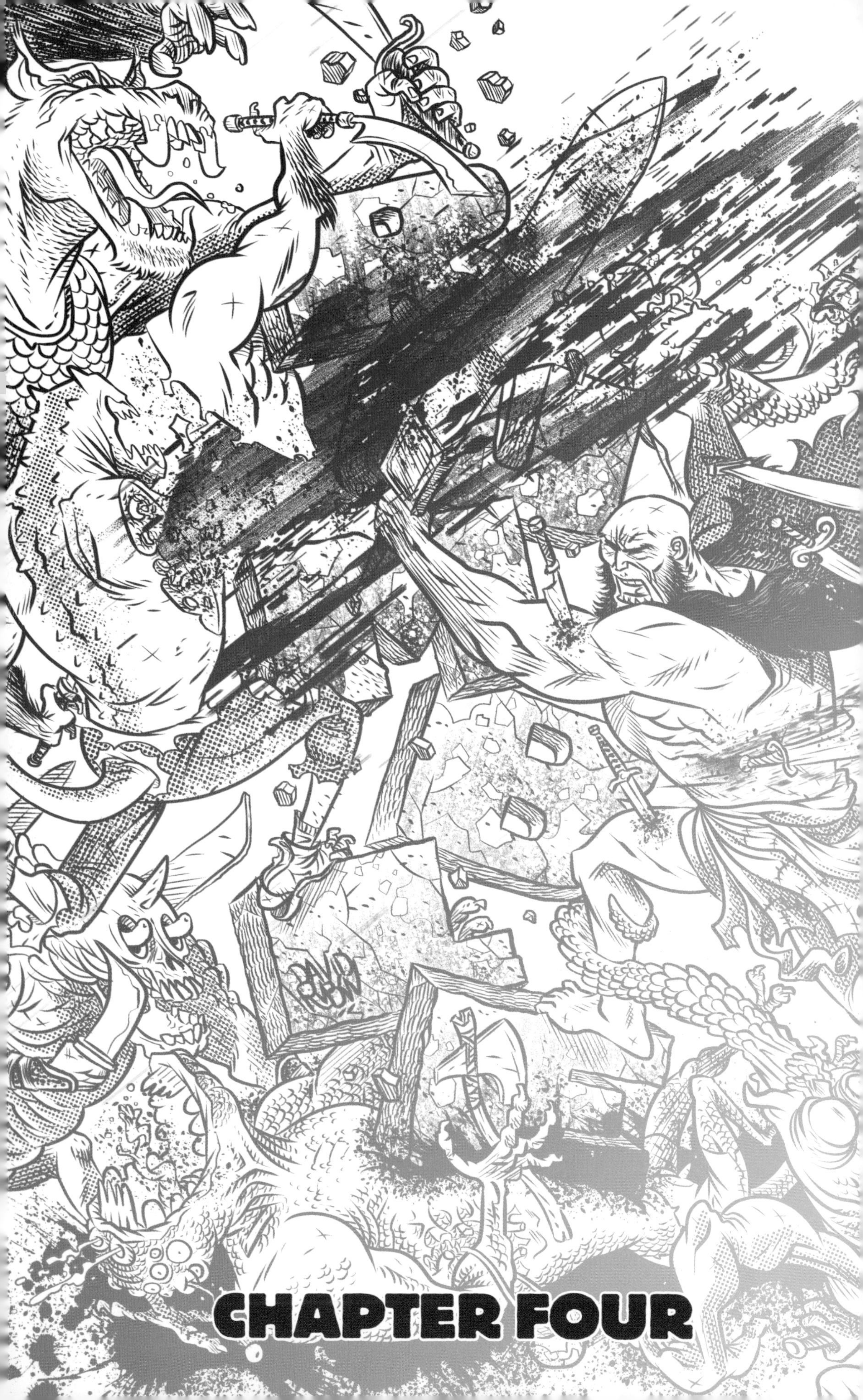

# CHAPTER FOUR

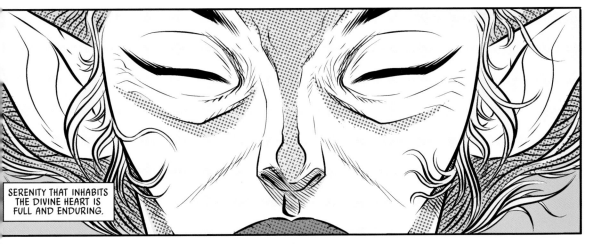

SERENITY THAT INHABITS THE DIVINE HEART IS FULL AND ENDURING.

PROVOKED BY NEITHER THOUGHT NOR ATTACHMENT, UNBOUND AND BOUNDLESS.

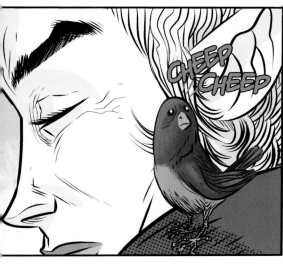

CHEEP CHEEP

SPLAT!

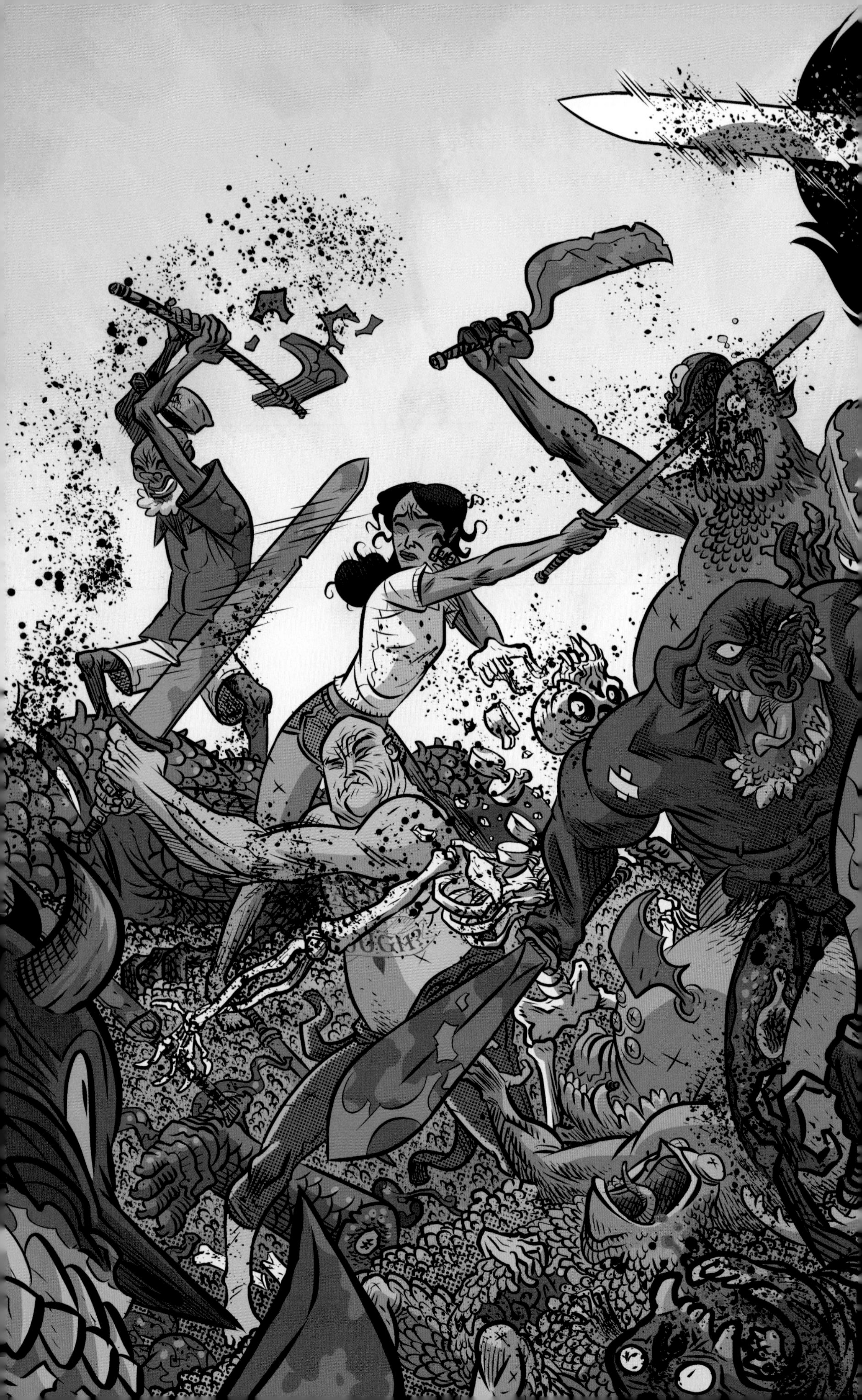

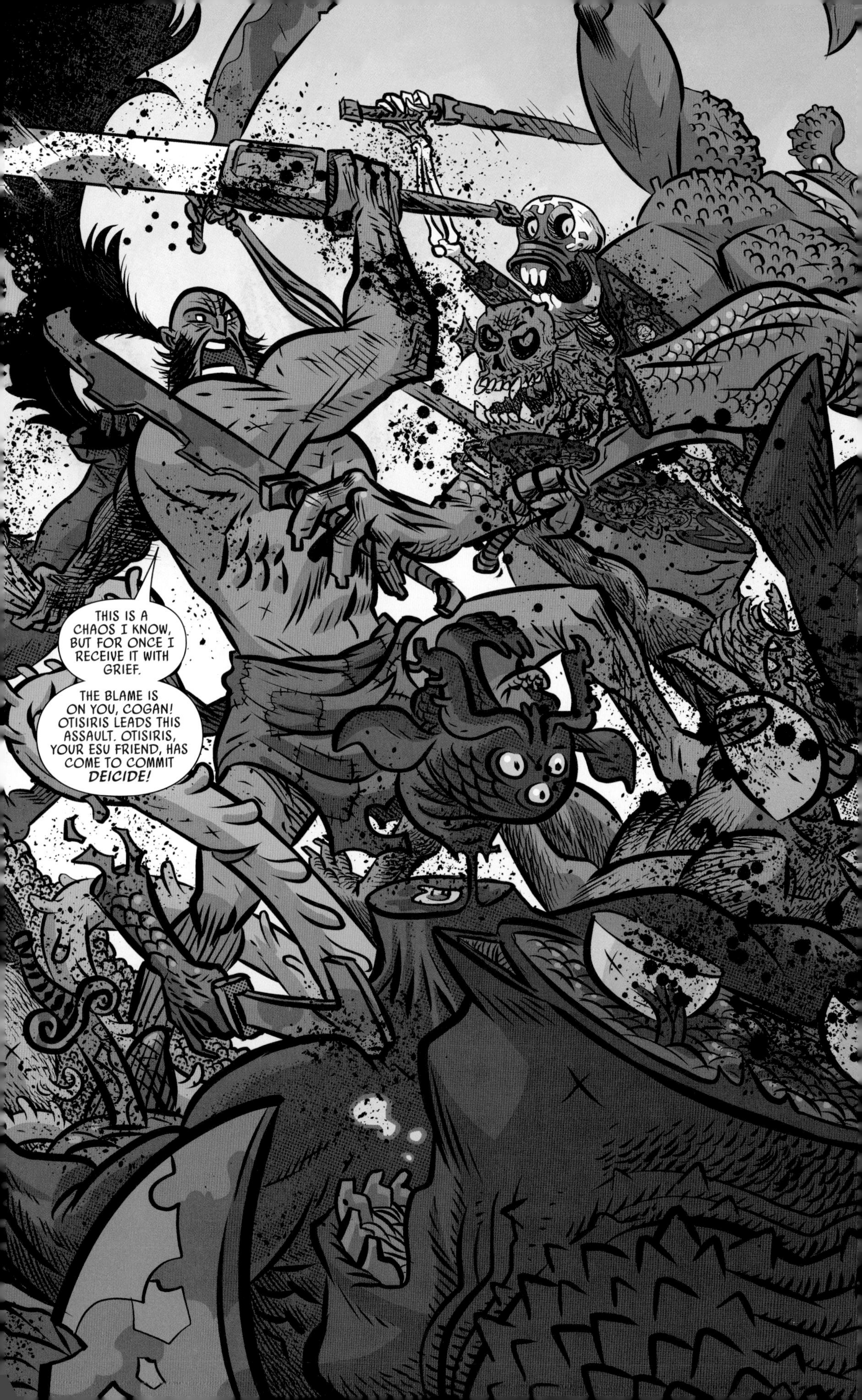
THIS IS A CHAOS I KNOW, BUT FOR ONCE I RECEIVE IT WITH GRIEF.
THE BLAME IS ON YOU, COGAN! OTISIRIS LEADS THIS ASSAULT. OTISIRIS, YOUR ESU FRIEND, HAS COME TO COMMIT *DEICIDE!*

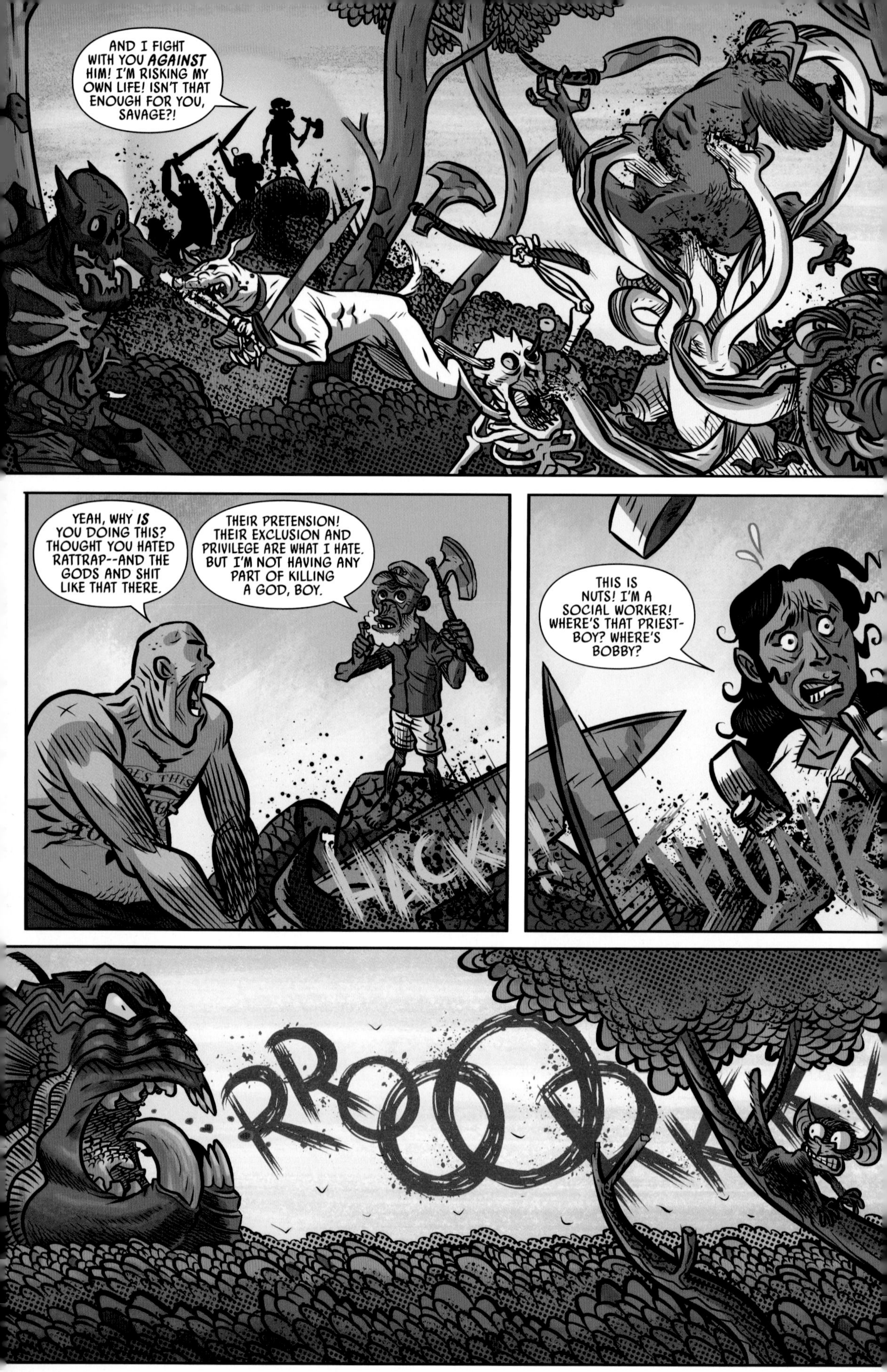
AND I FIGHT WITH YOU *AGAINST* HIM! I'M RISKING MY OWN LIFE! ISN'T THAT ENOUGH FOR YOU, SAVAGE?!
YEAH, WHY *IS* YOU DOING THIS? THOUGHT YOU HATED RATTRAP--AND THE GODS AND SHIT LIKE THAT THERE.
THEIR PRETENSION! THEIR EXCLUSION AND PRIVILEGE ARE WHAT I HATE. BUT I'M NOT HAVING ANY PART OF KILLING A GOD, BOY.
HACK!
THIS IS NUTS! I'M A SOCIAL WORKER! WHERE'S THAT PRIEST-BOY? WHERE'S BOBBY?

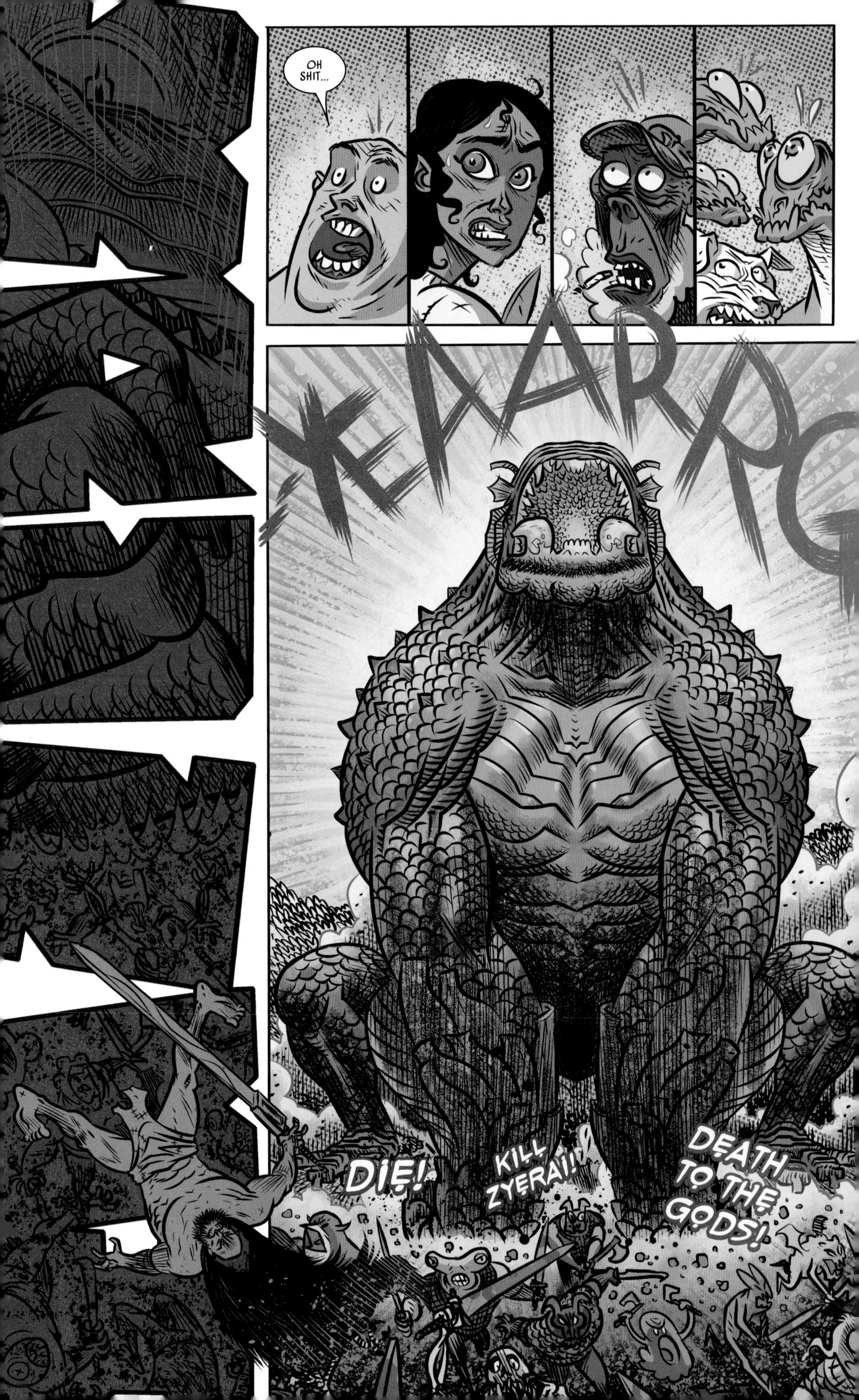
OH SHIT...
YEAARRG
DIE!
KILL ZYERAI!
DEATH TO THE GODS!

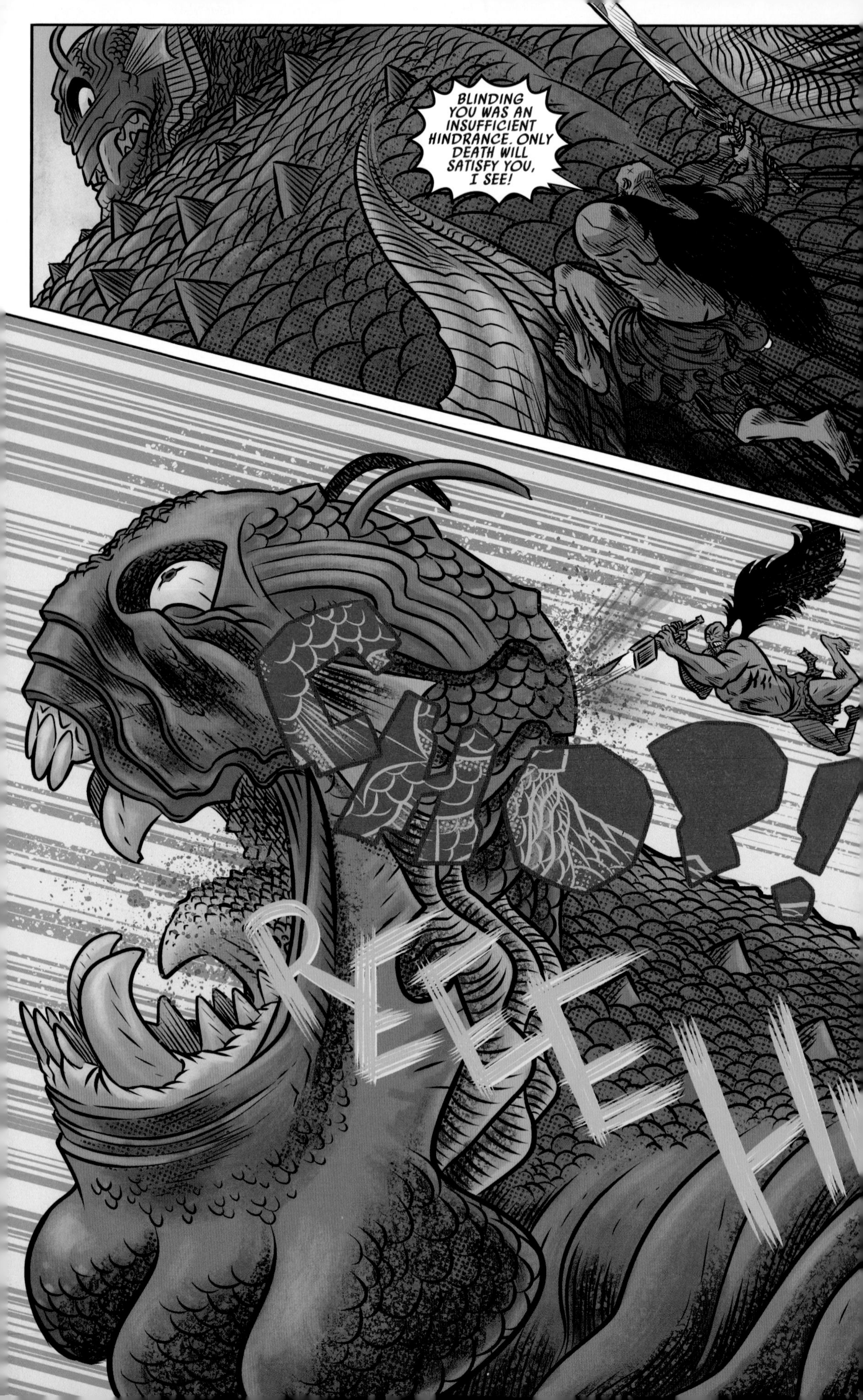
BLINDING YOU WAS AN INSUFFICIENT HINDRANCE. ONLY DEATH WILL SATISFY YOU, I SEE!

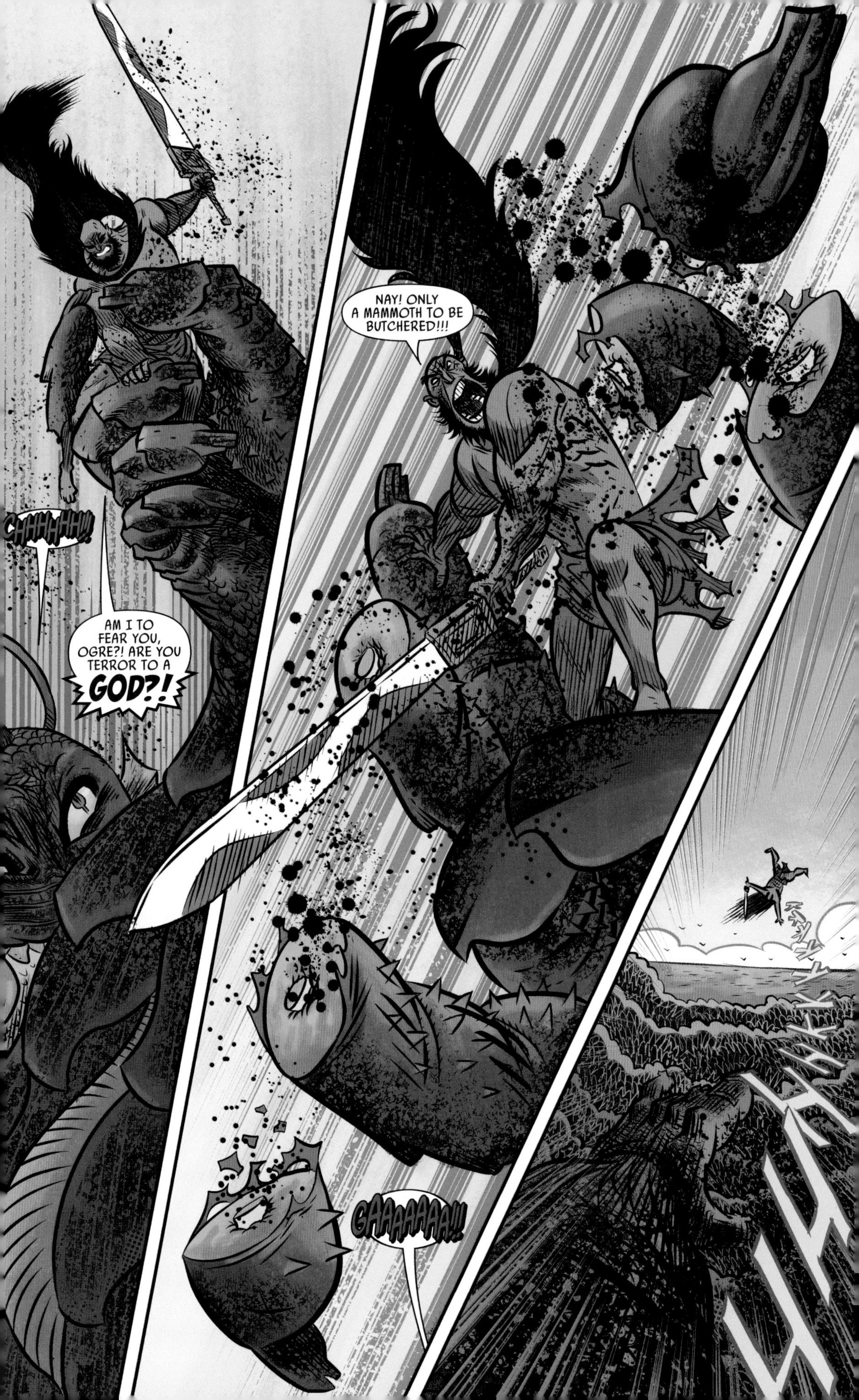
CHHHHHH!!!
AM I TO FEAR YOU, OGRE?! ARE YOU TERROR TO A GOD?!
NAY! ONLY A MAMMOTH TO BE BUTCHERED!!!
GAAAAAA!!!

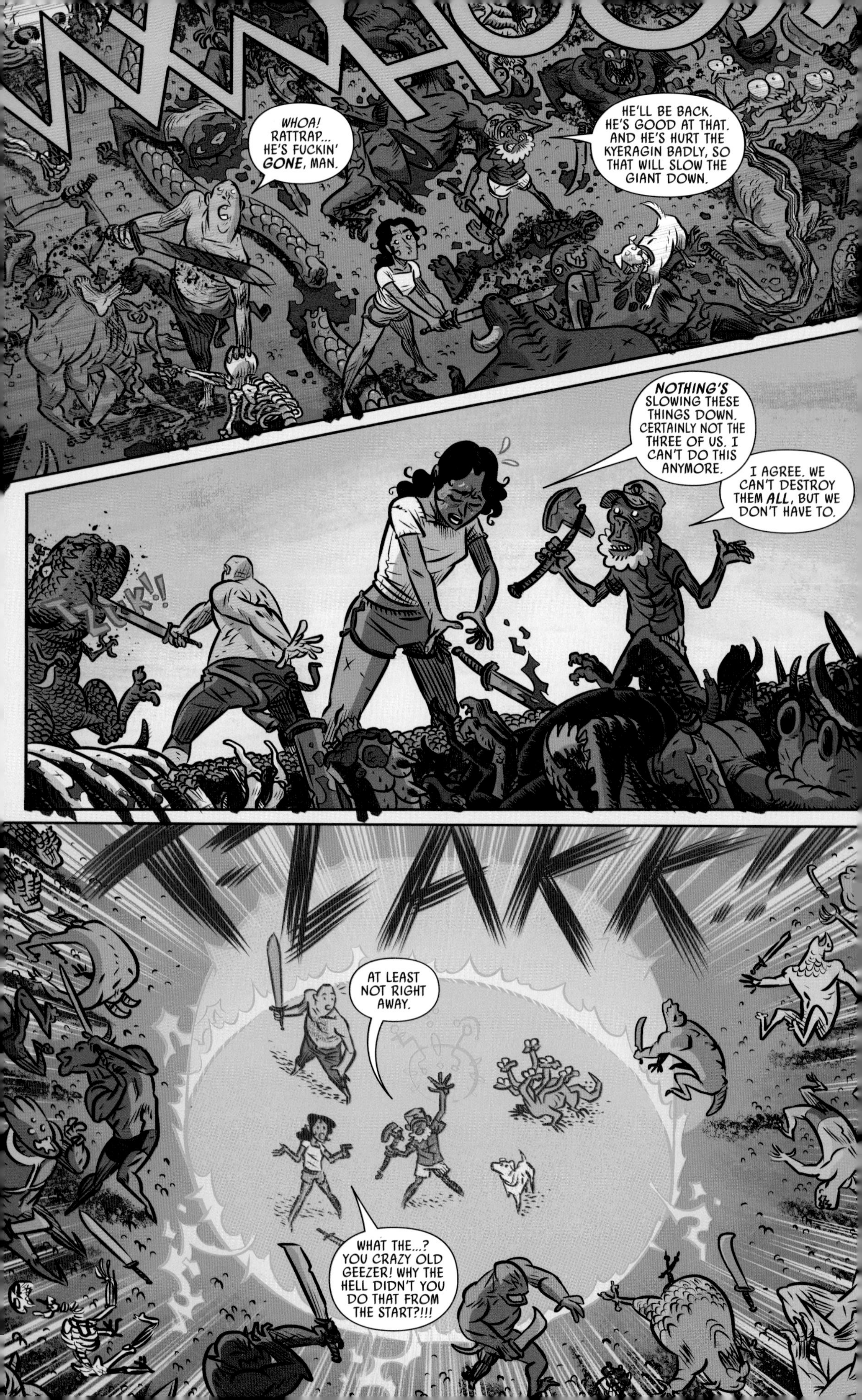
WHOA! RATTRAP... HE'S FUCKIN' GONE, MAN.
HE'LL BE BACK. HE'S GOOD AT THAT. AND HE'S HURT THE KYERAGIN BADLY, SO THAT WILL SLOW THE GIANT DOWN.
NOTHING'S SLOWING THESE THINGS DOWN. CERTAINLY NOT THE THREE OF US. I CAN'T DO THIS ANYMORE.
I AGREE. WE CAN'T DESTROY THEM ALL, BUT WE DON'T HAVE TO.
TZUK!!
KLAKK!!
AT LEAST NOT RIGHT AWAY.
WHAT THE...? YOU CRAZY OLD GEEZER! WHY THE HELL DIDN'T YOU DO THAT FROM THE START?!!!

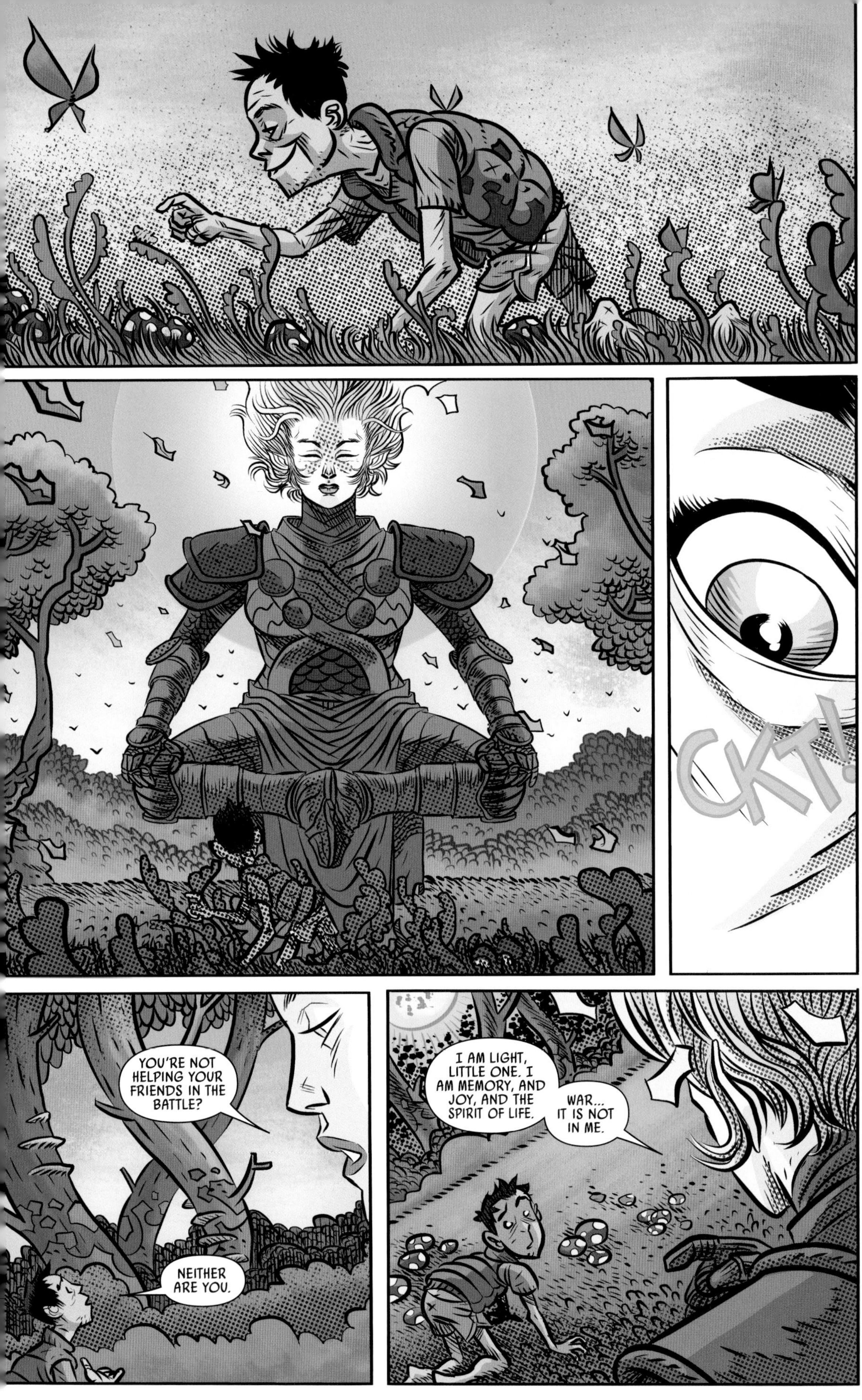
CKT!
YOU'RE NOT HELPING YOUR FRIENDS IN THE BATTLE?
NEITHER ARE YOU.
I AM LIGHT, LITTLE ONE. I AM MEMORY, AND JOY, AND THE SPIRIT OF LIFE.
WAR... IT IS NOT IN ME.

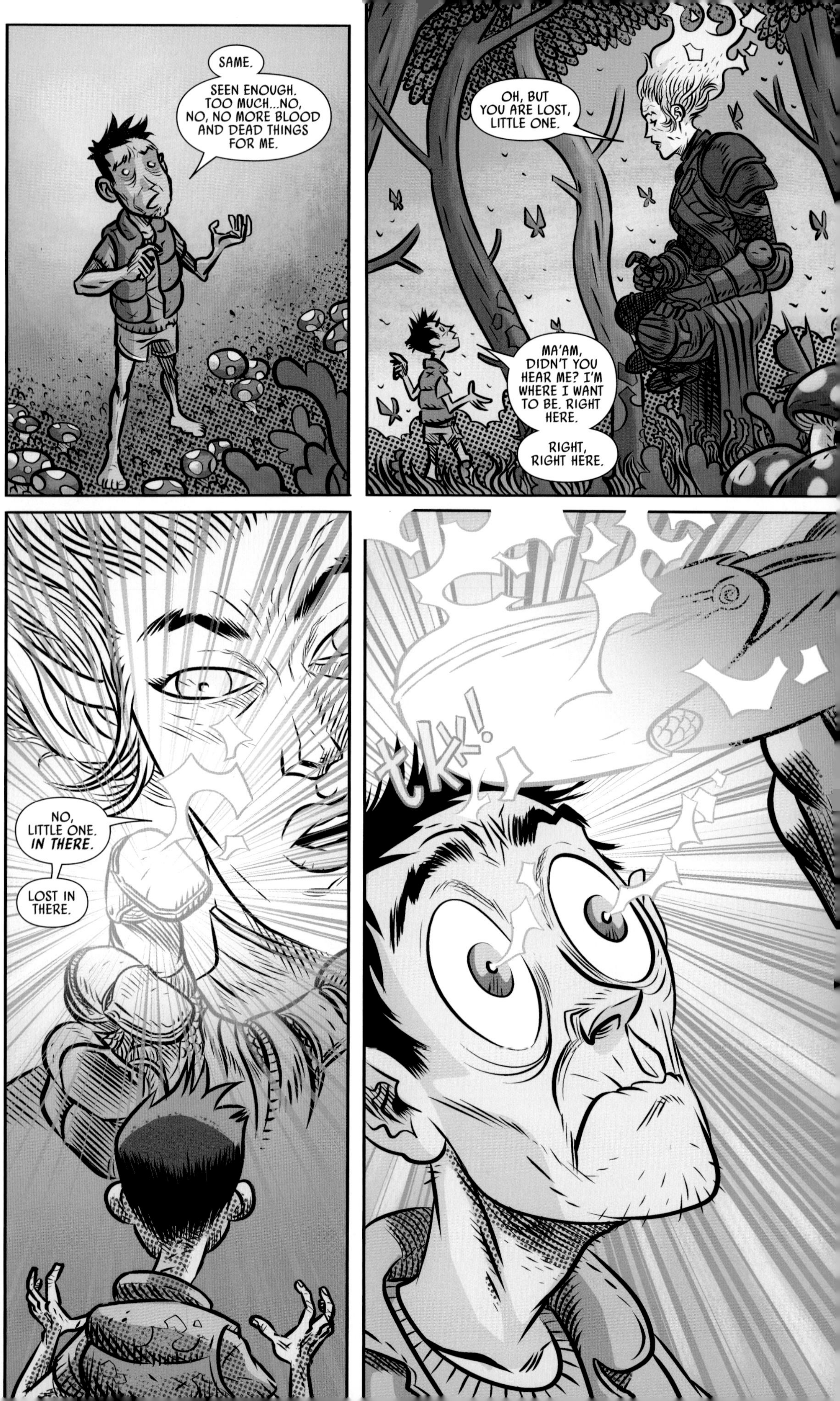
SAME.
SEEN ENOUGH. TOO MUCH...NO, NO, NO MORE BLOOD AND DEAD THINGS FOR ME.
OH, BUT YOU ARE LOST, LITTLE ONE.
MA'AM, DIDN'T YOU HEAR ME? I'M WHERE I WANT TO BE. RIGHT HERE.
RIGHT, RIGHT HERE.
NO, LITTLE ONE. *IN THERE.*
LOST IN THERE.
tk!

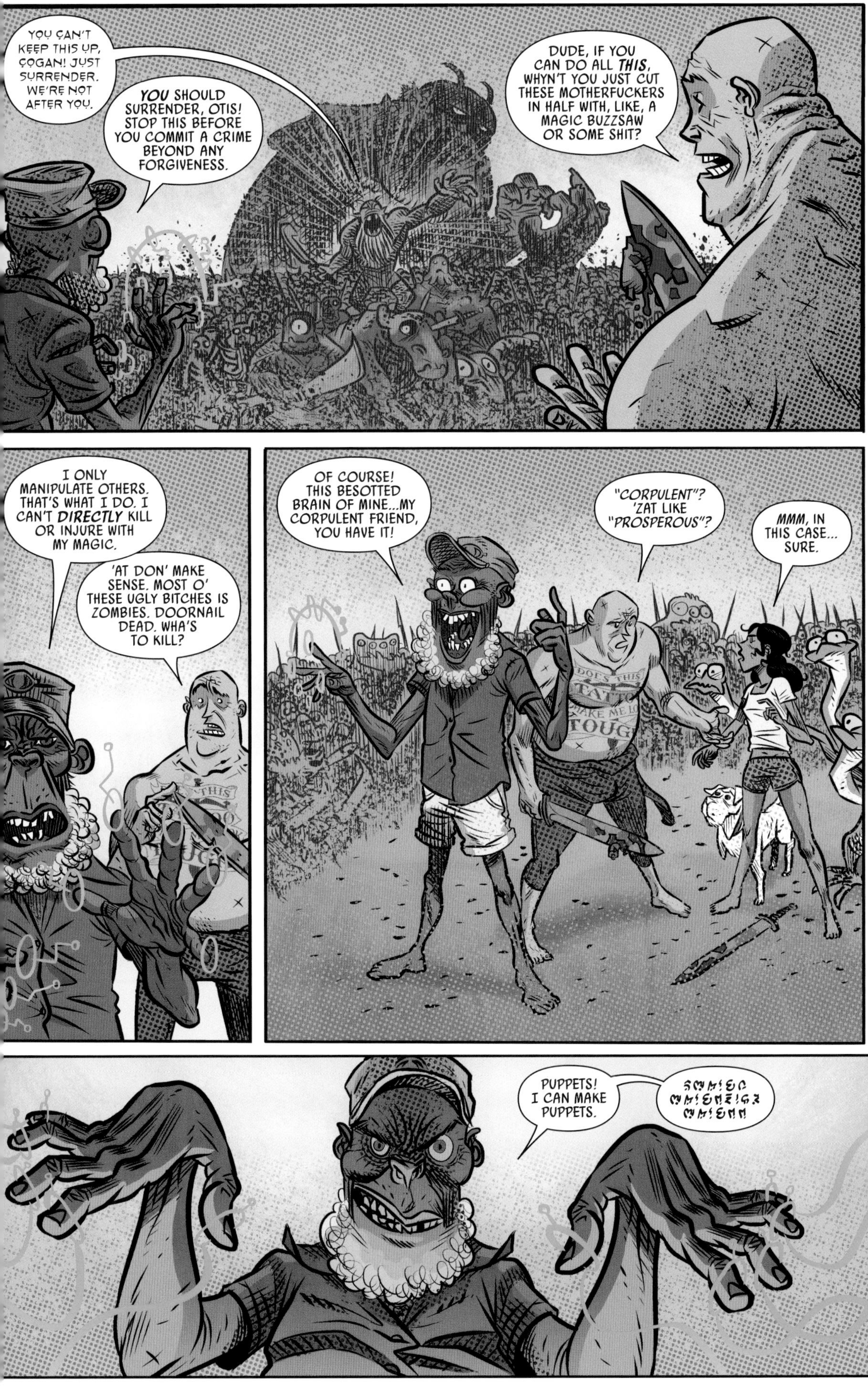
YOU CAN'T KEEP THIS UP, COGAN! JUST SURRENDER. WE'RE NOT AFTER YOU.
YOU SHOULD SURRENDER, OTIS! STOP THIS BEFORE YOU COMMIT A CRIME BEYOND ANY FORGIVENESS.
DUDE, IF YOU CAN DO ALL THIS, WHYN'T YOU JUST CUT THESE MOTHERFUCKERS IN HALF WITH, LIKE, A MAGIC BUZZSAW OR SOME SHIT?
I ONLY MANIPULATE OTHERS. THAT'S WHAT I DO. I CAN'T DIRECTLY KILL OR INJURE WITH MY MAGIC.
'AT DON' MAKE SENSE. MOST O' THESE UGLY BITCHES IS ZOMBIES. DOORNAIL DEAD. WHA'S TO KILL?
OF COURSE! THIS BESOTTED BRAIN OF MINE...MY CORPULENT FRIEND, YOU HAVE IT!
"CORPULENT"? 'ZAT LIKE "PROSPEROUS"?
MMM, IN THIS CASE... SURE.
PUPPETS! I CAN MAKE PUPPETS.

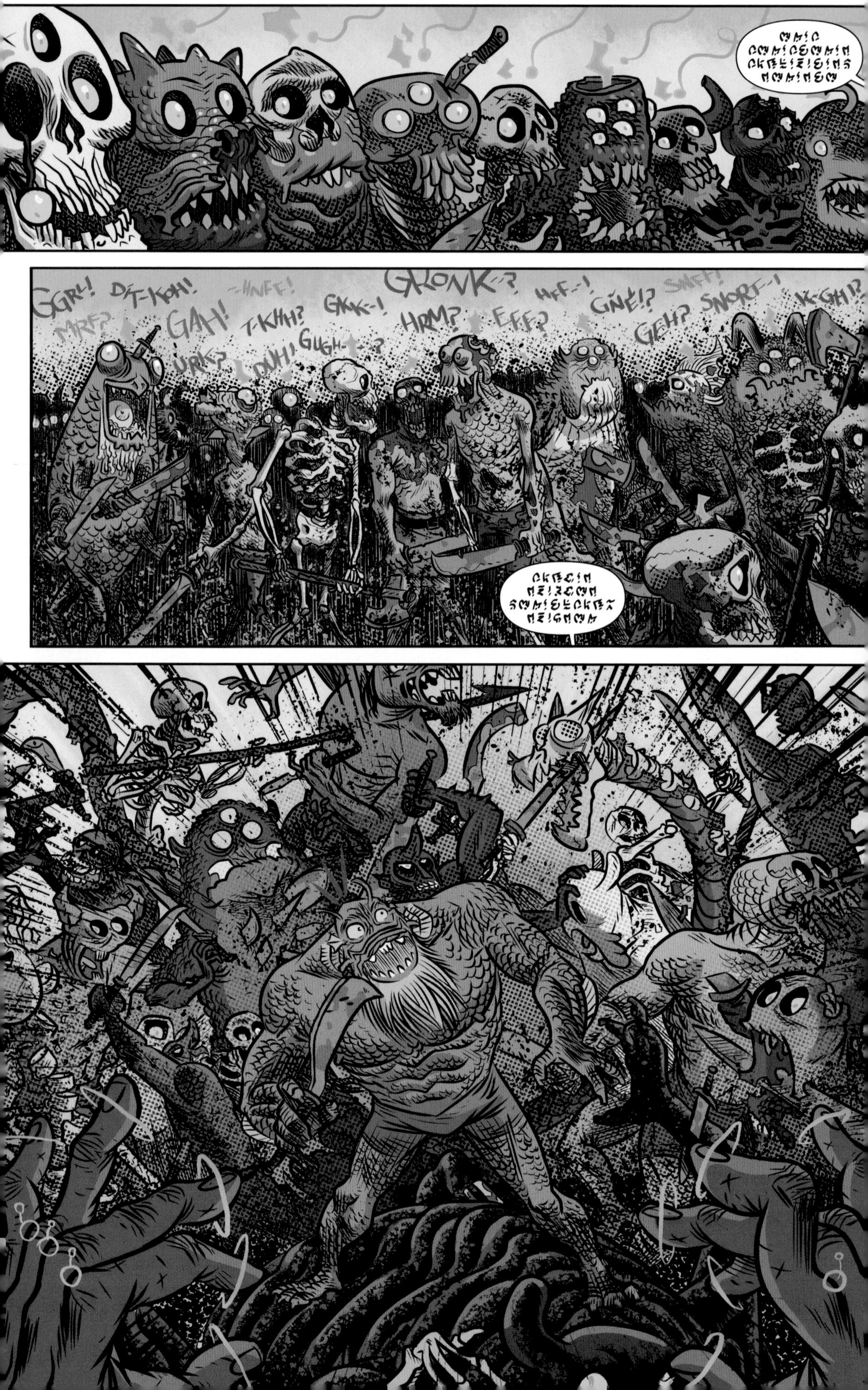
GGRL! DIT-KOH! -HNFF! GRONK--? HFF--! GNE!? SMFF! SNORT--! K-GH!?
MRF? GAH! T-KHH? GKK--! HRM? EFF? GEH?
URK? DUH! GUGH---?

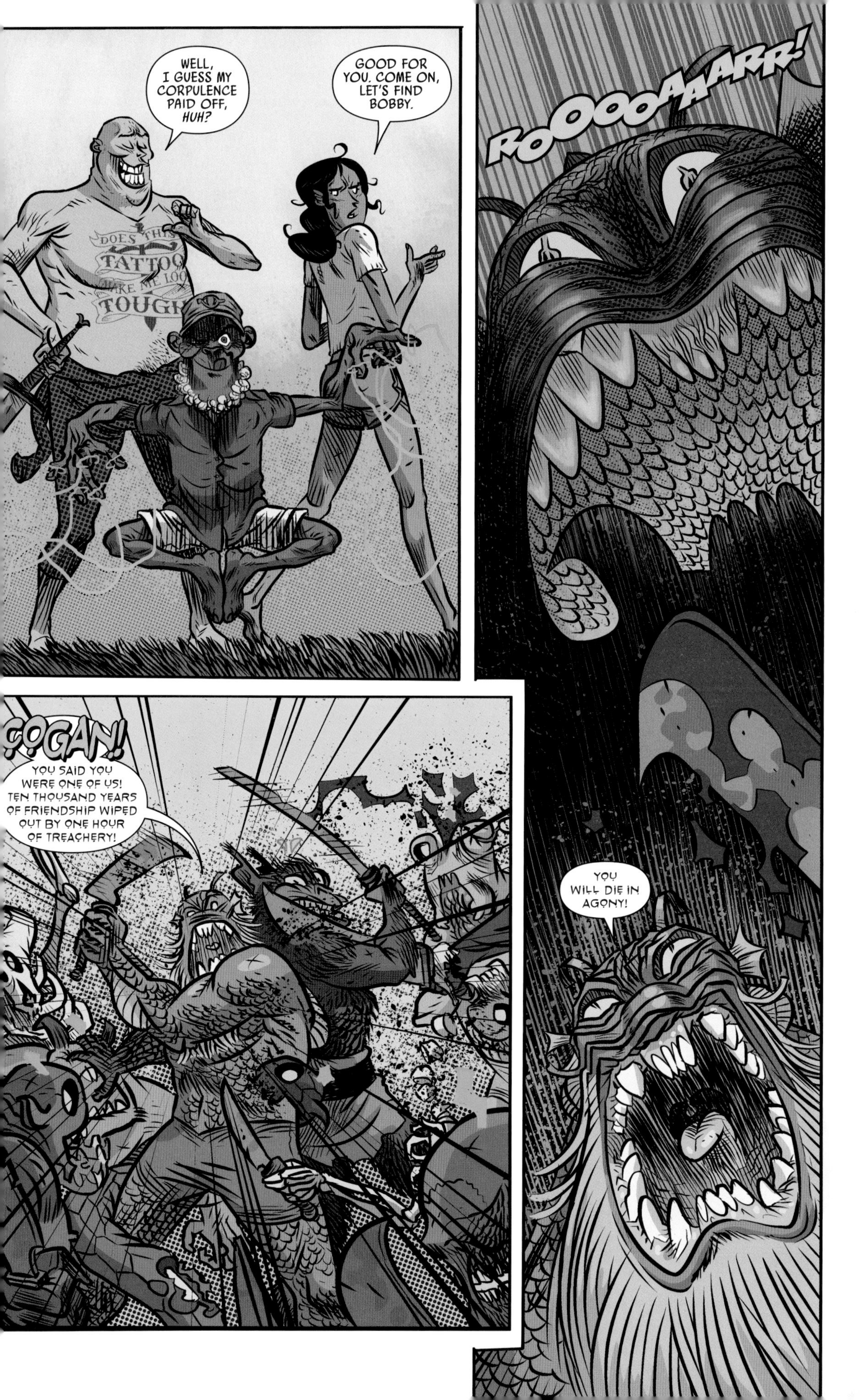
WELL, I GUESS MY CORPULENCE PAID OFF, HUH?
GOOD FOR YOU. COME ON, LET'S FIND BOBBY.
ROOOOOAAARR!
ÇOGAN!
YOU SAID YOU WERE ONE OF US! TEN THOUSAND YEARS OF FRIENDSHIP WIPED OUT BY ONE HOUR OF TREACHERY!
YOU WILL DIE IN AGONY!

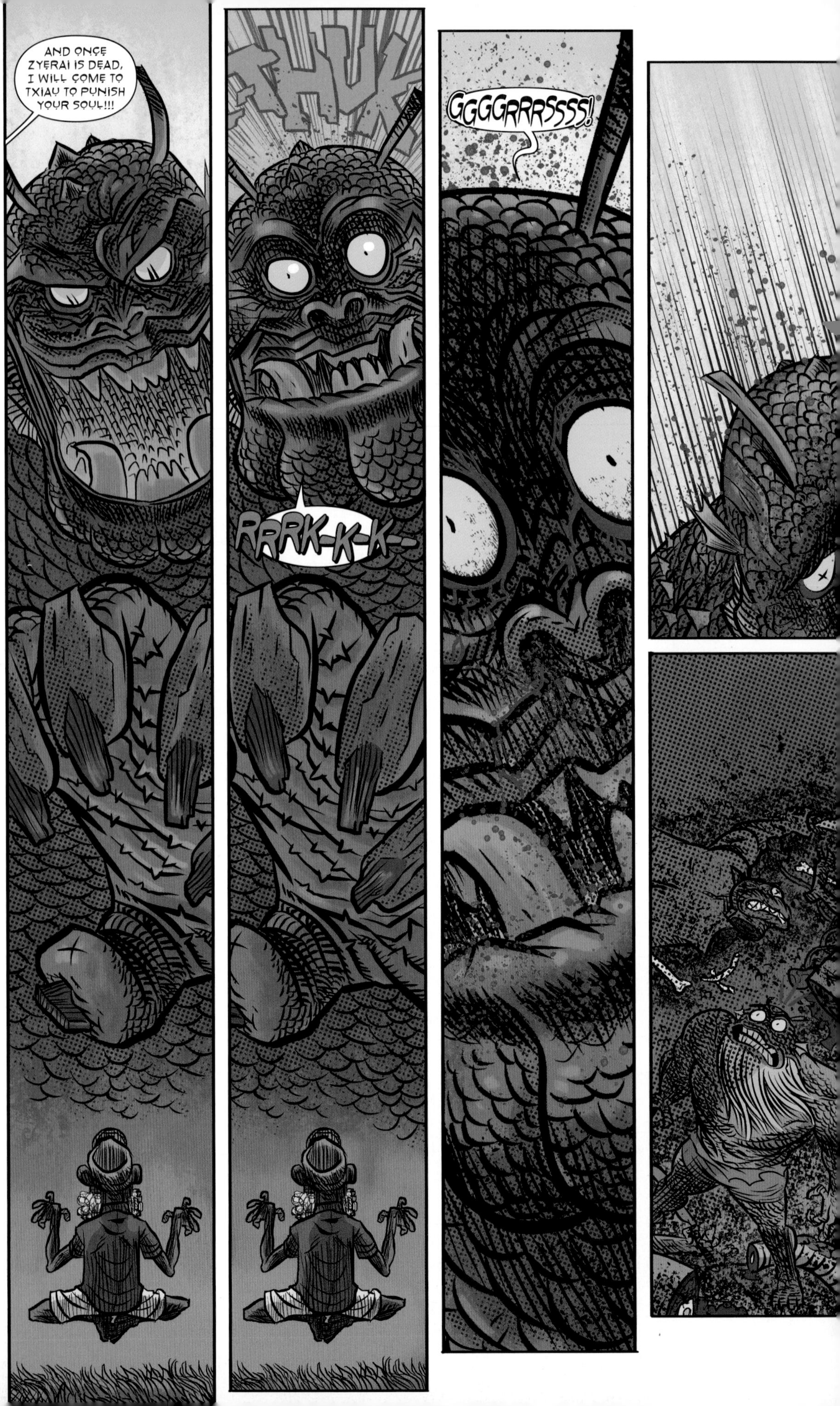
AND ONCE ZYERAI IS DEAD, I WILL COME TO TXIAU TO PUNISH YOUR SOUL!!!
THUK
RRRK-K-K-
GGGGRRRSSSS!

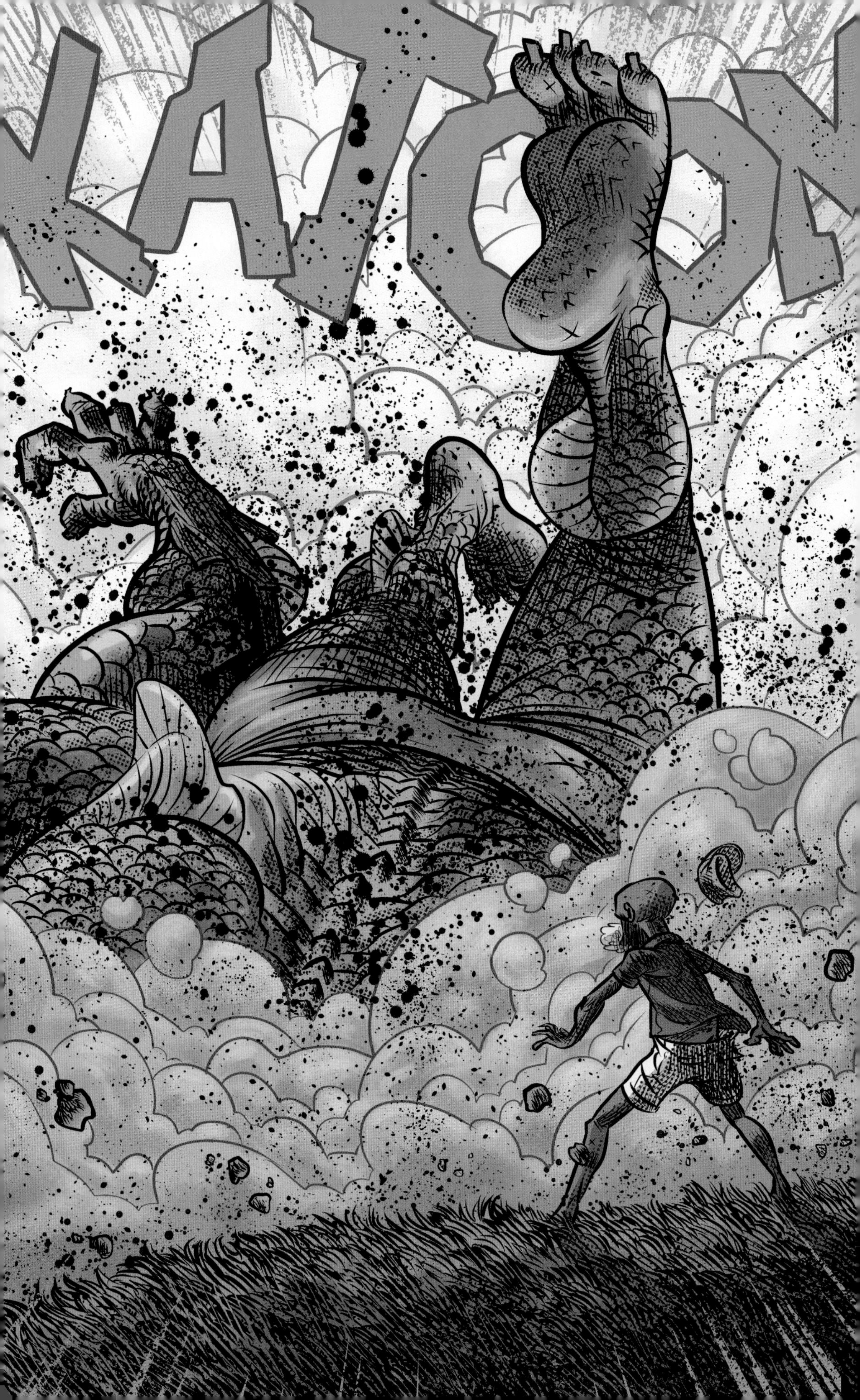

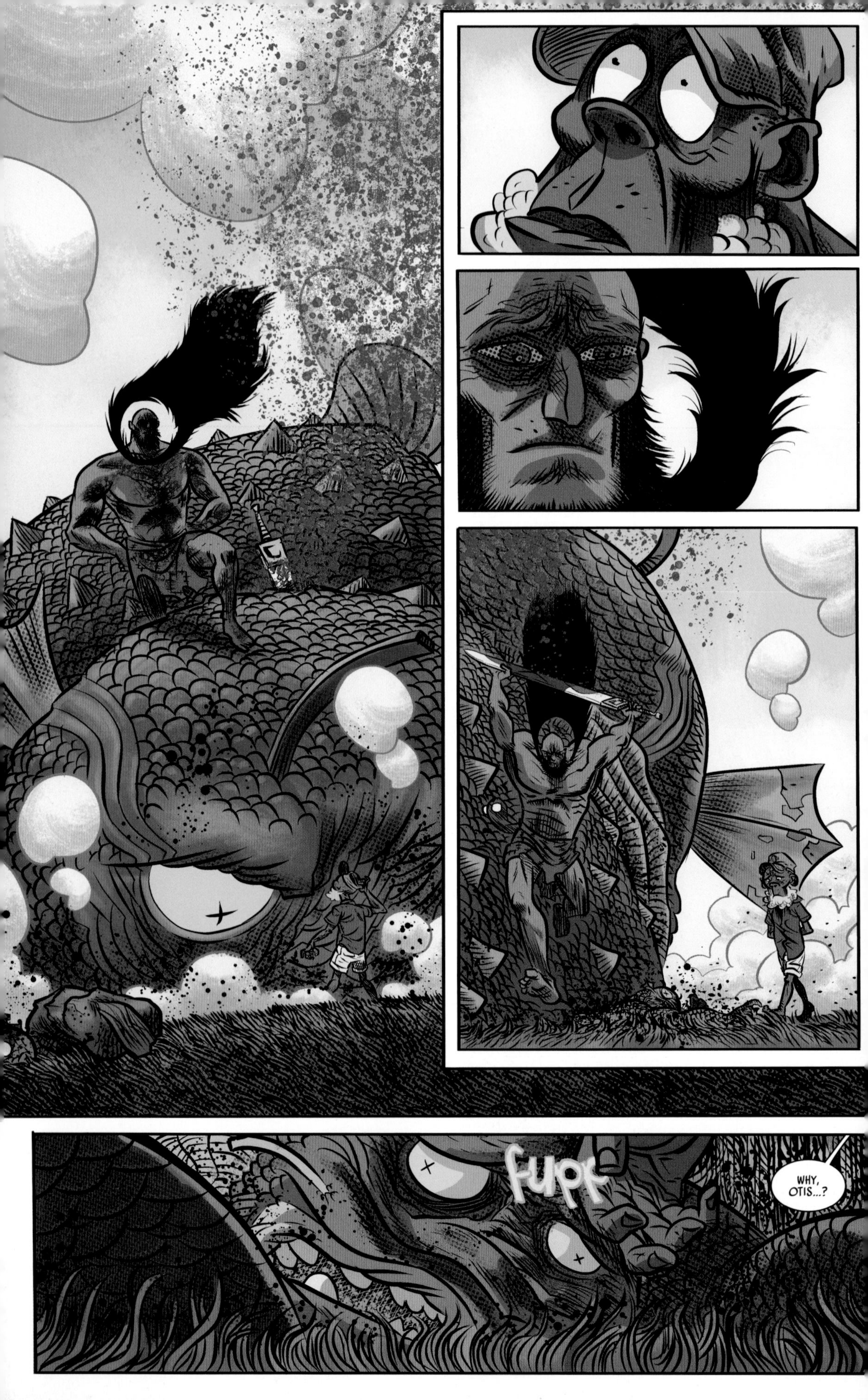
FUPF
WHY, OTIS...?

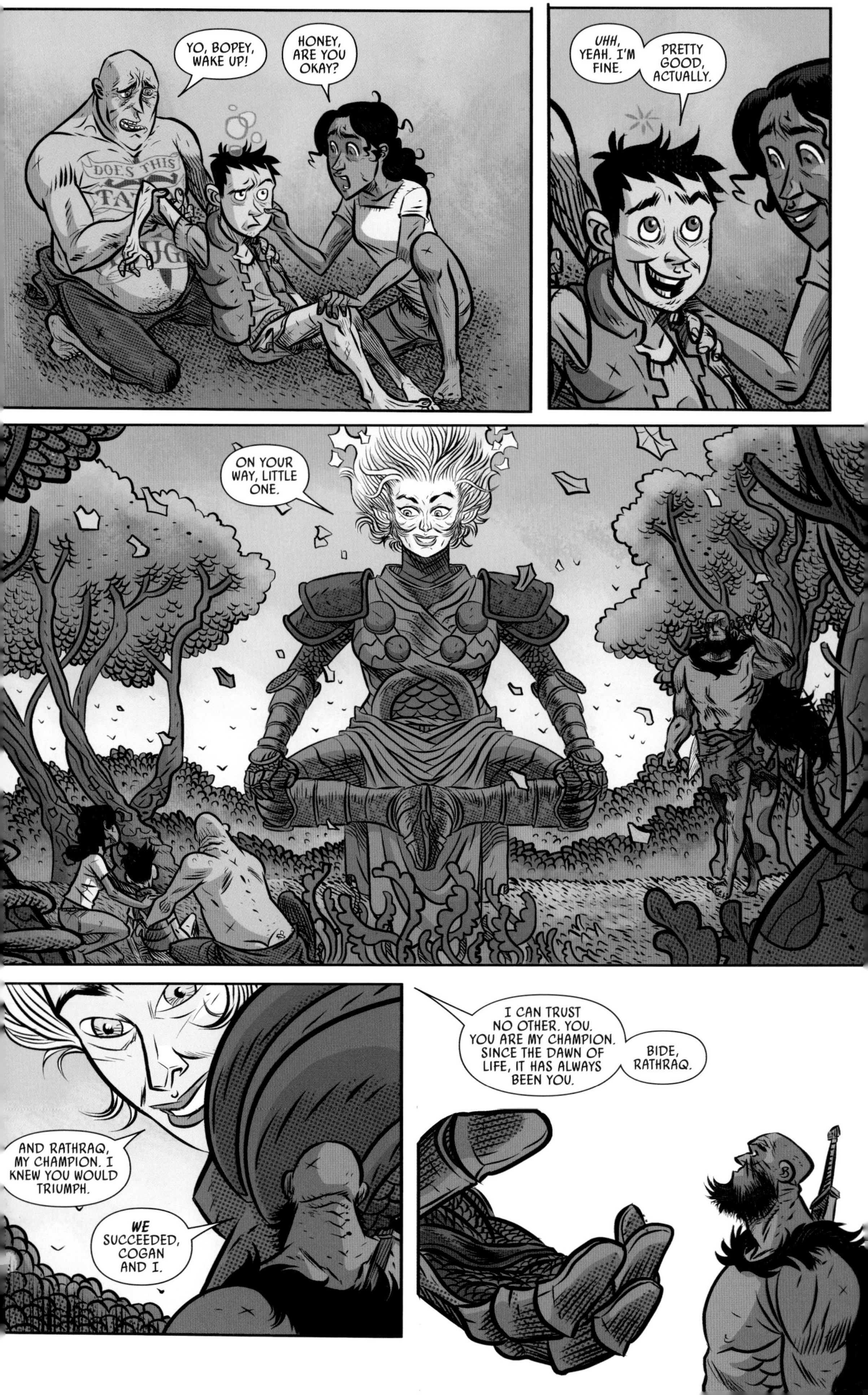
YO, BOPEY, WAKE UP!
HONEY, ARE YOU OKAY?
DOES THIS
UHH, YEAH. I'M FINE.
PRETTY GOOD, ACTUALLY.
ON YOUR WAY, LITTLE ONE.
AND RATHRAQ, MY CHAMPION. I KNEW YOU WOULD TRIUMPH.
*WE* SUCCEEDED, COGAN AND I.
I CAN TRUST NO OTHER. YOU. YOU ARE MY CHAMPION. SINCE THE DAWN OF LIFE, IT HAS ALWAYS BEEN YOU.
BIDE, RATHRAQ.

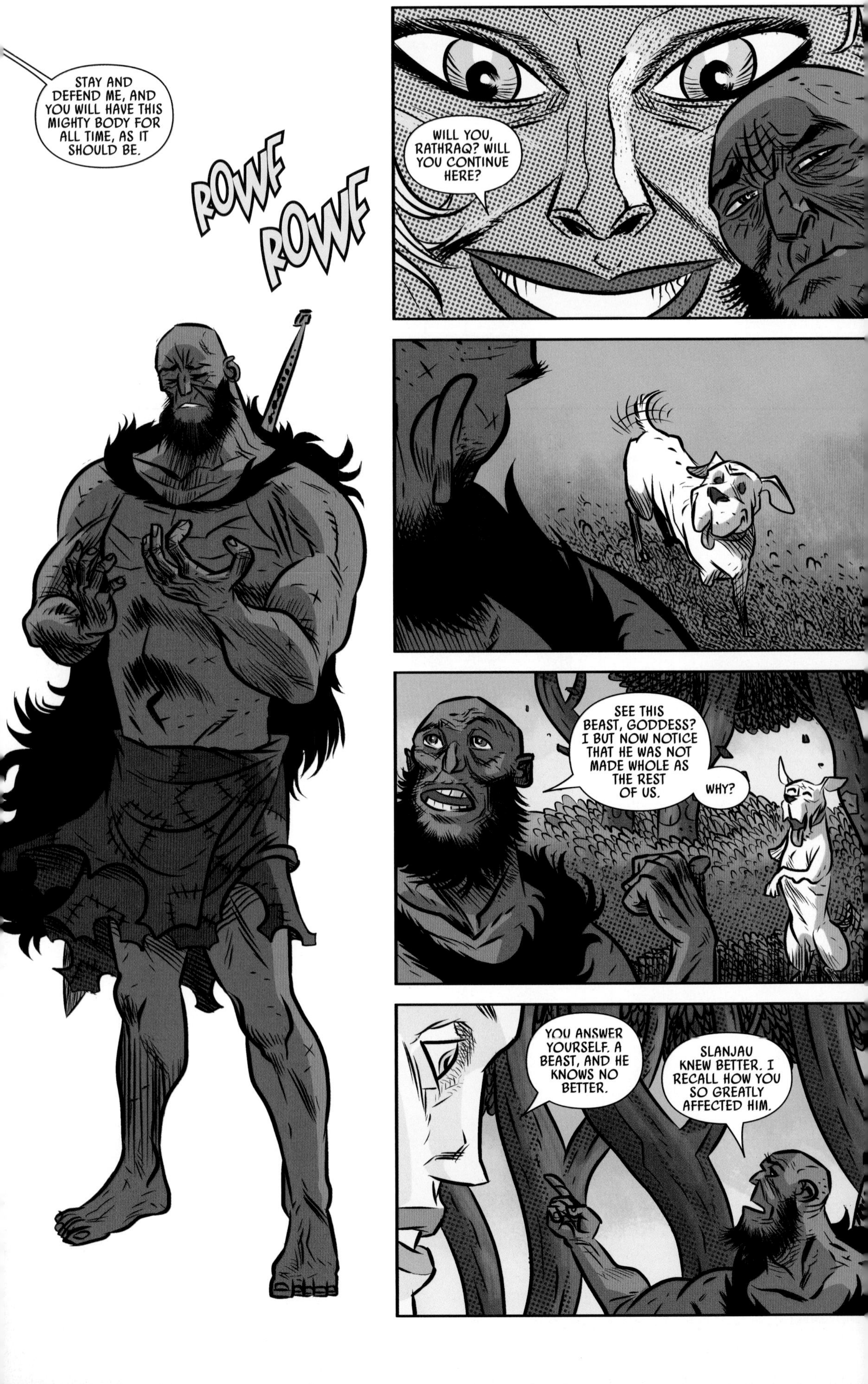
STAY AND DEFEND ME, AND YOU WILL HAVE THIS MIGHTY BODY FOR ALL TIME, AS IT SHOULD BE.
ROWF ROWF
WILL YOU, RATHRAQ? WILL YOU CONTINUE HERE?
SEE THIS BEAST, GODDESS? I BUT NOW NOTICE THAT HE WAS NOT MADE WHOLE AS THE REST OF US.
WHY?
YOU ANSWER YOURSELF. A BEAST, AND HE KNOWS NO BETTER.
SLANJAU KNEW BETTER. I RECALL HOW YOU SO GREATLY AFFECTED HIM.

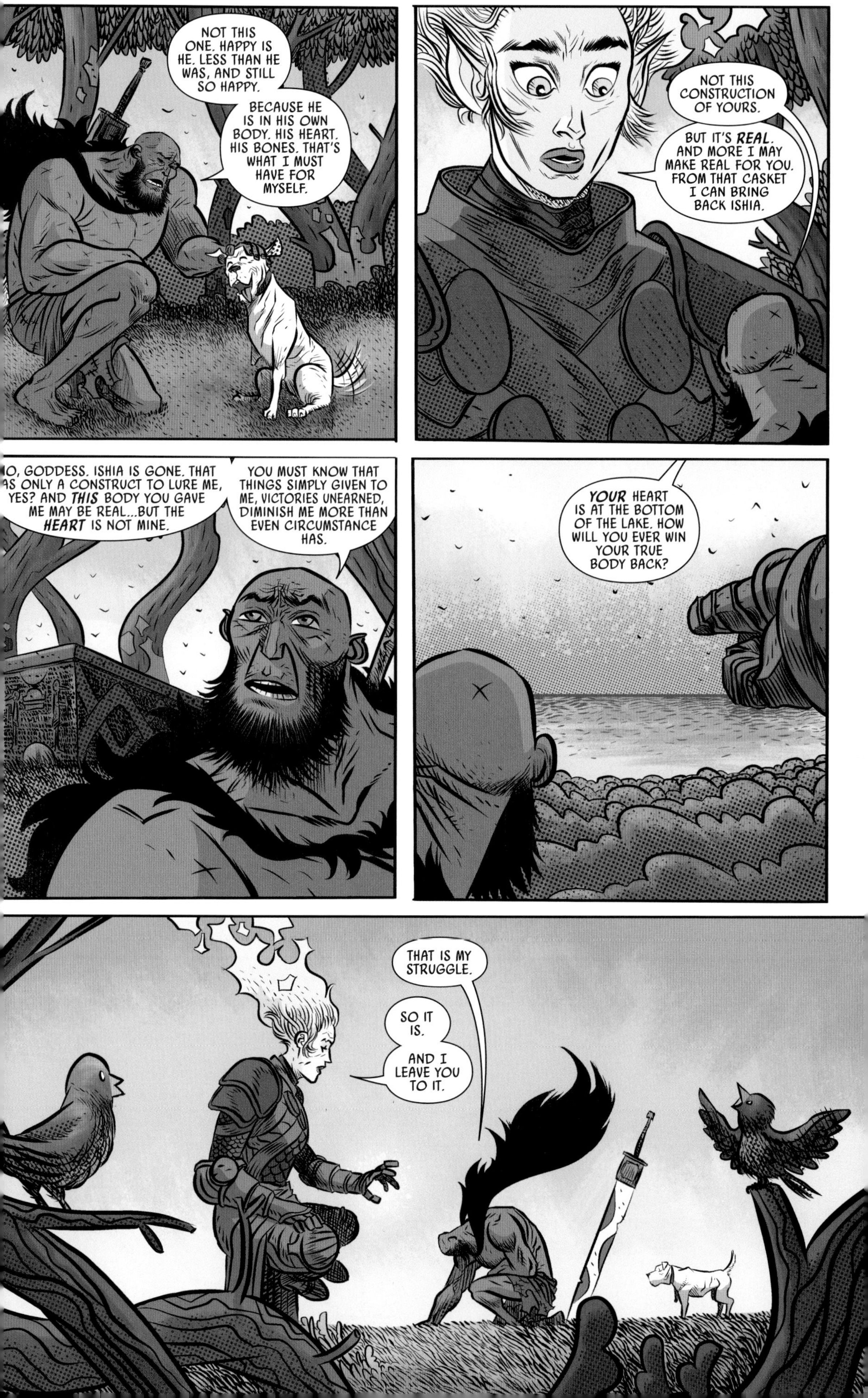
NOT THIS ONE. HAPPY IS HE. LESS THAN HE WAS, AND STILL SO HAPPY.
BECAUSE HE IS IN HIS OWN BODY. HIS HEART. HIS BONES. THAT'S WHAT I MUST HAVE FOR MYSELF.
NOT THIS CONSTRUCTION OF YOURS.
BUT IT'S REAL. AND MORE I MAY MAKE REAL FOR YOU. FROM THAT CASKET I CAN BRING BACK ISHIA.
O, GODDESS. ISHIA IS GONE. THAT AS ONLY A CONSTRUCT TO LURE ME, YES? AND THIS BODY YOU GAVE ME MAY BE REAL...BUT THE HEART IS NOT MINE.
YOU MUST KNOW THAT THINGS SIMPLY GIVEN TO ME, VICTORIES UNEARNED, DIMINISH ME MORE THAN EVEN CIRCUMSTANCE HAS.
YOUR HEART IS AT THE BOTTOM OF THE LAKE. HOW WILL YOU EVER WIN YOUR TRUE BODY BACK?
THAT IS MY STRUGGLE.
SO IT IS.
AND I LEAVE YOU TO IT.

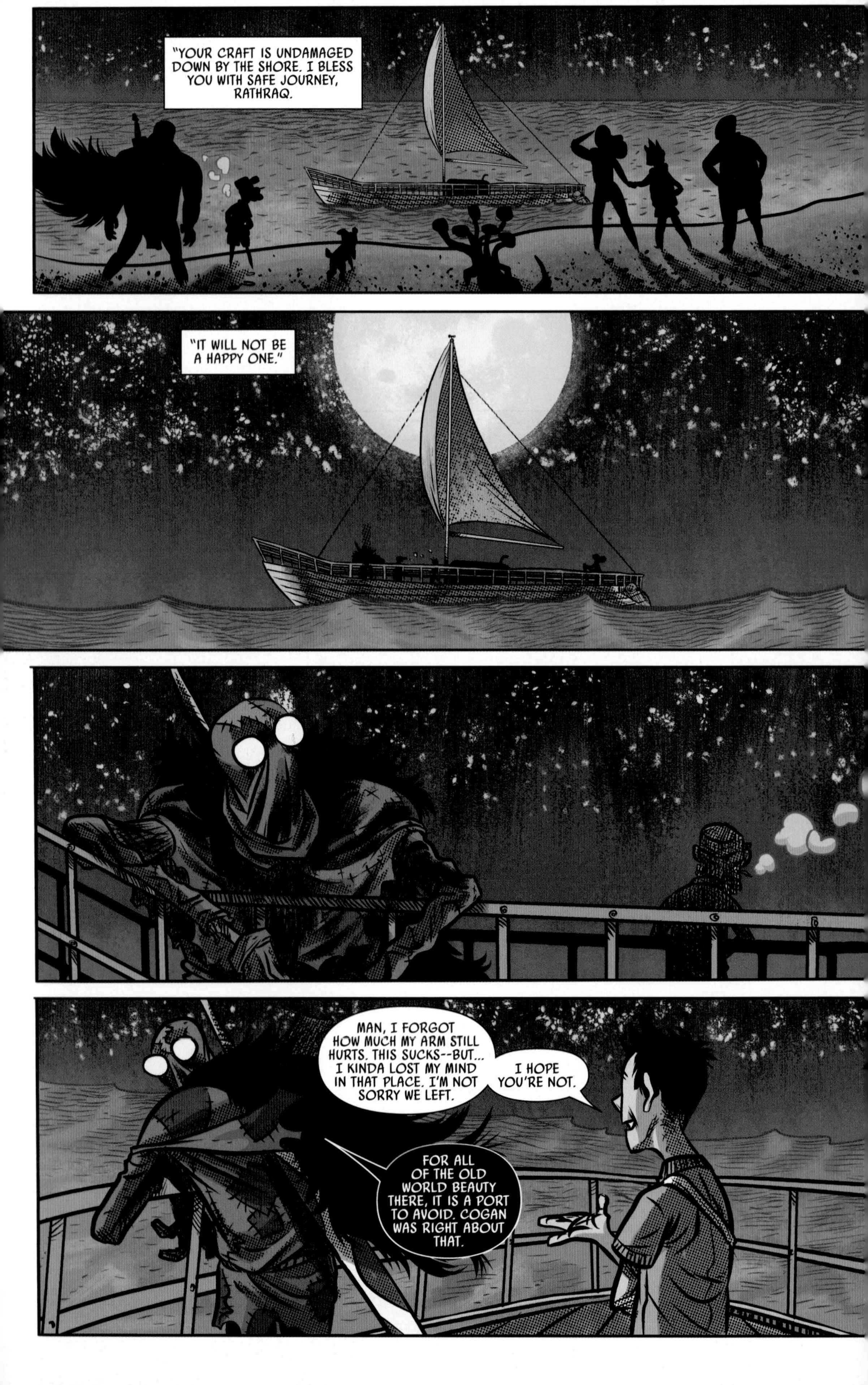
"YOUR CRAFT IS UNDAMAGED DOWN BY THE SHORE. I BLESS YOU WITH SAFE JOURNEY, RATHRAQ.
"IT WILL NOT BE A HAPPY ONE."
MAN, I FORGOT HOW MUCH MY ARM STILL HURTS. THIS SUCKS--BUT... I KINDA LOST MY MIND IN THAT PLACE. I'M NOT SORRY WE LEFT.
I HOPE YOU'RE NOT.
FOR ALL OF THE OLD WORLD BEAUTY THERE, IT IS A PORT TO AVOID. COGAN WAS RIGHT ABOUT THAT.

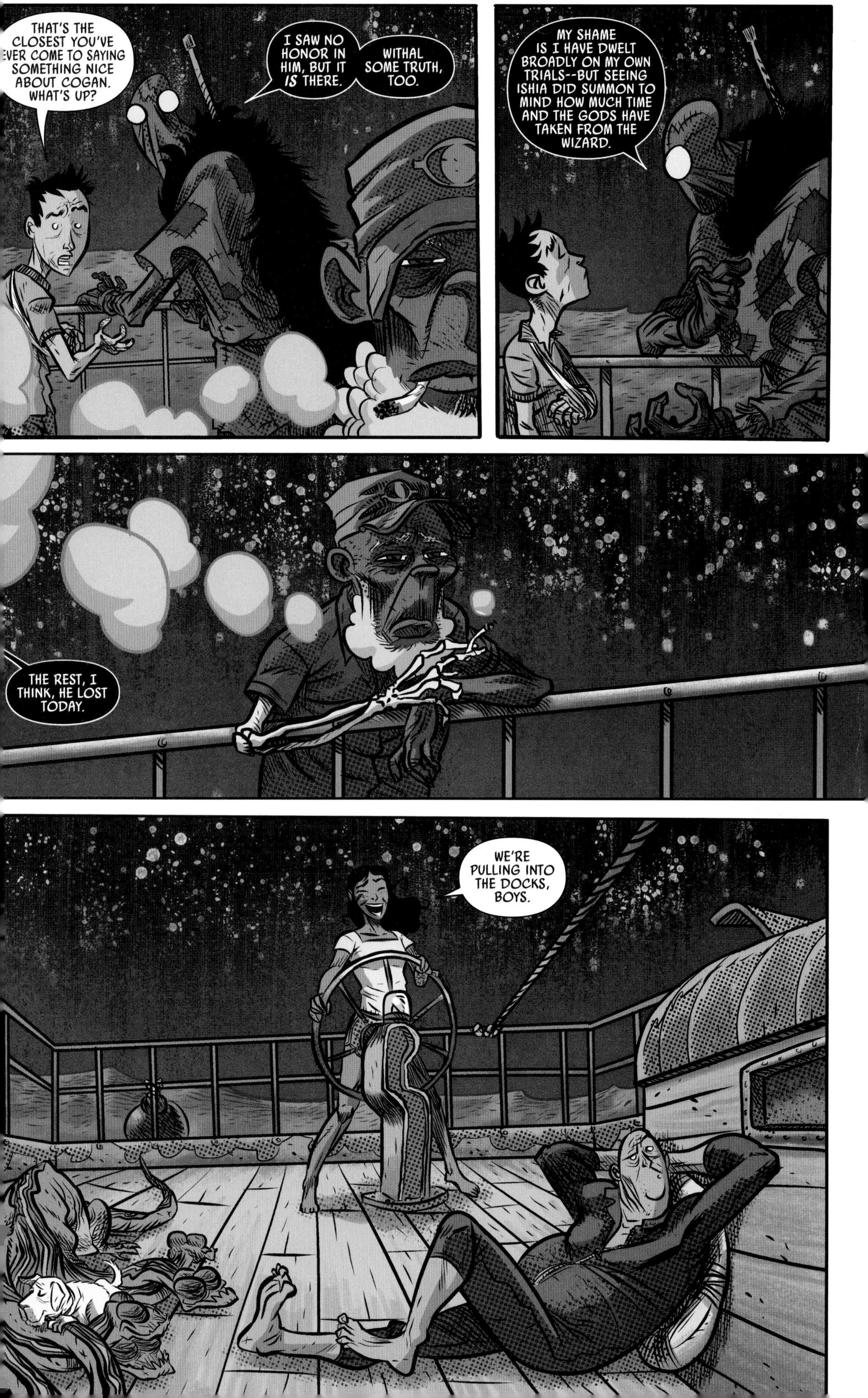
THAT'S THE CLOSEST YOU'VE EVER COME TO SAYING SOMETHING NICE ABOUT COGAN. WHAT'S UP?
I SAW NO HONOR IN HIM, BUT IT IS THERE.
WITHAL SOME TRUTH, TOO.
MY SHAME IS I HAVE DWELT BROADLY ON MY OWN TRIALS--BUT SEEING ISHIA DID SUMMON TO MIND HOW MUCH TIME AND THE GODS HAVE TAKEN FROM THE WIZARD.
THE REST, I THINK, HE LOST TODAY.
WE'RE PULLING INTO THE DOCKS, BOYS.

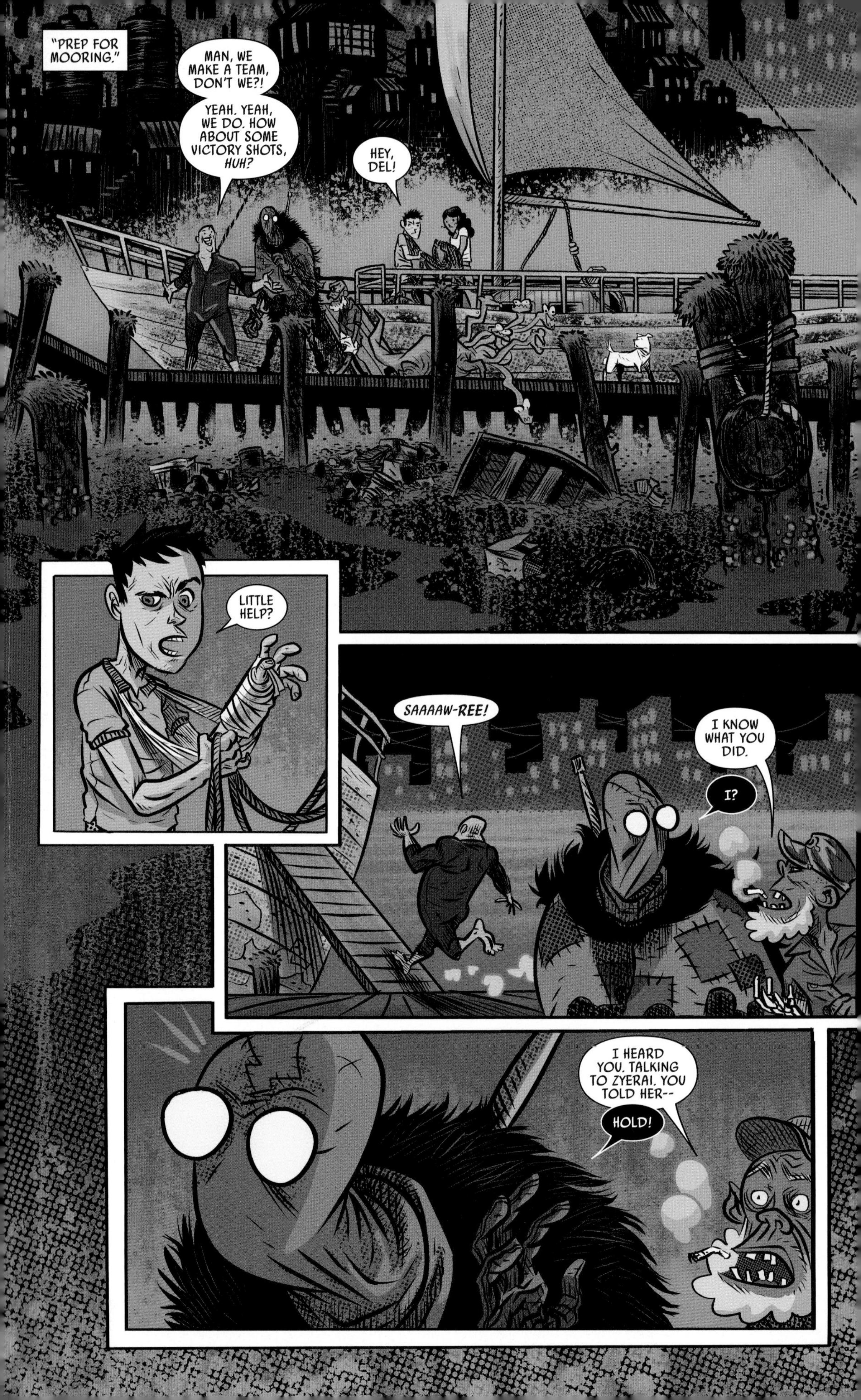
"PREP FOR MOORING."
MAN, WE MAKE A TEAM, DON'T WE?!
YEAH. YEAH, WE DO. HOW ABOUT SOME VICTORY SHOTS, HUH?
HEY, DEL!
LITTLE HELP?
SAAAAW-REE!
I KNOW WHAT YOU DID.
I?
I HEARD YOU. TALKING TO ZYERAI. YOU TOLD HER--
HOLD!

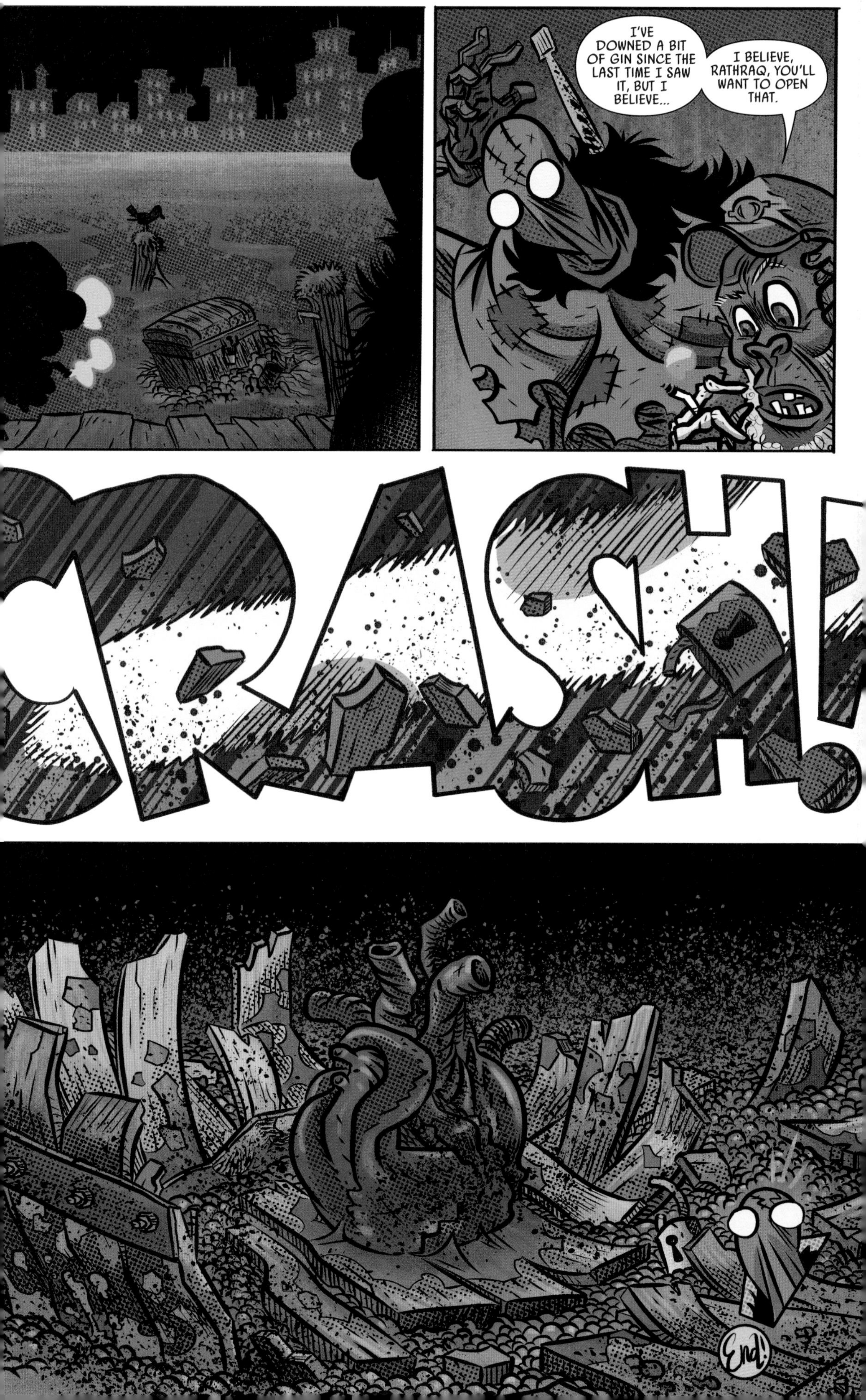
I'VE DOWNED A BIT OF GIN SINCE THE LAST TIME I SAW IT, BUT I BELIEVE...
I BELIEVE, RATHRAQ, YOU'LL WANT TO OPEN THAT.
CRASH!
End!

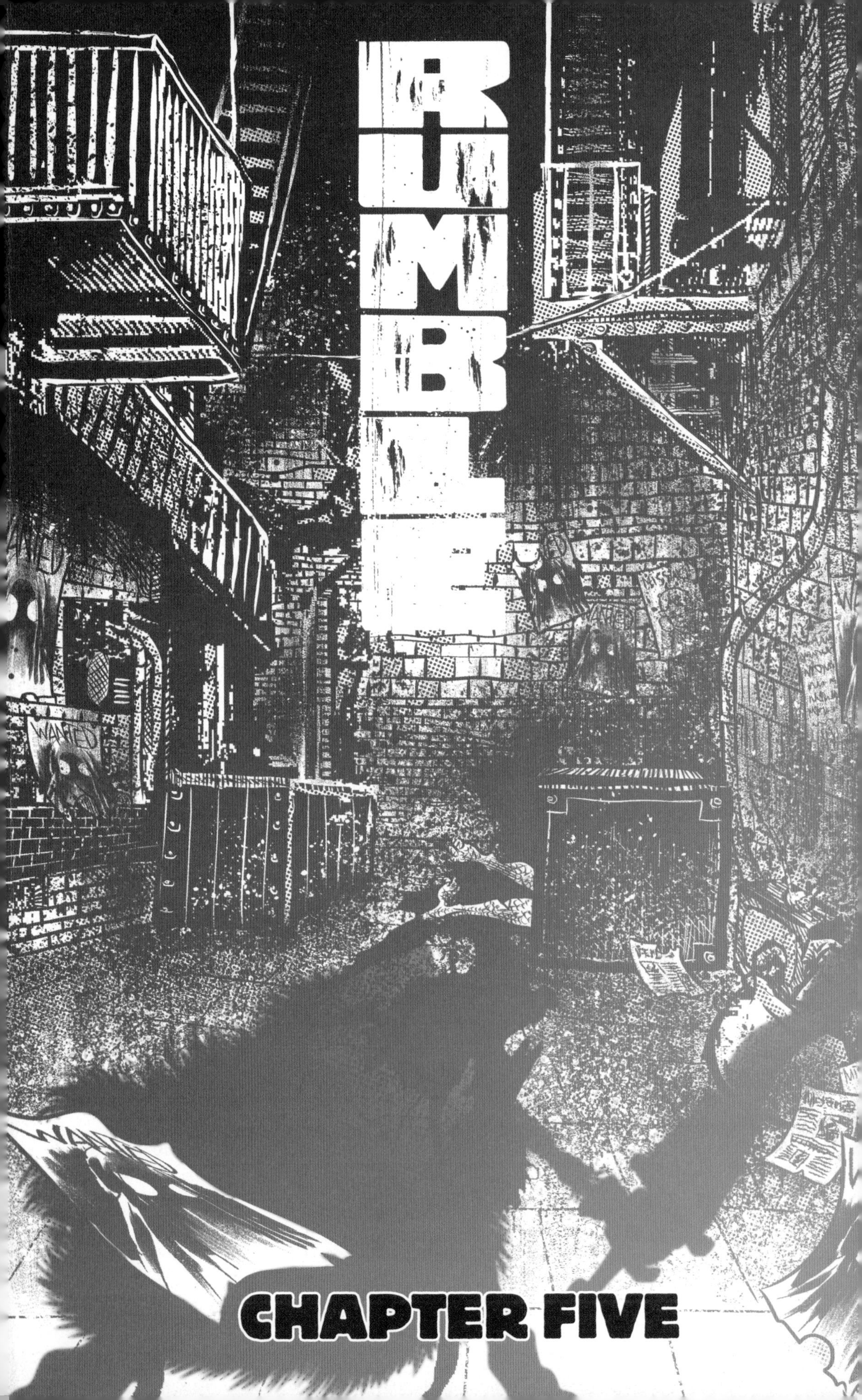
RUMBLE
CHAPTER FIVE

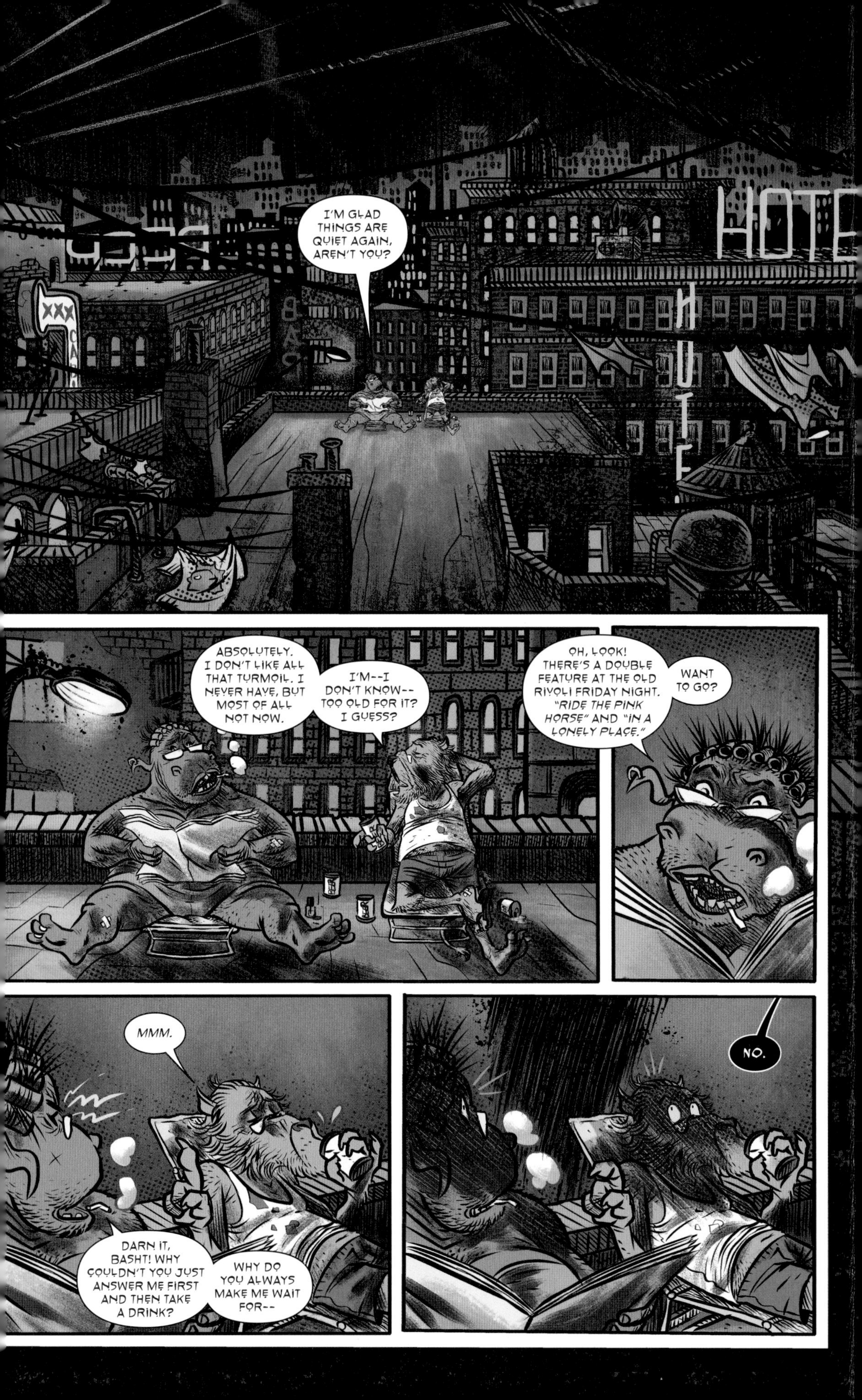

HOTE
I'M GLAD THINGS ARE QUIET AGAIN, AREN'T YOU?
ABSOLUTELY. I DON'T LIKE ALL THAT TURMOIL. I NEVER HAVE, BUT MOST OF ALL NOT NOW.
I'M--I DON'T KNOW--TOO OLD FOR IT? I GUESS?
OH, LOOK! THERE'S A DOUBLE FEATURE AT THE OLD RIVOLI FRIDAY NIGHT. "RIDE THE PINK HORSE" AND "IN A LONELY PLACE."
WANT TO GO?
MMM.
DARN IT, BASHT! WHY COULDN'T YOU JUST ANSWER ME FIRST AND THEN TAKE A DRINK?
WHY DO YOU ALWAYS MAKE ME WAIT FOR--
NO.

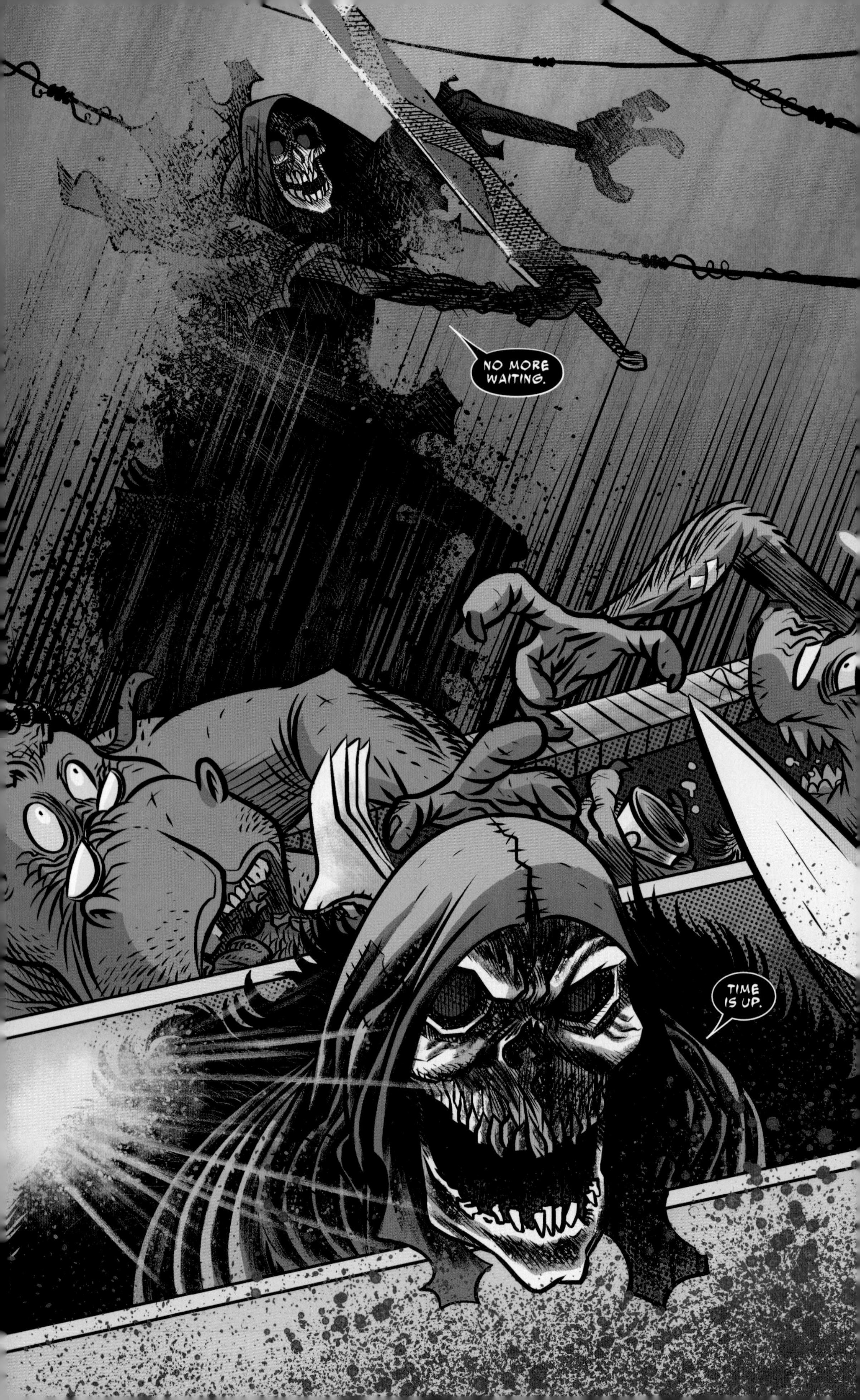
NO MORE WAITING.
TIME IS UP.

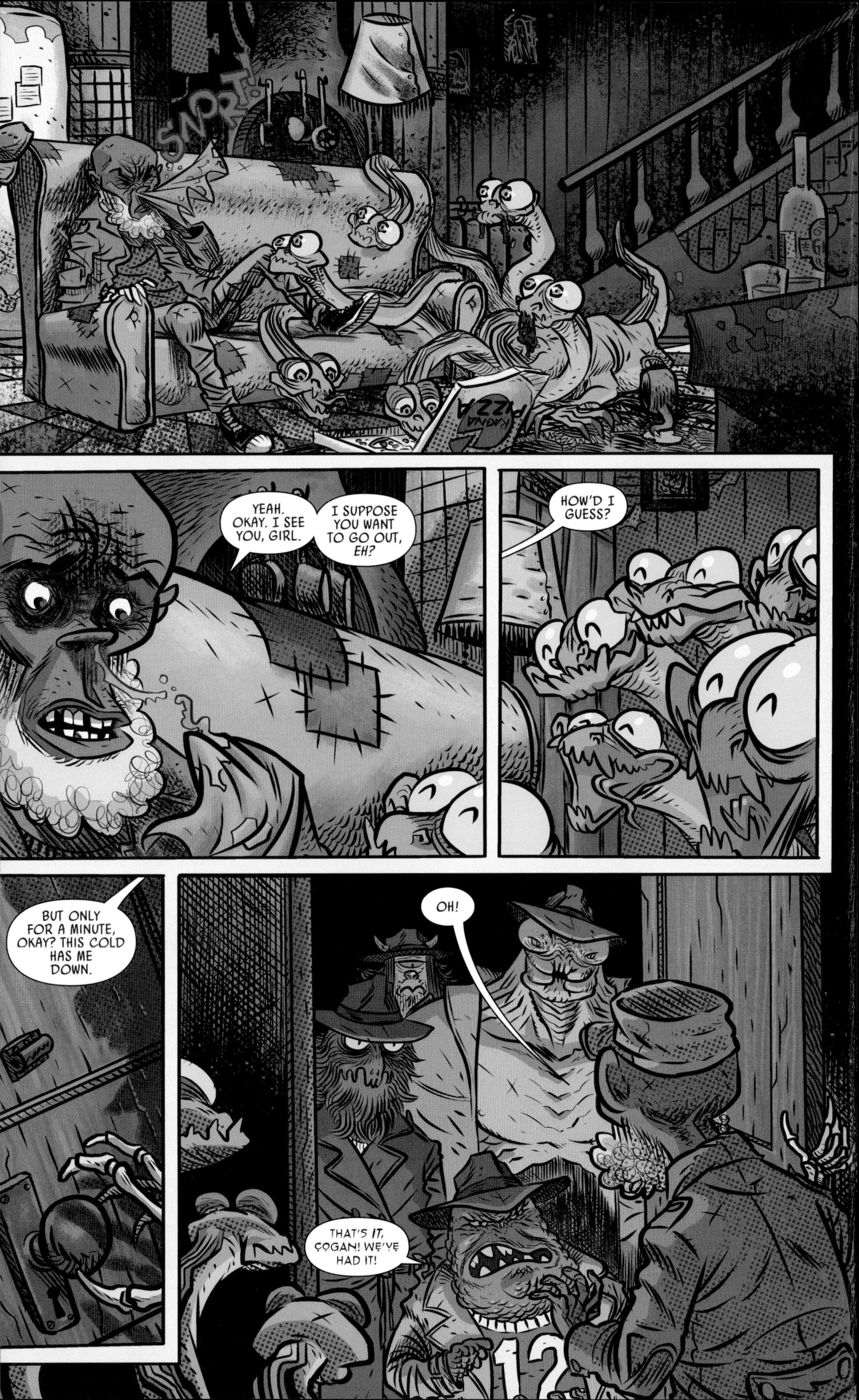
SNORT!
RAGNA PIZZA
YEAH. OKAY. I SEE YOU, GIRL.
I SUPPOSE YOU WANT TO GO OUT, EH?
HOW'D I GUESS?
BUT ONLY FOR A MINUTE, OKAY? THIS COLD HAS ME DOWN.
OH!
THAT'S IT, COGAN! WE'VE HAD IT!

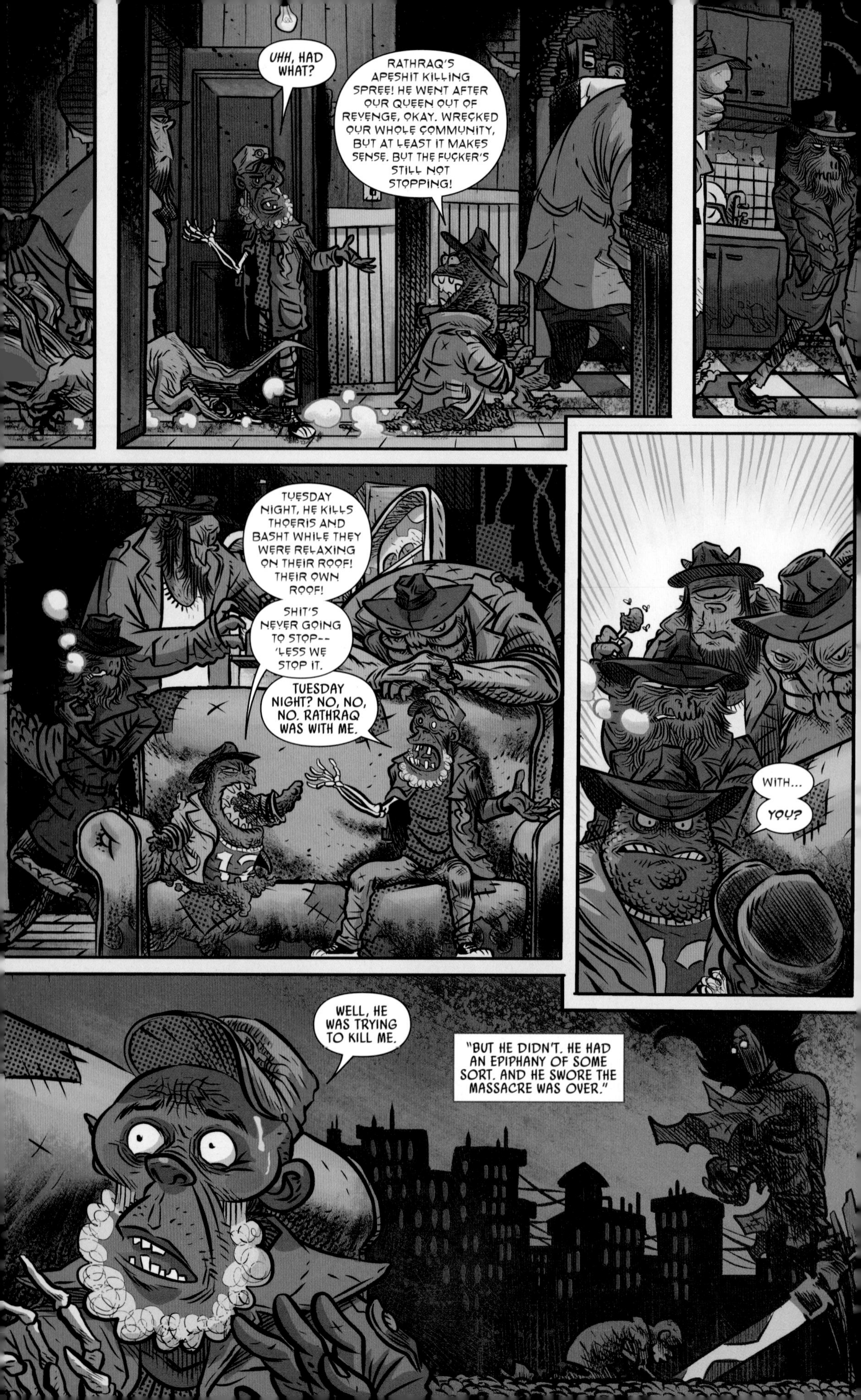
UHH, HAD WHAT?
RATHRAQ'S APESHIT KILLING SPREE! HE WENT AFTER OUR QUEEN OUT OF REVENGE, OKAY. WRECKED OUR WHOLE COMMUNITY, BUT AT LEAST IT MAKES SENSE. BUT THE FUCKER'S STILL NOT STOPPING!
TUESDAY NIGHT, HE KILLS THOERIS AND BASHT WHILE THEY WERE RELAXING ON THEIR ROOF! THEIR OWN ROOF!
SHIT'S NEVER GOING TO STOP-- 'LESS WE STOP IT.
TUESDAY NIGHT? NO, NO, NO. RATHRAQ WAS WITH ME.
WITH...
YOU?
WELL, HE WAS TRYING TO KILL ME.
"BUT HE DIDN'T. HE HAD AN EPIPHANY OF SOME SORT. AND HE SWORE THE MASSACRE WAS OVER."

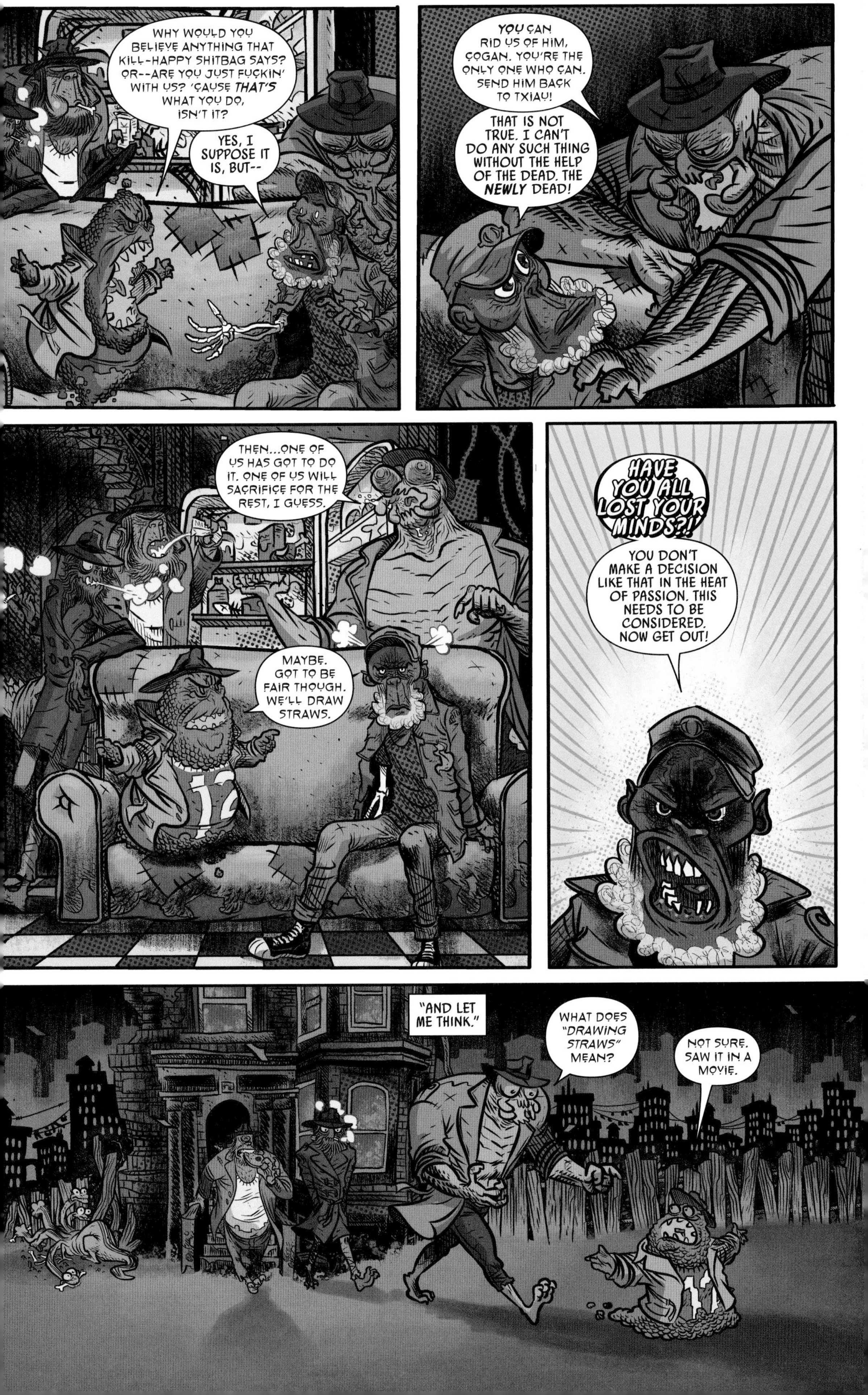
WHY WOULD YOU BELIEVE ANYTHING THAT KILL-HAPPY SHITBAG SAYS? OR--ARE YOU JUST FUCKIN' WITH US? 'CAUSE *THAT'S* WHAT YOU DO, ISN'T IT?
YES, I SUPPOSE IT IS, BUT--
*YOU* CAN RID US OF HIM, COGAN. YOU'RE THE ONLY ONE WHO CAN. SEND HIM BACK TO TXIAU!
THAT IS NOT TRUE. I CAN'T DO ANY SUCH THING WITHOUT THE HELP OF THE DEAD. THE *NEWLY* DEAD!
THEN...ONE OF US HAS GOT TO DO IT. ONE OF US WILL SACRIFICE FOR THE REST, I GUESS.
MAYBE. GOT TO BE FAIR THOUGH. WE'LL DRAW STRAWS.
HAVE YOU ALL LOST YOUR MINDS?!
YOU DON'T MAKE A DECISION LIKE THAT IN THE HEAT OF PASSION. THIS NEEDS TO BE CONSIDERED. NOW GET OUT!
"AND LET ME THINK."
WHAT DOES "*DRAWING STRAWS*" MEAN?
NOT SURE. SAW IT IN A MOVIE.

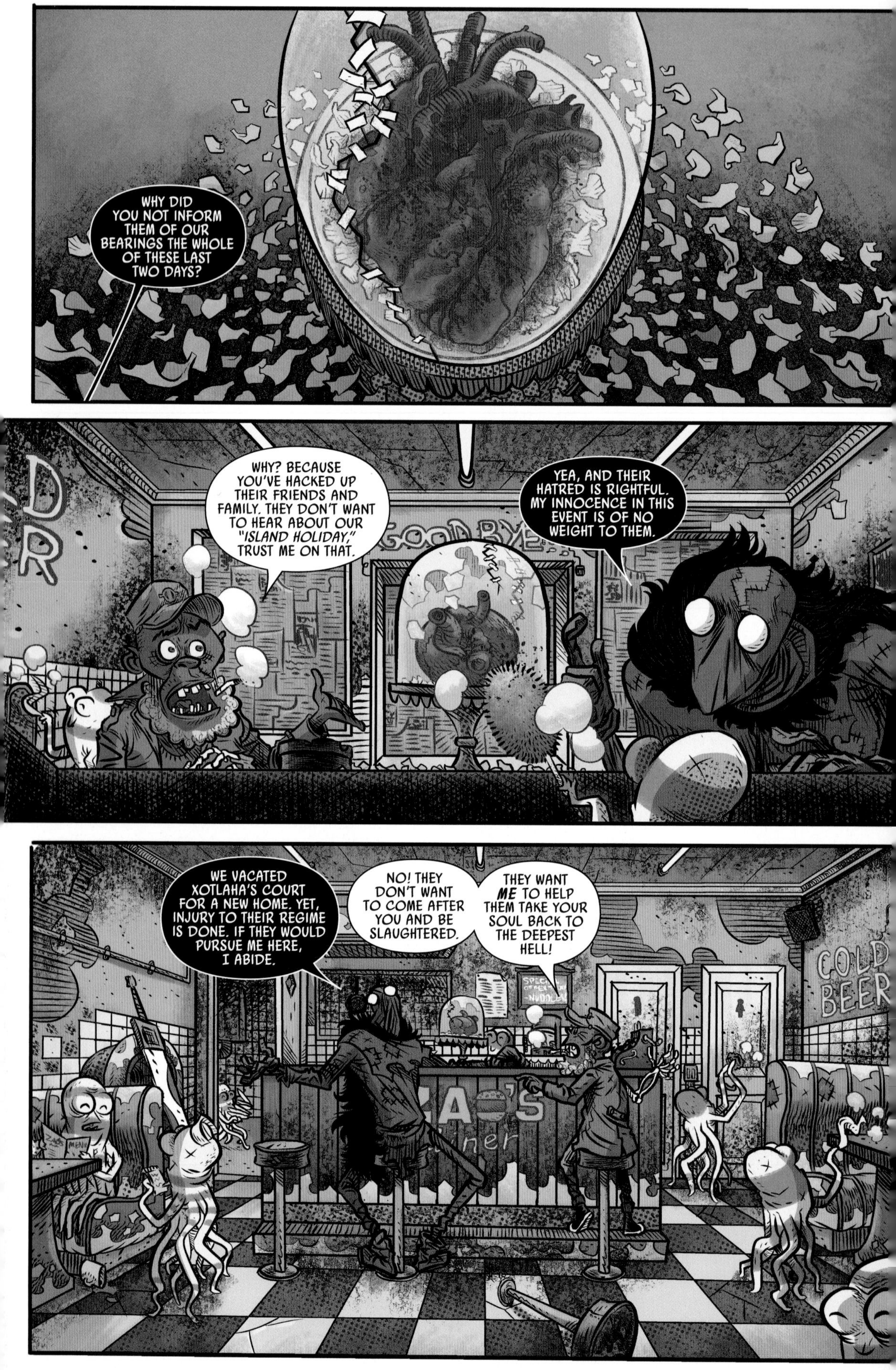
WHY DID YOU NOT INFORM THEM OF OUR BEARINGS THE WHOLE OF THESE LAST TWO DAYS?
WHY? BECAUSE YOU'VE HACKED UP THEIR FRIENDS AND FAMILY. THEY DON'T WANT TO HEAR ABOUT OUR *"ISLAND HOLIDAY,"* TRUST ME ON THAT.
GOOD BYE
YEA, AND THEIR HATRED IS RIGHTFUL. MY INNOCENCE IN THIS EVENT IS OF NO WEIGHT TO THEM.
WE VACATED XOTLAHA'S COURT FOR A NEW HOME. YET, INJURY TO THEIR REGIME IS DONE. IF THEY WOULD PURSUE ME HERE, I ABIDE.
NO! THEY DON'T WANT TO COME AFTER YOU AND BE SLAUGHTERED.
THEY WANT ***ME*** TO HELP THEM TAKE YOUR SOUL BACK TO THE DEEPEST HELL!
COLD BEER

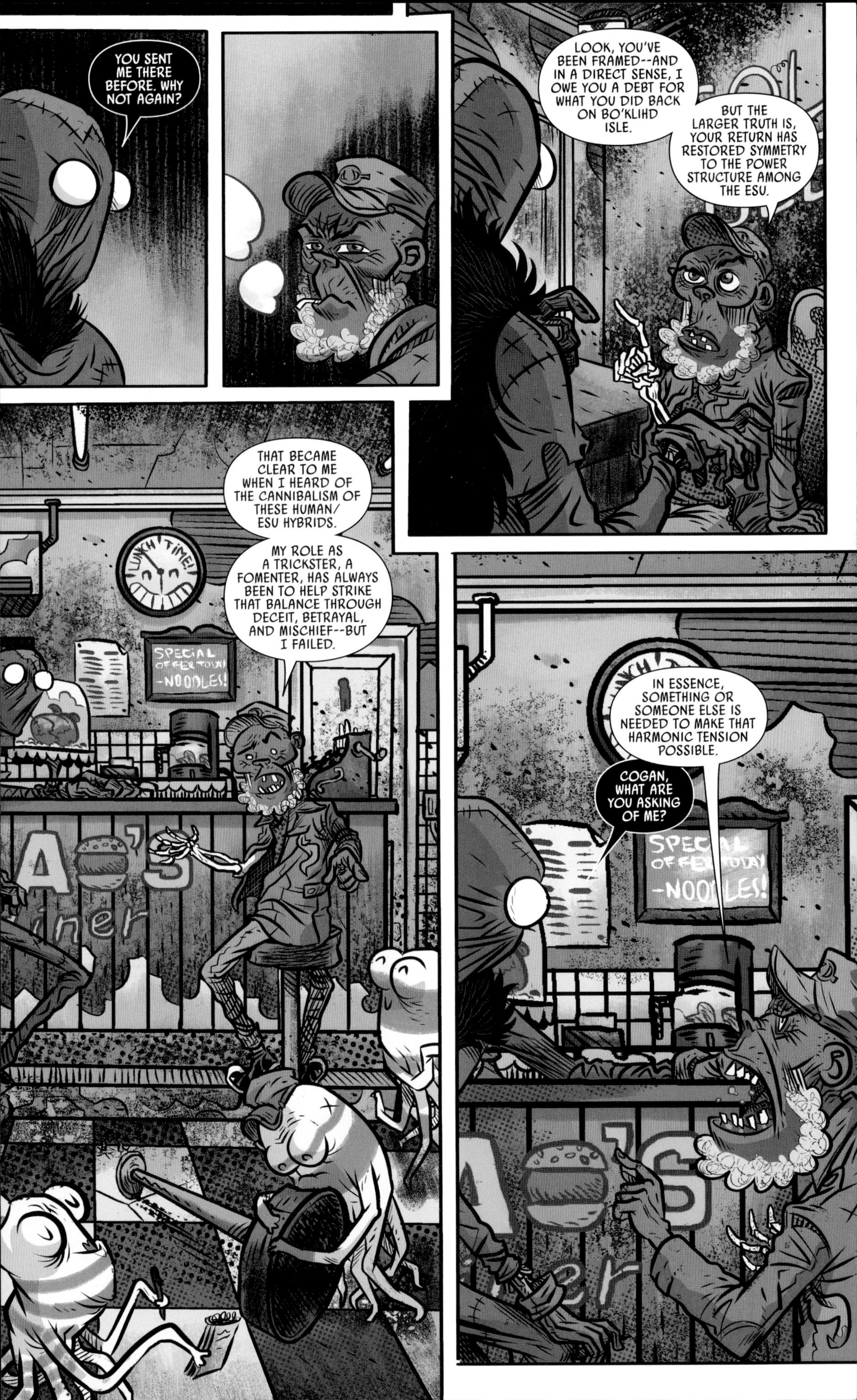
YOU SENT ME THERE BEFORE. WHY NOT AGAIN?
LOOK, YOU'VE BEEN FRAMED--AND IN A DIRECT SENSE, I OWE YOU A DEBT FOR WHAT YOU DID BACK ON BO'KLIHD ISLE.
BUT THE LARGER TRUTH IS, YOUR RETURN HAS RESTORED SYMMETRY TO THE POWER STRUCTURE AMONG THE ESU.
THAT BECAME CLEAR TO ME WHEN I HEARD OF THE CANNIBALISM OF THESE HUMAN/ ESU HYBRIDS.
MY ROLE AS A TRICKSTER, A FOMENTER, HAS ALWAYS BEEN TO HELP STRIKE THAT BALANCE THROUGH DECEIT, BETRAYAL, AND MISCHIEF--BUT I FAILED.
LUNCH TIME!
SPECIAL OFFER TODAY -NOODLES!
IN ESSENCE, SOMETHING OR SOMEONE ELSE IS NEEDED TO MAKE THAT HARMONIC TENSION POSSIBLE.
COGAN, WHAT ARE YOU ASKING OF ME?

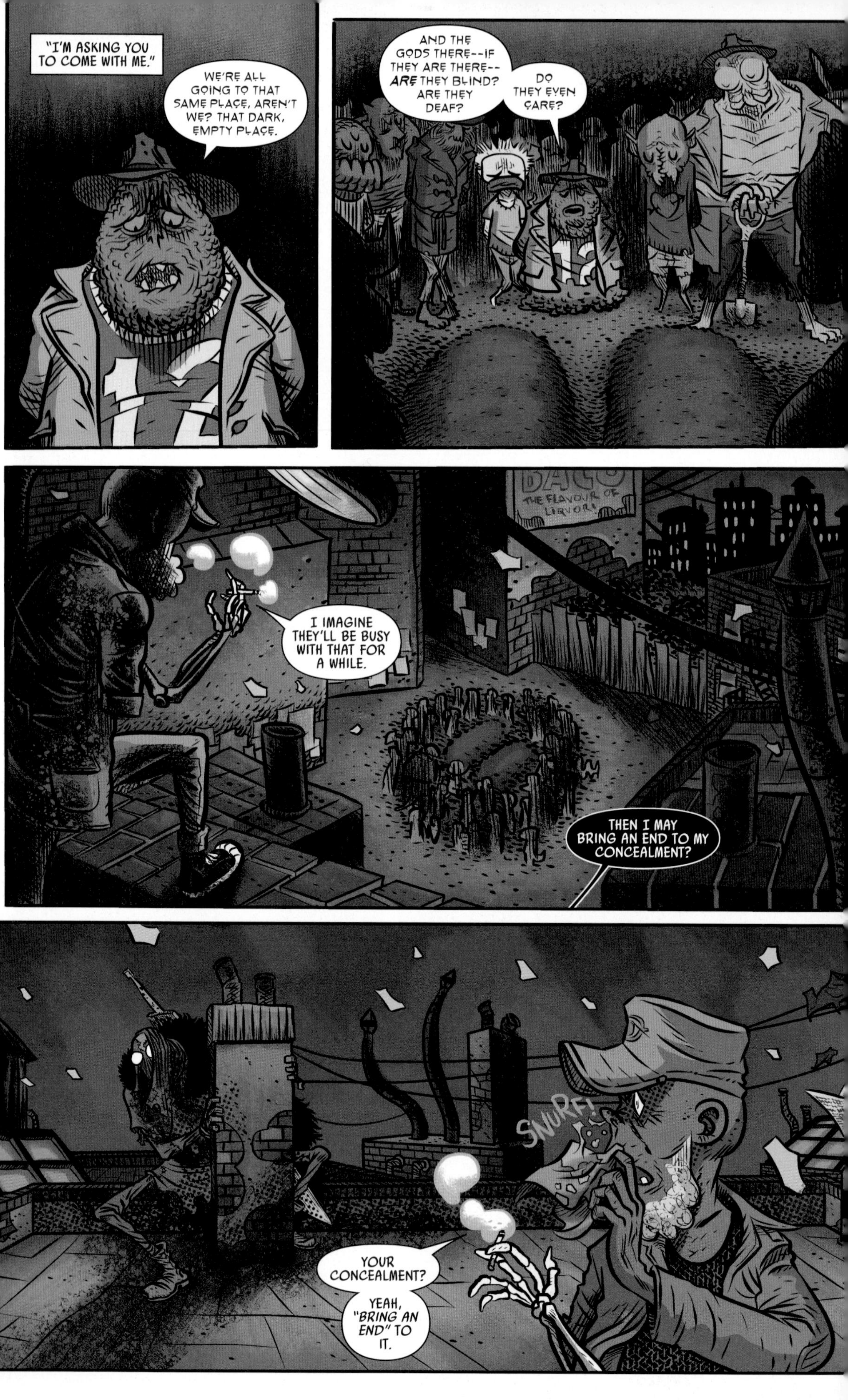
"I'M ASKING YOU TO COME WITH ME."
WE'RE ALL GOING TO THAT SAME PLACE, AREN'T WE? THAT DARK, EMPTY PLACE.
AND THE GODS THERE--IF THEY ARE THERE--ARE THEY BLIND? ARE THEY DEAF?
DO THEY EVEN CARE?
THE FLAVOUR OF LIQVOR!
I IMAGINE THEY'LL BE BUSY WITH THAT FOR A WHILE.
THEN I MAY BRING AN END TO MY CONCEALMENT?
SNURF!
YOUR CONCEALMENT?
YEAH, "BRING AN END" TO IT.

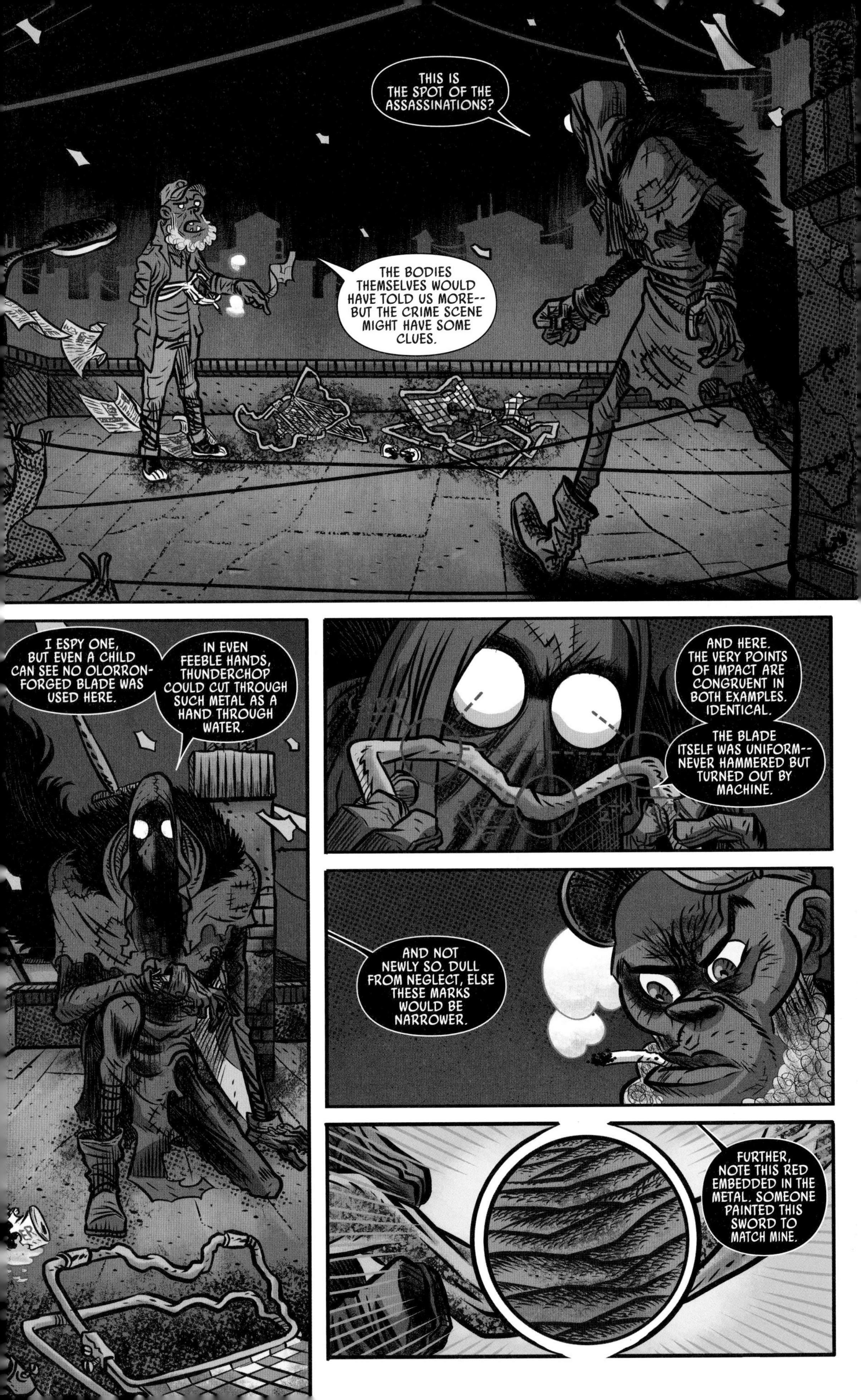
THIS IS THE SPOT OF THE ASSASSINATIONS?
THE BODIES THEMSELVES WOULD HAVE TOLD US MORE-- BUT THE CRIME SCENE MIGHT HAVE SOME CLUES.
I ESPY ONE, BUT EVEN A CHILD CAN SEE NO OLORRON-FORGED BLADE WAS USED HERE.
IN EVEN FEEBLE HANDS, THUNDERCHOP COULD CUT THROUGH SUCH METAL AS A HAND THROUGH WATER.
AND HERE. THE VERY POINTS OF IMPACT ARE CONGRUENT IN BOTH EXAMPLES. IDENTICAL.
THE BLADE ITSELF WAS UNIFORM-- NEVER HAMMERED BUT TURNED OUT BY MACHINE.
AND NOT NEWLY SO. DULL FROM NEGLECT, ELSE THESE MARKS WOULD BE NARROWER.
FURTHER, NOTE THIS RED EMBEDDED IN THE METAL. SOMEONE PAINTED THIS SWORD TO MATCH MINE.

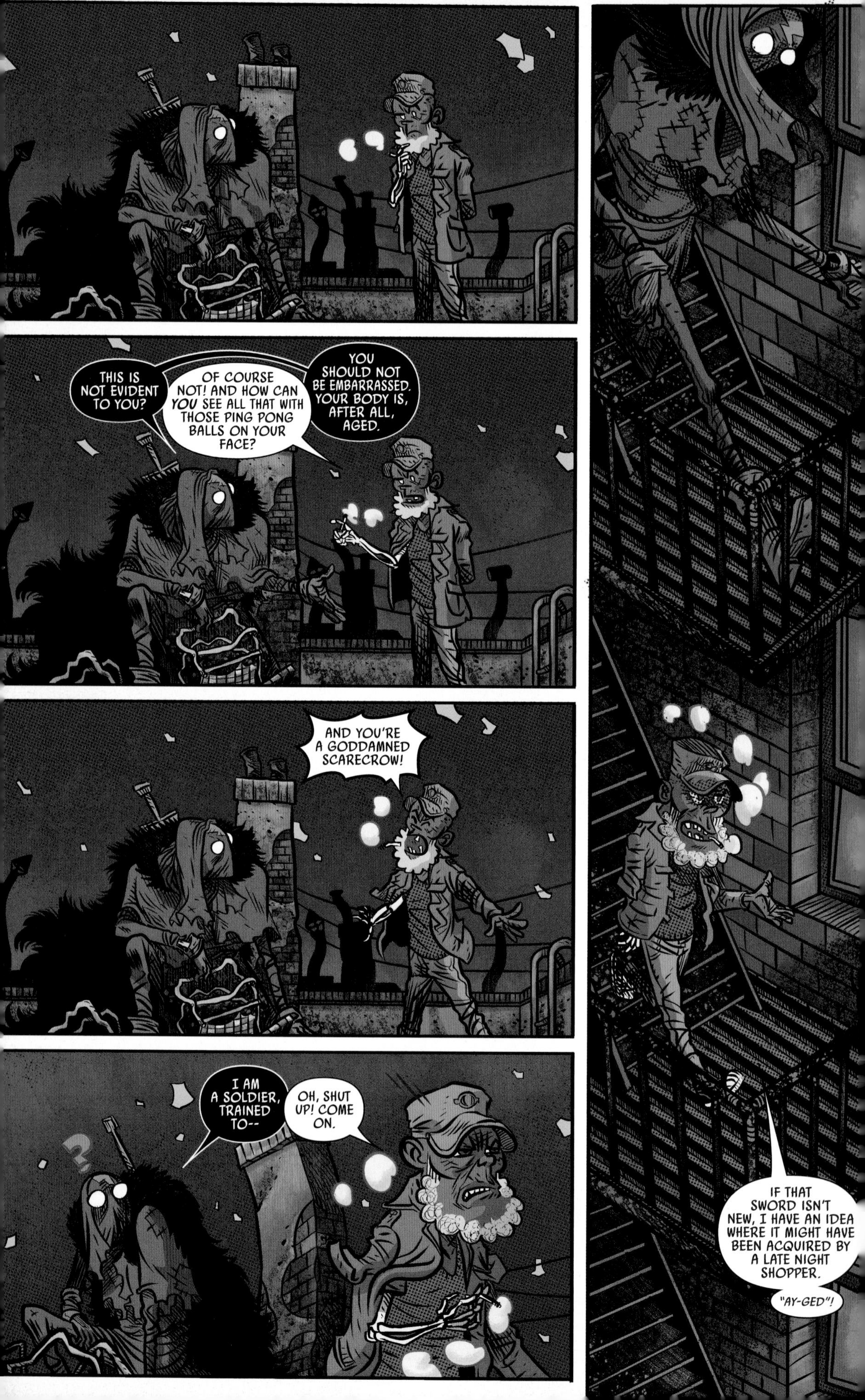
THIS IS NOT EVIDENT TO YOU?
OF COURSE NOT! AND HOW CAN YOU SEE ALL THAT WITH THOSE PING PONG BALLS ON YOUR FACE?
YOU SHOULD NOT BE EMBARRASSED. YOUR BODY IS, AFTER ALL, AGED.
AND YOU'RE A GODDAMNED SCARECROW!
I AM A SOLDIER, TRAINED TO--
OH, SHUT UP! COME ON.
?
IF THAT SWORD ISN'T NEW, I HAVE AN IDEA WHERE IT MIGHT HAVE BEEN ACQUIRED BY A LATE NIGHT SHOPPER.
"AY-GED"!

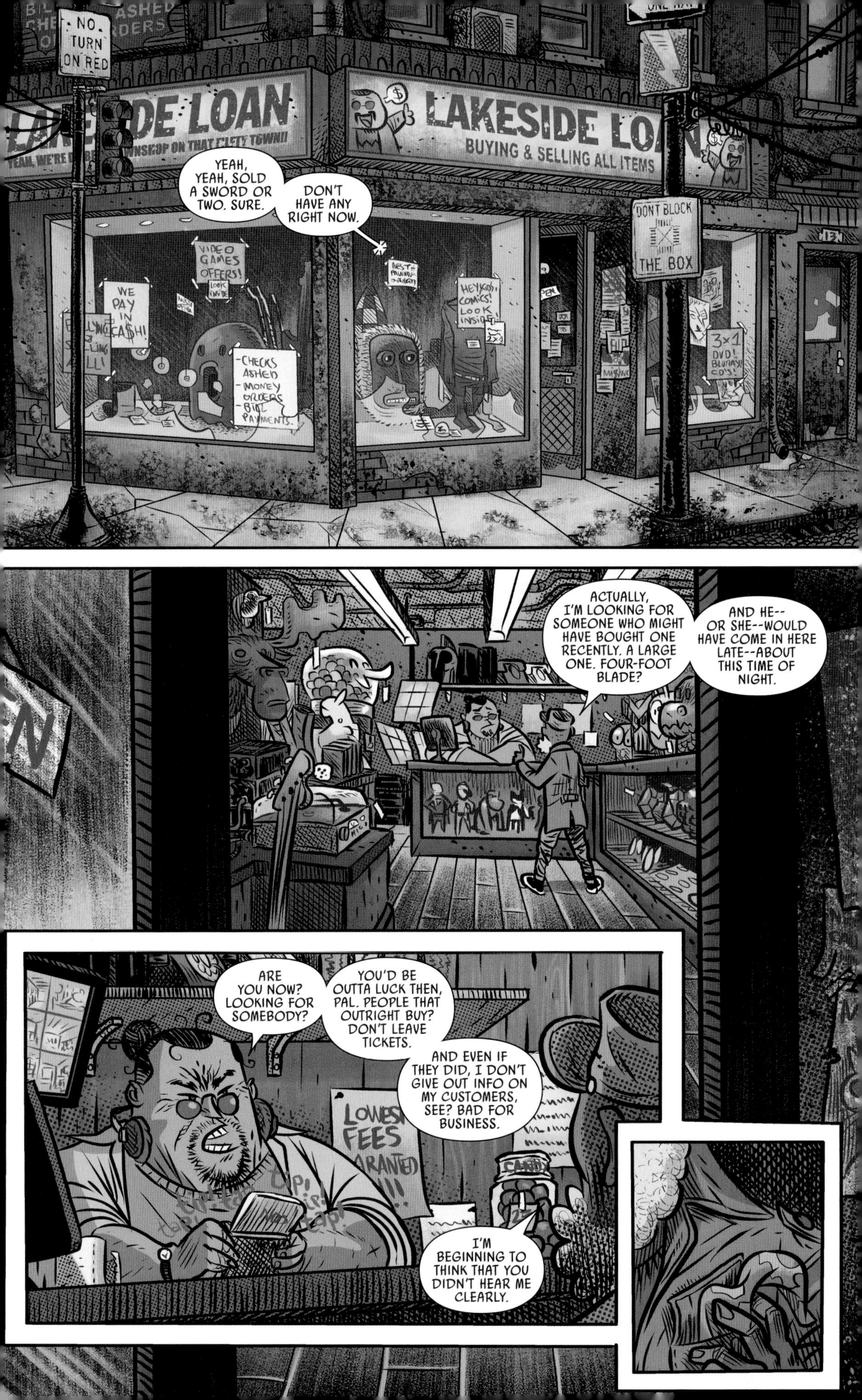
NO TURN ON RED
LAKESIDE LOAN
BUYING & SELLING ALL ITEMS
YEAH, YEAH, SOLD A SWORD OR TWO. SURE.
DON'T HAVE ANY RIGHT NOW.
DON'T BLOCK THE BOX
VIDEO GAMES OFFERS!
WE PAY IN CA$H!
HEY KIDS! COMICS! LOOK INSIDE!
3x1 DVD! BLURAY! CD'S!
ACTUALLY, I'M LOOKING FOR SOMEONE WHO MIGHT HAVE BOUGHT ONE RECENTLY. A LARGE ONE. FOUR-FOOT BLADE?
AND HE-- OR SHE--WOULD HAVE COME IN HERE LATE--ABOUT THIS TIME OF NIGHT.
ARE YOU NOW? LOOKING FOR SOMEBODY?
YOU'D BE OUTTA LUCK THEN, PAL. PEOPLE THAT OUTRIGHT BUY? DON'T LEAVE TICKETS.
AND EVEN IF THEY DID, I DON'T GIVE OUT INFO ON MY CUSTOMERS, SEE? BAD FOR BUSINESS.
I'M BEGINNING TO THINK THAT YOU DIDN'T HEAR ME CLEARLY.

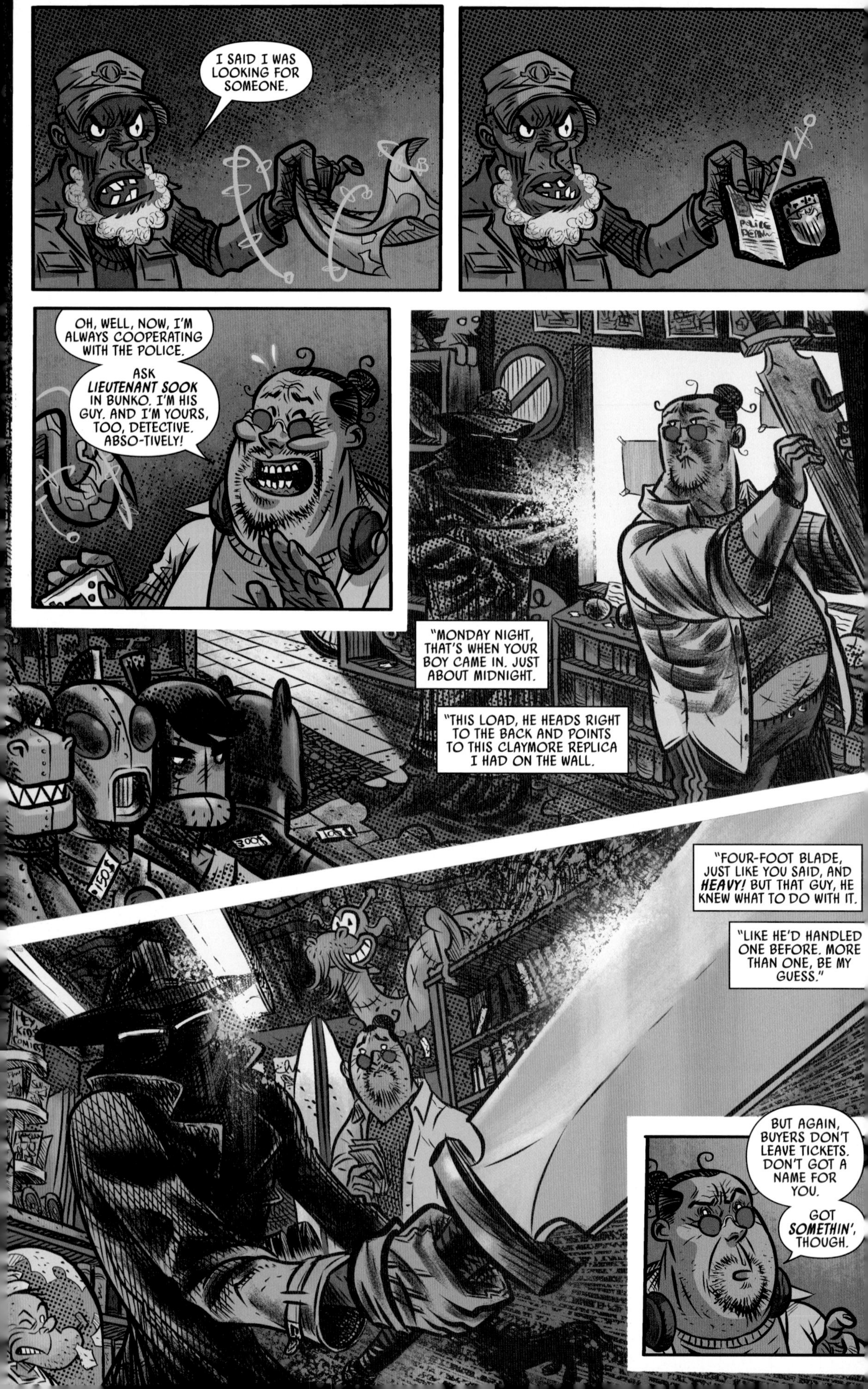

I SAID I WAS LOOKING FOR SOMEONE.
POLICE DEPARTMENT
OH, WELL, NOW, I'M ALWAYS COOPERATING WITH THE POLICE.
ASK ***LIEUTENANT SOOK*** IN BUNKO. I'M HIS GUY. AND I'M YOURS, TOO, DETECTIVE. ABSO-TIVELY!
"MONDAY NIGHT, THAT'S WHEN YOUR BOY CAME IN. JUST ABOUT MIDNIGHT.
"THIS LOAD, HE HEADS RIGHT TO THE BACK AND POINTS TO THIS CLAYMORE REPLICA I HAD ON THE WALL.
"FOUR-FOOT BLADE, JUST LIKE YOU SAID, AND ***HEAVY!*** BUT THAT GUY, HE KNEW WHAT TO DO WITH IT.
"LIKE HE'D HANDLED ONE BEFORE. MORE THAN ONE, BE MY GUESS."
BUT AGAIN, BUYERS DON'T LEAVE TICKETS. DON'T GOT A NAME FOR YOU.
GOT ***SOMETHIN'***, THOUGH.

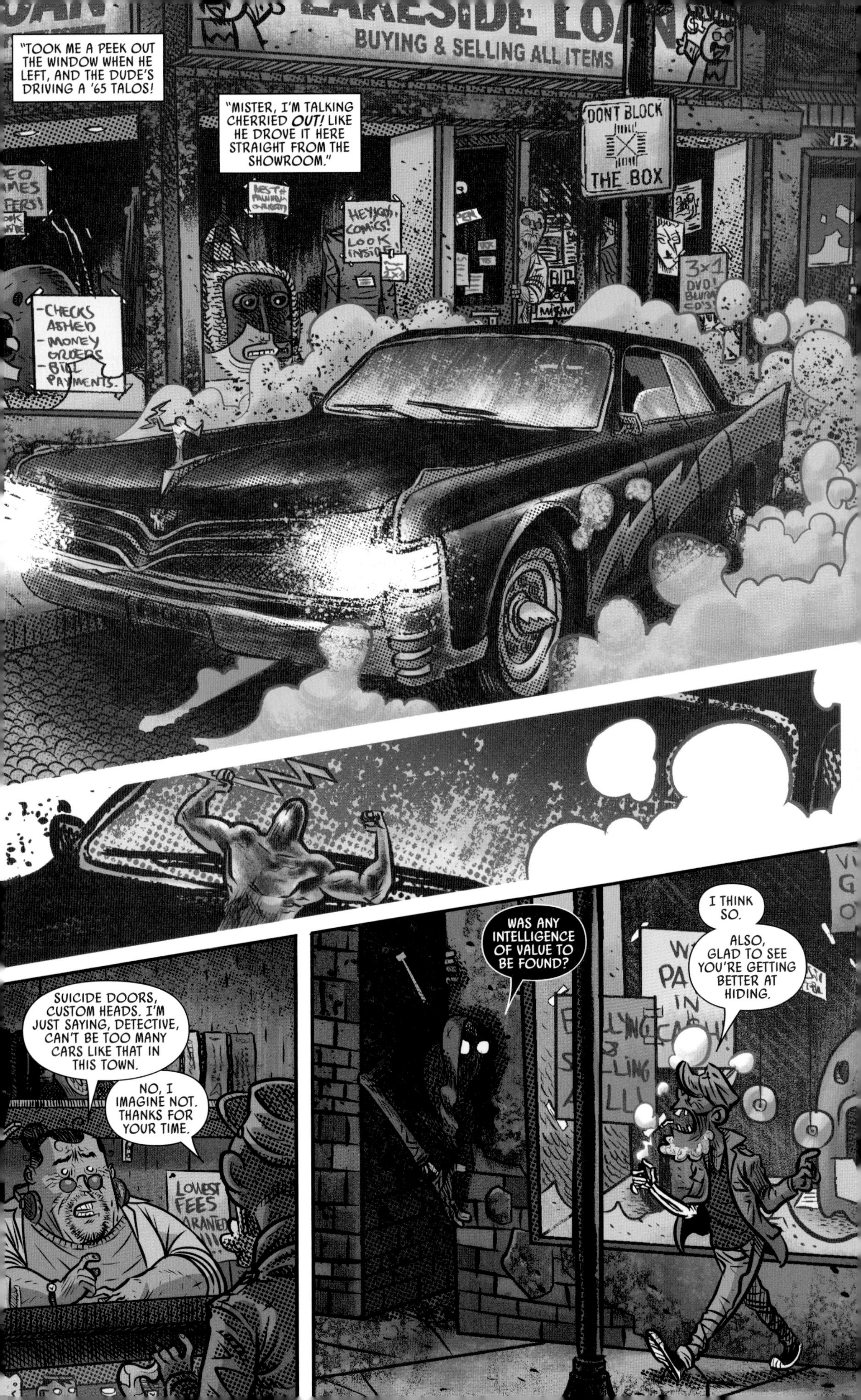
BUYING & SELLING ALL ITEMS
"TOOK ME A PEEK OUT THE WINDOW WHEN HE LEFT, AND THE DUDE'S DRIVING A '65 TALOS!
"MISTER, I'M TALKING CHERRIED OUT! LIKE HE DROVE IT HERE STRAIGHT FROM THE SHOWROOM."
DONT BLOCK THE BOX
HEY KIDS! COMICS! LOOK INSIDE
-CHECKS ASHED -MONEY ORDERS -BILL PAYMENTS.
3x1 DVD! CD'S
SUICIDE DOORS, CUSTOM HEADS. I'M JUST SAYING, DETECTIVE, CAN'T BE TOO MANY CARS LIKE THAT IN THIS TOWN.
NO, I IMAGINE NOT. THANKS FOR YOUR TIME.
LOWEST FEES
WAS ANY INTELLIGENCE OF VALUE TO BE FOUND?
I THINK SO.
ALSO, GLAD TO SEE YOU'RE GETTING BETTER AT HIDING.

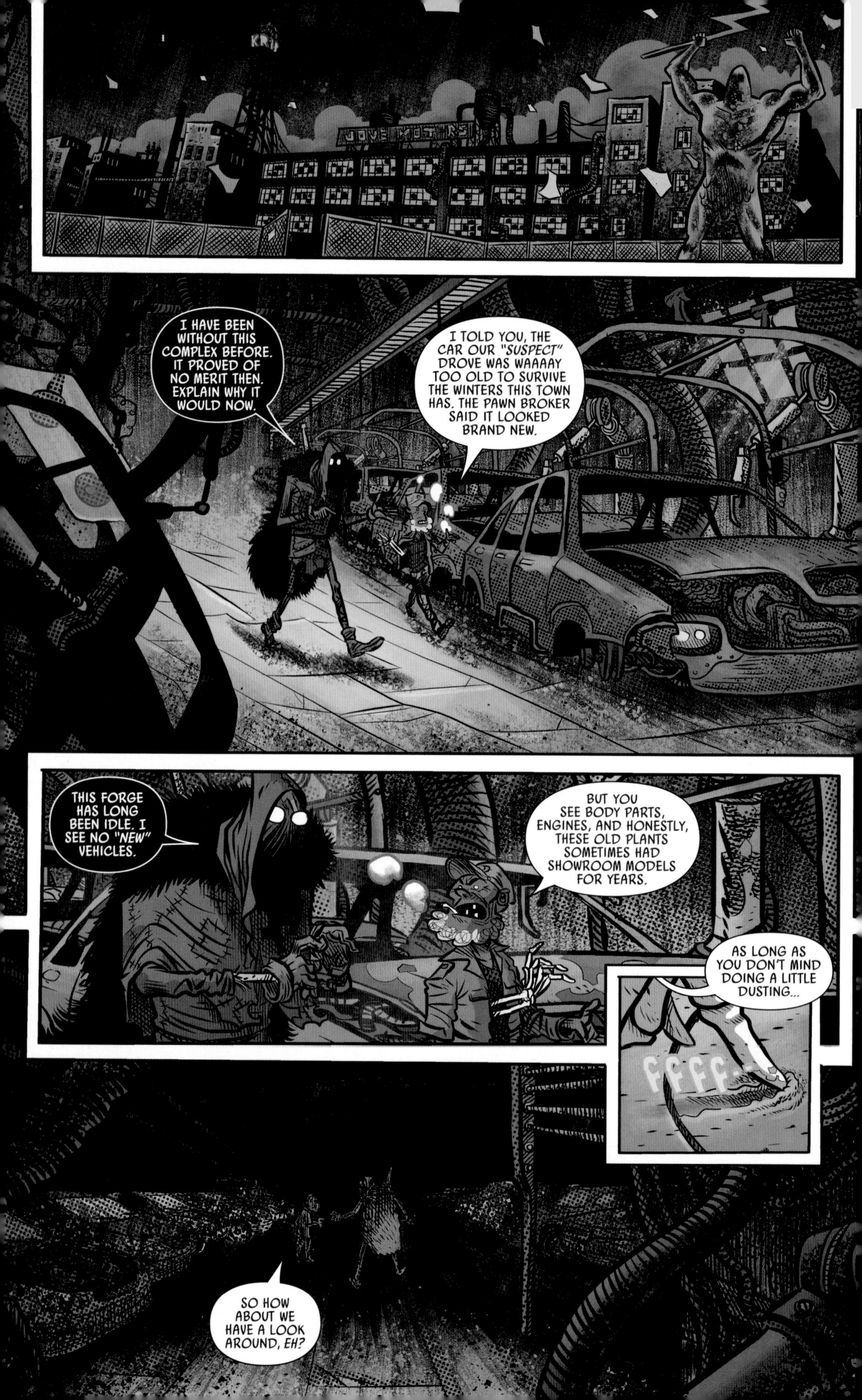
I HAVE BEEN WITHOUT THIS COMPLEX BEFORE. IT PROVED OF NO MERIT THEN. EXPLAIN WHY IT WOULD NOW.
I TOLD YOU, THE CAR OUR "SUSPECT" DROVE WAS WAAAAY TOO OLD TO SURVIVE THE WINTERS THIS TOWN HAS. THE PAWN BROKER SAID IT LOOKED BRAND NEW.
THIS FORGE HAS LONG BEEN IDLE. I SEE NO "NEW" VEHICLES.
BUT YOU SEE BODY PARTS, ENGINES, AND HONESTLY, THESE OLD PLANTS SOMETIMES HAD SHOWROOM MODELS FOR YEARS.
AS LONG AS YOU DON'T MIND DOING A LITTLE DUSTING...
FFFF...
SO HOW ABOUT WE HAVE A LOOK AROUND, EH?

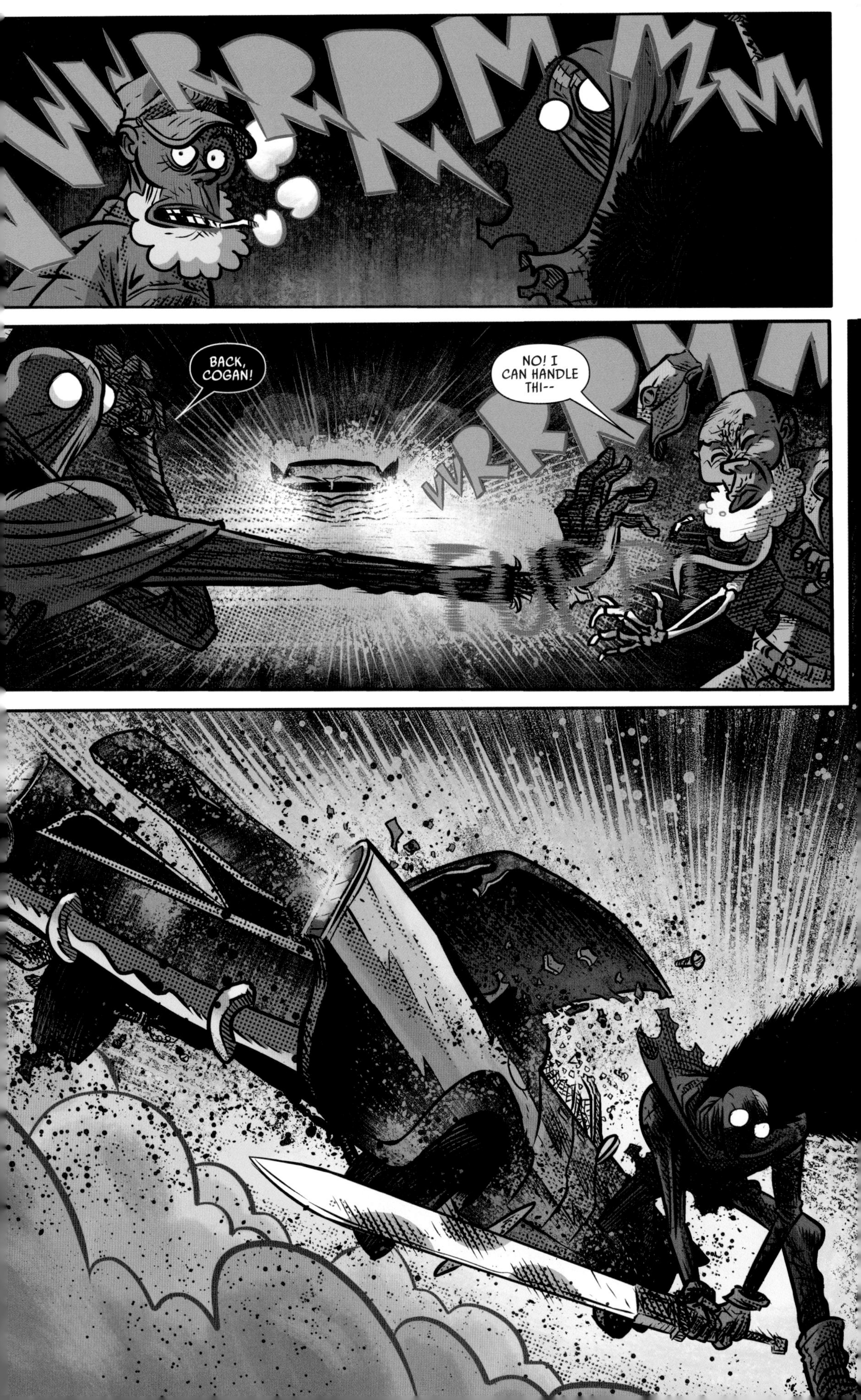
BACK, COGAN!
NO! I CAN HANDLE THI--

YOU DON'T WAIT FOR DEATH.
YOU COME TO MEET IT!

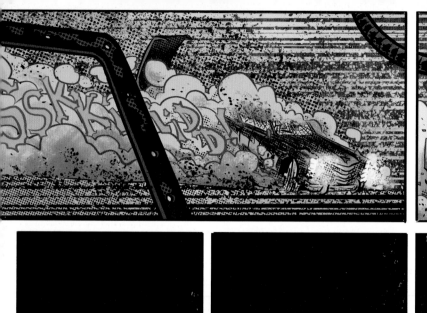

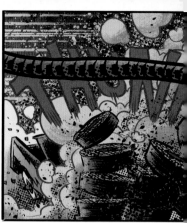

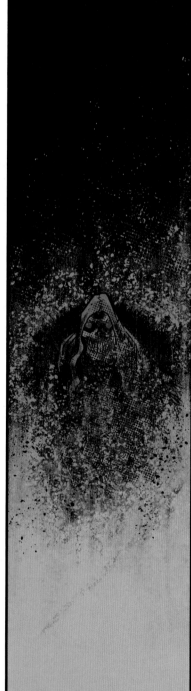

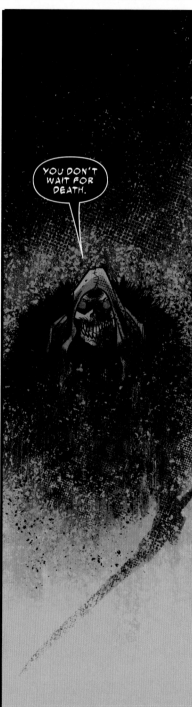

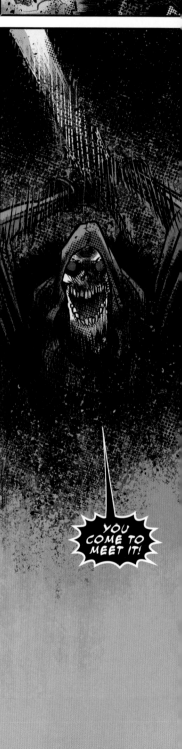

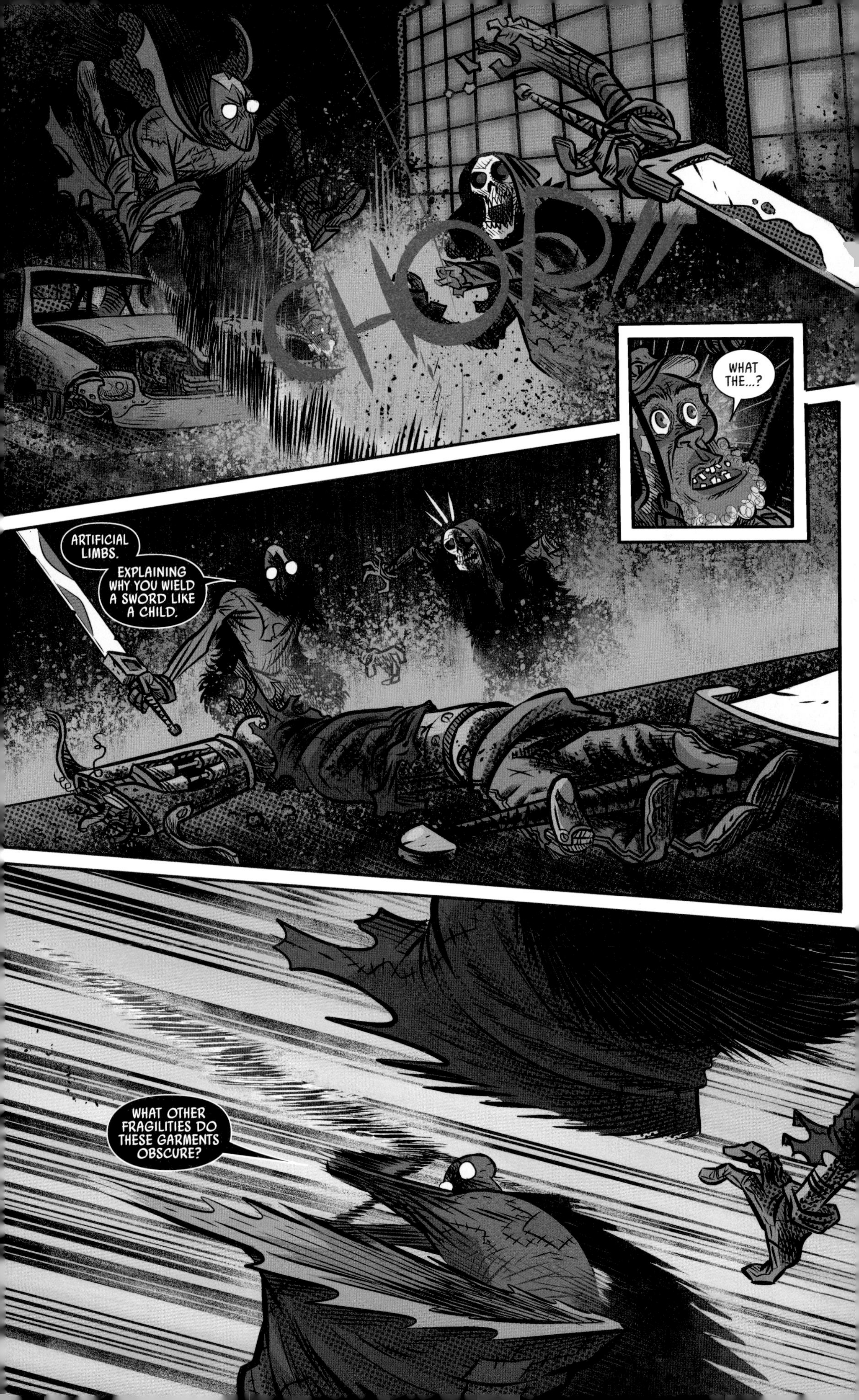
CHOP!!
WHAT THE...?
ARTIFICIAL LIMBS.
EXPLAINING WHY YOU WIELD A SWORD LIKE A CHILD.
WHAT OTHER FRAGILITIES DO THESE GARMENTS OBSCURE?

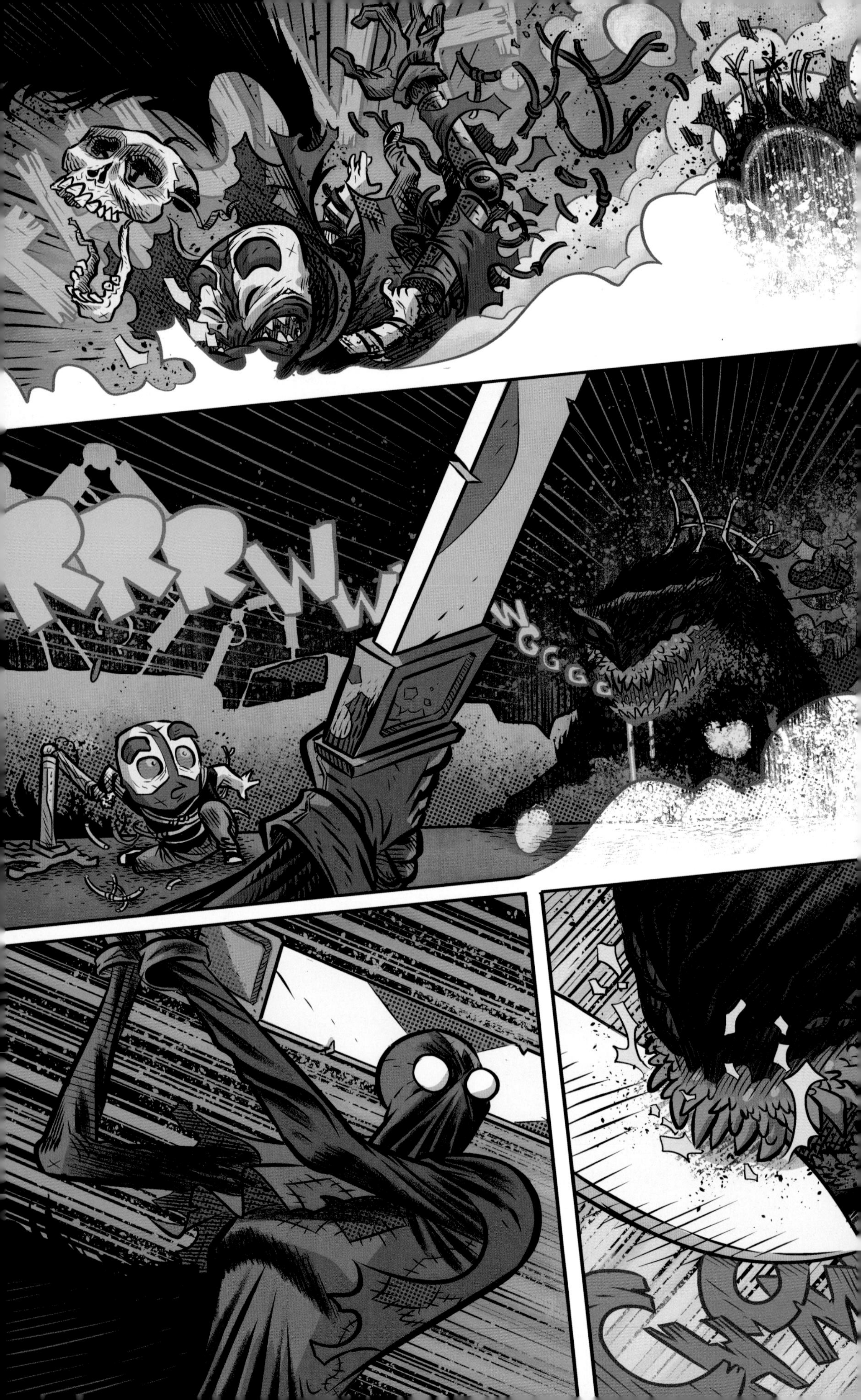
RRRWWW
WGGGG

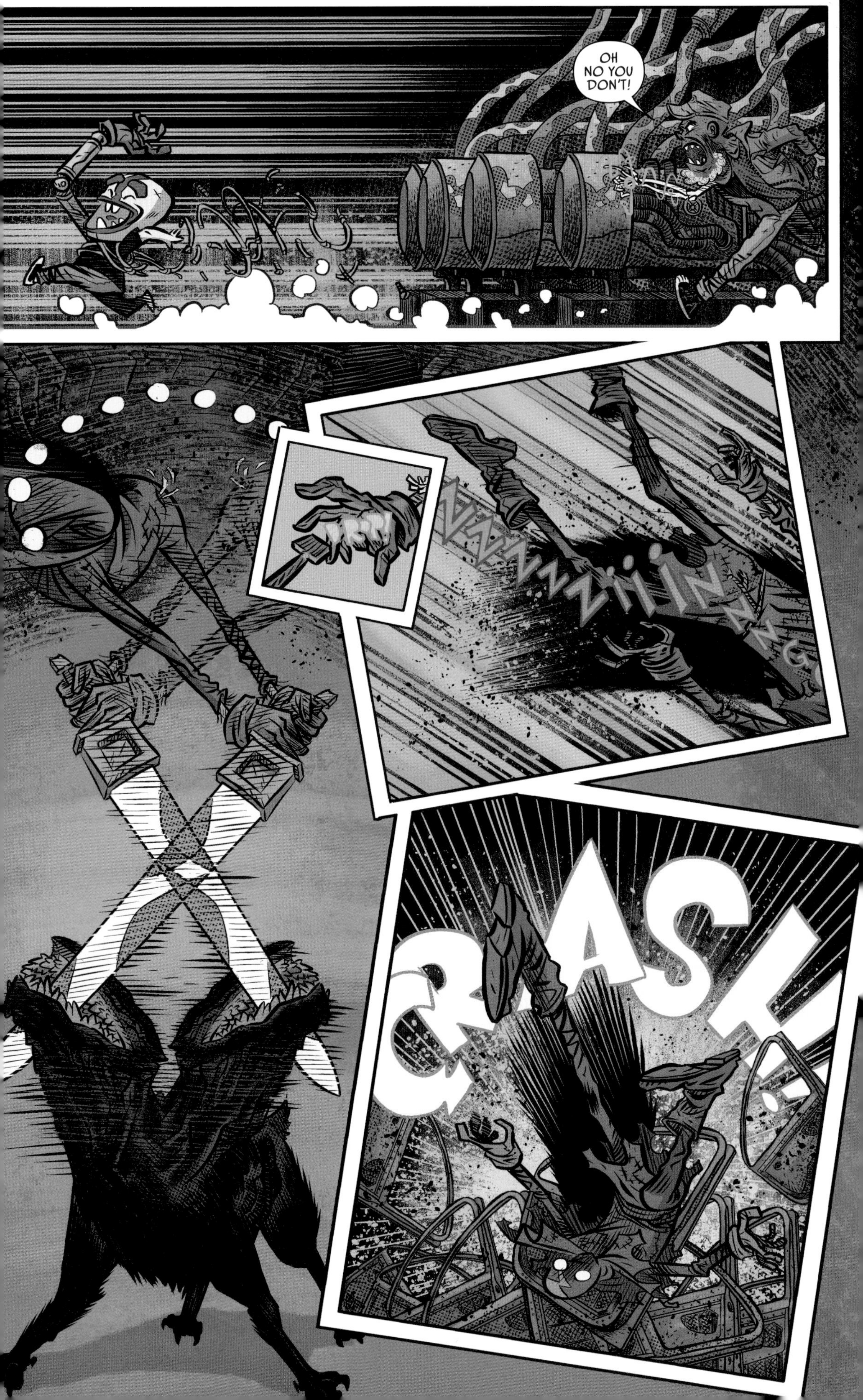

OH NO YOU DON'T!
CRASH!

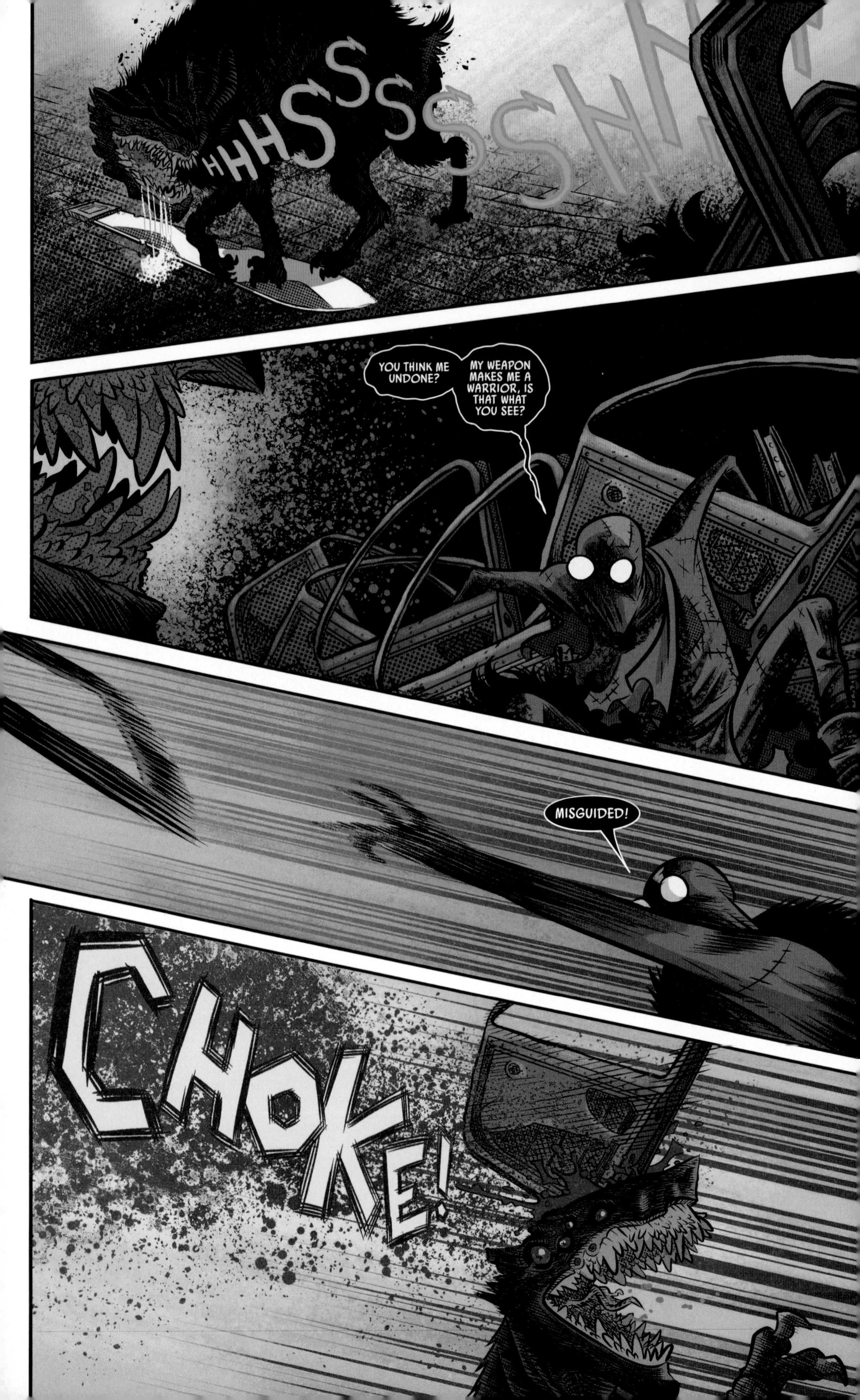
HHHSSSSSSHHH
YOU THINK ME UNDONE?
MY WEAPON MAKES ME A WARRIOR, IS THAT WHAT YOU SEE?
MISGUIDED!
CHOKE!

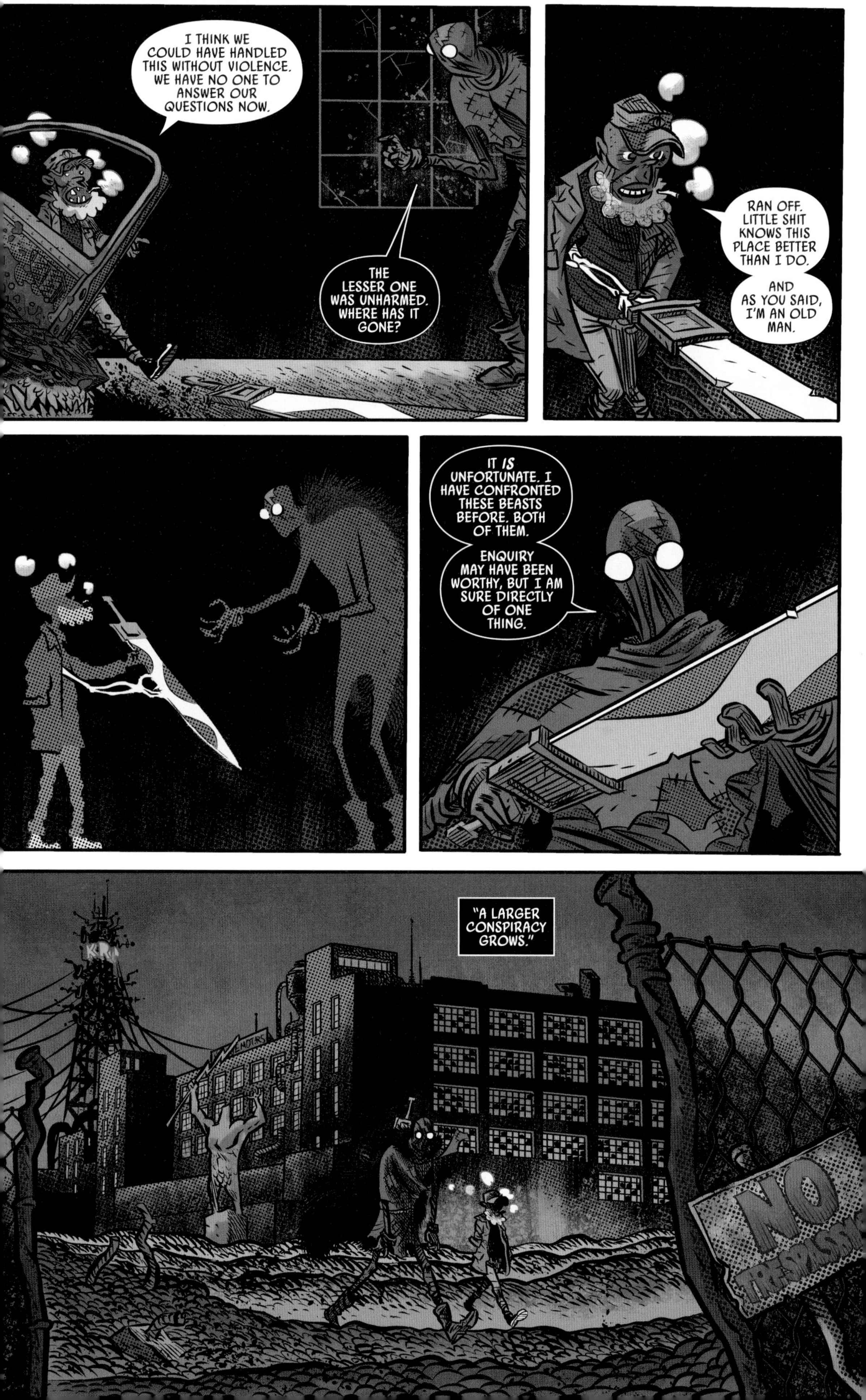

I THINK WE COULD HAVE HANDLED THIS WITHOUT VIOLENCE. WE HAVE NO ONE TO ANSWER OUR QUESTIONS NOW.
THE LESSER ONE WAS UNHARMED. WHERE HAS IT GONE?
RAN OFF. LITTLE SHIT KNOWS THIS PLACE BETTER THAN I DO.
AND AS YOU SAID, I'M AN OLD MAN.
IT *IS* UNFORTUNATE. I HAVE CONFRONTED THESE BEASTS BEFORE. BOTH OF THEM.
ENQUIRY MAY HAVE BEEN WORTHY, BUT I AM SURE DIRECTLY OF ONE THING.
"A LARGER CONSPIRACY GROWS."
NO

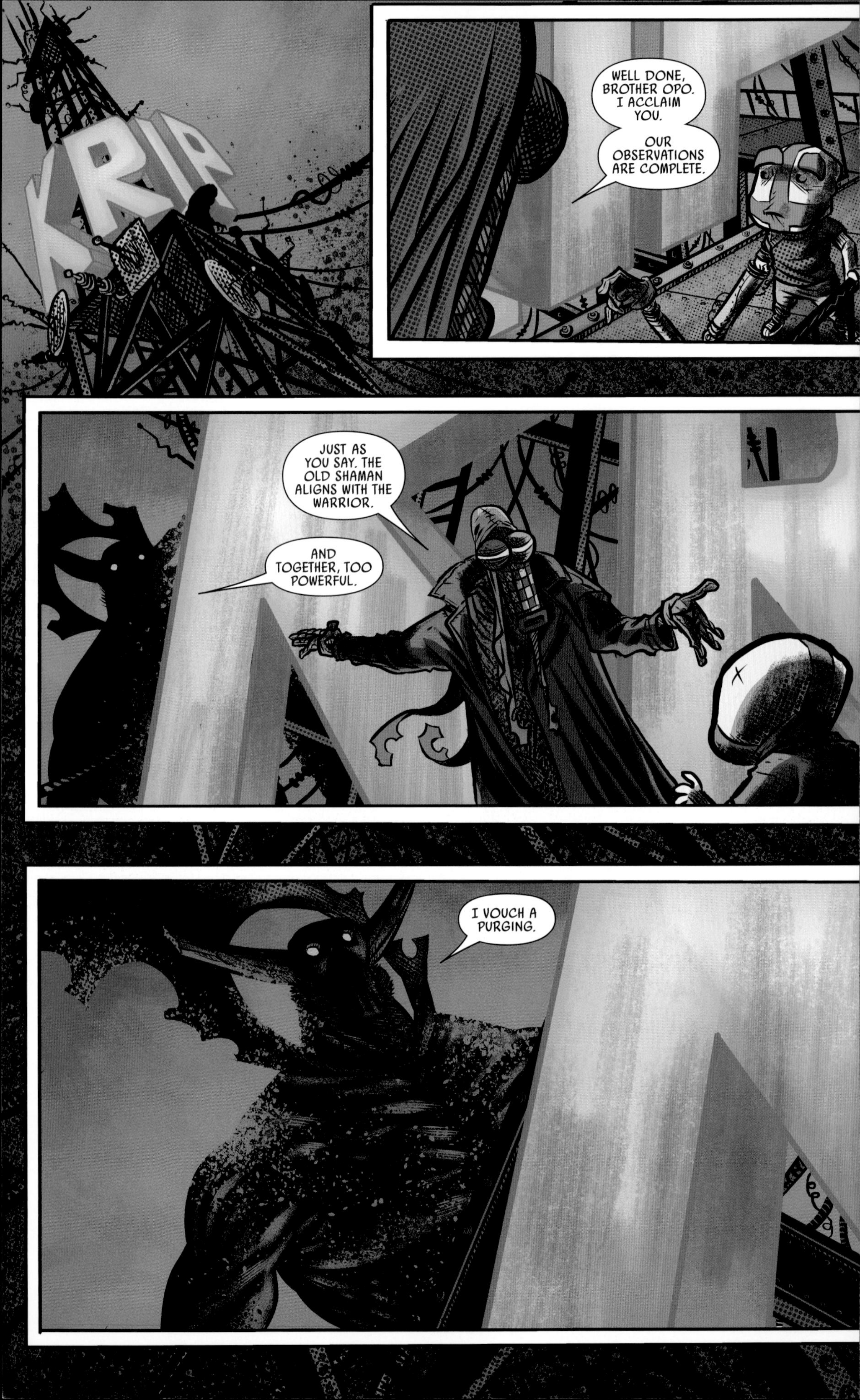

KRIP
WELL DONE, BROTHER OPO. I ACCLAIM YOU.
OUR OBSERVATIONS ARE COMPLETE.
JUST AS YOU SAY. THE OLD SHAMAN ALIGNS WITH THE WARRIOR.
AND TOGETHER, TOO POWERFUL.
I VOUCH A PURGING.

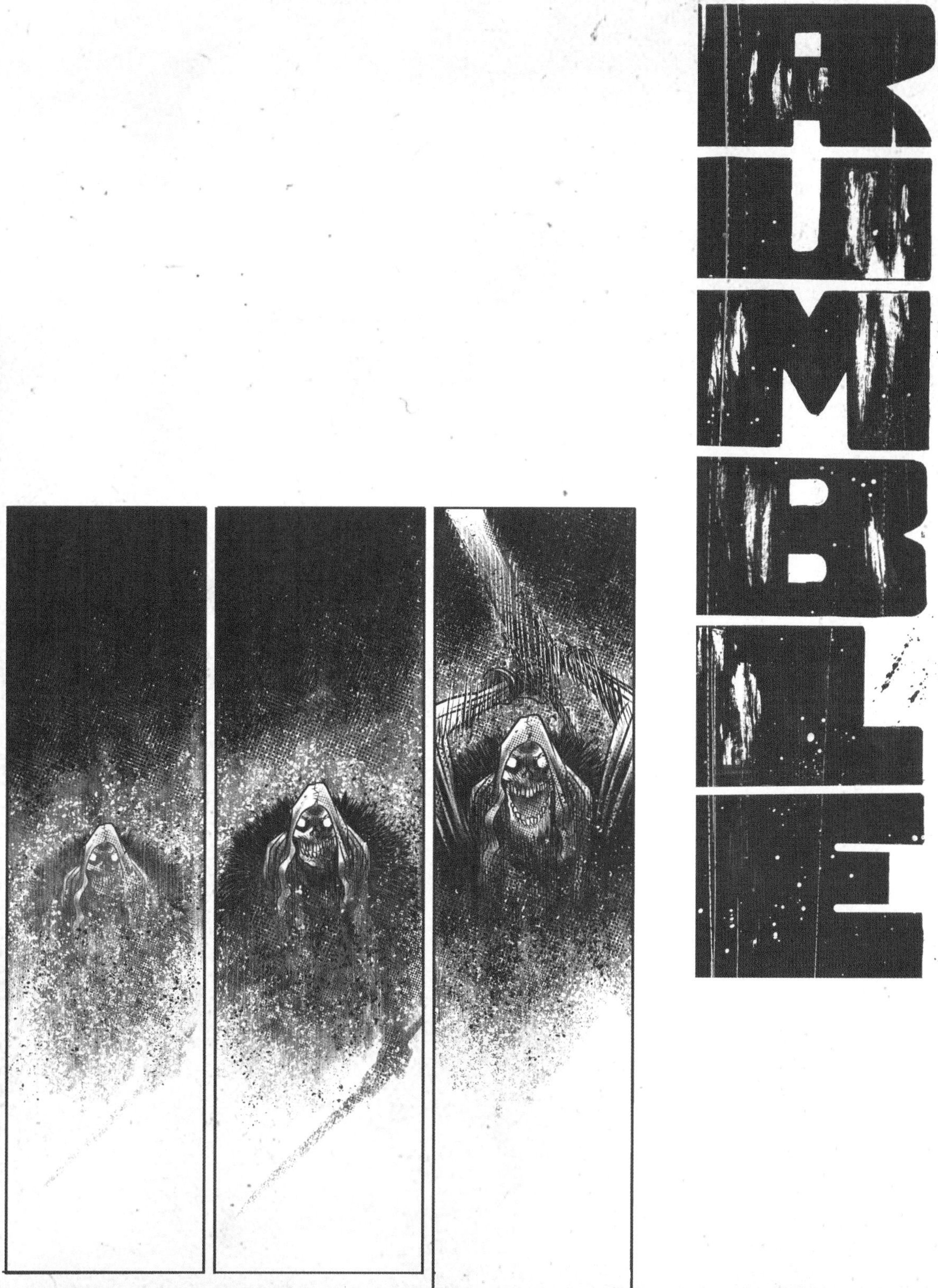
RUMBLE

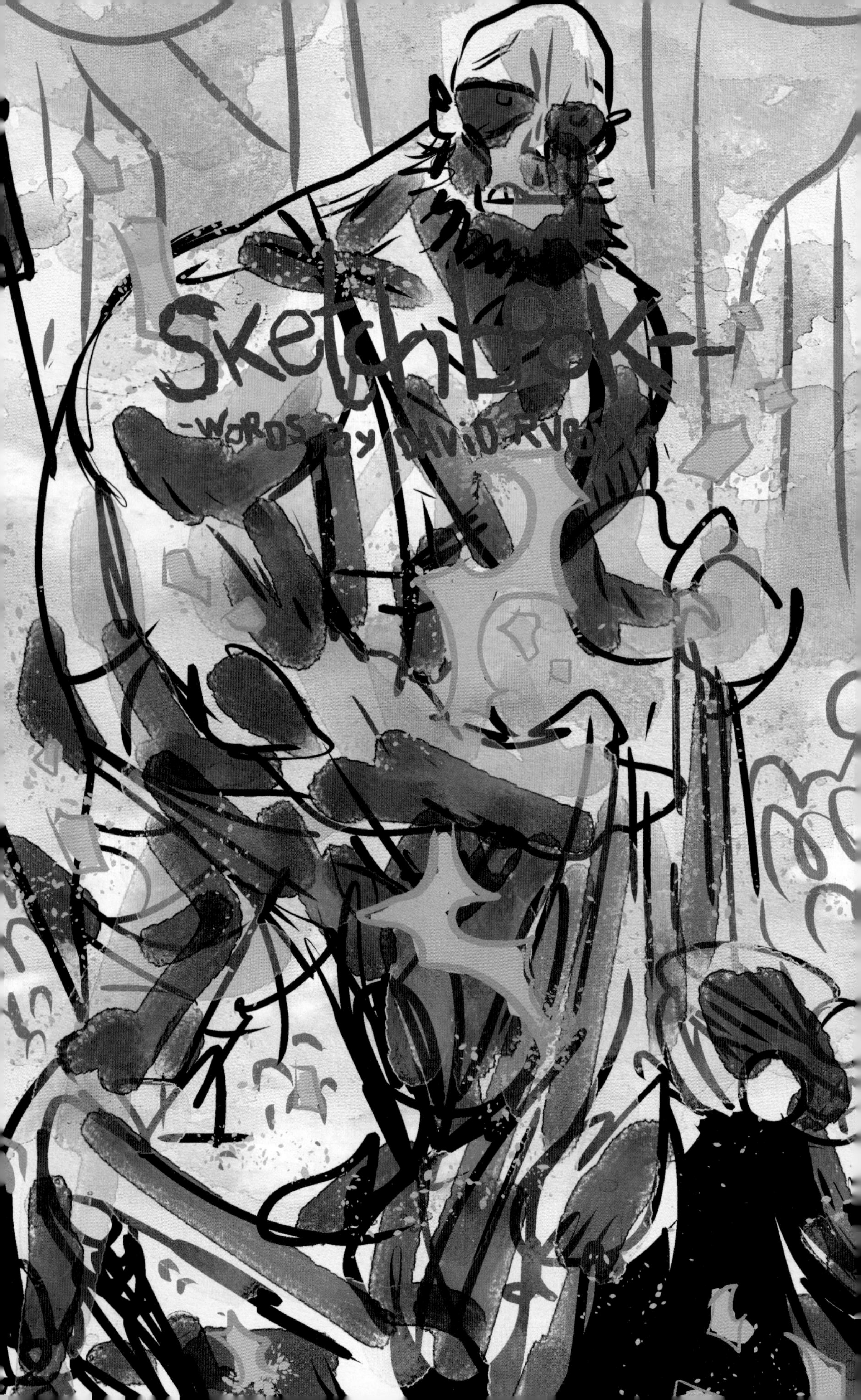
Sketchbook-
-WORDS BY DAVID RUB

## WELL, LET'S TALK ABOUT THE COVERS!!

THE COVER IS PERHAPS THE MOST IMPORTANT ELEMENT OF A MONTHLY COMIC. IT IS, AFTER ALL, THE FIRST POINT OF CONTACT BETWEEN THE READERS AND THE CREATORS' WORK. UNSURPRISINGLY, THERE'S A BIT OF A PROCESS TO GETTING THE COVER JUST RIGHT.

HERE'S THE ROUGH COVER OF THE TRADE PAPERBACK YOU NOW HAVE IN YOUR HANDS THAT INITIALLY WENT TO JOHN. THERE'S A LOT OF GRAPHIC INFORMATION HERE THAT I DELETED AS I WENT THROUGH THE NEXT STEPS. THAT'S ALL PART OF MY SEARCH TO FIND THE BEST AND MOST ICONIC IMAGE THAT BEST SERVES THE COVER OF A WHOLE COLLECTION.

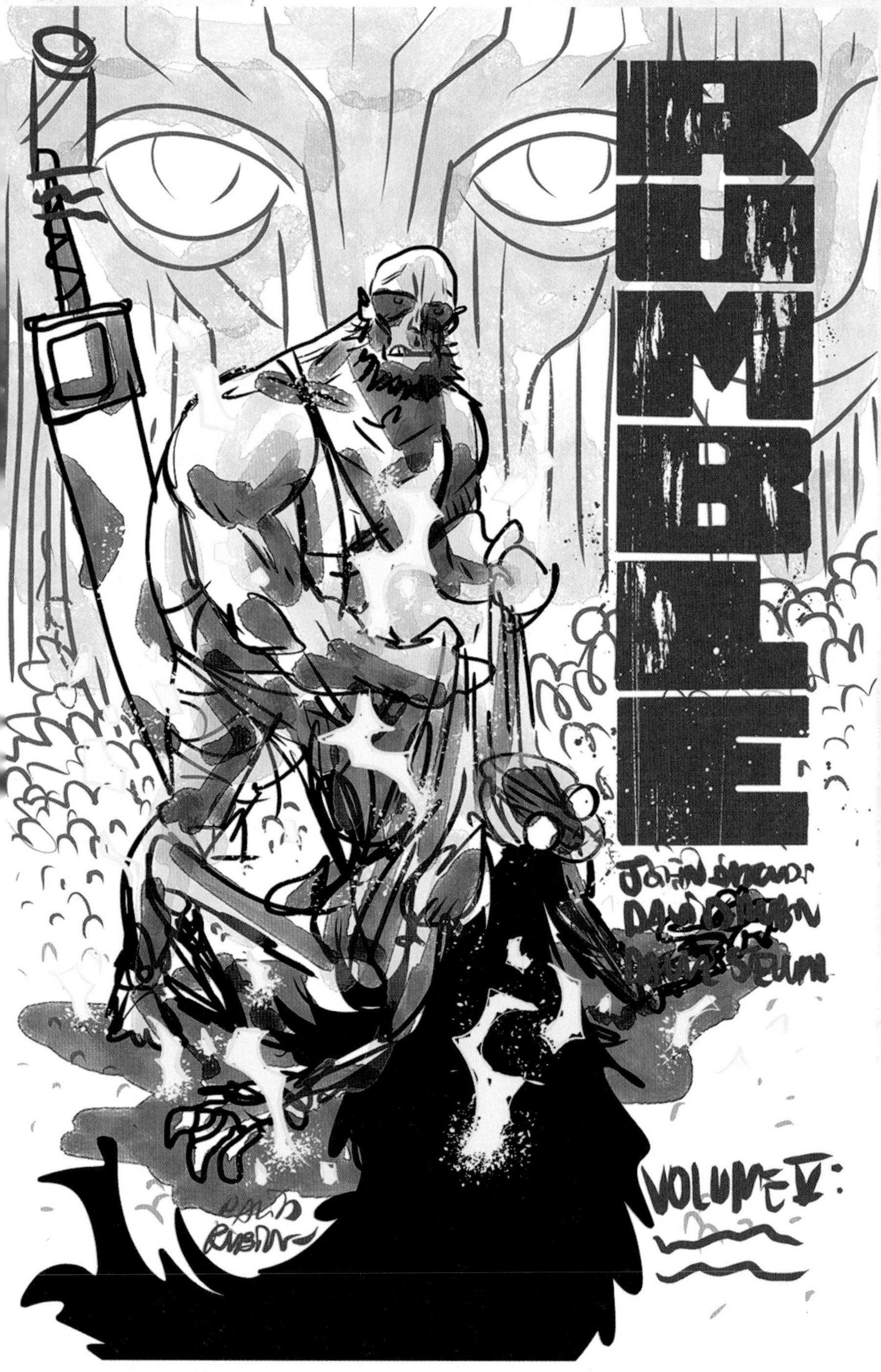
RUMBLE
VOLUME V:

NOTE: WHEN I WORK ON A ROUGH FOR A COVER, I ALWAYS INCLUDE THE LOGO AND OTHER DESIGN ELEMENTS. IT'S IMPORTANT FOR ME TO HAVE A SENSE OF HOW THE COVER WILL LOOK WITH ALL THE TRADE DRESS AND HOW THOSE THINGS WILL PLAY OUT AGAINST THE IMAGE. IT ALSO HELPS OTHERS TO VISUALIZE THE FINAL COVER AND SPEEDS UP THE APPROVAL PROCESS.

IN THE SECOND STEP, I DRAW UP THE COVER. I WORK DIGITALLY SO I CAN MORE EASILY FIX ANY PROBLEMS.

I LEARNED TO DRAW TRADITIONALLY–INK OVER PENCILS ON PAPER. SO WHEN I WORK DIGITALLY, I TRY TO USE WHATEVER NEW TOOLS I CAN TO REPRODUCE THE SAME LOOK OF TRADITIONAL ART. AS A RESULT, OTHER ARTISTS SOMETIMES ASK WHAT BRUSH OR PEN I USE ON RUMBLE AND ARE SURPRISED TO DISCOVER THAT I WORK DIGITALLY. THAT'S ALWAYS THE AIM. I DON'T WANT ANYBODY TO BE THINKING ABOUT HOW THE ART WAS PRODUCED WHEN THEY READ RUMBLE. THIS PRINTED COMIC SHOULD BE A GOLDEN TICKET TO THE FANTASY AND (HOPEFULLY) JOY OF ENTERING INTO ANOTHER WORLD. EVERYTHING ELSE IS SECONDARY.

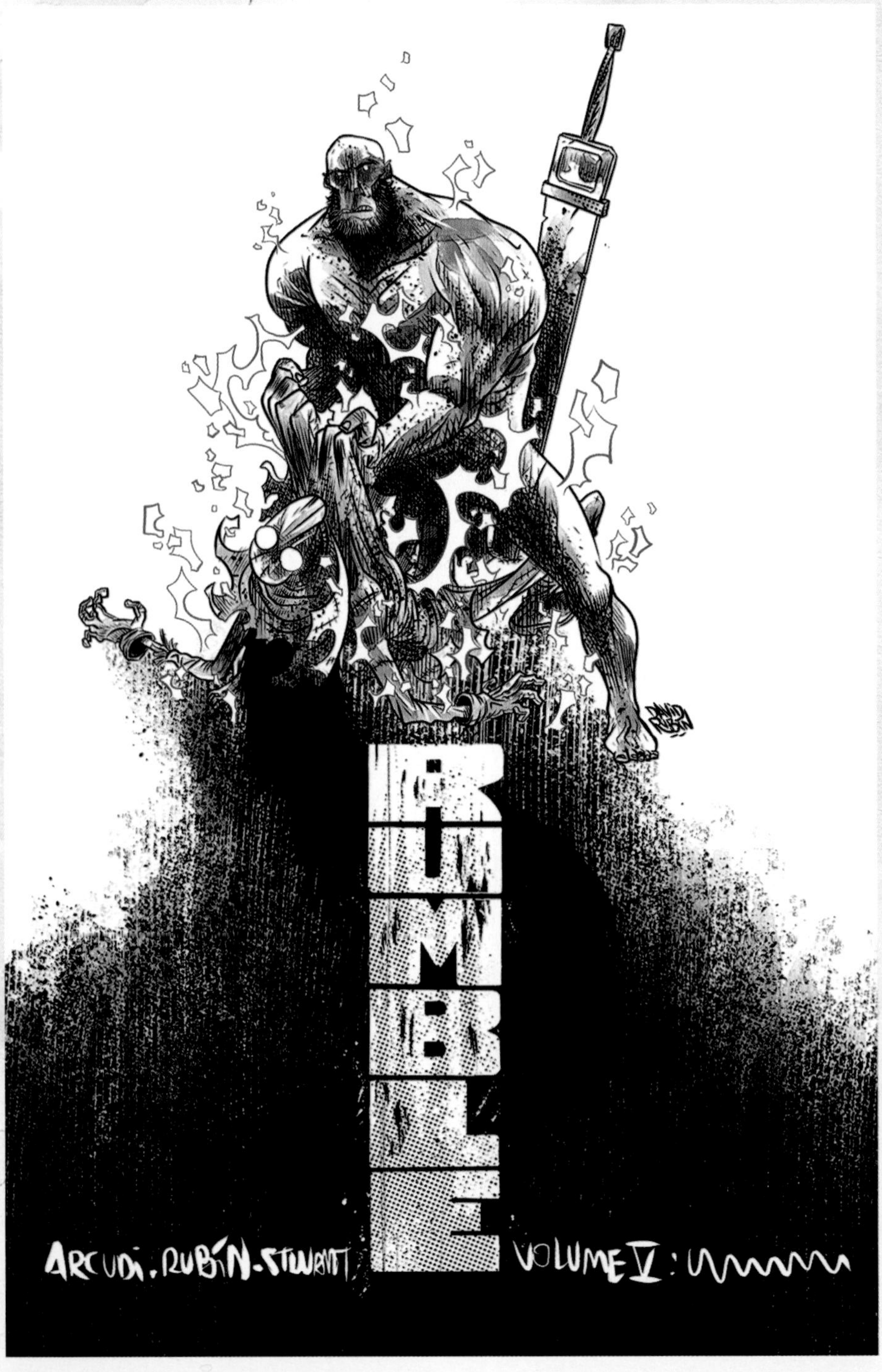

DAVID RUBIN
RUMBLE
ARCUDI . RUBIN . STEWART
VOLUME V :


NOTE: AS YOU CAN SEE, I CHANGED THE COMPOSITION FROM THE ROUGH, GOT RID OF THE BACKGROUND, AND CHANGED THE SIZE AND LOCATION OF THE LOGO–AND THE CHARACTERS, FOR THAT MATTER. IT'S SIMPLER AND BOLDER. THE FIRE YOU SEE HERE IS ON A SEPARATE LAYER AND I COLORED PINK TO GIVE ME AN IDEA OF HOW MY FINAL COLORS WILL PLAY OUT. I DO THE SAME THING WITH THE INTERIORS–WHICH ARE COLORED BY DAVE STEWART.

COLOR IS ONE OF MY FAVORITE PARTS! DAVE STEWART DOES MAGNIFICENT WORK ON THE INTERIORS, AND LIKE EVERYBODY ELSE, I LOVE HIS COLORS. BUT FOR THE COVERS, I PREFER TO DO THE COLORS MYSELF BECAUSE I REALLY LOVE DOING IT.

WHEN I FINISH THE LINE ART, I SEND THE B&W COVER TO THE FLATTER, KIKE J. DIAZ. I STARTED WORKING WITH KIKE THREE YEARS AGO AS MY FLATTER ON ETHER.

KIKE COMES BACK WITH THE FLAT COLORS ON A SEPARATE LAYER (A).

ORIGINALLY THE COVER WAS DONE UP RED (B), WHICH WORKED FINE, BUT JOHN REMINDED ME THAT THE PREVIOUS TRADE HAD A SIMILAR COLOR SCHEME, SO I SWITCHED IT TO BLUE (C), AND AT LAST WE HAVE THE COVER FOR RUMBLE VOLUME 5!

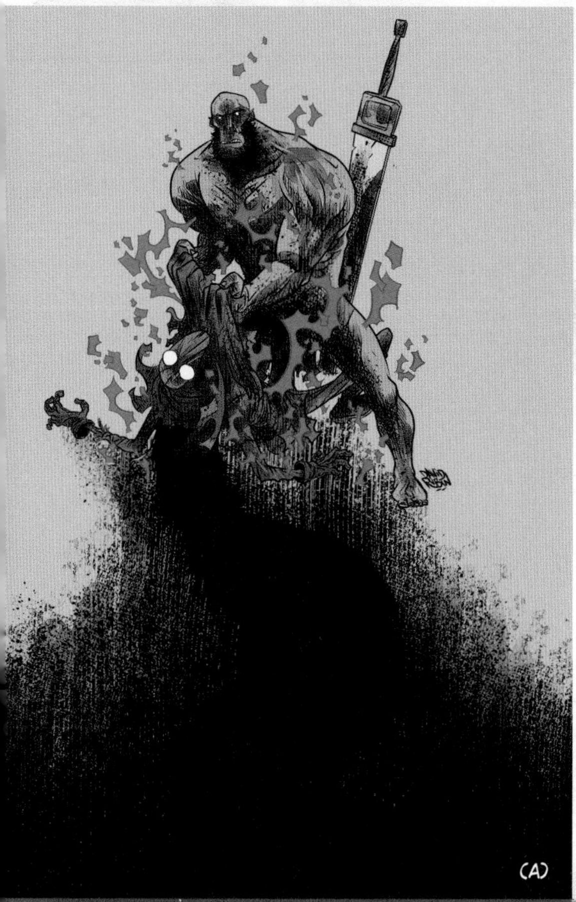
(A)

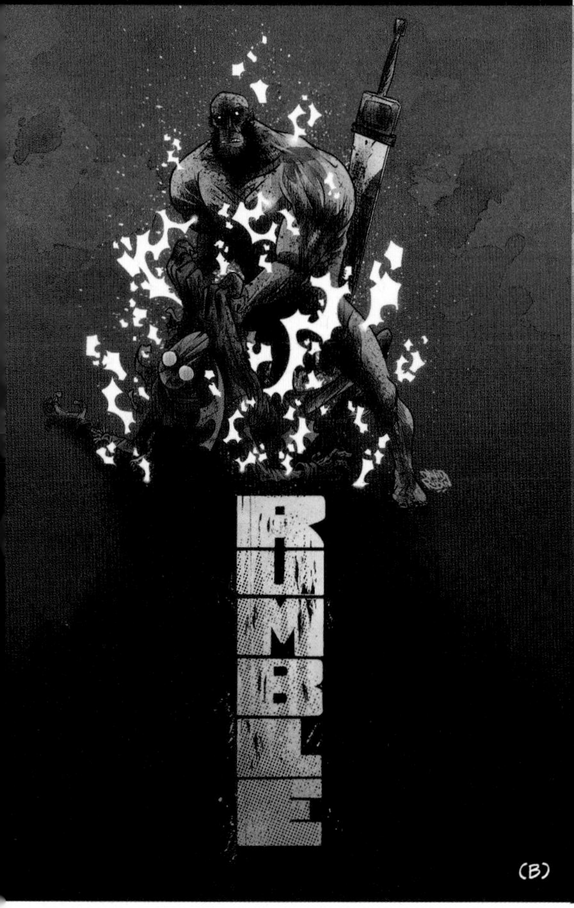
RUMBLE
(B)

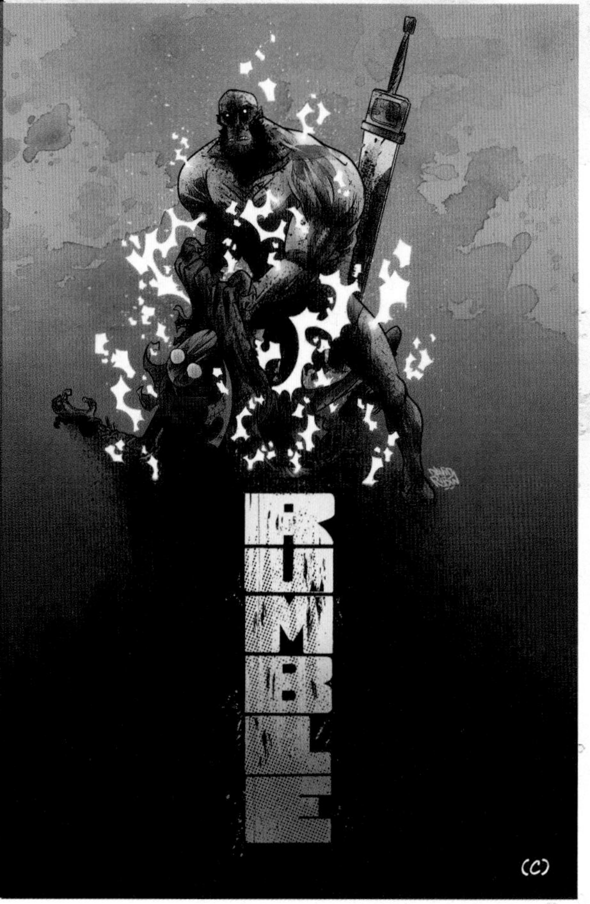
RUMBLE
(C)

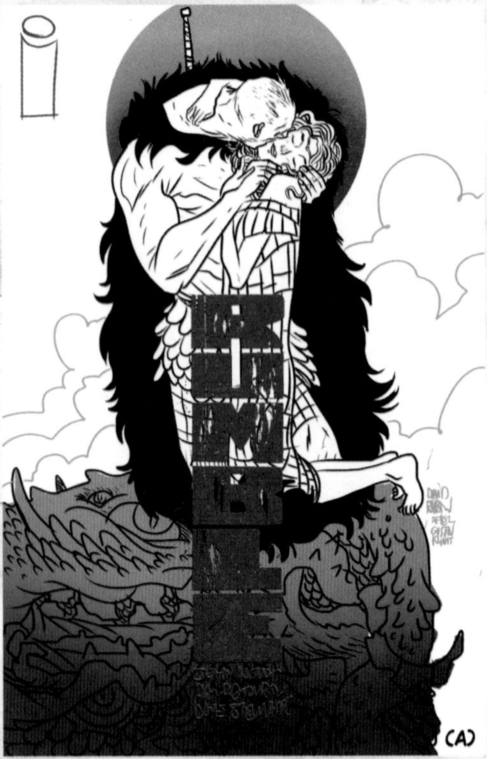
RUMBLE

(A)

HERE IS ONE OF MY FAVORITE COVERS OF THIS ARC (ISSUE #8). WHEN I STARTED THIS COVER I WAS THINKING ABOUT THE RELATIONSHIP BETWEEN GODRAQ (THAT'S WHAT JOHN AND I CALL THE WARRIOR GOD VERSION OF RATHRAQ) AND HIS WIFE, ISHIA. IT'S AN IMPORTANT PART OF THIS ISSUE, SO I FOCUSED ALL MY ATTENTION ON THEM.

RUMBLE HAS HAD A WONDERFUL VARIETY OF COVERS EVER SINCE THE AMAZING JAMES HARREN STARTED DOING THEM, AND I TRY TO CONTINUE THAT TRADITION. BUT I REALIZED THAT WE'VE NEVER HAD A ROMANCE COVER. THAT THOUGHT LED ME TO ONE OF THE GREATEST IMAGES REPRESENTING LOVE IN ALL ITS POWER AND BEAUTY: THE KISS BY AUSTRIAN PAINTER GUSTAV KLIMT.

(A) IS THE ROUGH WITH YOUNG GODRAQ AND ISHIA. AND SINCE IT'S KLIMT, JOHN LOVES THE IDEA, SO I'M ON TO STEP TWO.

WITH THE LINE ART (B), I TRIED TO BE FAITHFUL TO THE ORIGINAL PAINTING, BUT AT THE SAME TIME, I DIDN'T WANT IT TO BE JUST A COPY. IN OTHER WORDS, I WANTED IT TO BE AN HOMAGE, BUT 100% RUMBLESQUE TOO.

SO I DIDN'T CHANGE MY STYLE OR TRY TO APPROPRIATE KLIMT'S STYLE OR THE PROPORTIONS OF THE ORIGINAL CHARACTERS. I JUST USED KLIMT'S COMPOSITION.

HOWEVER, ISHIA'S DRESS IS A DIRECT REFERENCE TO KLIMT'S PAINTING. TO ME, THE SHAPE AND TEXTURE OF THAT DRESS ARE THE MOST IMPORTANT THINGS IN THE ORIGINAL, SO I MUST USE THEM–OF COURSE!

IN THE PAINTING, THE CHARACTERS EMBRACE OVER A COMPOSITION OF GRASS AND FLOWERS. I CHANGED THAT TO A COMPOSITION OF MONSTERS. I MEAN, THIS IS A COVER FOR RUMBLE, AFTER ALL!

NOTE: EACH COLOR YOU SEE HERE IS ON A SEPARATE LAYER.

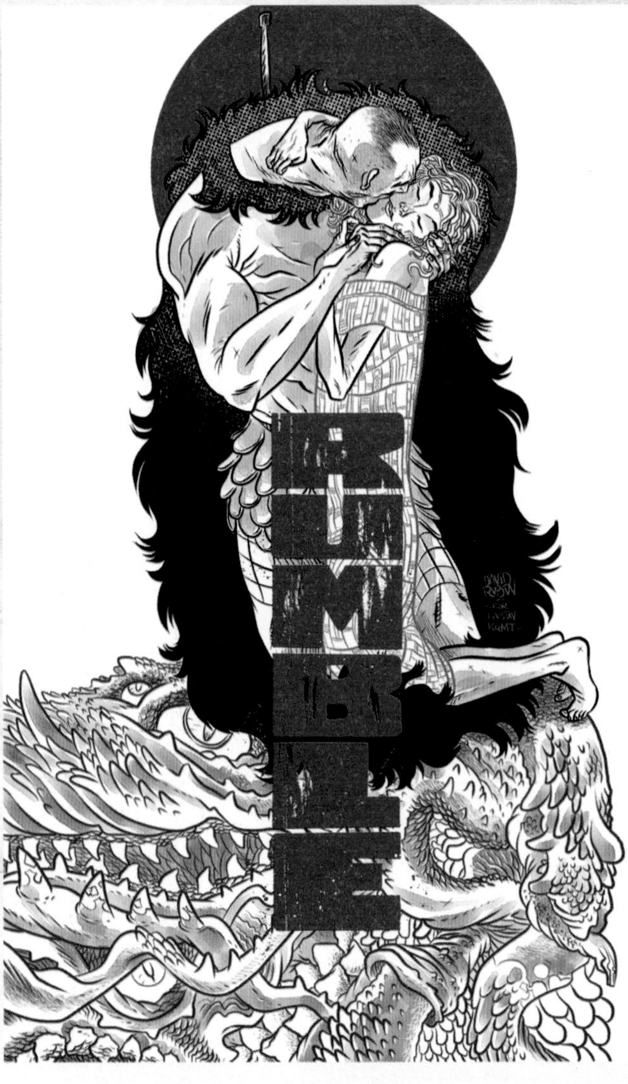
RUMBLE

(B)

(C)

AS WITH THE TRADE COVER, I SENT THE LINE ART TO KIKE FOR FLATTING. (C)

WHEN I GOT THE FLATS, I STARTED WORKING ON FINAL COLORS (D). THE MOST DIFFICULT PART WAS TRANSLATING THE BEAUTY OF THE GOLD PAINT INTO DIGITAL COLORS. KLIMT MADE HIS PAINT WITH ACTUAL GOLD DUST, AND I ONLY HAD PHOTOSHOP!

WHEN I FINISHED THE COLOR WORK, I LAYERED ON THE LOGO AGAIN. I CHANGED THE SIZE OF THE LOGO BECAUSE IT WOULD HAVE HIDDEN TOO MUCH OF THE GOLDEN DRESS.

ONE BIT OF ADVICE: WHEN DESIGNING A COVER, THINK OF YOURSELF AS A GRAPHIC DESIGNER AS MUCH AS AN ARTIST.

BELIEVE ME, IT HELPS.

WELL, THAT'S IT!!

JOHN AND I HOPE YOU ENJOY THIS NEW RUMBLE ARC AND THAT THIS SKETCHBOOK SECTION GIVES YOU A PEEK BEHIND THE SCENES—AND MAYBE INSPIRES A FEW OF YOU IN WAYS YOU CAN WORK INTO YOUR OWN ILLUSTRATIONS AND COMICS!

DAVID RUBIN
(MADRID, 12/8/2018)

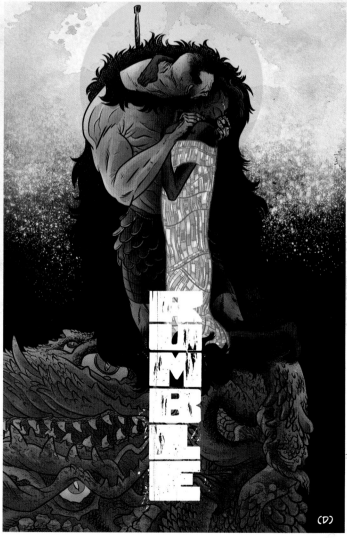

(D)

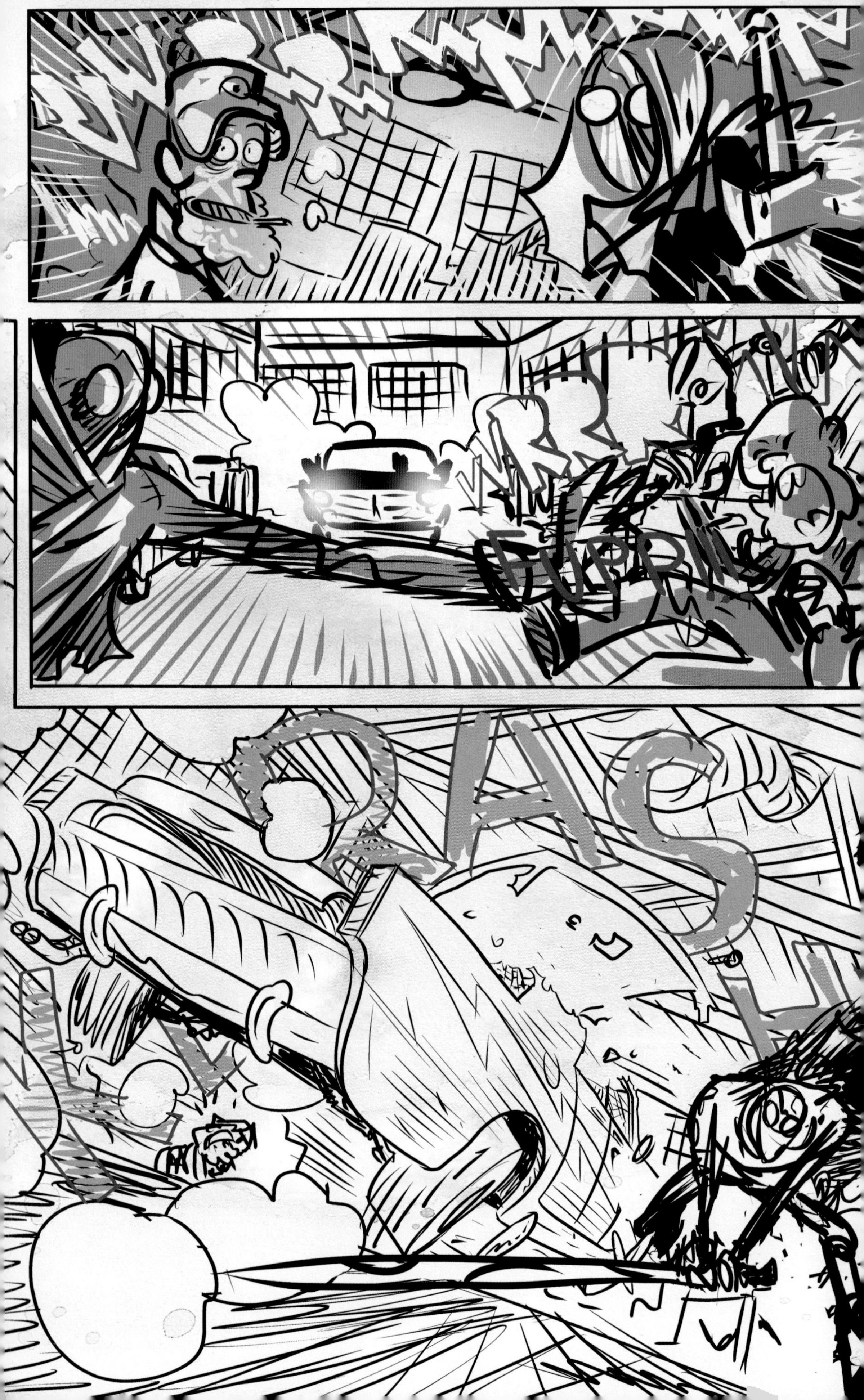
FUPP!!

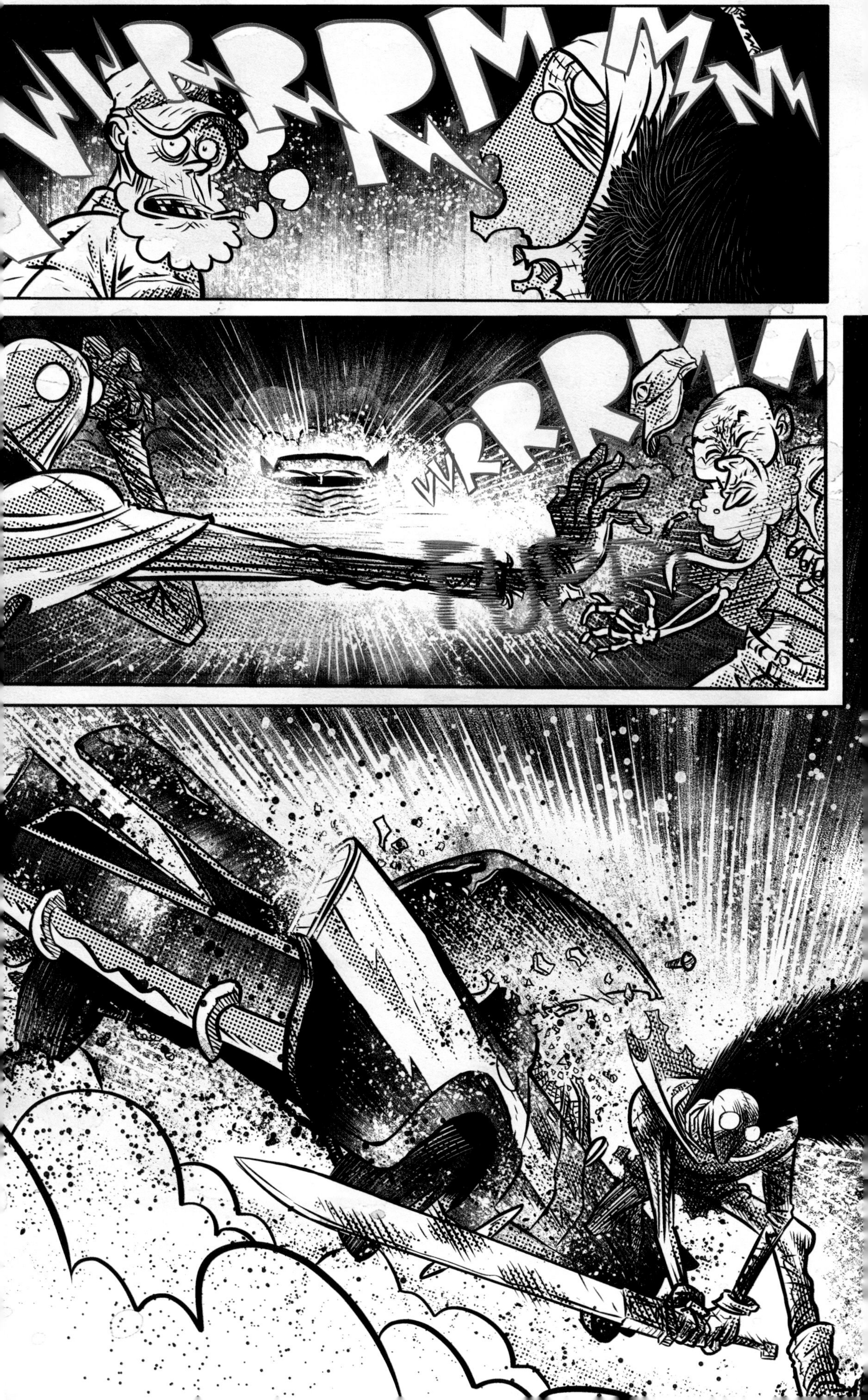
WRRRMMM
WRRRMM

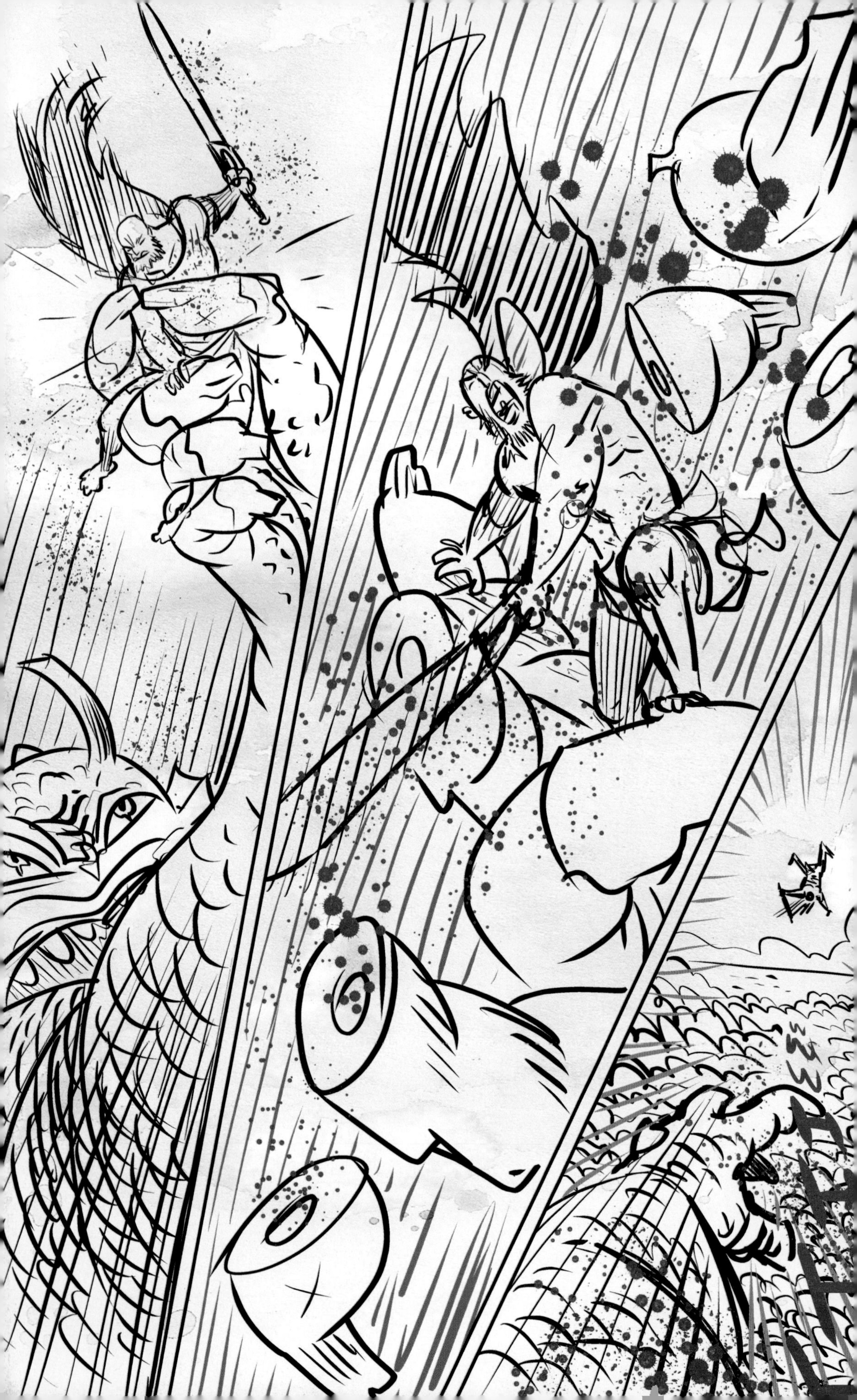

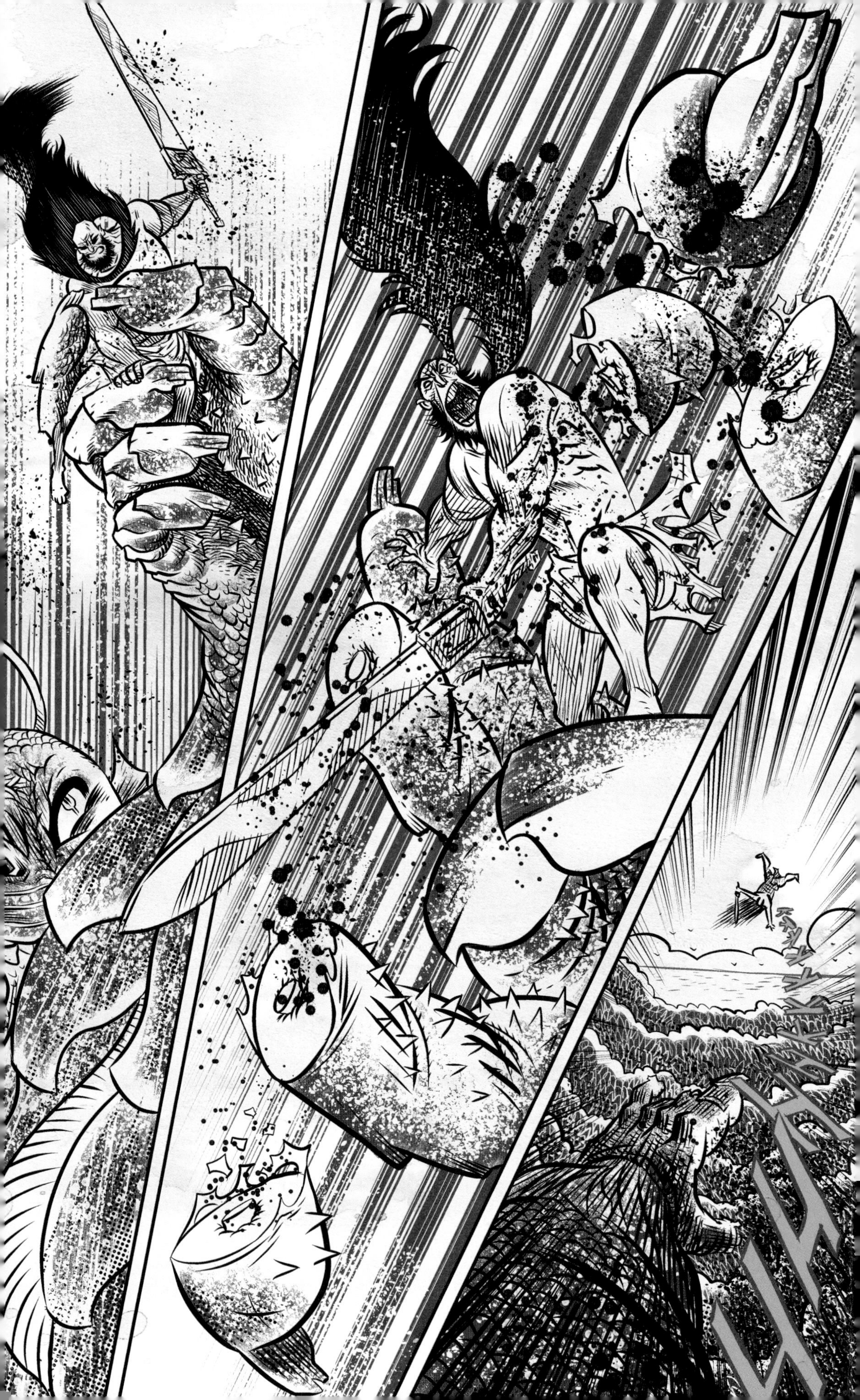

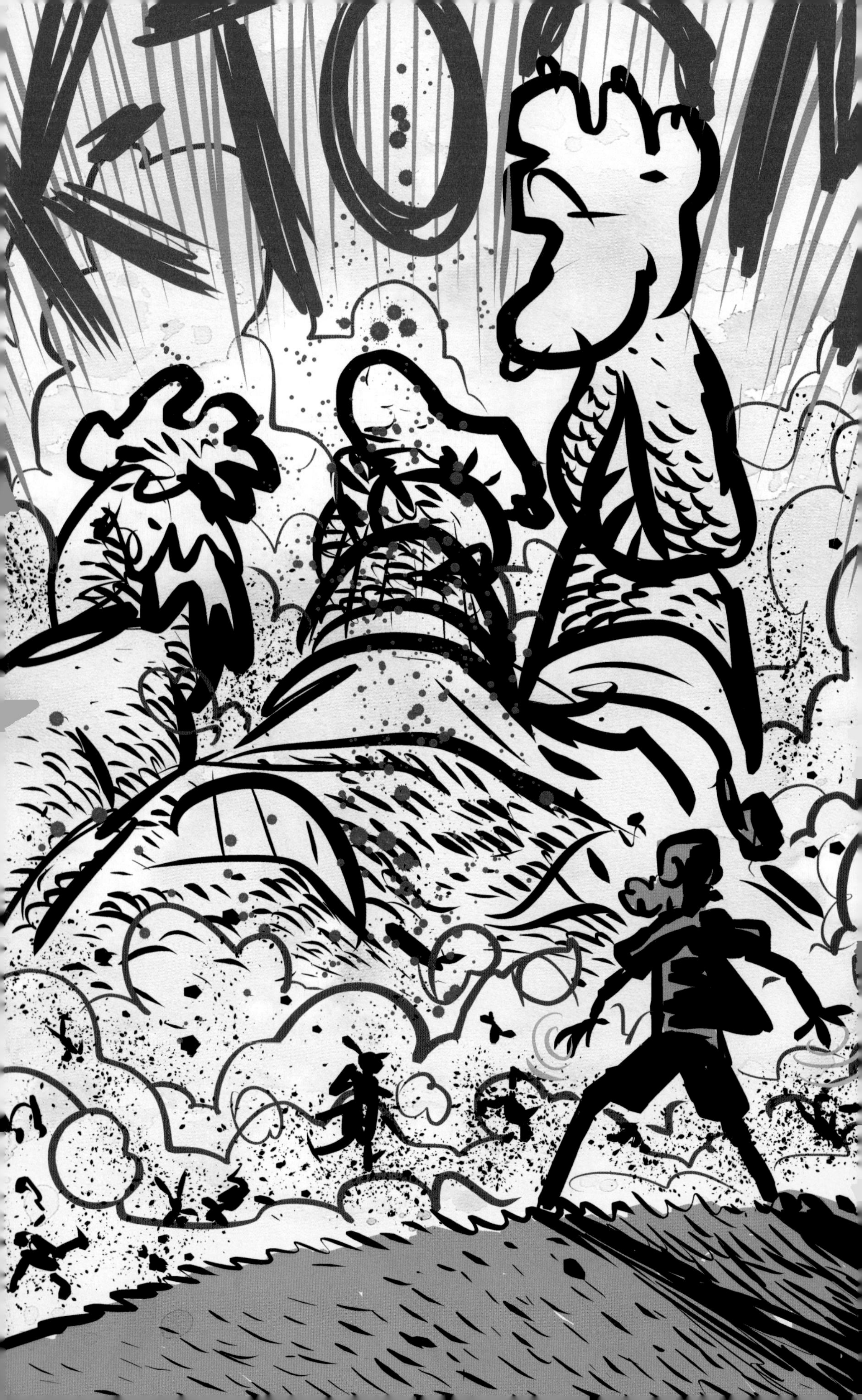

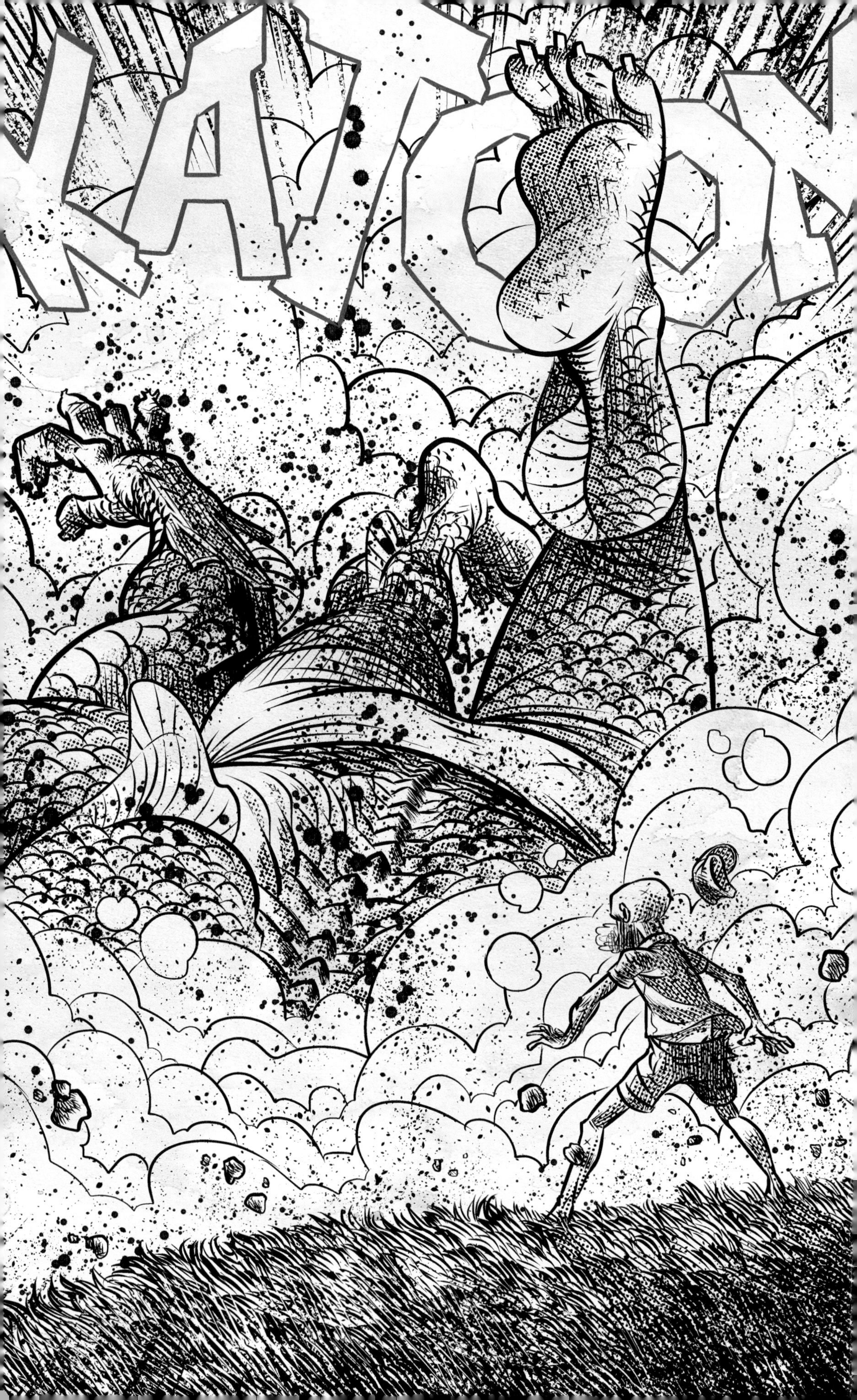

**1** art by **GONZALO RUGGIERI**
@gonzaloruggieri

**2** art by **VLAD LEGOSTAEV**
@vladlegostaev

**3** art by **IRRA**
@irra_1979

**4** art by **XURXO G PENALTA**
@xurxogpenalta

**5** art by **KIKE J. DÍAZ**
@kikejdiaz

**6** art by **JORGE MONLONGO**
@monlongo

**7** art by **ESDRAS CRISTÓBAL**
@esdrascomic

**8** art by **VALERIO GIANGIORDANO**
@valeriogiangiordanoart

**9** art by **VICTOR PUCHALSKI**
@victorpuchalski

**10** art by **JORDI PÉREZ**
@jordi_pz

**11** art by **JUAN GEDEON**
@juan_gedeon
colors by **CARLOS CABRERA**
@carloscabrera.art

**12** art by **AREMO MASSA**
@aremocreates

**13** art by **ROBERTO RICCI**
@roberto_ricci_art

**14** art by **FERNANDO BLANCO GONZÁLEZ**
@fernandoblancocomic

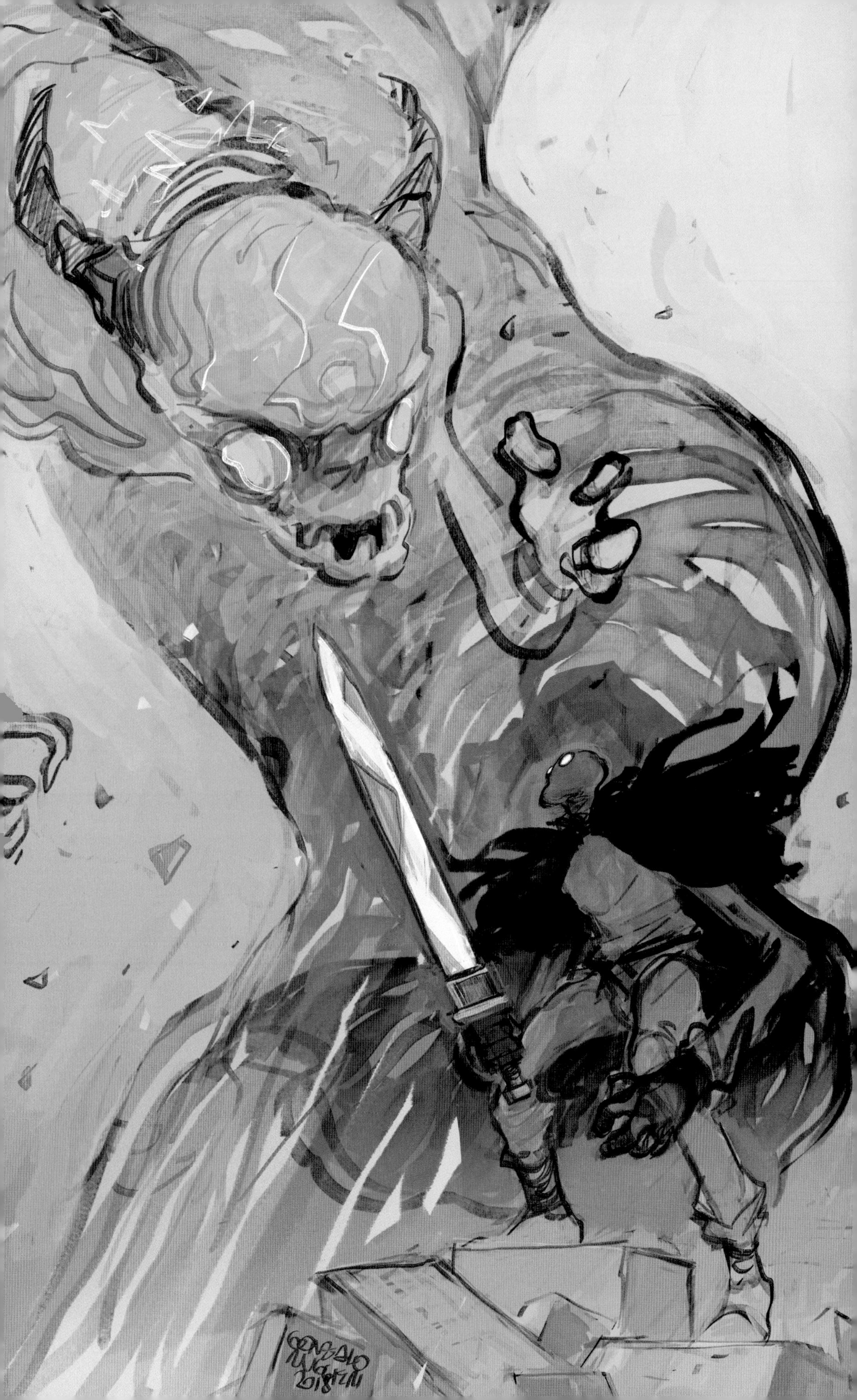

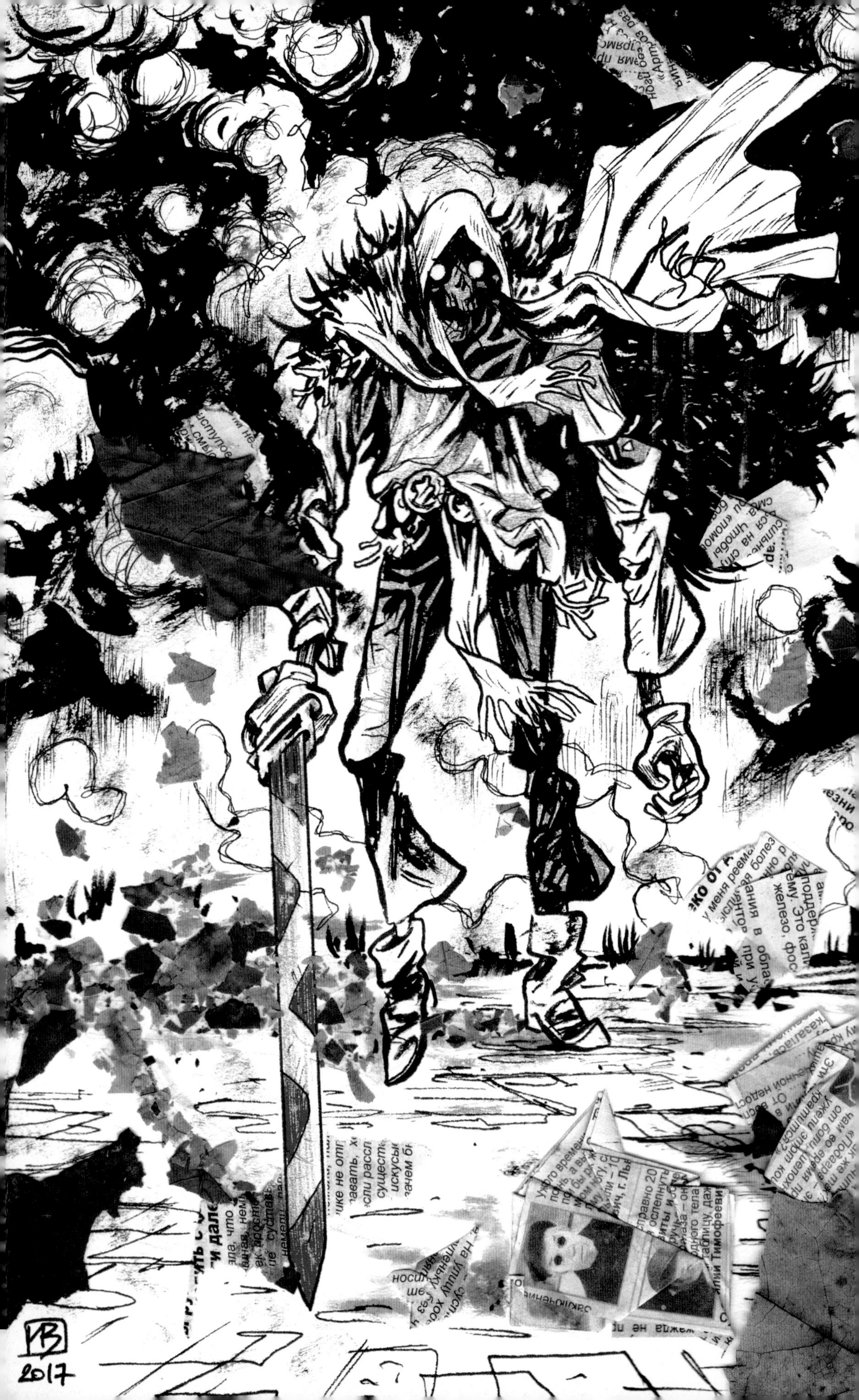
2017

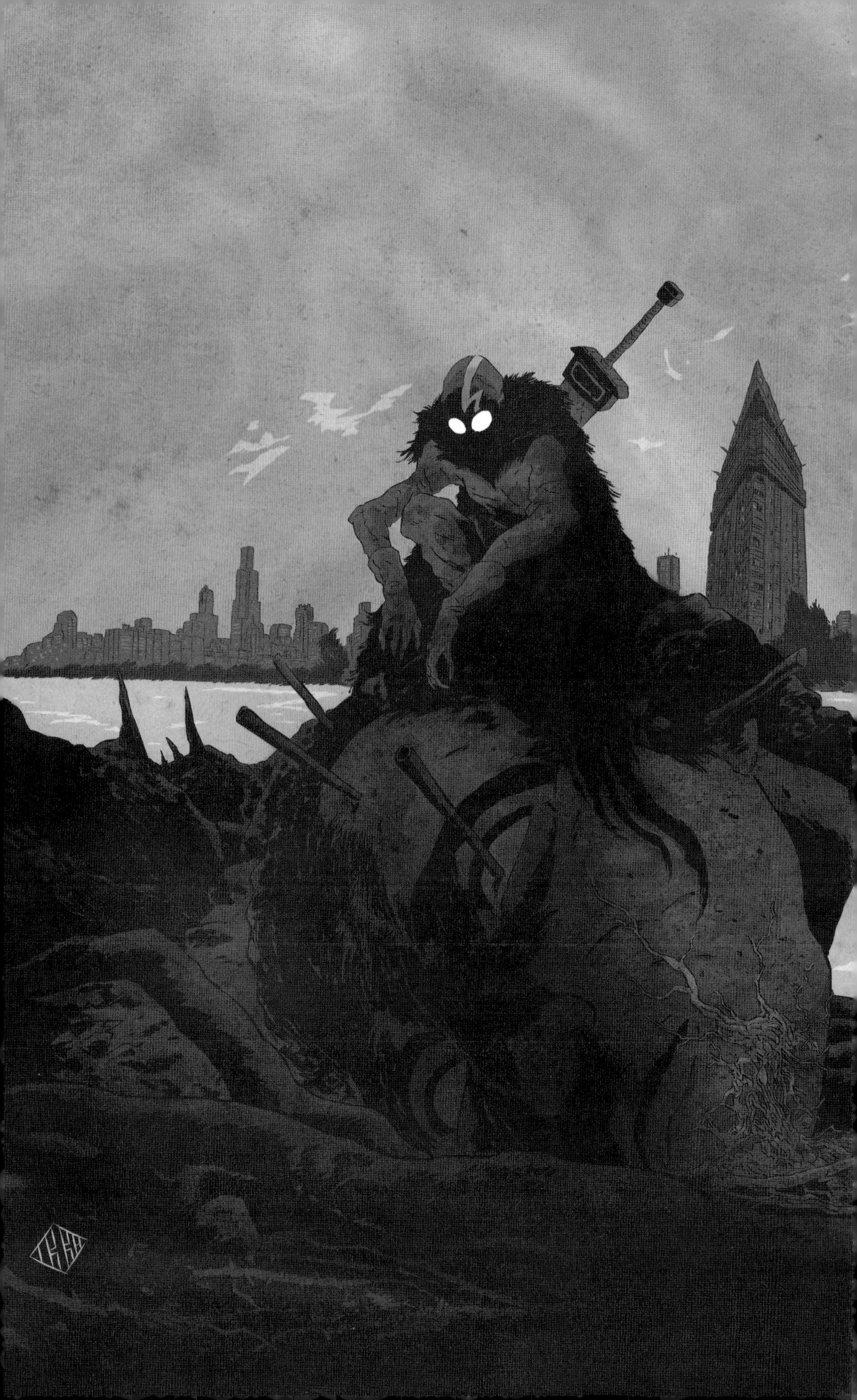

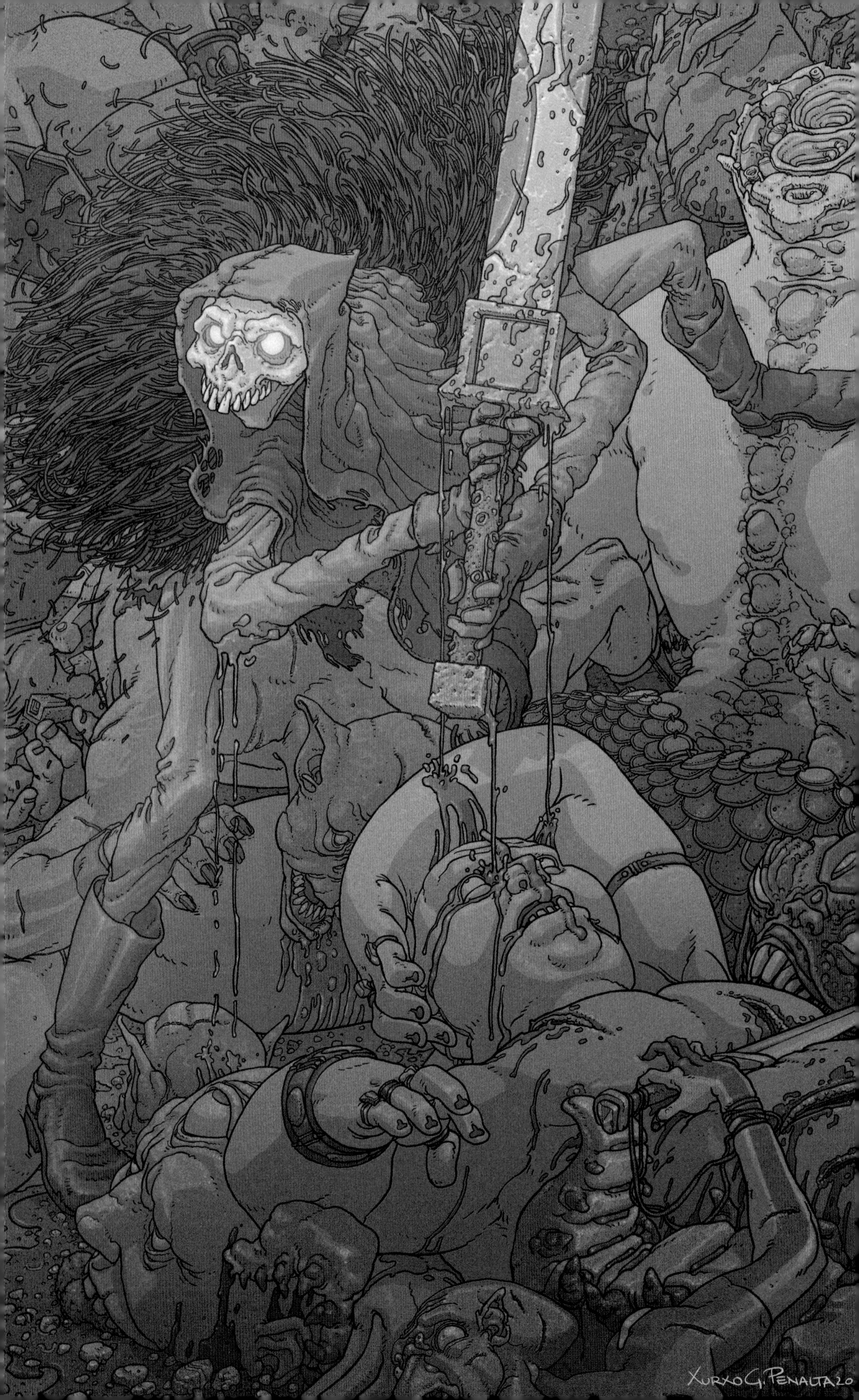
XURXO G. PENALTA 20

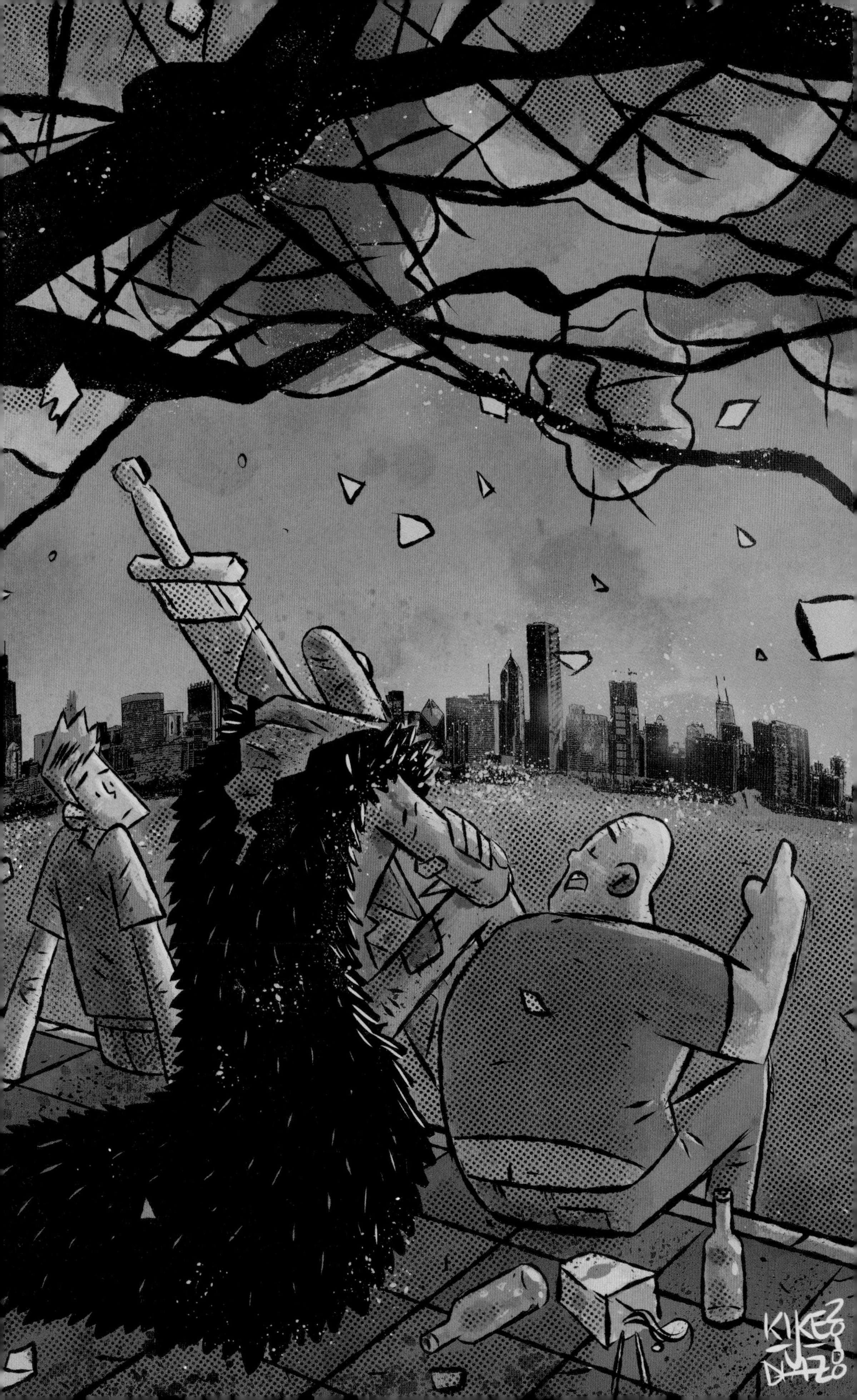

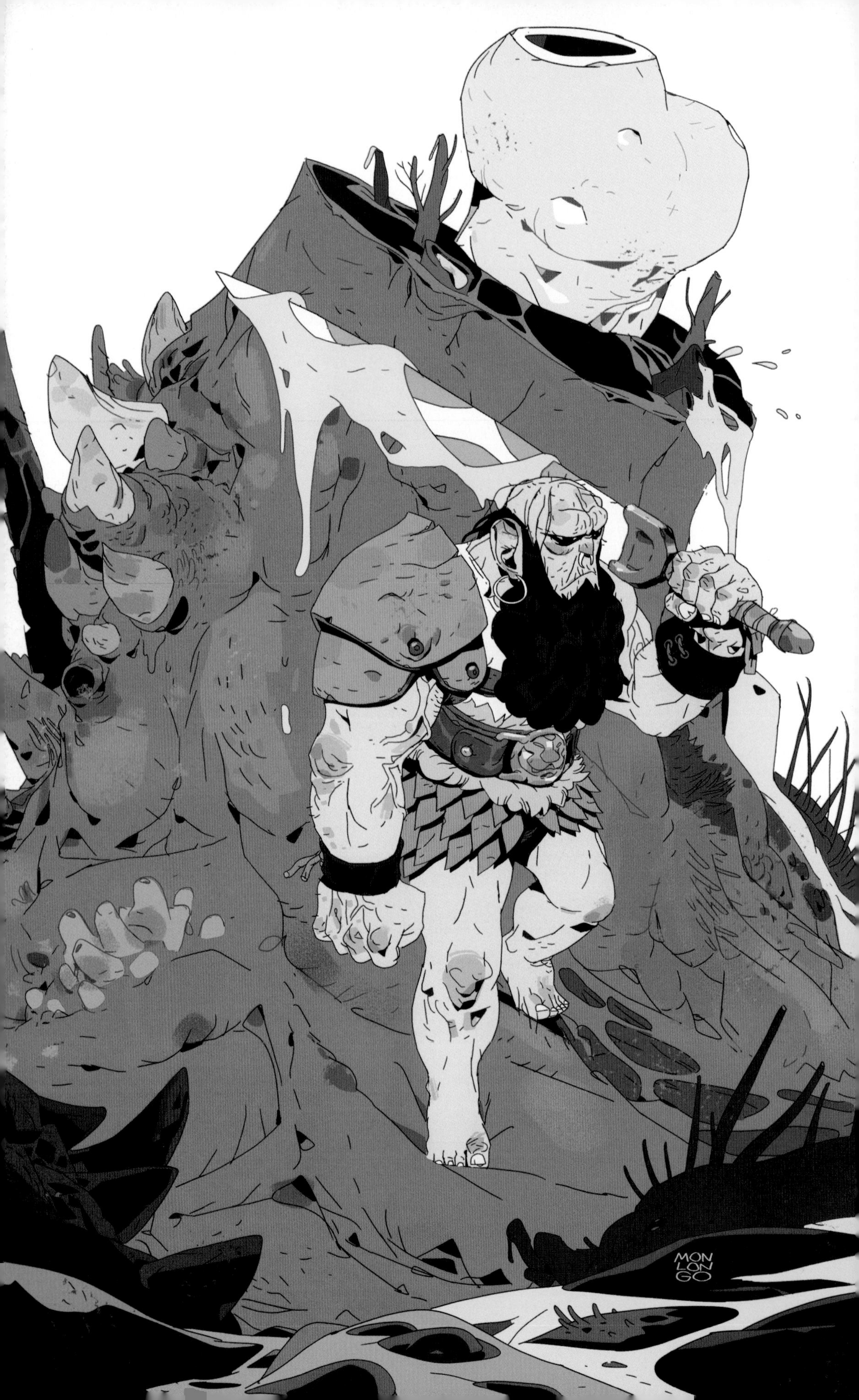
MON
LON
GO

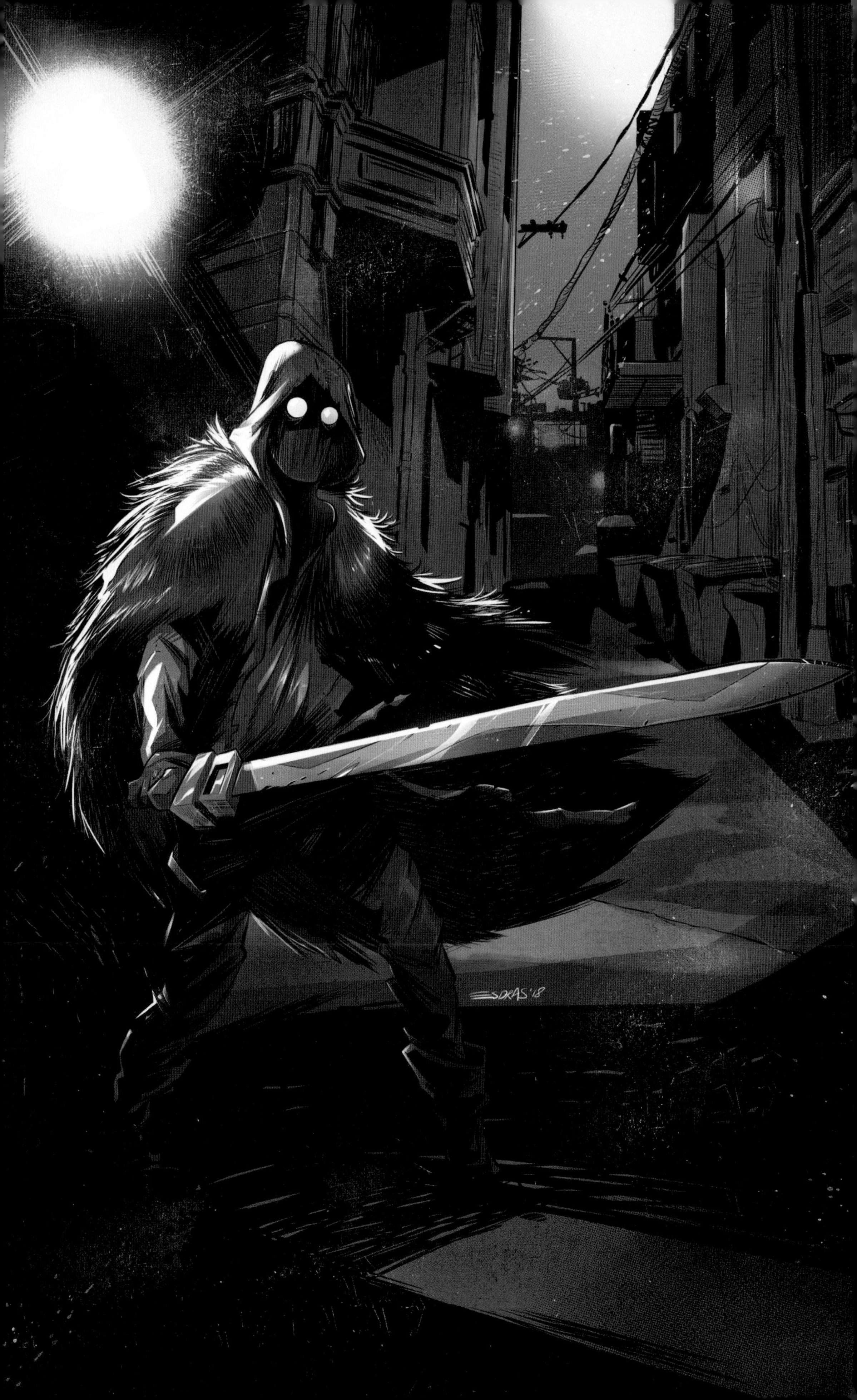
ESDRAS '18

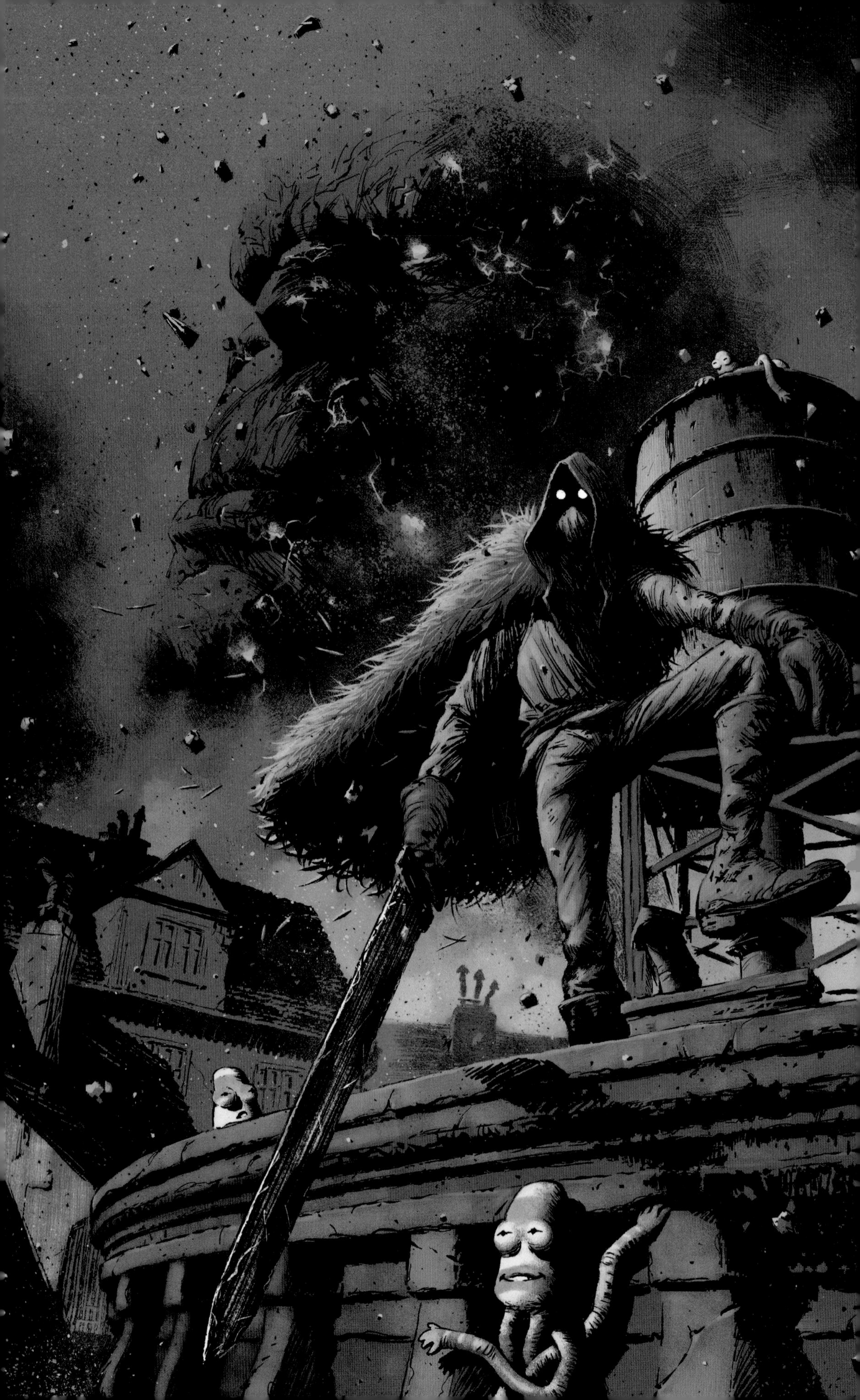

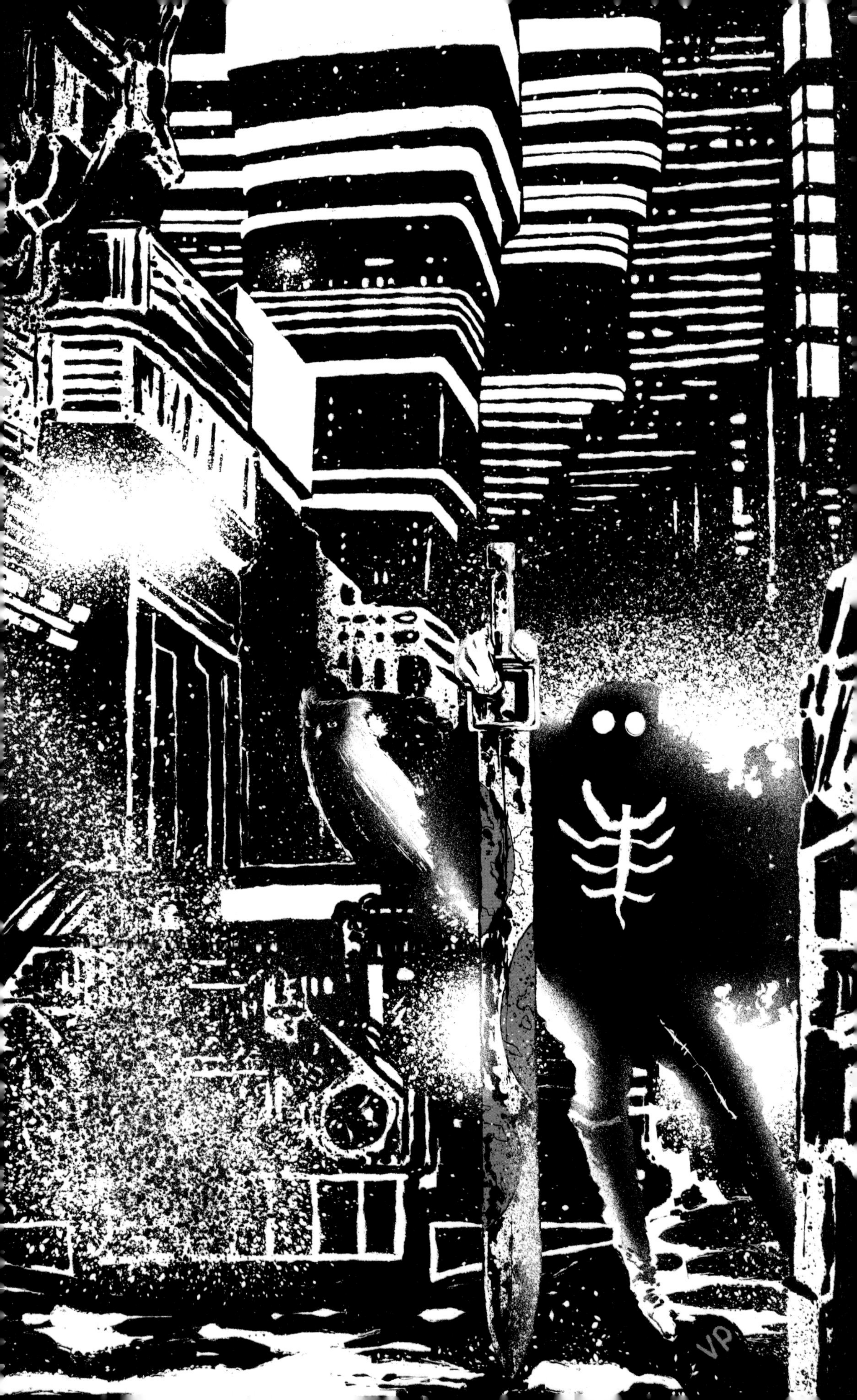

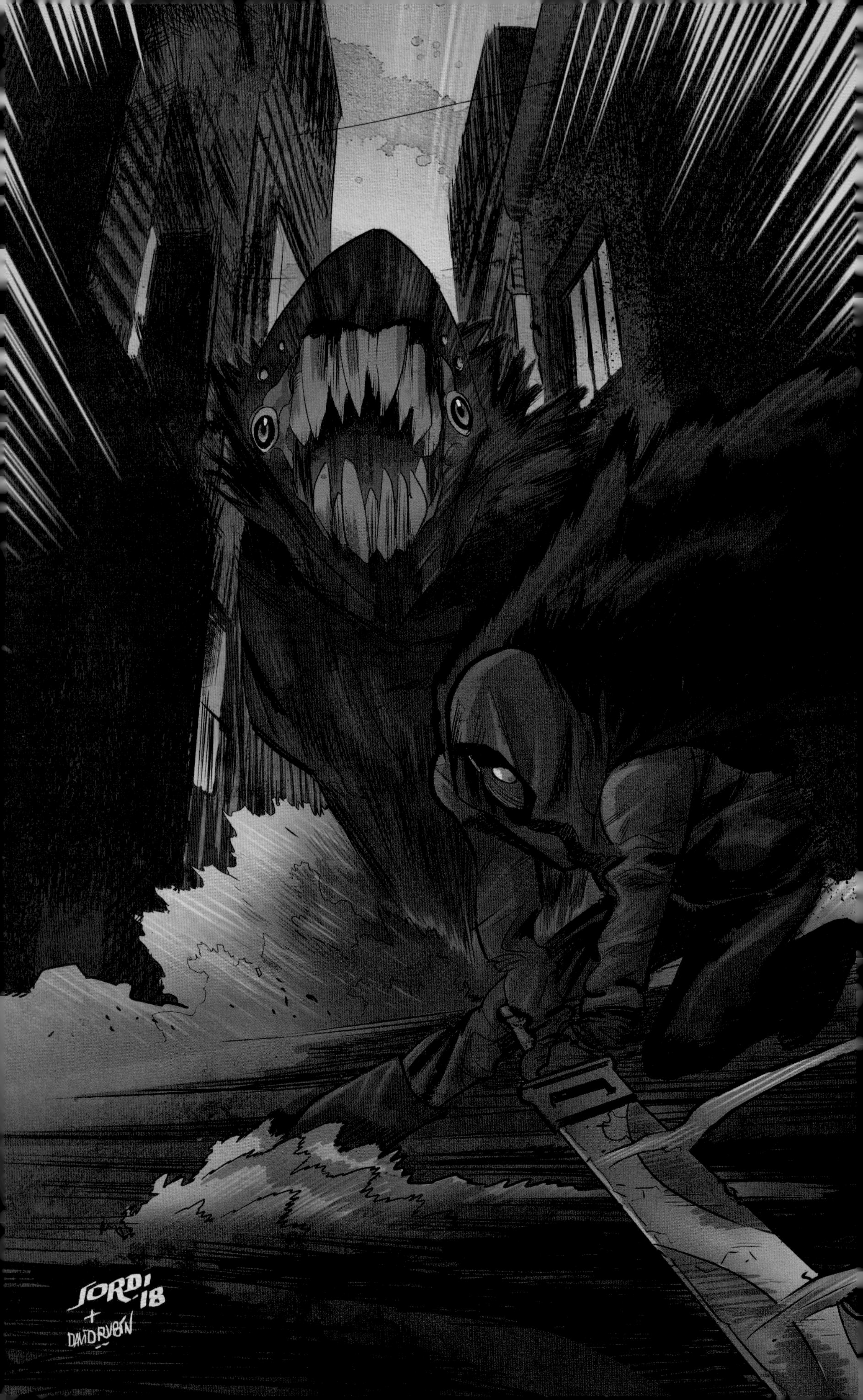
JORDI '18
+
DAVID RUBÍN

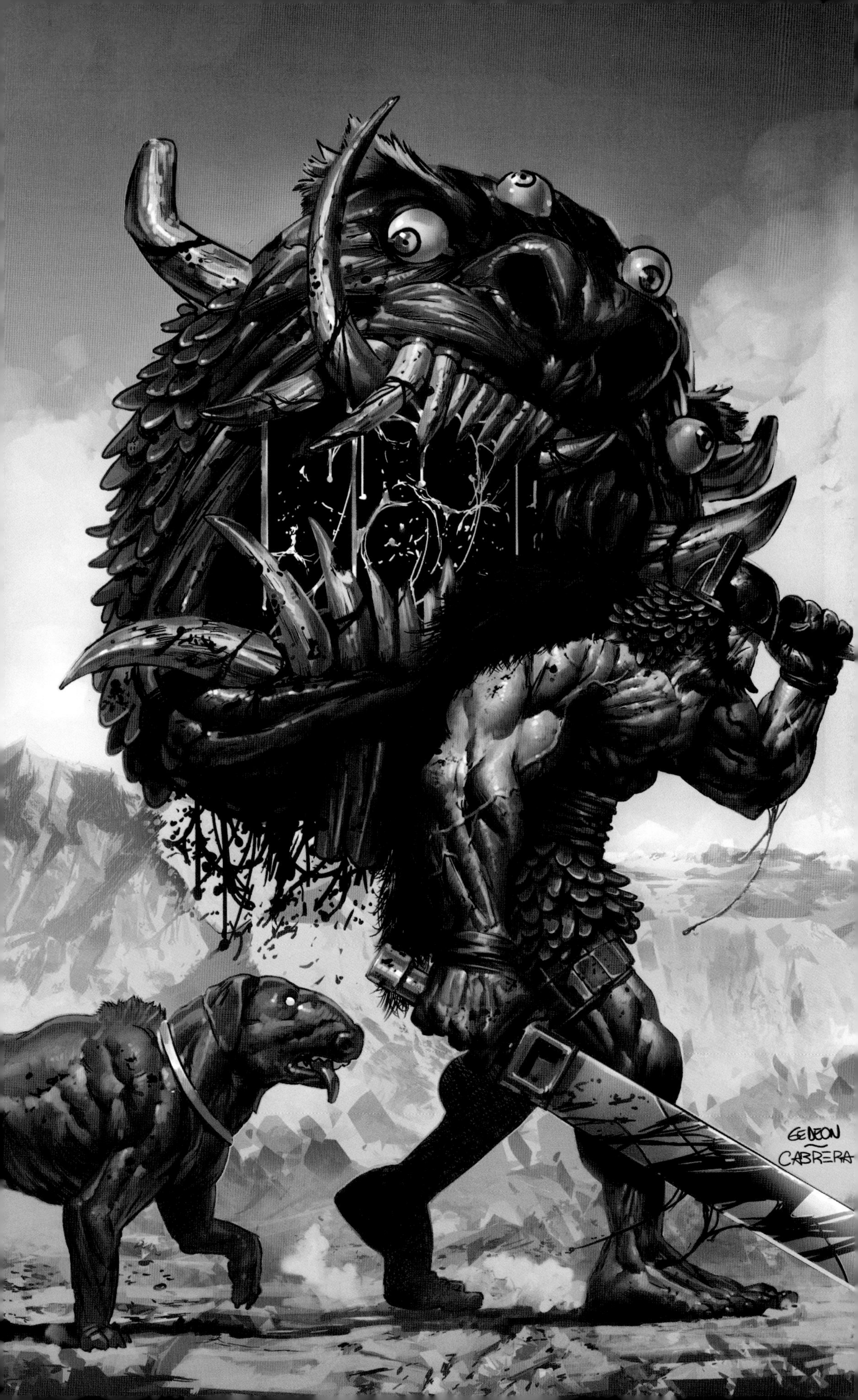
GEDEON
CABRERA

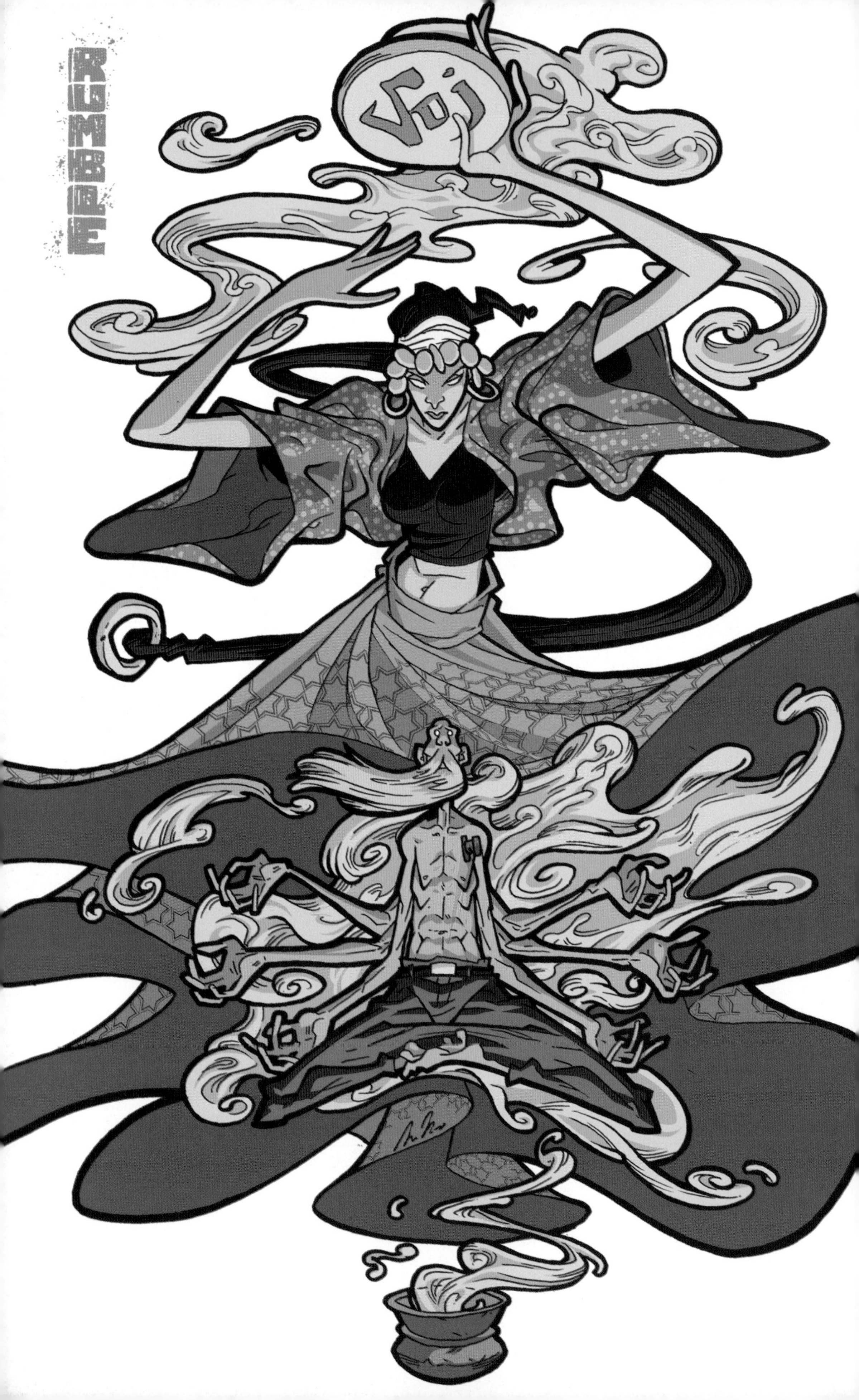
RUMBLE

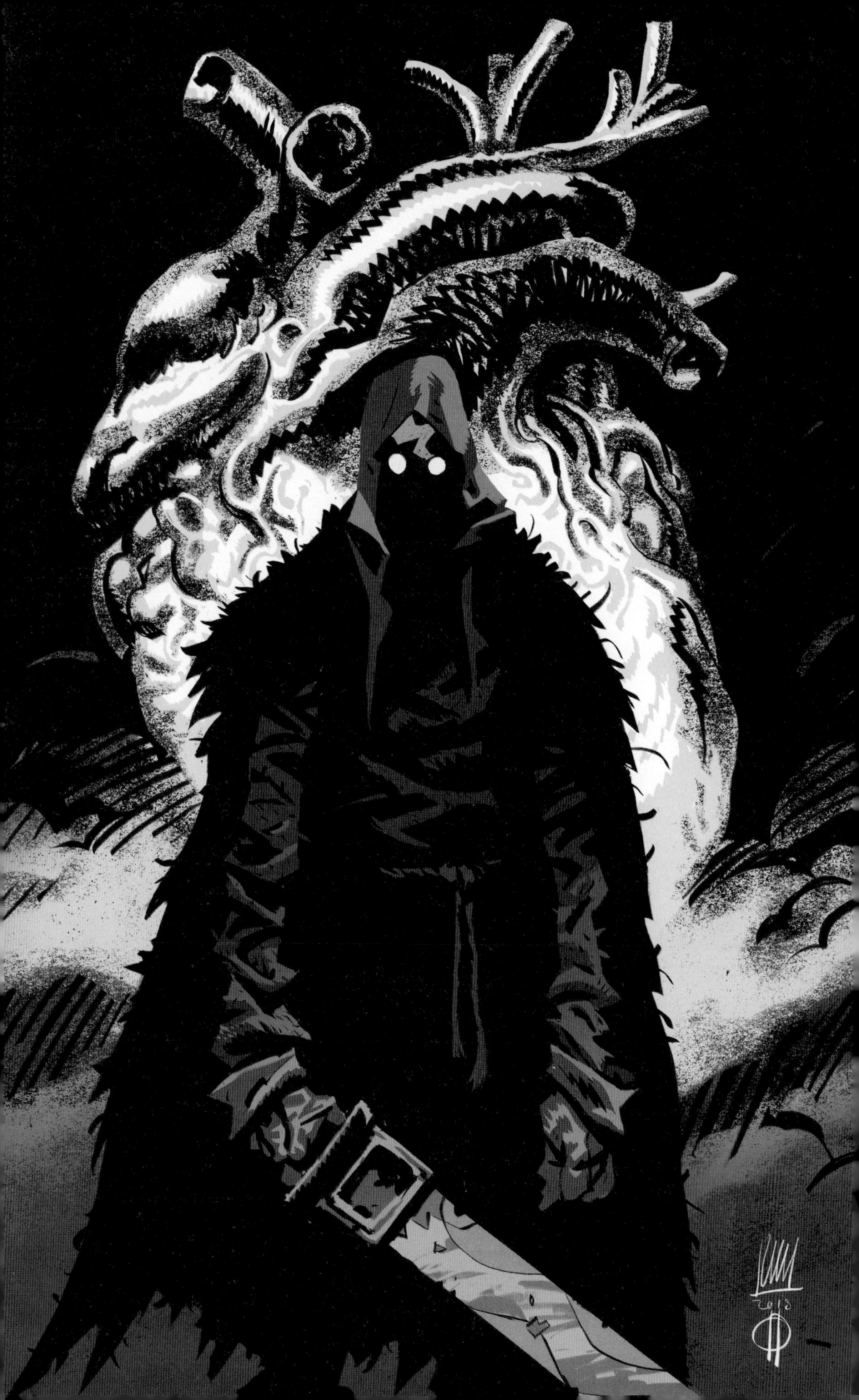

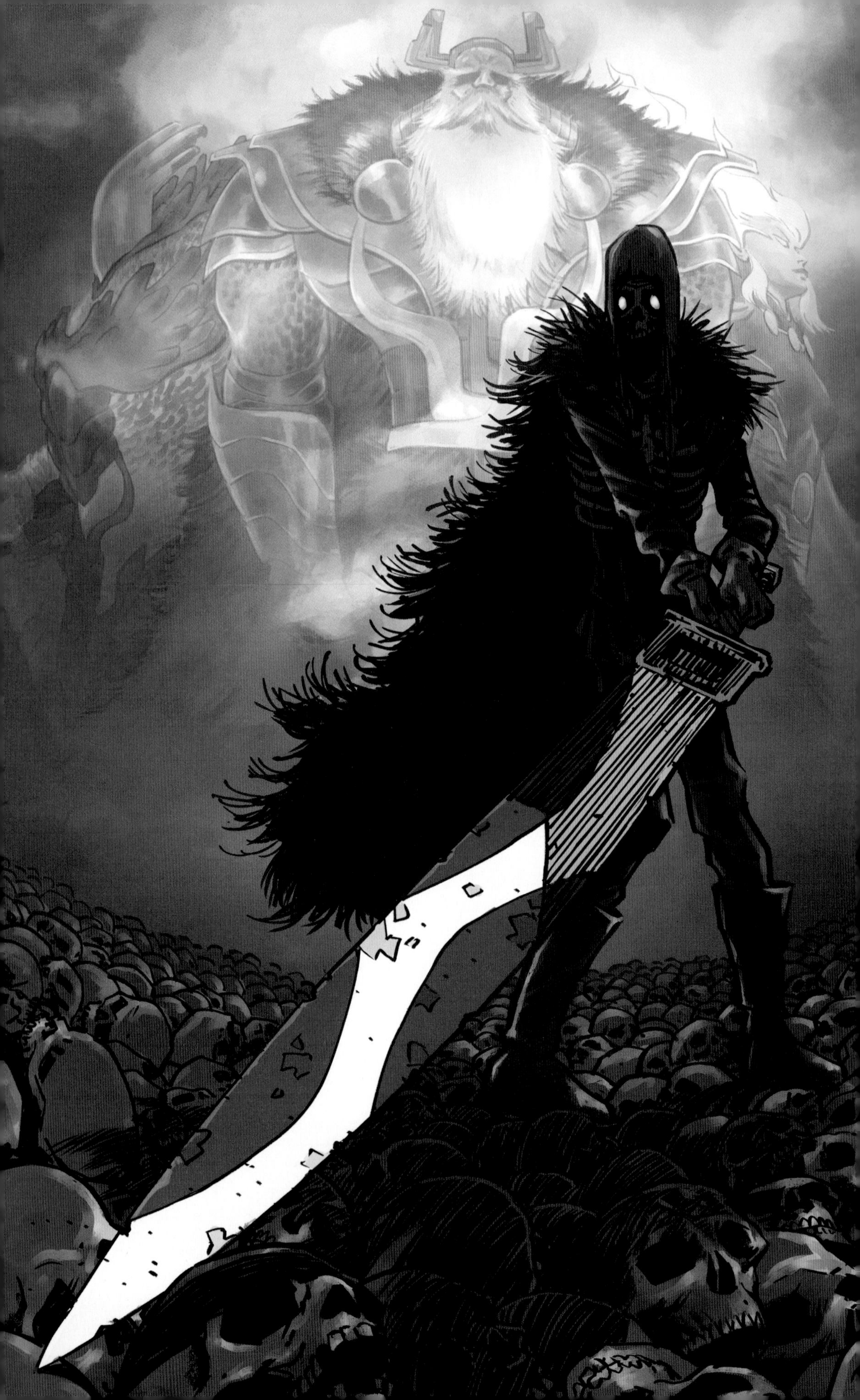

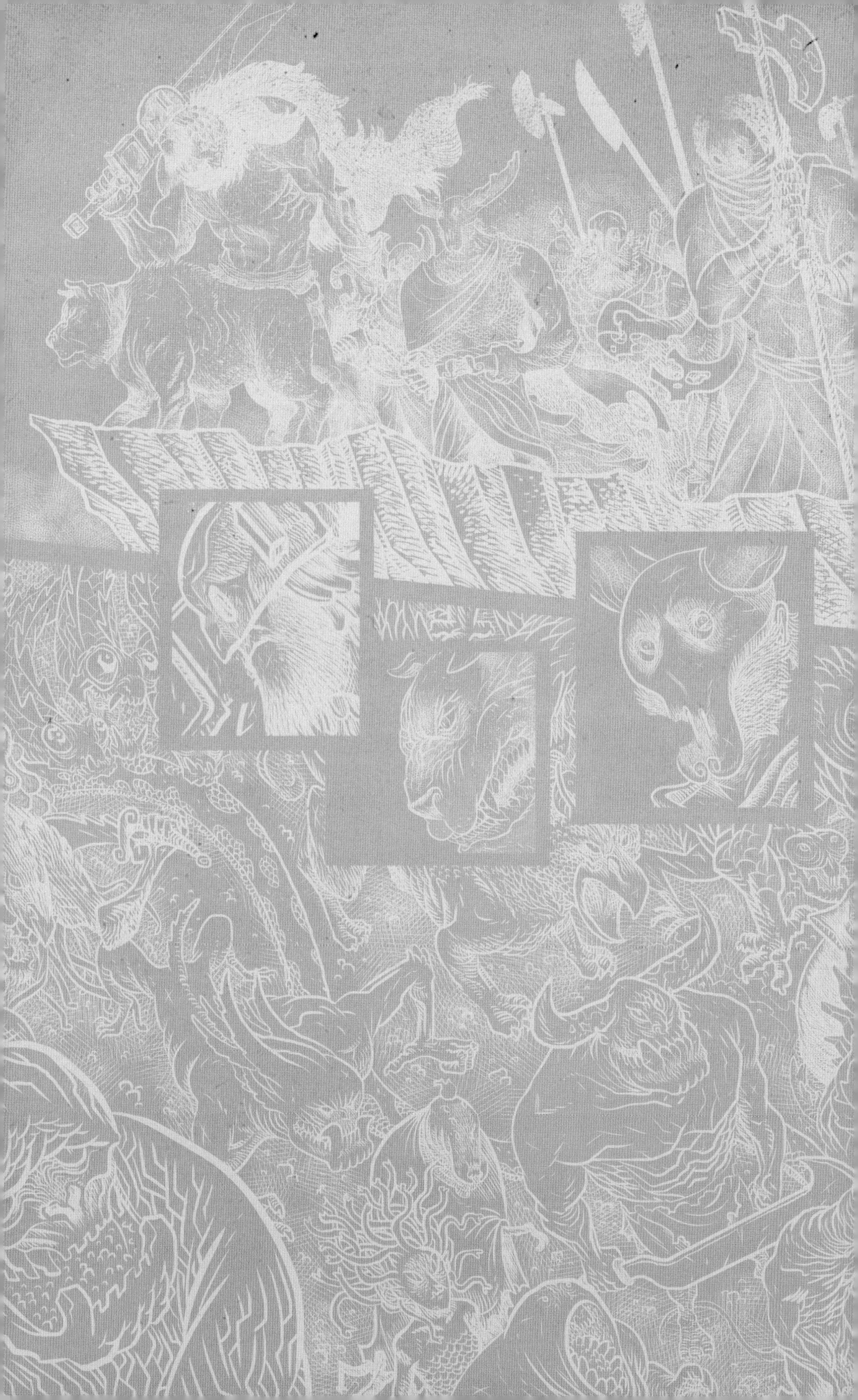

**1**
variant cover for issue #6
art by **PETER SNEJBJERG**
@peter_snejbjerg

**2**
variant cover for issue #7
art by **TONI FEJZULA**
@tonifejzula

**3**
comic code variant for issue #7
art by **DAVID RUBÍN**

**4**
variant cover for issue #8
art by **DAVID LAFUENTE**
@srdavidlafuente

**5**
variant cover for issue #9
art by **DUNCAN FEGREDO**
@duncanfegredo (Twitter)

**6**
variant cover for issue #10
art by **TROY NIXEY**

**7**
hero initiative variant for issue #10
art by **BRANDON GRAHAM**
@royalbrandon

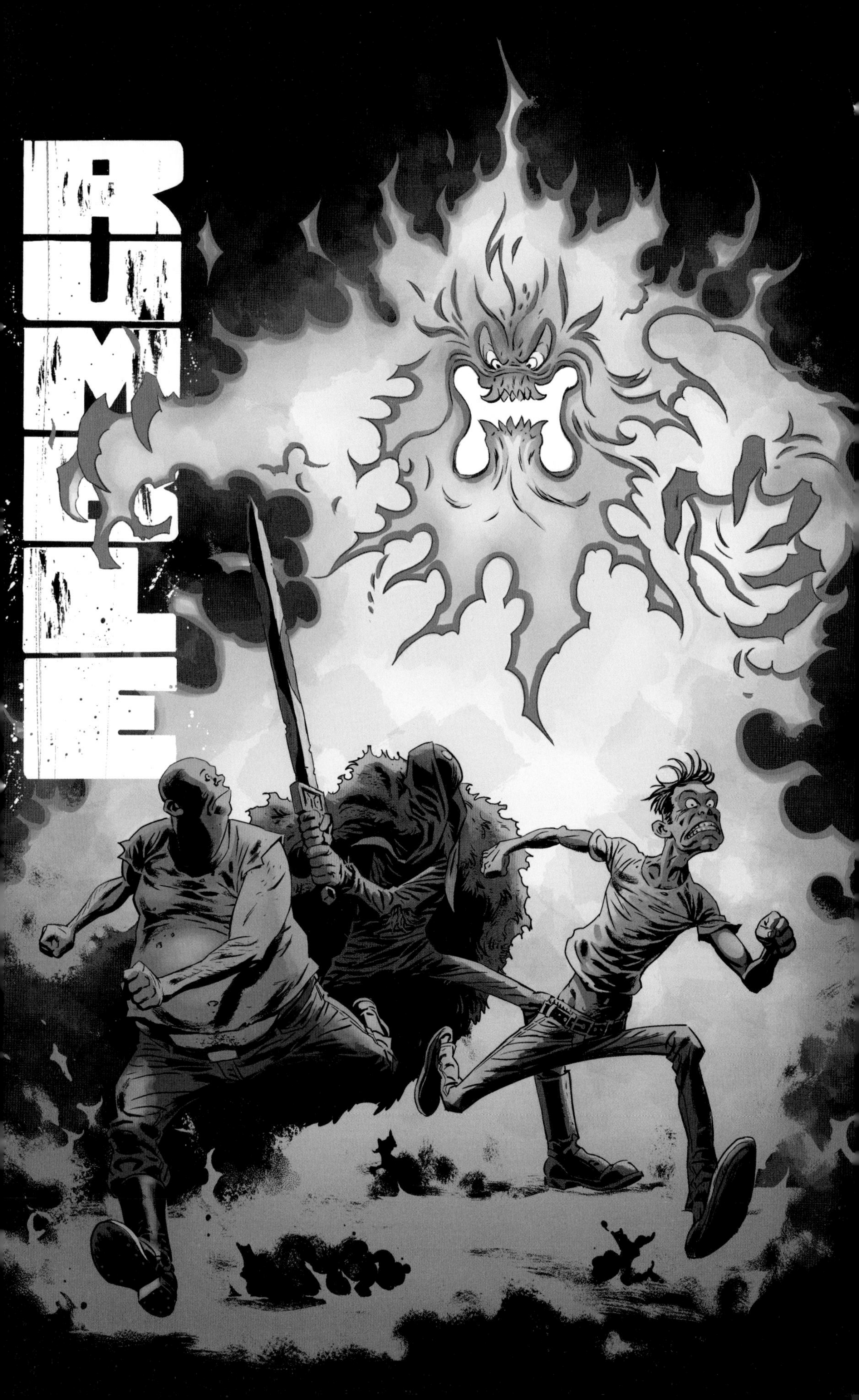
RUMBLE

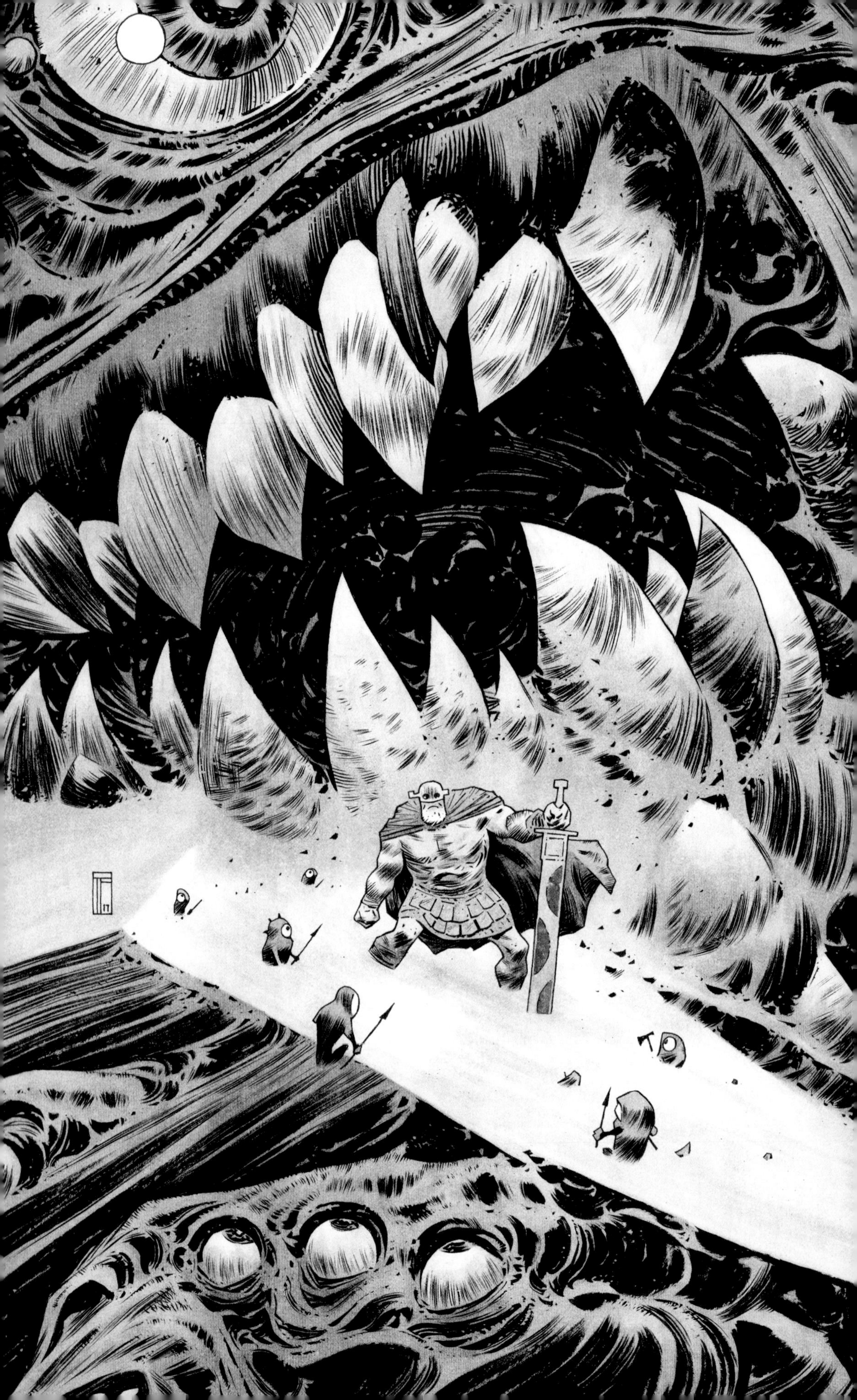

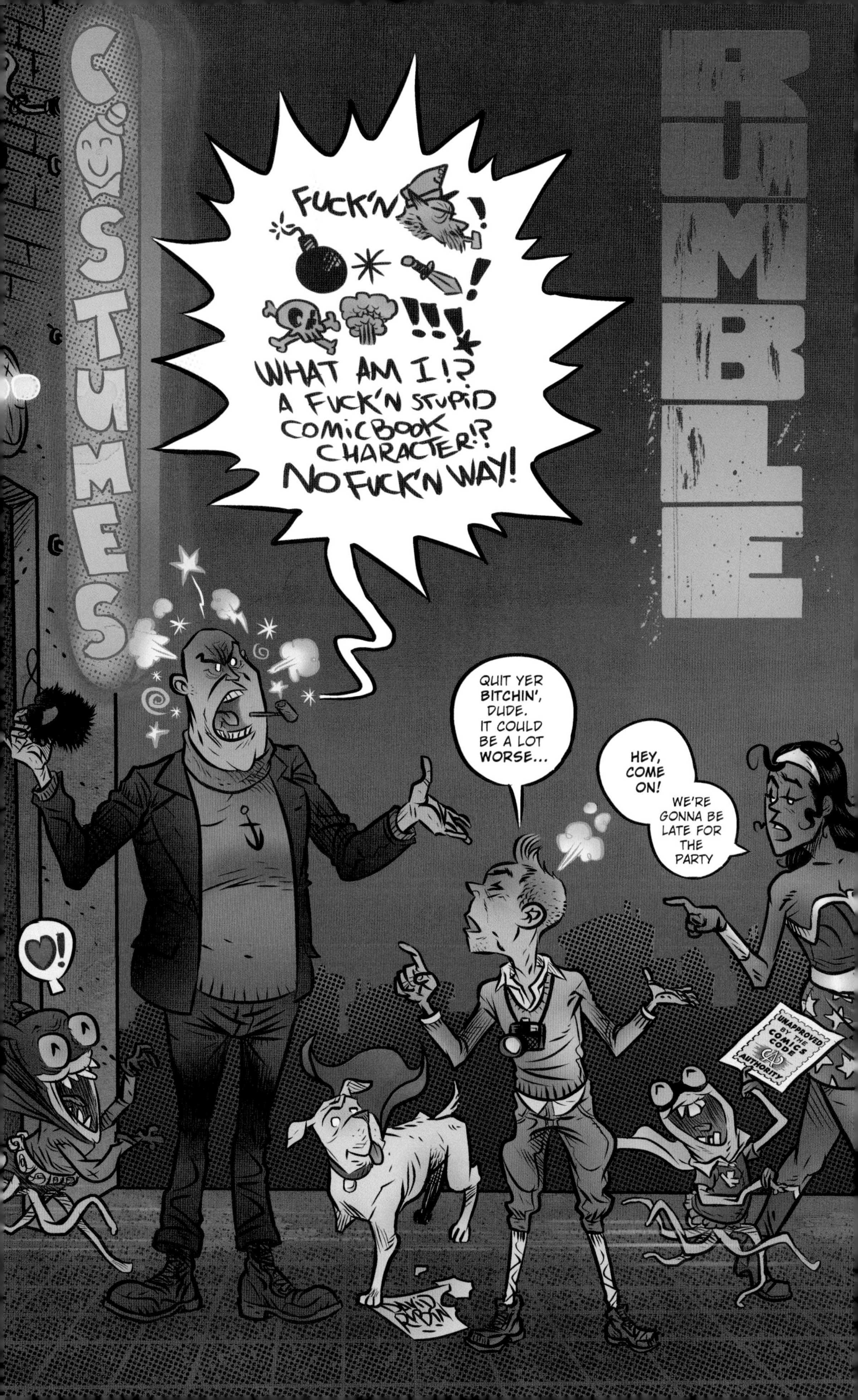

COSTUMES
RUMBLE
FUCK'N !
!
!!!
WHAT AM I!? A FUCK'N STUPID COMICBOOK CHARACTER!? NO FUCK'N WAY!
QUIT YER BITCHIN', DUDE. IT COULD BE A LOT WORSE...
HEY, COME ON!
WE'RE GONNA BE LATE FOR THE PARTY
UNAPPROVED BY THE COMICS CODE AUTHORITY

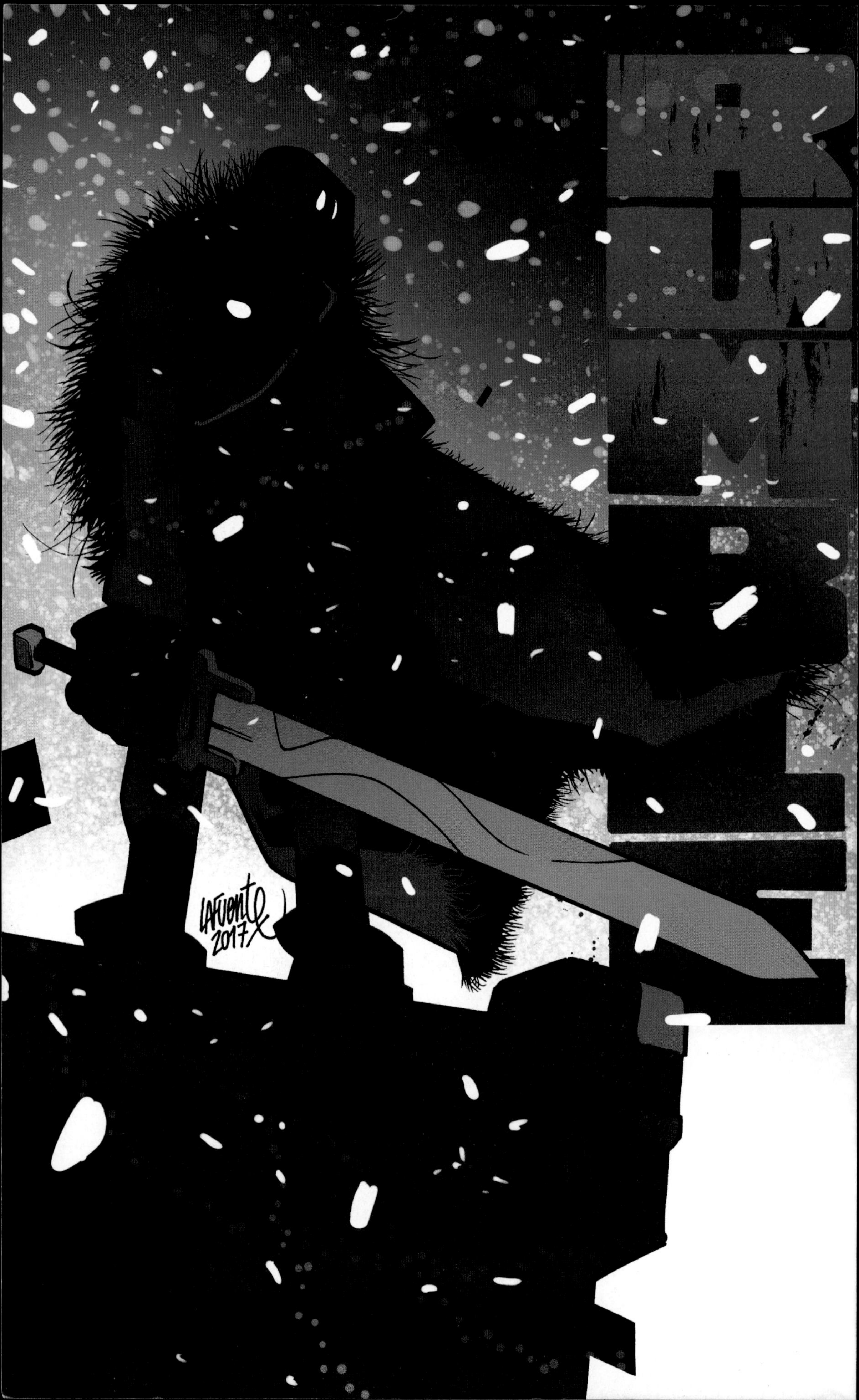
RUMBLE
LAFUENTE 2017

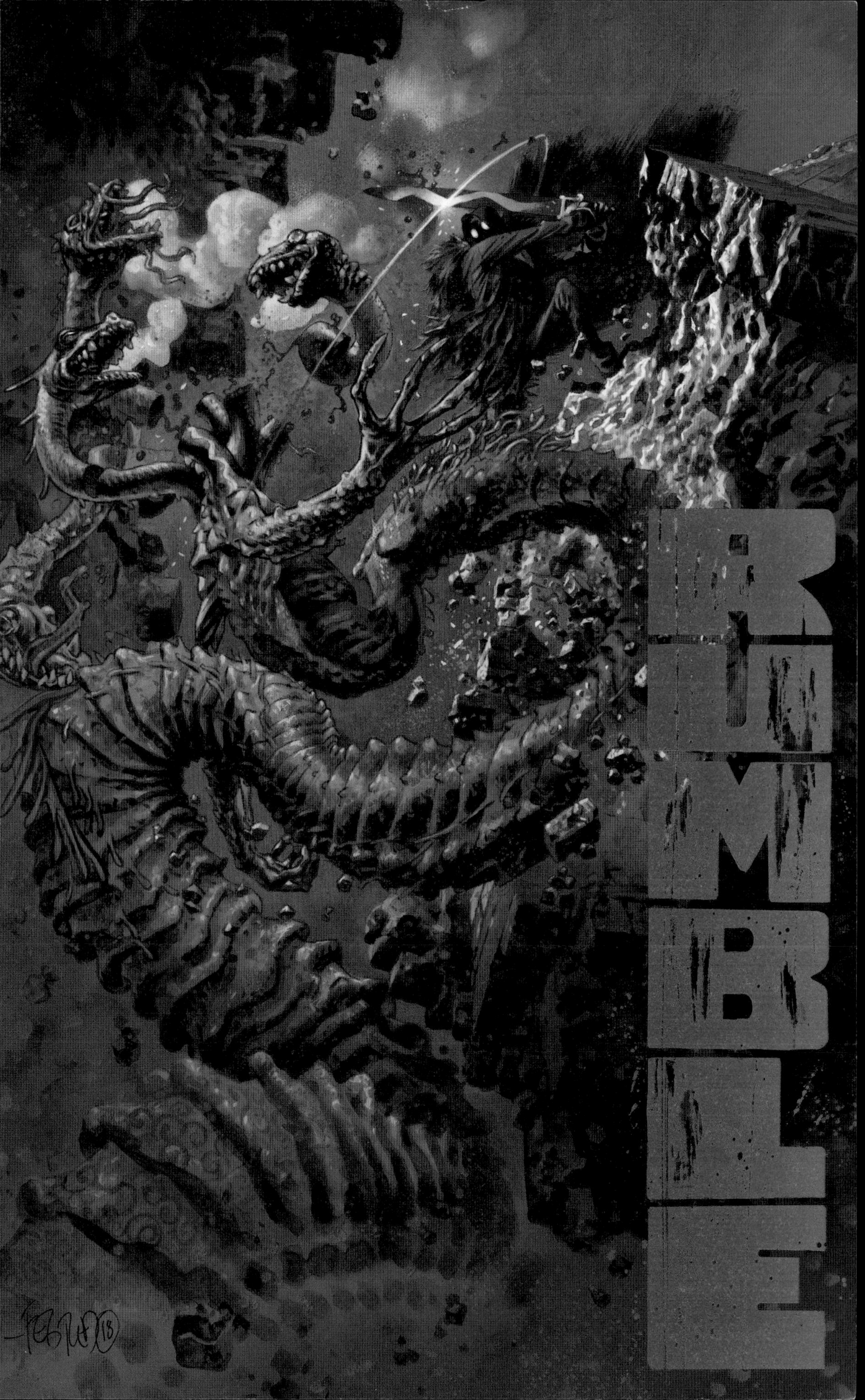
RUMBLE

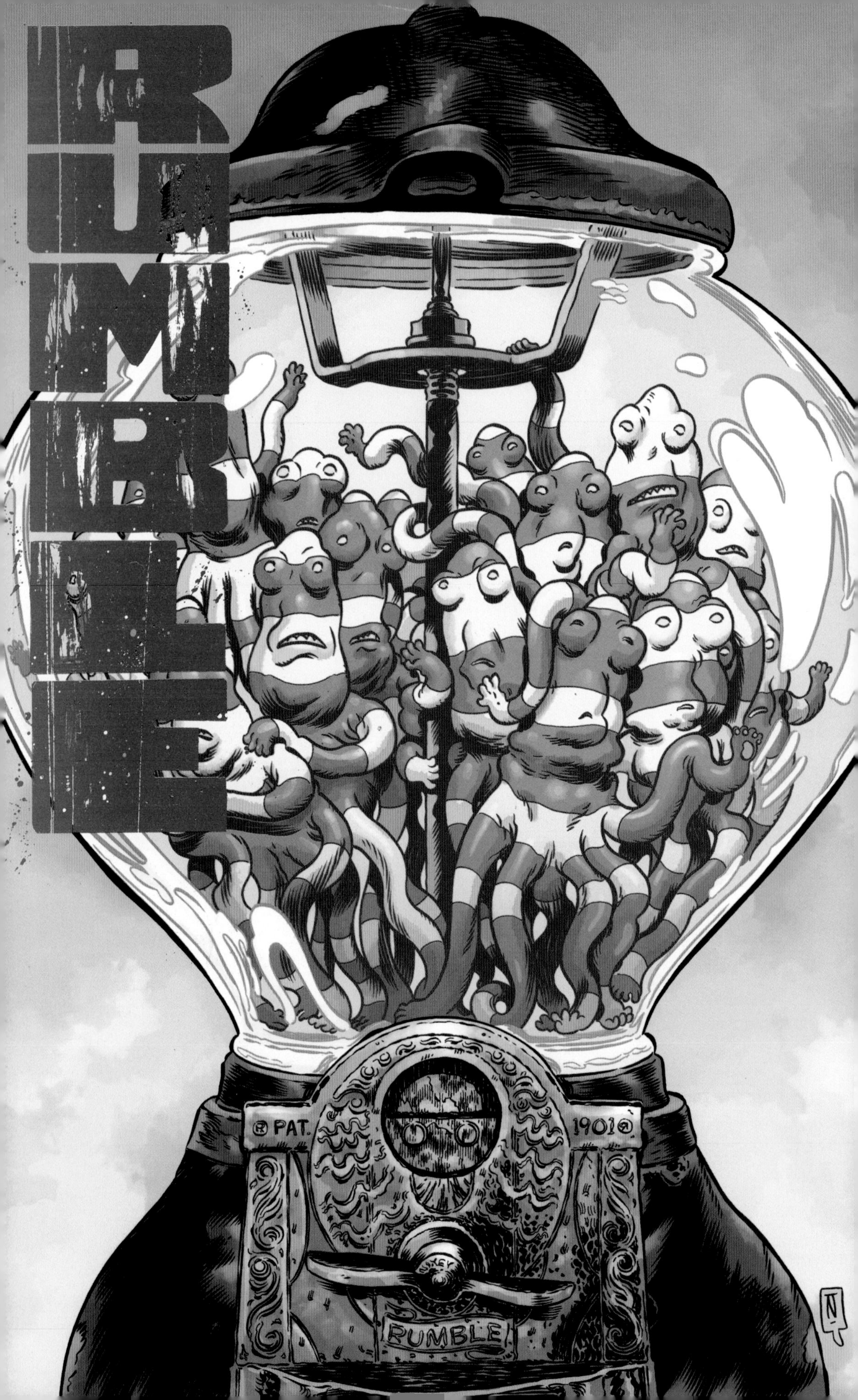
RUMBLE
® PAT.
1901®
RUMBLE

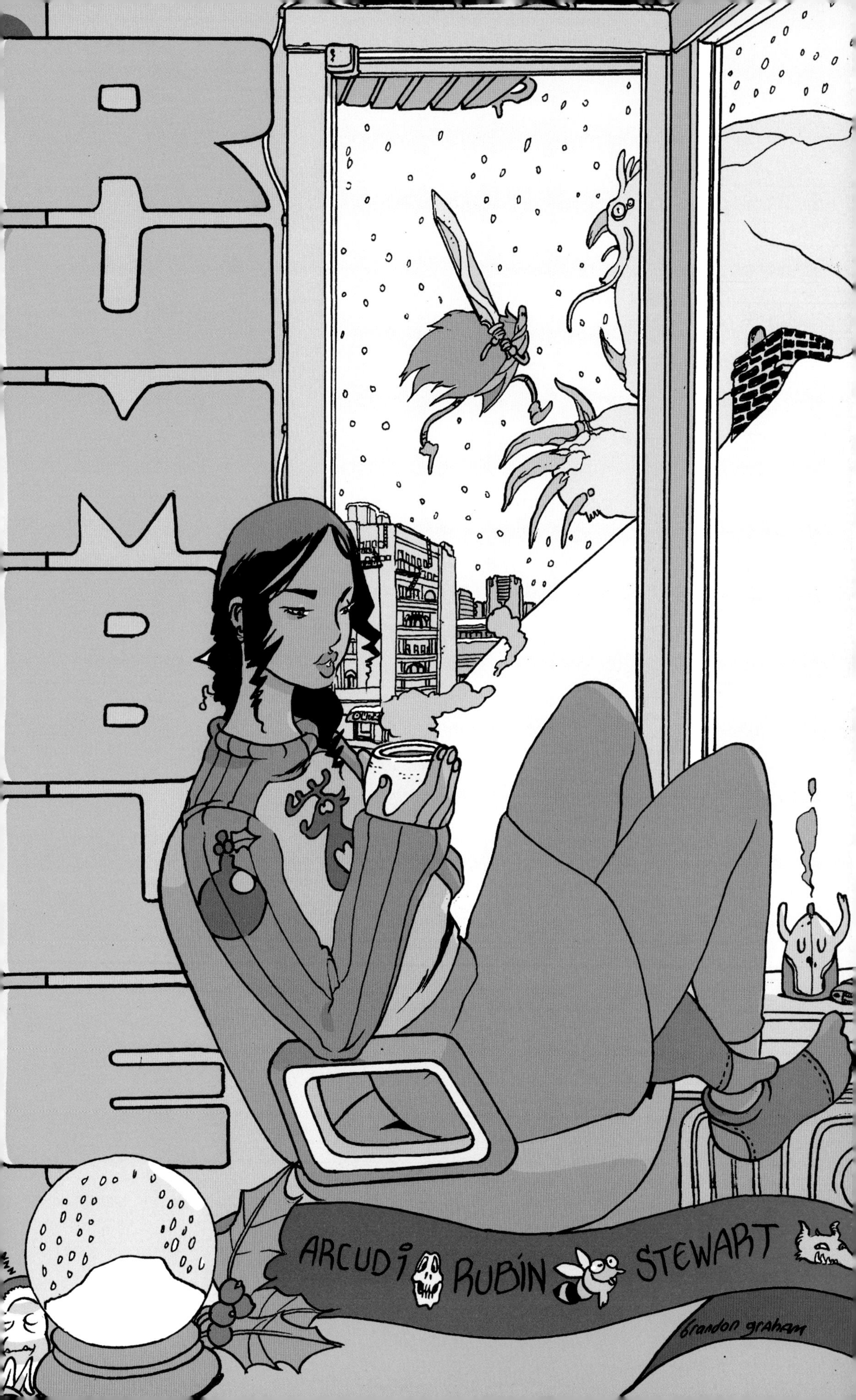
ARCUDI RUBIN STEWART
brandon graham

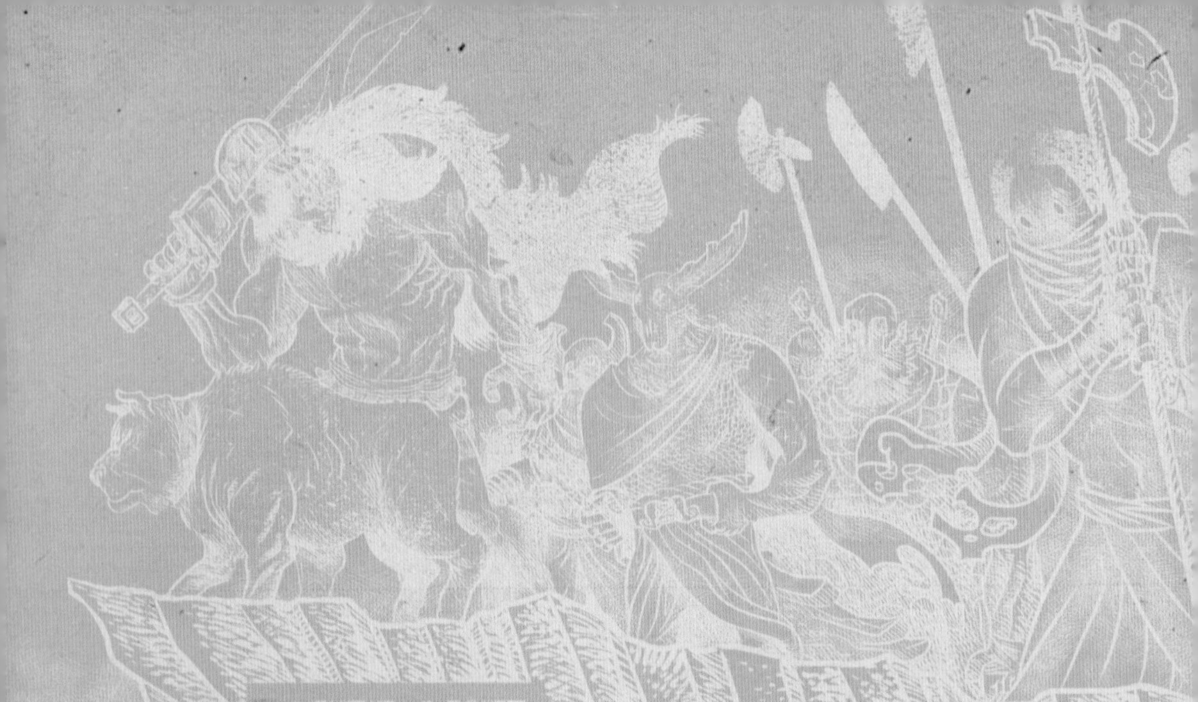

## JOHN ARCUDI

is made entirely of globally sourced materials, but that hasn't stopped him!

After years of writing comics like *The Mask*, *Doom Patrol*, *Major Bummer*, *The Creep*, and *BPRD*, John decided he wanted to fulfill his lifelong dream of writing a story about a monster-killing, sword-swinging scarecrow. That's what you have in your hands right now.

## DAVID RUBÍN

enjoys drawing all kinds of stuff: monsters, guts, action and intense dramatic "Douglas Sirkesques" sequences. He has worked on several other titles including *Black Hammer*, *Ether*, *The Fiction* and both *Aurora West* graphic novels.

He lives in Torrelodones, a suburb of Madrid, with his wife Sara, their little daughter Auria, and an old cat called Zemo. His dream is to travel to a planet better than our own...or at least one with fewer awful people. In the meantime, on Earth, David uses his cartoonist superpowers to build a better world.

## DAVE STEWART

was born on the high desert, while his mother danced to the chatter of a rattlesnake's tail. Despite a rare case of Sasquatch leg and the desire to run with any northbound moose migration, he found the coloring arts were a suitable profession to fuel the resources needed to build a moonshine still in the backwoods hills of Southest Portland. Much to his surprise he found that his coloring garnered him industry awards, unlike his feverish gathering of dry leaves for winter bedding. And he colors on.